19th Workshop of the Australasian Language Technology Association (ALTA 2021)

Online
8-10 December 2021

ISBN: 978-1-7138-9160-4

Printed from e-media with permission by:

Curran Associates, Inc.
57 Morehouse Lane
Red Hook, NY 12571

Some format issues inherent in the e-media version may also appear in this print version.

Printed with permission by Curran Associates, Inc. (2024)

Association for Computational Linguistics
209 N. Eighth Street
Stroudsburg, Pennsylvania 18360

Phone: 1-570-476-8006
Fax: 1-570-476-0860

acl@aclweb.org

Additional copies of this publication are available from:

Curran Associates, Inc.
57 Morehouse Lane
Red Hook, NY 12571 USA
Phone: 845-758-0400
Fax: 845-758-2633
Email: curran@proceedings.com
Web: www.proceedings.com

ALTA 2021

Proceedings of the 19th Workshop of the Australasian Language Technology Association

8–10 December, 2021

Online

Gold Sponsors:

Silver Sponsors:

Introduction

Welcome to the 19th edition of the Annual Workshop of the Australasian Language Technology Association (ALTA 2021). The purpose of ALTA is to promote language technology research and development in Australia and New Zealand. Every year ALTA hosts a workshop which is the key local forum for disseminating research in Natural Language Processing and Computational Linguistics, with presentations and posters from students, industry, and academic researchers. This year ALTA is hosted as a virtual workshop, due to the COVID-19 pandemic. In total we received 18 long, 8 short, and 2 abstract submissions and we accepted 15 long and 7 short papers to appear in the workshop, as well as the 2 extended abstracts. Each paper was reviewed by at least two members of the program committee, using a double-blind protocol. Great care was taken to avoid all conflicts of interest. Of all submissions, 25 were first-authored by students. We had submissions from a total of seven countries: Australia, New Zealand, Spain, France, Germany, Netherlands and United States. We are extremely grateful to the Programme Committee members for their time and their detailed and helpful comments and reviews. This year we had committee members from all over the globe including Australia, New Zealand, Japan, Sweden, Switzerland, United States and United Arab Emirates. Overall, there will be six oral presentation sessions and two virtual poster sessions. We also ran a shared task in Evidence Based Medicine (EBM) organised by Diego Mollá-Aliod (Macquarie University). Participants were invited to submit a system description paper, which are included in this volume with a light review by ALTA chairs. Finally, the workshop will feature keynotes from Barbara Plank (IT University of Copenhagen), Ben Hutchinson (Google) and Dirk Hovy (Bocconi University), following a tradition of bringing speakers from both academia and industry. ALTA 2021 is very grateful for the financial support generously offered by our sponsors. Without their contribution, the running of these events to bring together the NLP community of the Australasian region would have been a challenge. We would like to express sincere gratitude to our sponsors. We very much hope that you will have an enjoyable and inspiring time at ALTA 2021!

Afshin Rahimi, William Lane and Guido Zuccon

Brisbane, Australia

Dec 2021

Organisers:

Program co-chairs: Afshin Rahimi, William Lane and Guido Zuccon
Program Execs: Maria Kim, Sarvnaz Karimi, Meladel Mistica, Diego Mollá and Massimo Piccardi
Shared task chair: Diego Mollá

Program Committee:

Abeed Sarkar (Emory University)
Afshin Rahimi (The University of Queensland)
Andrea Schalley (Karlstad University)
Antonio Jimeno (RMIT University)
Diego Molla (Macquarie University)
Dominique Estival (Western Sydney University)
Fajri Koto (The University of Melbourne)
Gabriela Ferraro (CSIRO)
Gholamreza Haffari (Monash University)
Hamed Hassanzadeh (The Australian e-Health Research Centre, CSIRO)
Guido Zuccon (University of Queensland)
Hiyori Yoshikawa (Fujitsu Laboratories Ltd.)
Jennifer Biggs (Defence Science and Technology Group)
Jey Han Lau (University of Melbourne)
Karin Verspoor (RMIT University)
Kristin Stock (Massey University)
Lea Frermann (The University of Melbourne)
Lizhen Qu (Monash University)
Maria Kim (Defence Science and Technology Group)
Massimo Piccardi (University of Technology Sydney)
Mel Mistica (The University of Melbourne)
Nitin Indurkhya (The University of New South Wales)
Sarvnaz Karimi (CSIRO)
Scott Nowson (PwC Middle East)
Stephen Wan (CSIRO)
Sunghwan Mac Kim (Hara Research Lab)
Timothy Baldwin (The University of Melbourne)
Trevor Cohn (The University of Melbourne)
William Lane (Charles Darwin University)
Wray Lindsay Buntine (Monash University)
Xiang Dai (University of Copenhagen)

Invited Speakers:

Barbara Plank, IT University of Copenhagen
Ben Hutchinson, Google
Dirk Hovy, Bocconi University

Invited Talks

Barbara Plank: Tackling scarce and biased data for more inclusive Natural Language Processing

Deep neural networks have revolutionised our field in recent years. Particularly contextualised representations obtained from large-scale language models have pushed frontiers. Despite of these advances, many challenges and research problems remain, due to the rich variability of language and a dreadful lack and bias in resources. In this talk, I will outline possible ways to go about these challenges to tackle scarce data and label bias. I will draw upon recent research in cross-lingual learning, data selection and learning from disagreement and present (on-going) work applied to NLP tasks such as syntactic processing, named entity recognition and task-oriented dialogue, showing how weak supervision and multi-task learning can help remedy some of these challenges.

Ben Hutchinson: Putting NLP Ethics Into Context

In order to consider the societal and ethical consequences of biases in NLP models, it is necessary to consider how the models will be integrated into user-facing AI systems and products. We also need to consider who those systems will be used by, on and with. In the first part of this talk, I will adopt a wide lens and consider technology ethics within various social, cultural and historical contexts, using examples from my research. In the second part of this talk, I will zoom in to discuss practical challenges that arise when building NLP systems that are contextually appropriate and responsible.

Dirk Hovy: More than words – Integrating social factors into language modeling

Language is a social construct. We use it to achieve various conversational goals. Only one among them is to convey information. However, natural language processing has traditionally focused only on this informational aspect, ignoring all social aspects of language. That restriction was partially necessary to make modeling progress. However, I argue that as modeling power increases, we might want to revisit the issue. Social aspects of language can help disambiguate meaning, add more nuance to our models, and are becoming increasingly important in all aspects of generation. In this talk, I will outline several of the social dimensions that influence language use, how they affect NLP models, and what efforts are already underway to incorporate them. I will conclude with some open questions and ideas for future directions. If we manage to include social aspects of language into NLP, I believe we will open new research avenues, improve performance, and create fairer language technology.

8th December (Wednesday) Workshop Day 1 (all times AEDT)

14:00 Tutorial on Machine Translation and Summarization
Inigo Jauregi, Jacob Parnell, and Massimo Piccardi

16:30 Social Gathering/Mentoring – Kumospace

9th December (Thursday) Day 2

9:00 ALTA Keynote – Barbara Plank: Tackling scarce and biased data for more inclusive Natural Language

10:00 Social Gathering/Brunch/Mentorship – Kumospace

10:30 Welcome to Day 2

10:40 Oral Presentations 1 (Long: 10m + 3m QA, Short: 8m + 2m)

Combining Shallow and Deep Representations for Text-Pair Classification (long)
Vincent Nguyen, Sarvnaz Karimi and Zhenchang Xing

Robustness Analysis of Grover for Machine-Generated News Detection (long)
Rinaldo Gagiano, Maria Myung-Hee Kim, Xiuzhen Zhang and Jennifer Biggs

Using Word Embeddings to Quantify Ethnic Stereotypes in 12 years of Spanish News. (long)
Danielly Sorato, Diana Zavala-Rojas and Maria del Carme Colominas Ventura

Multi-modal Intent Classification for Assistive Robots with Large-scale Naturalistic Datasets (long)
Karun Varghese Mathew, Venkata S Aditya Tarigoppula and Lea Frermann

Does QA-based intermediate training help fine-tuning language models for text classification? (short)
Shiwei Zhang and Xiuzhen Zhang

Using Discourse Structure to Differentiate Entities in Literature (short)
Antonio Jimeno Yepes, Ameer Albahem and Karin Verspoor

11:52 Afternoon Break/Lunch/Social Gathering/Mentorship

14:00 Oral Presentations 2 (Long: 10m + 3m QA, Short: 8m + 2m)

An Approach to the Frugal Use of Human Annotators for Text Classification Tasks (long)
Li'An Chen and Hanna Suominen

Exploring the Vulnerability of NLP Models via Universal Adversarial Texts (long)
Xinzhe Li, Ming Liu, Xingjun Ma and Longxiang Gao

Phone Based Keyword Spotting for Transcribing Very Low Resource Languages (long)
Eric Le Ferrand, Steven Bird and Laurent Besacier

Exploring Story Generation with Multi-task Objectives in Variational Autoencoders (long)
Zhuohan Xie, Jey Han Lau and Trevor Cohn

14:52 Break: Social Gathering/Mentorship

15:07 Oral Presentations 3 (Long: 10m + 3m QA, Short: 8m + 2m)

Evaluating Hierarchical Document Categorisation (short)
Qian Sun, A. Shen, H. Yoshikawa, C. Ma, D. Beck, T. Iwakura and T. Baldwin

Cross-Domain Language Modeling: An Empirical Investigation (short)
Vincent Nguyen, Sarvnaz Karimi, Maciej Rybinski and Zhenchang Xing

BERT's The Word : Sarcasm Target Detection using BERT (short)
Pradeesh Parameswaran, Andrew Trotman, Veronica Liesaputra and David Eyers

A Computational Acquisition Model for Multi-modal Word Learning from Scratch (abstract)
Uri Berger, Gabriel Stanovsky, Omri Abend and Lea Frermann
Retrodiction as Delayed Recurrence: the Case of Adjectives in Italian and English (short)
Raquel G. Alhama, Francesca Zermiani and Atiqah Khaliq
Automatic Post-Editing for Translating Chinese Novels to Vietnamese (short)
Thanh Vu and Dai Quoc Nguyen

16:07 Poster Session (all papers in Oral presentations 1 and 2)
17:30 End of day 2

10th December (Friday) Day 3

10:00 Welcome to Day 3
10:05 Oral Presentations 4 (Long: 10m + 3m QA, Short: 8m + 2m)
Inductive Biases for Low Data VQA: A Data Augmentation Approach (abstract)
Narjes Askarian, Ehsan Abbasnejad, Ingrid Zukerman, Wray Buntine and Reza Haffari
Evaluation of Review Summaries via Question-Answering (long)
Nannan Huang and Xiuzhen Zhang
Curriculum Learning Effectively Improves Low Data VQA (long)
Narjes Askarian, Ehsan Abbasnejad, Ingrid Zukerman, Wray Buntine and Reza Haffari
Document Level Hierarchical Transformer (long)
Najam Zaidi, Trevor Cohn and Gholamreza Haffari

11:00 ALTA Keynote – Barbara Plank: Tackling scarce and biased data for more inclusive Natural Language
12:00 Break/Lunch/Social Gathering/Mentorship – Kumospace
13:30 Oral Presentations 5 (Long: 10m + 3m QA, Short: 8m + 2m)
Harnessing Privileged Information for Hyperbole Detection (long)
Rhys Biddle, Maciek Rybinski, Qian Li, Cecile Paris and Guandong Xu
Principled Analysis of Energy Discourse with Topic Labeling (long)
Thomas Scelsi, Alfonso Martinez Arranz and Lea Frermann
Generating and Modifying Natural Language Explanations (long)
Abdus Salam, Rolf Schwitter and Mehmet Orgun
Findings on Conversation Disentanglement (long)
Rongxin Zhu, Jey Han Lau and Jianzhong Qi

14:22 Oral Presentations 6 (shared task papers: 8m + 2m)
Overview of the 2021 ALTA Shared Task: Automatic Grading of Evidence, 10 Years Later (long)
Diego Molla-Aliod
Quick, get me a Dr. BERT: Automatic Grading of Evidence using Transfer Learning (long)
Pradeesh Parameswaran, Andrew Trotman, Veronica Liesaputra, David Eyers
An Ensemble Model for Automatic Grading of Evidence (long)
Yuting Guo, Yao Ge, Ruqi Liao, Abeed Sarker
Handling Variance of Pretrained Language Models in Grading Evidence in the Medical Literature (long)
Fajri Koto, Biaoyan Fang

15:02 ALTA General Meeting
15:17 Best Paper Awards
15:22 Poster Session (All papers in Oral sessions 3 and 4)
17:00 ALTA Keynote – Dirk Hovy: More than words – Integrating social factors into language modeling
18:00 Social Gathering/Mentorship – Kumospace
16:30 End of Day 3

Table of Contents

Long Papers

Short Papers

Shared Task Papers

Findings on Conversation Disentanglement

Rongxin Zhu, Jey Han Lau, Jianzhong Qi

School of Computing and Information System
The University of Melbourne
rongxinz1@student.unimelb.edu.au, {jeyhan.lau, jianzhong.qi}@unimelb.edu.au

Abstract

Conversation disentanglement, the task to identify separate threads in conversations, is an important pre-processing step in multi-party conversational NLP applications such as conversational question answering and conversation summarization. Framing it as a utterance-to-utterance classification problem — i.e. given an utterance of interest (UOI), find which past utterance it replies to — we explore a number of transformer-based models and found that BERT in combination with handcrafted features remains a strong baseline. We then build a multi-task learning model that jointly learns utterance-to-utterance and utterance-to-thread classification. Observing that the ground truth label (past utterance) is in the top candidates when our model makes an error, we experiment with using bipartite graphs as a post-processing step to learn how to best match *a set of UOIs* to past utterances. Experiments on the Ubuntu IRC dataset show that this approach has the potential to outperform the conventional greedy approach of simply selecting the highest probability candidate for each UOI independently, indicating a promising future research direction.

1 Introduction

In public forums and chatrooms such as Reddit and Internet Relay Chat (IRC), there are often multiple conversations happening at the same time. Figure 1 shows two threads of conversation (blue and green) running in parallel. *Conversation disentanglement*, a task to identify separate threads among intertwined messages, is an essential preprocessing step for analysing entangled conversations in multi-party conversational applications such as question answering (Li et al., 2020) and response selection (Jia et al., 2020). It is also useful in constructing datasets for dialogue system studies (Lowe et al., 2015).

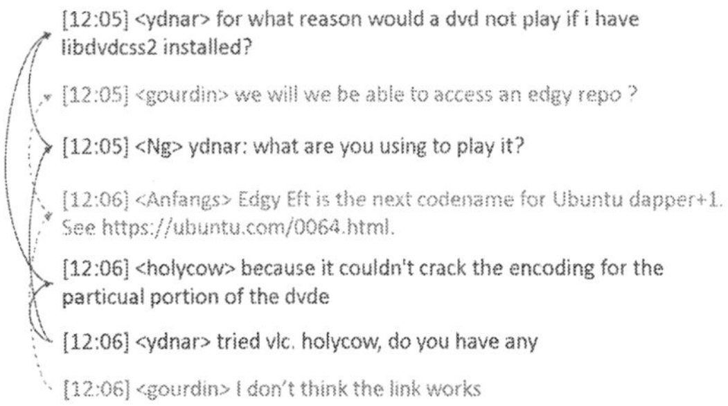

Figure 1: Ubuntu IRC chat log sample sorted by time. Each arrow represents a directed reply-to relation. The two conversation threads are shown in blue and green.

Previous studies address the conversation disentanglement task with two steps: *link prediction* and *clustering*. In link prediction, a confidence score is computed to predict a *reply-to* relation from an *utterance of interest* (UOI) to a past utterance (Elsner and Charniak, 2008; Zhu et al., 2020). In clustering, conversation threads are recovered based on the predicted confidence scores between utterance pairs. The most popular clustering method uses a greedy approach to group UOIs linked with their best past utterances to create the threads (Kummerfeld et al., 2019; Zhu et al., 2020).

In *link prediction*, the model that estimates the relevance between a pair of utterances plays an important role. To this end, we explore three transformer-based pretrained models: BERT (Devlin et al., 2019), ALBERT (Lan et al., 2019) and POLY-ENCODER (Humeau et al., 2019). These variants are selected by considering performance, memory consumption and speed. We found that BERT in combination with handcrafted features remains a strong baseline. Observing that utterances may be too short to contain sufficient information for disentanglement, we also build a multi-task learning model that learns to jointly link a UOI to a past utterance and a cluster of past utterances (i.e.

the conversation threads).

For *clustering*, we experiment with bipartite graph matching algorithms that consider how to best link a set of UOIs to their top candidates, thereby producing globally more optimal clusters. When the graph structure is known, we show that this approach substantially outperforms conventional greedy clustering method, although challenges remain on how to infer the graph structure.

To summarise:

- We study different transformer-based models for conversation disentanglement.
- We explore a multi-task conversation disentanglement framework that jointly learns utterance-to-utterance and utterance-to-thread classification.
- We experiment with bipartite graphs for clustering utterances and found a promising future direction.

2 Related Work

Conversation disentanglement methods can be classified into two categories: (1) two-step methods and (2) end-to-end methods.

In two-step methods, the first step is to measure the relations between utterance pairs, e.g., *reply-to* relations (Zhu et al., 2020; Kummerfeld et al., 2019) or *same thread* relations (Elsner and Charniak, 2008, 2010). Either feature-based models (Elsner and Charniak, 2008, 2010) or deep learning models (Kummerfeld et al., 2019; Zhu et al., 2020) are used. Afterwards a clustering algorithm is applied to recover separate threads using results from the first step. Elsner and Charniak (2008, 2010, 2011) use a greedy graph partition algorithm to assign an utterance u to the thread of u' which has the maximum relevance to u among candidates if the score is larger than a threshold. Kummerfeld et al. (2019); Zhu et al. (2020) use a greedy algorithm to recover threads following all reply-to relations independently identified for each utterance. Jiang et al. (2018) propose a graph connected component-based algorithm.

End-to-end methods construct threads incrementally by scanning through a chat log and either append the current utterance to an existing thread or create a new thread. Tan et al. (2019) use a hierarchical LSTM model to obtain utterance representation and thread representation. Liu et al. (2020) build a transition-based model that uses three LSTMs for utterance encoding, context encoding and thread state updating, respectively.

Symbol	Meaning
U	A chat log with N utterances
T	A set of disjoint threads in U
$\mathcal{T}$	A thread in T
u_i	An utterance of interest
u	An utterance in a chat log
C_i	A candidate (parent) utterance pool for u_i
t_i	The token sequence of u_i with n_i tokens

Table 1: A summary of symbols/notations.

3 Notations and Task Definition

Given a chat log U with N utterances $\{u_1, u_2, \cdots, u_N\}$ in chronological order, the goal of conversation disentanglement is to obtain a set of disjoint threads $T = \{\mathcal{T}^1, \mathcal{T}^2, \cdots, \mathcal{T}^m\}$. Each thread $\mathcal{T}^l$ contains a collection of topically-coherent utterances. Utterance u_i contains a list of n_i tokens $w_1^i, w_2^i, \cdots, w_{n_i}^i$.

The task can be framed as a *reply-to relation identification* problem, where we aim to find the *parent utterance* for every $u_i \in U$ (Kummerfeld et al., 2019; Zhu et al., 2020), i.e., if an utterance u_i replies to a (past) utterance u_j, u_j is called the parent utterance of u_i. When all reply-to utterance pairs are identified, T can be recovered unambiguously by following the reply-to relations.

Henceforth we call the target utterance u_i an *utterance of interest* (UOI). We use $u_i \rightarrow u_j$ to represent the reply-to relation from u_i to u_j, where u_j is the parent utterance of u_i. The reply-to relation is asymmetric, i.e., $u_i \rightarrow u_j$ and $u_j \rightarrow u_i$ do not hold at the same time. We use a *candidate pool* C_i to denote the set of candidate utterances from which the parent utterance is selected from. Table 1 presents a summary of symbols/notations.

4 Dataset

We conduct experiments on the Ubuntu IRC dataset (Kummerfeld et al., 2019), which contains questions and answers about the Ubuntu system, as well as chit-chats from multiple participants. Table 2 shows the statistics in train, validation and test sets. The four columns are the number of chat logs, the number of annotated utterances, the number of threads and the average number of parents for each utterance.

Split	Chat Logs	Ann. Utt	Threads	Avg. parent
Train	153	67463	17327	1.03
Valid	10	2500	495	1.04
Test	10	5000	964	1.04

Table 2: Statistics of training, validation and testing split of the Ubuntu IRC dataset. "Ann. Utt" is the number of annotated utterances. "Avg. parent" is the average number of parents of an utterance.

5 Experiments

We start with studying pairwise models that take as input a pair of utterances and decide whether a reply-to relation exists (Section 5.1). Then, we add dialogue history information into consideration and study a multi-task learning model (Section 5.2) built upon the pairwise models. In Section 5.3, we further investigate a globally-optimal approach based on bipartite graph matching, considering the top parent candidates of multiple UOIs together to help resolve conflicts in the utterance matches.

5.1 Pairwise Models

To establish a baseline, we first study the effectiveness of pairwise models that measure the confidence of a reply-to relation between an UOI and each candidate utterance independently without considering any past context (e.g., dialogue history). To find the parent utterance for u_i, we compute the relevance score r_{ij} between u_i and each $u_j \in C_i$:

$$r_{ij} = f(u_i, u_j, \boldsymbol{v_{ij}}), \forall\, u_j \in C_i \tag{1}$$

where $f(\cdot)$ is the pairwise model and $\boldsymbol{v_{ij}}$ represents additional information describing the relationship between u_i and u_j, such as manually defined features like time, user (name) mentions and word overlaps. We use transformer-based models to automatically capture more complex semantic relationships between utterances pairs, such as question-answer relation and coreference resolution which cannot be modeled by features very well.

Following Kummerfeld et al. (2019), we assume the parent utterance of a UOI to be within k_c history utterances in the chat log, and we solve a k_c-way multi-class classification problem where C_i contains exactly k_c utterances $[u_{i-k_c+1}, \cdots, u_{i-1}, u_i]$. UOI u_i is included in C_i for detecting self-links, i.e., an utterance that starts a new thread. The training loss is:

$$L_r = -\sum_{i=1}^{N}\sum_{j=1}^{k_c} \mathbb{1}[y_i = j] \log\, p_{ij} \tag{2}$$

where $\mathbb{1}[y_i = j] = 1$ if $u_i \to u_j$ holds, and 0 otherwise; p_{ij} is the normalized probability after applying softmax over $\{r_{ij}\}_{u_j \in C_i}$.

5.1.1 Models

We study the empirical performance of the following pairwise models. See more details of the models in Appendix 8.

LASTMENTION: A baseline model that links a UOI u_i to the last utterance of the user directly mentioned by u_i. If u_i does not contain a user mention, we link it to the immediately preceding utterance, i.e., u_{i-1}.

GLOVE+MF: Following Kummerfeld et al. (2019), this is a feedforward neural network (FFN) that uses the max and mean Glove (Pennington et al., 2014) embeddings of a pair of utterances and some handcrafted features[1] including time difference between two utterances, direct user mention, word overlaps, etc.

MF: An FFN model that uses only the handcrafted features in GLOVE+MF. This model is designed to test the effectiveness of the handcrafted features.[2]

BERT (Devlin et al., 2019): A pretrained model based on transformer (Vaswani et al., 2017) fine-tuned on our task. We follow the standard setup for sentence pair scoring in BERT by concatenating UOI u_i and a candidate u_j delimited by [SEP].

BERT+MF: A BERT-based model that also incorporates the handcrafted features in GLOVE+MF.

BERT+TD: A BERT-based model that uses the time difference between two utterances as the only manual feature, as preliminary experiments found that this is the most important feature.

ALBERT (Lan et al., 2019): A parameter-efficient BERT variant fine-tuned on our task.

POLY-ENCODER (Humeau et al., 2019): A transformer-based model designed for fast training and inference by encoding query (UOI) and candidate separately.[3] We use POLY-ENCODER

[1] See a full feature list in Kummerfeld et al. (2019).

[2] Note that MF is different from the manual features model in Kummerfeld et al. (2019) which uses a linear model.

[3] It is worthwhile to note that POLY-ENCODER showed strong performance on a related task, next utterance selection, which aims to choose the correct future utterance, but with two key differences: (1) their UOI incorporates the dialogue history which provides more context; (2) they randomly sample

in two settings: POLY-BATCH where the labels of UOIs in a batch is used as the shared candidate pool to reduce computation overhead, and POLY-INLINE where each query has its own candidate pool similar to the other models.

5.1.2 Results

Evaluation Metrics We measure the model performance in three aspects: (1) the *link prediction* metrics measure the precision, recall and F1 scores of the predicted reply-to relations; (2) the *clustering* metrics include variation information (VI, (Meilă, 2007)), one-to-one Overlap (1-1, (Elsner and Charniak, 2008)) and exact match F1; these evaluate the quality of the recovered threads;[4] and (3) the *ranking* metrics Recall@k ($k = \{1, 5, 10\}$) assess whether the ground truth parent utterance u_j is among the top-k candidates.[5]

Dataset construction In training and validation, we set C_i to contain exactly one parent utterance of an UOI u_i. We observe that 98.5% of the UOIs in the training data reply to a parent utterance within the 50 latest utterances and so we set $k_c = 50$ (i.e., $|C_i| = 50$). We discard training samples that do no contain the parent utterance of an UOI under this setting (1.5% in the training data). If there are more than one parent utterances in C_i (2.5% in training data), we take the latest parent utterance of u_i as the target "label". We do not impose these requirements in testing and so do not manipulate the test data.

Model configuration We clip both UOI u_i and a candidate u_j to at most 60 tokens. $|\boldsymbol{v_{ij}}|$ (manual feature dimension) $= 77$ in BERT+MF. In BERT+TD, $|\boldsymbol{v_{ij}}| = 6$. The dimensionality of word embeddings in MF is 50. All BERT-based models use the "bert-base-uncased" pretrained model. The batch size for POLY-INLINE, BERT, BERT+TD and BERT+MF is 64.[6] The batch sizes of POLY-BATCH and ALBERT are 96 and 256 respectively. We tune the batch size, the number of layers, and the hidden size in BERT+MF and BERT+TD according to recall@1 on the validation set.

negative examples to create the candidates, while we use k_c past utterances as candidates, which makes the next utterance selection task arguably an easier task.

[4]Exact Match F1 is calculated based on the number of recovered threads that perfectly match the ground truth ones (ignoring the ground truth threads with only one utterance).

[5]E.g., if u_j is in the top-5 candidates, recall@5 = 1.

[6]Actual batch size is 4 with a gradient accumulation of 16.

Results and discussions Table 3 shows that LASTMENTION is worse than all other models, indicating that direct user mentions are not sufficient for disentanglement. The manual features model (MF) has very strong results, outperforming transformer-based models (BERT, ALBERT and POLY-ENCODER) by a large margin, suggesting that the manual features are very effective.

The overall best model across all metrics is BERT+MF. Comparing BERT+MF to BERT, we see a large improvement when we incorporate the manual features. Interestingly though, most of the improvement appears to come from the time difference feature (BERT+MF vs. BERT+TD).

Looking at BERT and POLY-INLINE, we see that the attention between words in BERT is helpful to capture the semantics between utterance pairs better, because the only difference between them is that POLY-INLINE encodes two utterances separately first and uses additional attention layers to compute the final relevance score.

The performance gap between POLY-BATCH and POLY-INLINE shows that the *batch mode* (Humeau et al., 2019) strategy has a negative impact on the prediction accuracy. This is attributed to the difference in terms of training and testing behaviour, as at test time we predict links similar to the inline mode (using past k_c utterances as candidates).

The GPU memory consumption and speed of transformer-based models are shown in Table 4. POLY-BATCH is the most memory efficient and fastest model, suggesting that it is a competitive model in real-world applications where speed and efficiency is paramount.

5.2 Context Expansion by Thread Classification

The inherent limitation of the pairwise models is that they ignore the dialogue history of a candidate utterance. Intuitively, if the prior utterances from the same thread of candidate utterance u_j is known, it will provide more context when computing the relevance scores. However, the threads of candidate utterances have to be inferred, which could be noisy. Furthermore, the high GPU memory consumption of transformer-based models renders using a long dialogue history impractical.

To address the issues above, we propose a multi-task learning framework that (1) considers the dialogue history in a memory efficient manner and (2) does not introduce noise at test time.

Model	Link Prediction Precision	Recall	F1	Ranking R@1	R@5	R@10	Clustering 1-1	VI	F
Last Mention	37.1	35.7	36.4	-	-	-	21.4	60.5	4.0
GLOVE+MF	71.5	68.9	70.1	70.2	95.8	98.6	76.1	91.5	34.0
MF	71.1	68.5	69.8	70.2	94.0	97.3	75.0	91.3	31.5
POLY-BATCH	39.3	37.9	38.6	40.8	69.8	80.8	52.3	80.8	9.8
POLY-INLINE	42.2	40.7	41.4	42.8	70.8	81.3	62.0	84.4	13.6
ALBERT	46.1	44.4	45.3	46.8	77.3	88.4	68.6	87.9	22.4
BERT	48.2	46.4	47.3	48.8	75.4	84.7	74.3	89.3	26.3
BERT+TD	67.9	65.4	66.6	66.9	90.6	95.3	76.0	91.1	34.9
BERT+MF	**73.9**	**71.3**	**72.6**	**73.9**	**95.8**	**98.6**	**77.0**	**92.0**	**40.9**

Table 3: Results of pairwise models. *Ranking metrics* are not applicable to *Last Mention*. Best scores are **bold**.

Model	GPU Mem (GB)	Speed (ins/s)
BERT	18.7	9.4
ALBERT	14.6	9.4
POLY-INLINE	9.9	16.8
POLY-BATCH	5.1	36.4

Table 4: GPU memory consumption and speed of transformer-based models. GPU Mem (GB) shows the peak GPU memory consumption in GB during training. Speed (ins/s) is the number of instances processed per second during training. All experiments are conducted on a single NVIDIA V100 GPU (32G) with automatic mixed precision turned on and a batch size of 4.

Specifically, we maintain a candidate thread pool with k_t threads. A thread that contains multiple candidates would only be included once. This alleviates some of the memory burden, not to mention that k_t is much smaller than $|C_i|$. For the second issue, we train a shared BERT model that does reply-to relation identification and thread classification jointly, and during training we use the ground truth threads but at test time we only perform reply-to relation identification, avoiding the use of potentially noisy (predicted) threads.

5.2.1 Model Architecture

The model consists of a shared BERT module and separate linear layers for reply-to relation identification and thread classification. As shown in Figure 2, given u_i, we compute its relevance score s^r_{ij} to every candidate utterances in utterance candidate pool C_i and relevance score s^t_{il} to every thread in thread candidate pool T^c_i. We aim to minimize the following loss function during model training:

$$L = -\Big(\sum_{i=1}^{N}\sum_{j=1}^{k_c} \mathbb{1}(y_r = j)\log s^r_{ij} + \alpha \sum_{i=1}^{N}\sum_{l=1}^{k_t} \mathbb{1}(y_t = l)\log s^t_{il}\Big) \quad (3)$$

where $\mathbb{1}(y_r = j)$ is 1 if u_j is the parent utterance of u_i, and 0 otherwise. Similarly, $\mathbb{1}(y_t = l)$ tests whether u_i belongs to thread T^c_i. Hyper-parameter α is used to balance the importance of the two loss components.

Relevance score computation We compute the utterance relevance score s^r_{ij} between UOI u_i and each candidate utterance $u_j \in C_i$ in the same way as the BERT model shown in Section 5.1 does.

For thread classification, we consider a pool containing k_t threads before u_i, including a special thread $\{u_i\}$ for the case where u_i starts a new thread. The score s^t_{il} between u_i and thread T_l is computed using the shared BERT, following the format used by Ghosal et al. (2020):

$$[[\text{CLS}], w^1_1, \cdots w^1_{n_1}, w^2_1, \cdots w^2_{n_2}, w^k_1 \cdots w^k_{n_k}, [\text{SEP}], w^i_1, \cdots w^i_{n_i}[\text{SEP}]]$$

where w^p_q is the q-th token of the p-th utterance in T_l, and w^i_m is the m-th token of u_i. We take the embedding of [CLS] and use another linear layer to compute the final score.

5.2.2 Results and Discussion

For reply-to relation identification, we use the same configuration described in Section 5.1.2. For thread classification, we consider $k_t = 10$ thread candidates. Each thread is represented by (at most) five latest utterances. The maximum number of tokens in T_l and t_i are 360 and 60, respectively. We train the model using Adamax optimizer with learning rate 5×10^{-5} and batch size 64. As before we use "bert-base-uncased" as the pretrained model.

As Table 5 shows, incorporating an additional thread classification loss ("MULTI ($\alpha = k$)" models) improves link prediction substantially compared to BERT, showing that the thread classification objective provides complementary information

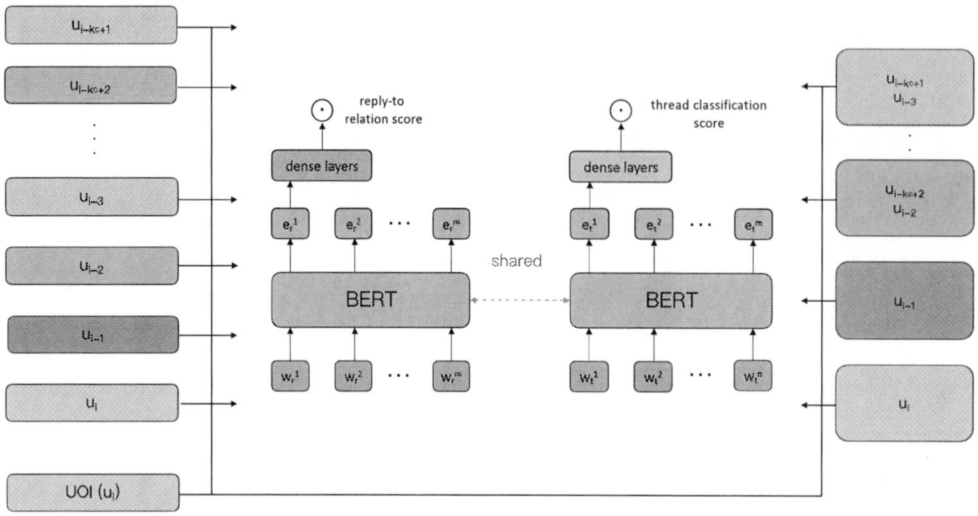

Figure 2: The architecture of the multi-task learning framework. On the left side, we use a BERT model with additional dense layers to calculate the relevance score between a UOI and each candidate utterance for reply-to relation identification. On the right side, we use the same BERT model but different dense layers on the top to calculate the relevance scores between the UOI and each candidate thread for thread classification.

	Link Prediction			Ranking			Clustering		
Model	Precision	Recall	F1	R@1	R@5	R@10	1-1	VI	F
BERT	48.2	46.4	47.3	48.8	75.4	84.7	74.3	89.3	26.3
BERT+MF	73.9	71.3	72.6	73.9	95.8	98.6	77.0	92.0	40.9
MULTI ($\alpha = 1$)	65.6	63.2	64.4	66.7	91.8	95.6	64.6	87.7	24.3
MULTI ($\alpha = 5$)	66.9	64.5	65.7	65.4	91.8	95.6	68.7	88.8	27.4
MULTI ($\alpha = 10$)	65.2	62.9	64.0	64.4	91.4	95.6	70.3	89.5	28.1
MULTI ($\alpha = 20$)	64.7	62.4	63.5	63.9	91.0	95.0	68.3	88.8	26.7
MULTI+MF ($\alpha = 1$)	72.8	70.2	71.5	71.9	94.0	96.4	76.3	91.8	36.1
MULTI+MF ($\alpha = 5$)	73.3	70.7	72.0	72.4	94.0	96.5	72.8	90.8	33.1
MULTI+MF ($\alpha = 10$)	72.2	69.6	70.8	70.4	93.4	96.4	71.8	90.2	29.9
MULTI+MF ($\alpha = 20$)	70.8	68.2	69.5	69.4	93.4	97.3	73.2	90.6	28.6

Table 5: Results of multi-task learning model.

to the reply-to relation identification task. Interestingly, when α increases from 5 to 10, both the link prediction and ranking metrics drop, suggesting that it is important not to over-emphasize thread classification, since it is not used at test time.

Adding thread classification when we have manual features (MULTI+MF vs. BERT+MF), however, does not seem to help, further reinforcing the effectiveness of these features in the dataset. That said, in situations/datasets where these manual features are not available, e.g. Movie Dialogue Dataset (Liu et al., 2020), our multi-task learning framework could be useful.

5.3 Bipartite Graph Matching for Conversation Disentanglement

After we have obtained the pairwise utterance relevance scores for every UOI, we need to link the candidate utterances with the UOIs to recover the threads. A greedy approach would use all reply-to relations that have been identified *independently* for each UOI to create the threads. As shown in Figure 3, the *reply-to* relations for u_{67} and u_{59} using greedy approach are $\{u_{67} \rightarrow u_{58}, u_{59} \rightarrow u_{58}\}$.

With such an approach, we observe that: (1) some candidates receive more responses than they should (based on ground truth labels); and (2) many UOIs choose the same candidate. Given the fact that over 95% of the UOIs' parents are within

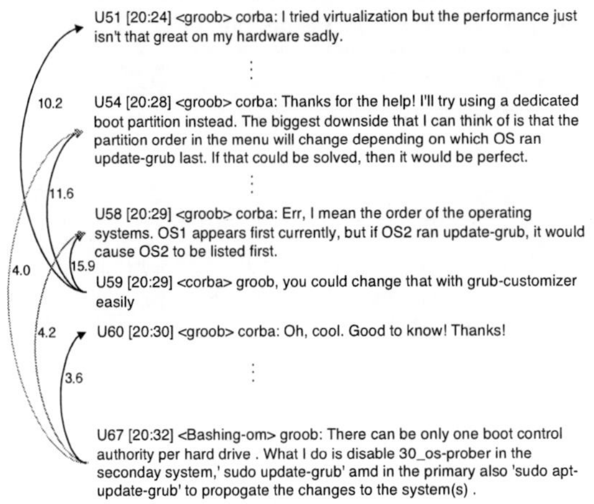

Figure 3: An example showing the difference between the greedy approach and the global decoding. Consider identifying the parent utterances of u_{59} and u_{67}. Each utterance contains ID (e.g., u_{51}), timestamp, user name and content. Both u_{59} and u_{67} have three candidates. The pairwise scores are labelled to the links, indicating the confidence of potential *reply-to* relations. The red link denotes the identified *reply-to* relation for u_{67} using the greedy approach, and the green link is the result of a global decoding algorithm.

the top-5 candidates in BERT+MF (R@5 in Table 3), we explore whether it is possible to get better matches if we constrain the maximum number of reply links each candidate receives and perform the linking of UOIs to their parent utterances together. In situations where a UOI u_i's top-1 candidate utterance u_j has a relevant score that is just marginally higher than other candidates but u_j is a strong candidate utterance for other UOIs, we may want to link u_j with the other UOIs instead of u_i. Using Figure 3 as example, if u_{58} can only receive one response, then u_{67} should link to the second best candidate u_{54} as its parent instead of u_{58}.

Based on this intuition, we explore using bipartite algorithms that treat the identification of all reply-to relations within a chat log as a *maximum-weight matching* (Gerards, 1995) problem on a bipartite graph. Note that this step is a post-processing step that can be applied to technically any pairwise utterance scoring models.

5.3.1 Graph Construction

Given a chat log U, we build a bipartite graph $G = \langle V, E, W\rangle$ where V is the set of nodes, E is the set of edges, and W is the set of edge weights. Set V consists of two subsets V_l and V_r representing two disjoint subsets of nodes of a bipartite. Subset $V_l = \{v_i^l\}_{i=1}^N$ represents the set of UOIs, i.e., each node v_i^l corresponds to a UOI u_i. Subset V_r represents the set of candidate utterances. Note that some UOIs may be candidate utterances of other UOIs. Such an utterance will have both a node in V_l and a node in V_r.

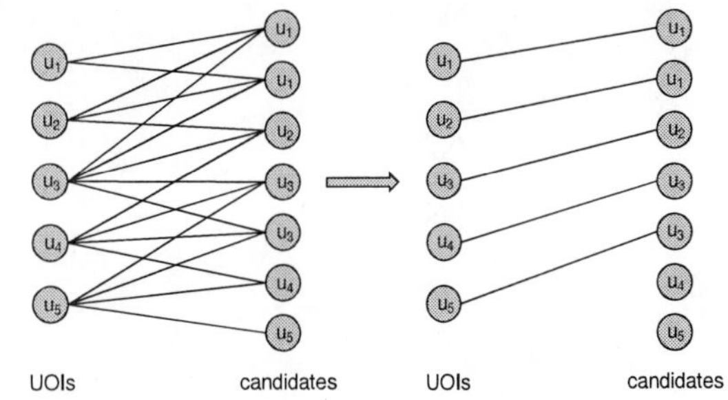

Figure 4: The left figure is an example bipartite graph built from a chat log with 5 UOIs. Each UOI u_i has $k_c = 3$ candidates $\{u_{i-2}, u_{i-1}, u_i\}$, except the first $k_c - 1$ UOIs (u_1 and u_2). Utterances u_1 and u_3 are duplicated twice because they receive 2 replies. The corresponding disentangled chat log is shown on the right figure with the following reply-to relations: $\{u_1 \rightarrow u_1, u_2 \rightarrow u_1, u_3 \rightarrow u_2, u_4 \rightarrow u_3, u_5 \rightarrow u_3\}$.

Some utterances may receive more than one reply, i.e., multiple nodes in V_l may link to the same node in V_r. This violates the standard assumption of a bipartite matching problem, where every node in V_r will only be matched with at most one node in V_l. To address this issue, we duplicate nodes in V_r. Let $\delta(u_j)$ denotes the number of replies u_j receives, then u_j is represented by $\delta(u_j)$ nodes in V_r. Now $V_r = \bigcup_{j=1}^N S(u_j)$, where $S(u_j)$ is a set of duplicated nodes $\{v_{j,1}^r, v_{j,2}^r, \cdots v_{j,\delta(u_j)}^r\}$ for u_j.

Sets E and W are constructed based on the pairwise relevance scores obtained from the link prediction phase. Specifically, $E = \bigcup_{i=1}^N R(u_i)$ where $R(u_i)$ is the set of edges between u_i and all its k_c candidates: $\bigcup_{m=1}^{k_c}\{\langle v_i^l, v_m\rangle\}_{v_m \in S(u_m)}$. For each UOI-candidate pair (u_i, u_j), if $\delta(u_j) > 0$, a set of edges $\{\langle v_i^l, v_{j,k}^r\rangle\}_{k=1}^{\delta(u_j)}$ are constructed, each with weight $w(i, j)$, which is the relevance score between u_i and u_j. An example bipartite graph is shown on the left side of Figure 4.

5.3.2 Integer Programming Formulation

Given the bipartite formulation above, we solve the conversation disentanglement problem as a maximum-weight bipartite matching problem, which is formulated as the following constrained optimization problem:

$$
\begin{aligned}
& \max \sum_{\langle v_i, v_j\rangle \in E} x(i,j) \cdot w(i,j) \\
\text{s.t.} \\
& \sum_{v_l \in neighbors(v_i)} x(i,l) = 1, \quad \forall v_i \in V_l \\
& \sum_{v_p \in neighbors(v_j)} x(p,j) \leq 1, \ \forall v_j \in V_r \\
& x(i,j) \in \{0,1\}
\end{aligned} \tag{4}
$$

Here, $neighbors(v_x)$ is the set of adjacent nodes of v_x (i.e., nodes directly connected to v_x) in G. For each edge in G, we have a variable $x(i,j)$, which takes value 1 if we include the edge $\langle v_i, v_j\rangle$ in the final matched bipartite, and 0 otherwise. Intuitively, we are choosing a subsect of E to maximize the total weight of the chosen edges, given the constraints that (1) each node in set V_l is connected to exactly one edge (each UOI has exactly one parent); and (2) each node in V_r is connected to at most one edge.

5.3.3 Node Frequency Estimation in V_r

Since the number of replies received by an utterance u_j, i.e., $\delta(u_j)$, is unknown at test time, we estimate $\delta(u_j)$ for each candidate utterance u_j. We experiment with two different estimation strategies: heuristics method and regression model.

In the heuristics method, we estimate $\delta(u_j)$ based on the total relevance scores accumulated by u_j from all UOIs, using the following equation:

$$
\begin{aligned}
r_{ij}{}' &= \frac{\exp(r_{ij})}{\sum_{u_k \in C_i} \exp(r_{ik})} \\
S_j &= \sum_i r_{ij}{}' \\
\hat{\delta}(u_j) &= \text{RND}(\alpha S_j + \beta)
\end{aligned}
$$

where $\hat{\delta}(u_j)$ is the estimation, RND is the $round(\cdot)$ function, and α and β are scaling parameters.

In the regression model, we train an FFN to predict $\delta(u_j)$ using mean squared error as the training loss. The features are normalized scores of u_j from all UOIs, as well as the sum of those scores. We also include textual features using BERT (based on the [CLS] vector), denoted as BERT+FFN. We use the same RND function to obtain an integer from the prediction of the regression models.

	Precision	Recall	F1
Oracle	88.4	85.2	86.8
Rule-Based	73.7	70.9	72.3
FFN	73.8	71.0	72.3
BERT+FFN	72.9	70.3	71.5

Table 6: Link prediction results using bipartite matching. *Oracle* is a model that uses ground truth node frequencies for V_r.

5.3.4 Experiments and Discussion

We obtain the performance upper bound by solving the maximum weight bipartite matching problem using the ground truth node frequencies for all nodes in V_r. This approach is denoted as "Oracle" in Table 6. We found that when node frequencies are known, bipartite matching significantly outperforms the best greedy methods (F1 score 86.8 vs. 72.6 of BERT+MF in Table 3).

When using estimated node frequencies, the heuristics method and FFN achieve very similar results, and BERT+FFN is worse than both. Unfortunately, these results are all far from Oracle, and they are ultimately marginally worse than BERT+MF (72.6; Table 3). Overall, our results suggest that there is much potential of using bipartite matching for creating the threads, but that there is still work to be done to design a more effective method for estimating the node frequencies.

6 Conclusion

In this paper, we frame conversation disentanglement as a task to identify the past utterance(s) that each utterance of interest (UOI) replies to, and conduct various experiments to explore the task. We first experiment with transformer-based models, and found that BERT combined with manual features is still a strong baseline. Next we propose a multi-task learning model to incorporate dialogue history into BERT, and show that the method is effective especially when manual features are not available. Based on the observation that most utterances' parents are in the top-ranked candidates when there are errors, we experiment with bipartite graph matching that matches a set of UOIs and candidates together to produce globally more optimal clusters. The algorithm has the potential to outperform standard greedy approach, indicating a promising future research direction.

7 Acknowledgement

We would like to thank the anonymous reviewers for their helpful comments.

References

Jacob Devlin, Ming-Wei Chang, Kenton Lee, and Kristina Toutanova. 2019. BERT: Pre-training of deep bidirectional transformers for language understanding. In *Proceedings of the 2019 Conference of the North American Chapter of the Association for Computational Linguistics: Human Language Technologies, Volume 1 (Long and Short Papers)*, pages 4171–4186, Minneapolis, Minnesota. Association for Computational Linguistics.

Micha Elsner and Eugene Charniak. 2008. You talking to me? a corpus and algorithm for conversation disentanglement. In *Proceedings of ACL-08: HLT*, pages 834–842, Columbus, Ohio. Association for Computational Linguistics.

Micha Elsner and Eugene Charniak. 2010. Disentangling chat. *Computational Linguistics*, 36(3):389–409.

Micha Elsner and Eugene Charniak. 2011. Disentangling chat with local coherence models. In *Proceedings of the 49th Annual Meeting of the Association for Computational Linguistics: Human Language Technologies*, pages 1179–1189, Portland, Oregon, USA. Association for Computational Linguistics.

AMH Gerards. 1995. Matching. *Handbooks in operations research and management science*, 7:135–224.

Deepanway Ghosal, Navonil Majumder, Rada Mihalcea, and Soujanya Poria. 2020. Utterance-level dialogue understanding: An empirical study. *arXiv preprint arXiv:2009.13902*.

Samuel Humeau, Kurt Shuster, Marie-Anne Lachaux, and Jason Weston. 2019. Poly-encoders: Architectures and pre-training strategies for fast and accurate multi-sentence scoring. In *International Conference on Learning Representations*.

Qi Jia, Yizhu Liu, Siyu Ren, Kenny Zhu, and Haifeng Tang. 2020. Multi-turn response selection using dialogue dependency relations. In *Proceedings of the 2020 Conference on Empirical Methods in Natural Language Processing (EMNLP)*, pages 1911–1920.

Jyun-Yu Jiang, Francine Chen, Yan-Ying Chen, and Wei Wang. 2018. Learning to disentangle interleaved conversational threads with a siamese hierarchical network and similarity ranking. In *Proceedings of the 2018 Conference of the North American Chapter of the Association for Computational Linguistics: Human Language Technologies, Volume 1 (Long Papers)*, pages 1812–1822.

Jonathan K. Kummerfeld, Sai R. Gouravajhala, Joseph J. Peper, Vignesh Athreya, Chulaka Gunasekara, Jatin Ganhotra, Siva Sankalp Patel, Lazaros C Polymenakos, and Walter Lasecki. 2019. A large-scale corpus for conversation disentanglement. In *Proceedings of the 57th Annual Meeting of the Association for Computational Linguistics*, pages 3846–3856, Florence, Italy. Association for Computational Linguistics.

Zhenzhong Lan, Mingda Chen, Sebastian Goodman, Kevin Gimpel, Piyush Sharma, and Radu Soricut. 2019. Albert: A lite bert for self-supervised learning of language representations. In *International Conference on Learning Representations*.

Jiaqi Li, Ming Liu, Min-Yen Kan, Zihao Zheng, Zekun Wang, Wenqiang Lei, Ting Liu, and Bing Qin. 2020. Molweni: A challenge multiparty dialogues-based machine reading comprehension dataset with discourse structure. In *Proceedings of the 28th International Conference on Computational Linguistics*, pages 2642–2652, Barcelona, Spain (Online). International Committee on Computational Linguistics.

Hui Liu, Zhan Shi, Jia-Chen Gu, Quan Liu, Si Wei, and Xiaodan Zhu. 2020. End-to-end transition-based online dialogue disentanglement. In *IJCAI*, volume 20, pages 3868–3874.

Ryan Lowe, Nissan Pow, Iulian Vlad Serban, and Joelle Pineau. 2015. The ubuntu dialogue corpus: A large dataset for research in unstructured multi-turn dialogue systems. In *Proceedings of the 16th Annual Meeting of the Special Interest Group on Discourse and Dialogue*, pages 285–294.

Marina Meilă. 2007. Comparing clusterings—an information based distance. *Journal of multivariate analysis*, 98(5):873–895.

Jeffrey Pennington, Richard Socher, and Christopher D Manning. 2014. Glove: Global vectors for word representation. In *Proceedings of the 2014 conference on empirical methods in natural language processing (EMNLP)*, pages 1532–1543.

Ming Tan, Dakuo Wang, Yupeng Gao, Haoyu Wang, Saloni Potdar, Xiaoxiao Guo, Shiyu Chang, and Mo Yu. 2019. Context-aware conversation thread detection in multi-party chat. In *Proceedings of the 2019 Conference on Empirical Methods in Natural Language Processing and the 9th International Joint Conference on Natural Language Processing (EMNLP-IJCNLP)*, pages 6456–6461.

Ashish Vaswani, Noam Shazeer, Niki Parmar, Jakob Uszkoreit, Llion Jones, Aidan N Gomez, Łukasz Kaiser, and Illia Polosukhin. 2017. Attention is all you need. In *Advances in neural information processing systems*, pages 5998–6008.

Henghui Zhu, Feng Nan, Zhiguo Wang, Ramesh Nallapati, and Bing Xiang. 2020. Who did they respond to? conversation structure modeling using masked hierarchical transformer. In *Proceedings of the AAAI Conference on Artificial Intelligence*, volume 34, pages 9741–9748.

8 Appendix

8.1 Models

BERT : The pairwise score is computed as follows:

$$\begin{aligned}&[\boldsymbol{e_1}, \boldsymbol{e_2}, \cdots, \boldsymbol{e_m}] = \text{BERT}(concat(t_i, t_j))\\ &\boldsymbol{e} = agg([\boldsymbol{e_1}, \boldsymbol{e_2}, \cdots, \boldsymbol{e_m}])\\ &r_{ij} = \boldsymbol{W}\boldsymbol{e} + \boldsymbol{b}\end{aligned} \tag{5}$$

Here, $concat(t_i, t_j)$ means to concatenate the two sub-word sequences t_i and t_j corresponding to u_i and u_j into a single sequence $[[\text{CLS}], w_1^i, \cdots, w_{n_i}^i, [\text{SEP}], w_1^j, \cdots, w_{n_j}^j, [\text{SEP}]]$, where [CLS] is a special beginning token and [SEP] is a separation token. Denote the number of tokens in this sequence by m. Then, $\boldsymbol{e_k} \in \mathbb{R}^{d_{BERT}}$ is the encoded embedding of the k-th ($k \leq m$) token in t_{ij}. Following (Devlin et al., 2019), we use the encoded embedding of [CLS] as the aggregated representation of u_i and u_j. Another linear layer is applied to obtain score $r_{ij} \in \mathbb{R}$ using learnable parameters $\boldsymbol{W} \in \mathbb{R}^{1 \times d_{BERT}}$ and $\boldsymbol{b} \in \mathbb{R}$.

8.2 BERT+MF

We obtain the encoded embedding of [CLS] in the same way as BERT, denoted as $\boldsymbol{e}$. Then, we compute the pairwise relevance score r_{ij} as follows:

$$\boldsymbol{h} = \boldsymbol{W_e}\,\boldsymbol{e} + \boldsymbol{b_e} \tag{6}$$

$$\boldsymbol{z} = [\boldsymbol{h}; \boldsymbol{v_{ij}}] \tag{7}$$

$$\boldsymbol{o} = softsign(\boldsymbol{W_z}\boldsymbol{z} + \boldsymbol{b_z}) \tag{8}$$

$$\boldsymbol{x} = softsign(\boldsymbol{W_o}\boldsymbol{o} + \boldsymbol{b_o}) \tag{9}$$

$$r_{ij} = sum(\boldsymbol{x}) \tag{10}$$

where $\boldsymbol{W_e} \in \mathbb{R}^{d_{mid} \times d_{BERT}}$ and $\boldsymbol{b_e} \in \mathbb{R}^{d_{mid}}$ are parameters of a linear layer to reduce the dimensionality of the BERT output; $[\boldsymbol{h}; \boldsymbol{v_{ij}}]$ is the concatenation of $\boldsymbol{h}$ and the pairwise vector of hand-crafted features $\boldsymbol{v_{ij}} \in \mathbb{R}^{d_f}$; $\boldsymbol{W_z} \in \mathbb{R}^{d_o \times d_z}$, $\boldsymbol{b_z} \in \mathbb{R}^{d_o}$, $\boldsymbol{W_o} \in \mathbb{R}^{d_x \times d_o}$ and $\boldsymbol{b_o} \in \mathbb{R}^{d_x}$ are parameters of two dense layers with the *softsign* activation function; $sum(\boldsymbol{x})$ represents the sum of values in vector $\boldsymbol{x}$.

In BERT+TD. The time difference feature between u_i and u_j is a 6-d vector:

$$[n', x_1, x_2, x_3, x_4, x_5]$$

where $n' = (i - j)/100$ representing the relative distance between two utterances in the candidate pool; $x_1, \cdots, x_5$ are binary values indicating whether the time difference in minutes between u_i and u_j lies in the ranges of $[-1, 0), [0, 1), [1, 5), [5, 60)$ and $(60, \infty)$ respectively.

8.3 Pairwise Models Settings

Model architecture and training We choose the best hyper-parameters according to the *ranking* performance Recall@1 on validation set. All models are evaluated every 0.2 epoch. We stop training if Recall@1 on validation set does not improve in three evaluations consecutively.

The final settings are as follows. In MF, we use a 2-layer FFN with *softsign* activation function. Both layers contain 512 hidden units. We train it using Adam optimizer with learning rate 0.001. For all transformer-based models (BERT, BERT+MF, ALBERT and POLY-ENCODER), we use Adamax optimizer with learning rate 5×10^{-5}, updating all parameters in training. We use automatic mixed precision to reduce GPU memory consumption provided by Pytorch[7]. All experiments are implemented in Parlai[8].

8.4 BGMCD Set Up

Setup Both node frequency estimation and graph construction are based on the relevance scores from BERT+MF. In the rule-based method, we choose α in $\{0.9, 1, 1, 1.3, 1.5, 1.7, 1.9\}$ and β in $\{0.1, 0.2, 0.3, 0.4, 0.5\}$. The optimal values $\alpha = 1.3$ and $\beta = 0.2$ yield the best link prediction F1 on the validation set. The regression mode is a 2-layer fully connected neural network. Both layers contain 128 hidden units, with the ReLU activation function. We choose hidden layer size from $\{64, 128, 256\}$ and the number of layers from $\{2, 3\}$. We train the model using Adam optimizer with batch size 64. Hyper-parameters are chosen to minimize mean squared error on the validation set. The integer programming problem is solved using pywraplp[9]. We observe that sometimes the integer programming problem is infeasible due to underestimation of the frequencies of some nodes. We relax Equation 4 in experiments as follows to

[7]https://pytorch.org/

[8]https://parl.ai/

[9]`https://google.github.io/or-tools/python/ortools/linear_solver/pywraplp.html`

avoid infeasibility:

$$
\begin{aligned}
&\max \sum_{\langle v_i, v_j \rangle \in E} x(i,j) \cdot w(i,j) \\
\text{s.t.} \quad & \\
&\sum_{v_l \in neighbors(v_i)} x(i,l) \leq 1, \quad \forall v_i \in V_l \\
&\sum_{v_p \in neighbors(v_j)} x(p,j) \leq 1, \ \forall v_j \in V_r \\
&x(i,j) \in \{0,1\}
\end{aligned}
\tag{11}
$$

An Approach to the Frugal Use of Human Annotators to Scale up Auto-coding for Text Classification Tasks

Li'An Chen[1], Hanna Suominen[1,3,4]
firstname.lastname@anu.edu.au
[1] ANU, Centre for the Public Awareness of Science / Canberra, Australia
[2] The Australian National University (ANU), School of Computing (SoCo) / Canberra, Australia
[3] Data61, Commonwealth Scientific and Industrial Research Organisation / Canberra, Australia
[4] University of Turku / Turku, Finland
[*] Address for Correspondence: ANU CPAS, 42A Linnaeus Way, Canberra, ACT 2601, Australia

Abstract

Human annotation for establishing the training data is often a very costly process in natural language processing (NLP) tasks, which has led to frugal NLP approaches becoming an important research topic. Many research teams struggle to complete projects with limited funding, labor, and computational resources. Driven by the Move-Step analytic framework theorized in the applied linguistics field, our study offers a rigorous approach to the frugal use of two human annotators to scale up auto-coding for text classification tasks. We applied the Linear Support Vector Machine algorithm to text classification of a job ad corpus. Our Cohen's Kappa for inter-rater agreement and Area Under the Curve (AUC) values reached averages of 0.76 and 0.80, respectively. The calculated time consumption for our human training process was 36 days. The results indicated that even the strategic and frugal use of only two human annotators could enable the efficient training of classifiers with reasonably good performance. This study does not aim to provide generalizability of the results. Rather, it is proposed that the annotation strategies arising from this study be considered by our readers only if they are fit for one's specific research purposes.

1 Introduction

In natural language processing (NLP), human annotation is an indispensable and decisive step. The human annotation process directly influences the quality of the training data in NLP tasks, and consequently, it influences the quality of machine-generated results. In this regard, Song et al. (2020) have revealed how significant the risk of reaching an incorrect conclusion could be if the quality of human annotation used for validation cannot be guaranteed. Unfortunately, the science of annotation is progressing very slowly (Hovy and Lavid, 2010; Song et al., 2020). In many NLP studies, methodological details concerning the human annotation process have not been fully disclosed (Song et al., 2020). Such a lack of disclosure may hinder readers' judgment of the soundness of human annotation procedures (Hovy and Lavid, 2010; Song et al., 2020). It is time for NLP researchers to attach greater importance to the methodological rigor of human annotation in NLP tasks.

Where the funding and labor are limited, institutions or researchers might have to turn to the 'frugal' use of human annotators for text labelling tasks. For instance, Andreotta et al. (2019) acknowledged the limitation of not being able to afford high computational and labor costs in their machine learning (ML)-assisted analysis of Tweeter commentary. Johnson et al. (2018) also point out cost control that many engineering teams may need to deal with and emphasize the importance of minimizing labor cost and required training data to meet target results in NLP projects. Therefore, well-planned investment of labor and training resources for NLP and ML tasks is a topic worth considerable scholarly attention. We need to investigate how to make the best use of limited labor and monetary resource to achieve the optimal machine-generated outcomes, while preserving methodological rigor.

Crowdsourcing is often put forward as a solution to the human coder resource problem. Aside from the fact that crowds are often not experts, this kind of human annotation is allowed only in some national contexts, such as in the US (e.g., Munro et al., 2010; Pavlick et al., 2014). This solution is not broadly applicable and has ethical implications with respect to researchers exploiting free or cheap labor. For instance, such option does not conform to the requirement for minimum hourly salaries under employment laws in national contexts such as Australia (Australian Government, 2020). Under circumstances of regulatory limitations and within ethical constraints, it becomes necessary to resort to the frugal use of human annotators to scale up data analyses.

Unlike human annotation tasks for ordinary image annotation (e.g., dog vs. cat recognition), many text annotations require expert knowledge because they are simply more demanding. For instance, the labelling of research skills in job ads involved human annotators who worked as researchers and educators at universities in Mewburn et al. (2020). These researchers point out that it can be extremely time and money-consuming to hire multiple expert human annotators. In many cases, if annotation procedures were well-devised, the frugal option generated results that were as good as the more costly option (Chang et al., 2017; Cocos et al., 2015). From the perspective of cost control, a better option would be to also involve non-expert annotators with well-designed annotation schemes to reach the optimal annotation outcomes (Chang et al., 2017). Therefore, it is in the interest of textual-data scientists to investigate if there is a way to guarantee the quality of manual annotation with the frugal use of human coders for automatic textual data analyses at scale. As many social science disciplines (e.g., applied linguistics or sociology) have a record of excellent human annotation frameworks, it is worth considering if annotation frameworks in any of these fields could help us enhance the methodological soundness for human annotation process in NLP tasks.

The research questions of this study are posed as follows:

1. For automatic text classification tasks, how could we design human annotators' workshop frugally and at the same time maintain good performance of the machine?

2. How could we design the human annotators' workshop to enable easy identification and fixation of problems in the human annotation schema?

3. If multiple human annotators were involved, which annotator's labelled data should be adopted for training?

The primary outcomes of this study were as follows:

1. The frugal use of an expert annotator and a non-expert annotator generated an averaged Cohen's Kappa of 0.76.

2. The total time investment of our frugal approach to human annotation was 376 hours (the time consumed by two human annotators).

3. The frugal use of only two human annotators plus a limited amount of labelled data resulted in an averaged area under the receiver operating characteristic (ROC) curve (AUC) score of 0.80.

4. Differentiation of coarse-grained and fine-grained labels allowed for enhanced interpretability of the ML performance. It also allowed for strategically hybrid use of multiple human annotators' labels to optimize the ML performance.

2 Methods

2.1 Data

Our human coders annotated job ad data from a corpus of high research skill intensive job ads of computing and healthcare positions[1]. In total, 1,800 job ads were chosen randomly from a large corpus consisted of health-domain and computing-domain job postings. The word counts of the 1,800 job ads reached 680,367. The randomly chosen job ads contained 900 health-domain job ads and 900 computing-domain job ads. As we aimed to minimize the labor and time cost, as well as the amount of data used for training and validation, the selection of only 1,800 job ads was based on a balanced consideration of the machine's performance and the time investment on manual annotation.

The job ad corpus was purchased from Burning Glass Technology Inc. Due to legal constraints, the data used for this study cannot be shared. However, it is assumed that our audience would be those who do not necessarily need to conduct analyses of job ads, but potentially other text classification tasks. Alternatively, readers interested in obtaining the same data for a verification of the results could contact Burning Glass Technology Inc. directly.

2.2 Ethics

We went through necessary ethics procedures to avoid potential conflict of interests. We obtained the approval for the data to be used for our research purpose. The manuscript of the paper was read by a legal consultant in our team and a representative from Burning Glass Technology Inc. to ensure our publication met contractual agreements. We also signed an agreement with our human annotators for clarification of responsibilities and task specifications. The agreement with the human annotators was approved by our ethics delegate. Thus, we believe that ethical issues were mitigated to the best of our abilities.

[1] We only analyzed computing-domain and health-domain job postings because the current paper is part of a large project to contextualize high-RSI job requirements for pedagogical purposes.

2.3 Human Annotators' Workshop

Our study involved two human annotators for the labelling of requirements in job ads. The first human annotator N1was one of the authors of the paper. N1 was an expert annotator and a PhD candidate who held a master's degree in applied linguistics with extensive experience in identifying job requirements from textual data. The second annotator N2 was hired as a volunteer for our task. N2 held a master's degree in finance with experience in classifying news information, her experience was less relevant compared to N1. Hence, N2 played the role of a novice human annotator in the annotators' team.

Before assigning the job ads to N1 and N2, the job ad texts were segmented into sentences to be labelled by the annotators. The purpose of segmenting the job ad data into sentences was to reduce cognitive burdens for both annotators.

It was decided that there should be both coarse-grained labels and fine-grained labels. The decision was theoretically driven and inspired by an inductive analytic framework called 'Move-Step analysis' pioneered by the renowned applied linguist John Swales (1990). Move-Step analysis is a widely adopted linguistic approach to the systematic examination of different genres (or text types). Genre theorists (Miller, 1984; Bhatia, 2014; Moreno and Swales, 2018) advocate that writing is a social action, and so a specific genre serves as a tool to achieve a social purpose that is shared among a community of practice. In our case, the purpose of the job ad genre is the communication of various skills, qualifications and capabilities required of a particular job vacancy, by the employer to potential hirees. To achieve an overarching purpose of a genre, writers need to involve conventionally acknowledged components in their writing (Swales, 1990). Swalesian genre theorists differentiated the conventional textual components of a genre into coarse-grained moves and fine-grained steps. The intention of differentiating granularity levels derives from the pedagogical orientation shared among the Swalesian genre theorists (Bhatia, 2014; Maswana et al., 2015; Moreno and Swales, 2018) for clarifying concepts more clearly in class. Move-step analysis has previously been applied by NLP researchers such as Chen et al. (2020) for projects with a strong pedagogical orientation. As argued by Chen et al. (2020), the provision of coarse-grained and fine-grained conventions embedded in the writing of a genre would allow students to learn more efficiently. The pedagogical orientation of move-step analysis aligns well with our intention to identify job requirements to enrich employability training[2].

To give the readers a clearer sense of what we meant by a coarse-grained/move-level job requirement label and its associated fine-grained/step-level labels, we give the example of the job requirement 'Continuous education' below:

Coarse-grained/Move-step label:

- Continuous education.

Its associated fine-grained labels:

- Passion & Self-motivation,
- Participation in training,
- Sharing of knowledge,
- Seeking advice, and
- Self-reflection.

Moreover, we assumed that the differentiation between coarse-grained and fine-grained labels might have other potential benefits. Having coarse- and fine-grained labels may speed up the annotation process. In this regard, Tange et al. (1998) showed that the combination of coarse and fine-grained labels helped the readers of informatics process information faster and more accurately.

After introducing move-step analysis and assigning the task to the two annotators, N1 conducted the first round of annotation of 200 job ads, as she had the expert skills and knowledge relevant to the task. It was then decided that the unit to be annotated could contain multiple labels, as N1 found that the employers sometimes put multiple requirements in one sentence. Hence, our task was multi-label text classification. After N1 finished the first round of annotation, she came up with a coding schema that listed all the coarse-grained and fine-grained job requirement categories, and she gave the schema to N2. From the second to the last round of annotation, both N1 and N2 were involved in the task. N1 and N2 conducted their annotation tasks individually. The two annotators used the annotation tool Dataturks to label the texts.

Overall, there were nine rounds of annotation. In between every two rounds of annotation, the

[2]How to use the identified job requirements to enrich employability training is not covered in the current paper. Our main focus in this study is still the demonstration of the frugal use of human annotators. The point of mentioning the alignment between our pedagogical aim and the use of move-step analysis is to advocate a well-justified selection of analytic framework to be used in human annotators' workshop to fit one's specific research aim.

two annotators met once to discuss their compared results. If a high level of inconsistency measured by Cohen's Kappa was found regarding a particular fine-grained label (e.g., Continuous education - Passion & Self-motivation), N1 and N2 would randomly scan through several inconsistent instances and give their justifications about why they labeled in their ways. If the agreement was reached concerning how to label similar instances in the future, both of them would write the agreed approach in their notepads. However, if an agreement was not reached after their justifications were given, they would note down the dubious items and leave them for the next meeting when they labeled more data and had further justifications to convince each other.

The inter-rater reliability between the two human annotators was measured by Cohen's Kappa. For assessing coders' agreement on the annotation of categorical variables, Hallgren (2013) recommends Cohen's Kappa as the measurement. The Cohen's Kappa equation was given in (1) as follows:

$$K = \frac{P(a) - P(e)}{1 - P(e)} \tag{1}$$

where P(a) denotes the observed percentage of the human annotators' agreement and P(e) refers to the probability that the agreement is met by chance.

After the Kappa was calculated for each coarse-grained and fine-grained category, we also calculated the standard error for the calculation of the 95% confidence intervals for the Kappa. The standard error equation is given in (2) as follows:

$$\alpha_K = \sqrt{\frac{P(a)(1 - P(e))}{N(1 - P(e))^2}} \tag{2}$$

where N refers to the overall numbers of classified tokens.

2.4 Machine Learning Methods

The algorithm chosen for running the auto-coding task was the Support Vector Machine (SVM) (Cortes and Vapnik, 1995) with the linear kernel. Linear SVM is a good choice in a low-resource context (Zhang et al., 2012), such as in ours. Linear SVM had also a low computational cost and at the same time good prediction results (Vijayan et al., 2017). For multi-label text classification tasks, Linear SVM could have good ability to generate prediction results close to those generated by manual efforts (Qin and Wang, 2009; Yang et al., 2009; Wang and Chiang, 2011).

We involved several steps in preprocessing the data. As mentioned in the description of the human coders' workshop, we segmented the job ad texts into sentences as labeling units. The classification task hence was also at sentence level. There were 63,504 sentence units overall. The average number of labels per sentence was 1.8. The segmentation into sentences supported calculation of the job requirements more accurately. Additionally, we removed stop words (e.g., conjunctions, articles) from the texts via the stop-word list given in the Natural Language Toolkit (NLTK) corpus v.3.5. The data were then put in a machine-readable format with the word representation tool TfidfVectorizer (term frequency times inverse document frequency) from the Scikit-learn v0.24.1.

We separated the processed data into 70%, 15%, and 15% chunks for the training, testing, and validation purposes. The ratio of the training/test/validation sets was based on the conventional practice suggested in Muller and Guido (2016) and Ng (2020). We were aware of other validation approaches such as K-fold cross-validation (CV). Considering that the tuning of the hyper-parameters (e.g., K value and ratio) in other CV approaches could be time-consuming and computationally expensive whilst their gain limited (as in Anguita et al., 2012 and Racz et al., 2021), we chose to proceed with the frugal option of 70%, 15% ,15% split of the data for train/test/validation.

For the parameter-tuning function of the Linear SVM classifier, we adopted the GridSearchCV tool from the Scikit-Learn v0.24.1. More specifically, the parameters tuned were 1) Loss, 2) Max-iteration, 3) Tolerance, 4) Fit intercept, and 5) Intercept scaling.

The performance of the Linear SVM classifier was measured by the AUC. The reason that we chose the AUC is that it, compared to the accuracy, F1 or other such measurements, was less prone to biased results from class imbalance (Suominen et al., 2008; Narkhede, 2018).

After the AUC values were calculated, we also computed the 95% confidence intervals for our automatic classifier.

3 Results

The inter-rater agreement measured by Cohen's K reached an average of 0.76 (see Section 3.1), meaning that most of our manually labeled categories can be used for making at least tentative conclusions. The results related to the total time investment in the human annotation process (see Section 3.2) suggested that two human annotators, each working 5 hours a day, would need approximately 36 days to complete the task. Section 3.3 is concerned with the performance of the two automatic classifiers trained with data labeled by our two annotators. Although the two classifiers both reached an averaged AUC of 0.80, a closer examination of fine-grained categories revealed potential room for further improvement to the human annotation schema. These findings posed the question of whether high-inter rater agreement is more important than the ML results' interpretability. Moreover, strategic hybrid use of the two classifiers for optimization was introduced in Section 3.3.

3.1 Inter-rater Agreement

The averaged inter-rater reliability measured by Kappa for all the identified categories reached 0.76 (see Table 1). For the fine-grained categories, the Kappa ranged from the minimum 0.60 to the maximum of 0.94. At the coarse-grained level, the Kappa range from 0.68 to 0.83. Based on the Kappa interpretation guidelines suggested by Krippendorff (2018), Kappa values under 0.67 indicate that any conclusion should not be counted. Values ranging from 0.67 to 0.80 point to tentative conclusions to be made. Values above 0.80 indicate that definite conclusions can be made. Based on Krippendorff's guidelines, it is safe to claim that only 9 out of 72, or 12.5% of the fine-gained categories, did not reach the standards for making a tentative conclusion. The rest 87.5% of fine-grained categories reached the 'Pass' Kappa threshold defined by Krippendorff, which has been deemed among the strictest (Hallgren, 2013). If we use guidelines defined by Landis and Koch (1977), who viewed Kappa under 0.61 as enough for the indication of a moderate agreement between two annotators, most of our fine-grained categories can be used for making at least tentative conclusions.

3.2 Time Investment in Human Annotation

The annotators reported that averagely they spent ten seconds annotating each sentence token in the task when they were fully concentrating on the task. The two annotators both labelled 63,504 sentence tokens. Therefore, the total time investment in the completion of a single-person annotation task was

Coarse-grained	Fine-grained	*Kappa* (Fine)	*95% CI* (Fine)	*Kappa* (Coarse)
People skills	Peer practitioners	0.76	(0.72 - 0.80)	0.70
	Interpersonal skills	0.77	(0.71 - 0.82)	
	Multidisciplinary collaboration	0.76	(0.72 - 0.81)	
	Decision makers	0.64	(0.59 - 0.69)	
	Public sectors	0.71	(0.68 - 0.74)	
	Private sectors	0.60	(0.55 - 0.66)	
	Business partners	0.71	(0.68 - 0.74)	
	General public	0.60	(0.54 - 0.66)	
	Research participants	0.70	(0.67 - 0.74)	
	Research institutions	0.78	(0.75 - 0.81)	
Empathy with	Clients	0.87	(0.81 - 0.93)	0.83
	Less experienced	0.73	(0.69 - 0.77)	
	Ethnic minorities	0.83	(0.80 - 0.87)	
	Children	0.89	(0.86 - 0.92)	
	Public welfare	0.65	(0.61 - 0.69)	
	Clients' families	0.85	(0.81 - 0.90)	
	Aging population	0.86	(0.82 - 0.91)	
	Disabled	0.88	(0.85 - 0.92)	
	Women	0.77	(0.73 - 0.91)	
	LGBTQI+	0.94	(0.91 - 0.99)	
Personal attributes	Leadership skills	0.82	(0.78 - 0.86)	0.77
	Time efficiency	0.79	(0.74 - 0.83)	
	Commercial orientation	0.69	(0.65 - 0.74)	
	Safety awareness	0.81	(0.77 - 0.85)	
	High-pressure management	0.72	(0.67 - 0.77)	
	Personal impact	0.81	(0.77 - 0.84)	
	Result orientation	0.82	(0.77 - 0.86)	
	Attention to details	0.77	(0.74 - 0.81)	
	Independence	0.80	(0.76 - 0.85)	
	Agility	0.71	(0.68 - 0.75)	
Continuous education	Passion & Motivation	0.78	(0.73 - 0.82)	0.78
	Knowledge sharing	0.83	(0.80 - 0.87)	
	Participation in training	0.80	(0.77 - 0.84)	
	Seeking advice	0.77	(0.72 - 0.81)	
	Self-reflection	0.70	(0.64 - 0.75)	
Cognitive abilities	Analytic skills	0.80	(0.77 - 0.84)	0.81
	Problem understanding & solving	0.83	(0.77 - 0.88)	
	Needs interpretation	0.76	(0.72 - 0.80)	
	Innovation	0.85	(0.81 - 0.89)	
Pursuit of job quality	Organisational environment	0.82	(0.78 - 0.86)	0.77
	Long-term contract	0.76	(0.72 - 0.79)	
	Specified payment	0.74	(0.69 - 0.79)	
	Unspecified payment	0.73	(0.70 - 0.77)	
	Surrounding environment	0.80	(0.75 - 0.84)	
Proof of qualification	Registration in institutions	0.79	(0.76 - 0.82)	0.77
	Writing skills	0.72	(0.68 - 0.75)	
	Oral & Presentation skills	0.79	(0.73 - 0.84)	
	Residency	0.80	(0.77 - 0.83)	
	Tertiary degree	0.81	(0.75 - 0.87)	
	Years of industry experience	0.80	(0.76 - 0.83)	
	General IT skills	0.70	(0.64 - 0.77)	
Professional standards	Policy & Regulation familiarisation	0.82	(0.78 - 0.85)	0.78
	Background check	0.88	(0.84 - 0.92)	
	Ethical conduct	0.61	(0.57 - 0.65)	
	Awareness of confidentiality	0.79	(0.75 - 0.84)	
Aesthetics	Detecting defects & debugging	0.77	(0.72 - 0.83)	0.81
	Refined design	0.85	(0.81 - 0.89)	
	Maintenance of environment	0.80	(0.72 - 0.87)	
Courage	Change management	0.79	(0.76 - 0.83)	0.72
	Risk management	0.77	(0.71 - 0.83)	
	Execution from concept	0.60	(0.56 - 0.64)	
	Travelling & Driving	0.81	(0.75 - 0.87)	
	On-call availability	0.69	(0.61 - 0.77)	
	Conflict management	0.68	(0.62 - 0.73)	
	Working in harsh environment	0.70	(0.62 - 0.77)	
Resource management	Capital & Budget management	0.70	(0.66 - 0.75)	0.71
	Configuration management	0.81	(0.77 - 0.84)	
	Resource allocation	0.63	(0.60 - 0.67)	
Hiring procedure	ASAP orientation	0.65	(0.61 - 0.69)	0.70
	Quality selection process	0.75	(0.70 - 0.81)	
Subject knowledge	Computer science subject knowledge	0.75	(0.70 - 0.80)	0.68
	Medical science subject knowledge	0.60	(0.56 - 0.65)	
None category	* Step tokens with no information about job requirements	0.92	(0.90 - 0.93)	N/A

Table 1: Cohen's K and the respective 95% confidence interval (CI) for the inter-rater agreement.

approximately 177 hours. Suppose a research team hires two annotators to do the coding task concurrently, and both the annotators work five hours a day. A project of a size comparable to ours might need about 36 days for the manual labeling to be completed. We considered such a time span as reasonably moderate. In addition, if the hired annotators could work for over five hours each day, the completion of the manual labeling process could be even faster. The exact hours allocated to a human annotator per day might vary based on different research teams' consideration.

The total labeling hours of the two annotators were 354 hours. Our corpus contained 826,891 words. Therefore, the approximate time investment per word for our labelling task was 1.6s. There were nine rounds of meetings (one hour for every meeting) plus the two-hour orientation time. Hence, two-person efforts for orientation and meetings cost 22 hours. In total, our two-annotator labeling task incurred a 376-hour time investment. Any team who also wants to use a similar frugal approach to their human-labeling task would find our results of interest.

3.3 Performance of the Automatic Classifier

The two automatic classifiers trained and tested with the data labeled by our two human annotators both reached an averaged gold-standard AUC value of 0.80. Table 2 suggest that 58% of the coarse-grained categories reached AUC values above 0.80 with Machine N1 on data labeled by N1. Around 57% of step-level categories reached AUC values above 0.8 with Machine N2 on data labeled by N2. The scores of AUC given by the machine trained and tested from data labeled by annotator N1 ranged from 0.52 to 1.00. The scores of AUC given by the machine trained and tested from data labeled by annotator N2 ranged from 0.58 to 0.99. Interestingly, when we calculated the average of the AUC results given by Machine N1 trained and tested on Data N1 for all the fine-grained categories, the value reached 0.80. Similarly, the averaged AUC results given by Machine N2 trained and tested on Data N2 reached 0.80, too. This reminded us of the likelihood that even when a machine's performance seems outstanding at a coarse-grained level, potential problems at a fine-grained level might be invisible.

Certain coarse-grained categories such as 'Decision makers' and 'Public welfare' were low in AUC scores. We would pay particular attention to these categories in our future attempt for continuous improvement. Our approach of identifying both the fine- and coarse-grained categories proved to be one that could increase the interpretability of the results. More specifically, if we had not differentiated between the fine- and coarse-grained categories, we would not have been able to know where the problem lay in the human annotation schema. With the information about which fine-grained categories did well and which did not, we could allow more efficient future attempts to drive continuous improvement on the human coding schema.

When classifier Ni was tested with data labeled by Nj, most of our fine-grained categories did not show a large decrease in the AUC. When the drop was small, we assumed that the two ML classifiers trained by the two annotators performed almost equally well. We only found 15 fine-grained categories to have a relatively large decrease in the AUC. We used an averaged decrease of 0.05 as the threshold (a threshold used in Hiissa et al., 2006) to denote a large decrease in classifier Ni's performance when tested with data labeled by Nj.

These 15 fine-grained categories, which showed a large decrease in performance were 'Peer practitioners', 'Interpersonal skills', 'Safety awareness', 'Agility', 'Passion Motivation', 'Problem understanding & solving', 'Unspecific payment', 'Residency', 'Refined design', 'Change management', 'Risk management', 'Conflict management', 'Working in harsh environment', 'Resource allocation', and 'Medical science subject knowledge' (Table 2).

These 15 fine-grained categories had good performance with Machine Ni tested on data labeled by Ni, but Machine Ni on data labeled by Nj gave a worse performance. This could indicate that the two human annotators' inner-rater reliability was high, but their inter-rater reliability was not as high. When human annotators face categories like these 15 ones in our study, we recommend a check regarding which features the human annotator Ni deemed as relevant to a category, but the human annotator Nj deemed as not. For the rest categories that did not show a large decrease, we recommend that researchers put Machine Ni into the formal use if Machine Ni on Data Nj results in less decrease in the AUC whilst Machine Ni's performance on Data Ni is also good. Instead of relying on the use of a single classifier for classifying all the fine-grained categories, the hybrid usage of Machine N1 and Machine N2 could optimize the classifier's performance even if the annotators' workshop was frugally designed.

4 Discussion

Our study showed that even the frugal use of only two human annotators plus a limited amount of labeled data resulted in an averaged AUC score of 0.80. Nonetheless, the differentiation between the fine-grained and coarse-grained categories in our coding schema revealed even the averaged AUC of 0.80 did not necessarily mean the quality of human annotation was as good [3]. The differentiation of fine and coarse granularities could enhance the interpretability of the results. In particular, such a differentiation provided a straightforward indication as to where the machine performed well or not and also where the problems lay in the human annotators' coding schema.

Our study had limitations. Although we provided justifications for all the choices we made in our methods, there is room to refine our project's design (e.g., involving classification of other genres) when we have more resources. Compared to most previous coding schemas where no differentiation of granularity levels was made, our approach could allow more to-the-point and efficient fixation of the human annotation for continuous improvement. Our findings regarding the benefits of having two granularity levels echo the results in Chen et al. (2020). Our choice of making the differentiation between granularity levels counters the suggestion given by Hovy and Lavid (2010). They argue that coarser granularity would improve the accuracy of human annotation results. Nonetheless, Hovy and Lavid (2010) have mostly used examples of semantic recognition tasks such as verb-sense annotation to support their argument. Our task of text classification is different from semantic recognition. Therefore, it is worth further investigating whether it is reasonable to always opt for 'neutering' for all NLP tasks only for the sake of reaching a high inter-rater agreement regardless of the research purpose.

Our frugal use of one expert annotator and one non-expert annotators proved to cost moderate annotation time whilst generating reasonably good results. Compared to the recruitment of multiple expert-annotators, our approach certainly was much less costly. The strategically hybrid use of automatic classifiers trained by our two annotators is perhaps comparable to a classifier trained by only expert annotators. However, such an assumption is subject to future investigations where appropriate measures are involved.

Future scholarly attempts could explore this topic of frugal hybrids of machines and human experts further to verify our assumption. In this regard, Fort (2016) and Chen et al. (2020) echo our thoughts by arguing that a well-devised non-expert annotator workshop could allow the labeling quality to be as good as when only expert annotators generate the labeling. Chang et al. (2017) expressed the concern that writing guidelines for even simple concepts for non-expert coders can be very prohibitive, but our approach of mixing both expert and non-expert coders is less likely to incur uncertainties and unexpected costs. To drive the progress of the science of annotation, scholars in the future might find it interesting to compare labeling results generated by pure experts, a mixture of experts non-experts, and crowdsourced workers for the same NLP project.

5 Conclusion

In this study, we advocate a methodologically sound approach to the frugal use of two annotators to conduct human annotation tasks for NLP projects. Our approach has multiple benefits. Specifically, the time and resource consumption of our frugal approach were moderate compared to the more expensive choice of hiring multiple expert annotators. Having multiple rounds of annotation activities and ongoing meetings makes it possible to make timely justification and adjustments for the annotation schema. Moderate cost, timely communication of dubious labels, joint development of the annotation schema, and reasonably good ML outcomes are the features of our frugal but theoretically sound approach to human annotation. These features make the frugal use of minimally two hu-

[3] The point of constantly mentioning the coarse-grained categories in this paper is to emphasize how coarse granularity alone was unable to ensure the optimal performance for our specific annotation task. Single granularity level has been pervasively used in many text classication tasks (Chen et al., 2018; Da San Martino et al., 2019; Heinisch and Cimiano, 2021). Nonetheless, recent studies (Chen et al., 2018; Da San Martino et al., 2019; Heinisch and Cimiano, 2021) suggest that single granularity cannot guarantee the optimal performance for certain tasks, which echo our findings here. In addition, we feel it necessary to keep the coarse granularity because the high-level categories are always useful when presenting complex results to the public

Coarse-grained	Fine-grained	AUC (Machine N1 on N1)	AUC (Machine N2 on N2)	AUC (Machine N1 on N2)	AUC (Machine N2 on N1)	Drop (Machine N1)	Drop (Machine N2)	95% CI (Machine N1)	95% CI (Machine N2)
People skills	Peer practitioners	0.82	0.84	0.77	0.77	0.05	0.07	(0.74 - 0.86)	(0.76 - 0.89)
	Interpersonal skills	0.85	0.83	0.76	0.81	0.09	0.02	(0.82 - 0.88)	(0.80 - 0.87)
	Multidisciplinary collaboration	0.86	0.84	0.84	0.78	0.02	0.06	(0.80 - 0.92)	(0.78 - 0.90)
	Decision makers	0.69	0.65	0.62	0.65	0.07	0.00	(0.63 - 0.74)	(0.60 - 0.70)
	Public sectors	0.69	0.65	0.66	0.69	0.03	0.00	(0.59 - 0.78)	(0.55 - 0.74)
	Private sectors	0.68	0.70	0.70	0.72	0.00	0.00	(0.59 - 0.79)	(0.61 - 0.80)
	Business partners	0.79	0.72	0.80	0.71	0.00	0.01	(0.73 - 0.84)	(0.67 - 0.78)
	General public	0.67	0.62	0.61	0.60	0.06	0.02	(0.61 - 0.72)	(0.55 - 0.69)
	Research participants	0.73	0.70	0.78	0.72	0.00	0.00	(0.67 - 0.79)	(0.64 - 0.77)
	Research institutions	0.81	0.83	0.88	0.79	0.00	0.04	(0.75 - 0.87)	(0.77 - 0.89)
Empathy with	Clients	0.88	0.92	0.87	0.88	0.01	0.04	(0.84 - 0.92)	(0.88 - 0.95)
	Less experienced	0.82	0.75	0.84	0.76	0.00	0.00	(0.77 - 0.86)	(0.70 - 0.79)
	Ethnic minorities	0.87	0.82	0.83	0.79	0.04	0.03	(0.82 - 0.91)	(0.77 - 0.86)
	Children	0.92	0.89	0.87	0.86	0.05	0.03	(0.88 - 0.96)	(0.84 - 0.93)
	Public welfare	0.52	0.58	0.60	0.56	0.00	0.02	(0.47 - 0.58)	(0.53 - 0.64)
	Clients' families	0.88	0.85	0.91	0.86	0.00	0.00	(0.84 - 0.92)	(0.80 - 0.89)
	Aging population	0.89	0.87	0.86	0.90	0.03	0.00	(0.83 - 0.94)	(0.81 - 0.93)
	Disabled	0.97	0.92	0.91	0.96	0.06	0.00	(0.94 - 0.99)	(0.87 - 0.97)
	Women	0.82	0.88	0.79	0.78	0.03	0.10	(0.76 - 0.88)	(0.82 - 0.94)
	LGBTQI+	1.00	0.99	0.98	0.98	0.02	0.01	(0.99 - 1.00)	(0.97 - 0.99)
Personal attributes	Leadership skills	0.85	0.84	0.89	0.88	0.00	0.00	(0.79 - 0.90)	(0.78 - 0.89)
	Time efficiency	0.80	0.83	0.76	0.79	0.04	0.04	(0.76 - 0.85)	(0.78 - 0.88)
	Commercial orientation	0.75	0.72	0.70	0.77	0.05	0.00	(0.70 - 0.81)	(0.66 - 0.77)
	Safety awareness	0.92	0.91	0.89	0.83	0.03	0.08	(0.88 - 0.96)	(0.87 - 0.95)
	High-pressure management	0.71	0.72	0.69	0.70	0.02	0.02	(0.66 - 0.77)	(0.66 - 0.76)
	Personal impact	0.83	0.85	0.86	0.82	0.00	0.03	(0.79 - 0.87)	(0.80 - 0.89)
	Result orientation	0.76	0.73	0.71	0.69	0.05	0.04	(0.70 - 0.81)	(0.69 - 0.78)
	Attention to details	0.78	0.78	0.75	0.77	0.03	0.01	(0.75 - 0.83)	(0.75 - 0.83)
	Independence	0.83	0.81	0.85	0.86	0.00	0.00	(0.79 - 0.87)	(0.77 - 0.85)
	Agility	0.84	0.82	0.72	0.75	0.12	0.07	(0.76 - 0.93)	(0.73 - 0.90)
Continuous education	Passion & Motivation	0.87	0.85	0.77	0.79	0.10	0.06	(0.83 - 0.91)	(0.80 - 0.89)
	Knowledge sharing	0.84	0.85	0.82	0.84	0.02	0.01	(0.79 - 0.88)	(0.80 - 0.90)
	Participation in training	0.87	0.84	0.81	0.85	0.06	0.00	(0.83 - 0.91)	(0.79 - 0.88)
	Seeking advice	0.71	0.72	0.78	0.77	0.00	0.00	(0.67 - 0.76)	(0.68 - 0.77)
	Self-reflection	0.70	0.69	0.76	0.68	0.00	0.01	(0.60 - 0.81)	(0.59 - 0.80)
Cognitive abilities	Analytic skills	0.77	0.74	0.82	0.78	0.00	0.00	(0.72 - 0.83)	(0.69 - 0.79)
	Problem understanding & solving	0.94	0.92	0.90	0.84	0.04	0.08	(0.91 - 0.97)	(0.88 - 0.95)
	Needs interpretation	0.78	0.82	0.71	0.79	0.07	0.03	(0.73 - 0.84)	(0.77 - 0.86)
	Innovation	0.90	0.91	0.86	0.89	0.04	0.02	(0.86 - 0.94)	(0.87 - 0.95)
Pursuit of job quality	Organisational environment	0.91	0.91	0.88	0.90	0.03	0.01	(0.86 - 0.96)	(0.86 - 0.96)
	Long-term contract	0.73	0.70	0.75	0.74	0.00	0.00	(0.64 - 0.81)	(0.61 - 0.78)
	Specified payment	0.79	0.77	0.71	0.75	0.08	0.02	(0.69 - 0.88)	(0.67 - 0.87)
	Unspecified payment	0.76	0.78	0.73	0.70	0.03	0.08	(0.70 - 0.83)	(0.71 - 0.85)
	Surrounding environment	0.61	0.66	0.65	0.70	0.00	0.00	(0.54 - 0.68)	(0.59 - 0.74)
Proof of qualification	Registration in institutions	0.84	0.84	0.87	0.81	0.00	0.03	(0.80 - 0.88)	(0.80 - 0.88)
	Writing skills	0.79	0.75	0.74	0.72	0.05	0.03	(0.74 - 0.83)	(0.70 - 0.80)
	Oral & Presentation skills	0.81	0.81	0.80	0.79	0.01	0.02	(0.75 - 0.87)	(0.75 - 0.87)
	Residency	0.96	0.89	0.84	0.85	0.12	0.04	(0.92 - 0.99)	(0.85 - 0.94)
	Tertiary degree	0.88	0.91	0.88	0.85	0.00	0.06	(0.81 - 0.95)	(0.83 - 0.98)
	Years of industry experience	0.84	0.84	0.81	0.82	0.03	0.02	(0.79 - 0.88)	(0.79 - 0.88)
	General IT skills	0.70	0.71	0.73	0.69	0.00	0.02	(0.65 - 0.76)	(0.66 - 0.77)
Professional standards	Policy & Regulation familiarisation	0.89	0.87	0.83	0.81	0.06	0.06	(0.85 - 0.93)	(0.92 - 0.91)
	Background check	0.92	0.96	0.88	0.90	0.04	0.06	(0.88 - 0.95)	(0.93 - 0.99)
	Ethical conduct	0.64	0.68	0.62	0.67	0.02	0.01	(0.60 - 0.68)	(0.64 - 0.72)
	Awareness of confidentiality	0.85	0.87	0.88	0.80	0.00	0.07	(0.80 - 0.91)	(0.82 - 0.92)
Aesthetics	Detecting defects & debugging	0.81	0.83	0.80	0.78	0.01	0.05	(0.76 - 0.85)	(0.78 - 0.87)
	Refined design	0.93	0.92	0.86	0.87	0.07	0.05	(0.89 - 0.97)	(0.88 - 0.96)
	Maintenance of environment	0.84	0.86	0.81	0.79	0.03	0.07	(0.78 - 0.91)	(0.80 - 0.93)
Courage	Change management	0.87	0.88	0.79	0.82	0.08	0.06	(0.83 - 0.91)	(0.84 - 0.92)
	Risk management	0.85	0.83	0.77	0.78	0.08	0.05	(0.80 - 0.91)	(0.78 - 0.88)
	Execution from concept	0.66	0.70	0.68	0.63	0.00	0.07	(0.60 - 0.72)	(0.64 - 0.76)
	Travelling & Driving	0.85	0.88	0.81	0.82	0.04	0.06	(0.79 - 0.90)	(0.82 - 0.93)
	On-call availability	0.73	0.74	0.77	0.69	0.00	0.05	(0.68 - 0.77)	(0.69 - 0.78)
	Conflict management	0.77	0.74	0.69	0.71	0.08	0.03	(0.73 - 0.82)	(0.70 - 0.79)
	Working in harsh environment	0.77	0.73	0.70	0.68	0.07	0.05	(0.70 - 0.85)	(0.66 - 0.80)
Resource management	Capital & Budget management	0.75	0.77	0.71	0.72	0.04	0.05	(0.70 - 0.81)	(0.72 - 0.83)
	Configuration management	0.83	0.84	0.77	0.82	0.06	0.02	(0.79 - 0.88)	(0.80 - 0.89)
	Resource allocation	0.73	0.71	0.68	0.62	0.05	0.09	(0.68 - 0.78)	(0.66 - 0.76)
Hiring procedure	ASAP orientation	0.70	0.69	0.70	0.66	0.00	0.03	(0.64 - 0.76)	(0.64 - 0.75)
	Quality selection process	0.81	0.84	0.87	0.78	0.00	0.06	(0.75 - 0.86)	(0.78 - 0.89)
Subject knowledge	Computer science subject knowledge	0.81	0.79	0.76	0.77	0.05	0.02	(0.73 - 0. 88)	(0.71 - 0.86)
	Medical science subject knowledge	0.69	0.71	0.60	0.63	0.09	0.08	(0.61 - 0.78)	(0.62 - 0.80)

Table 2: AUC values and respective 95% confidence intervals (IC) & Drop from Machine Ni tested on Nj.

man annotators a good alternative to crowdsourcing and expert annotation. Regarding whether or not to differentiate granularity levels and whether or not to resort to human annotation frameworks from non-NLP disciplines in the human annotation process, our suggestion is that researchers should make the decision based on specific research purposes. We hope this study could serve as a point to drive reflection upon the science of annotation within our NLP community.

Acknowledgement

We are grateful for the support from Emsi Burning Glass Inc, PostAc®, and ANU CV Discovery Translation Fund2.0. Our thanks also go to Prof. Inger Mewburn, Dr. Will Grant, and the anonymous paper reviewers for their insightful comments on this paper. We thank Dr. Lindsay Hogan and Chenchen Xu for offering us advise on the technical and legal requirements involved in this study. We appreciate the anonymous annotator's contribution in our coders' workshop. Finally, the first author would like to thank Australian Government Research Training Program International Scholarship for supporting her PhD studies.

References

Andreotta, M., Nugroho, R., Hurlstone, M., Boschetti, F., Farrell, S., Walker, I., and Paris, C. (2019). Analyzing social media data: A mixed-methods framework combining computational and qualitative text analysis. *Behavior Research Methods*, 51(4):1776–1781.

Anguita, D., Ghelardoni, L., Ghio, A., Oneto, L., and Ridella, S. (2012). The 'k' in k-fold cross validation. In *Proceedings of the 2012 European Symposium on Artificial Neural Networks, Computational Intelligence and Machine Learning*, pages 441–446.

Australian Government (2020). Fair work: Minimum wages. Accessed: 2021-07-23.

Bhatia, V. (2014). *Analysing genre: Language use in professional settings*. Routledge, London, UK.

Chang, C. J., Amershi, S., and Kamar, E. (2017). Revolt: Collaborative crowdsourcing for labeling machine learning datasets. In *Proceedings of the 2017 CHI Conference on Human Factors in Computing Systems*, pages 2334–2346.

Chen, L., Liang, J., Xie, C., and Xiao, Y. (2018). Short text entity linking with fine-grained topics. In *Proceedings of the 27th ACM International Conference on Information and Knowledge Management*, pages 457–466.

Chen, L., Suominen, H., and Mewburn, I. (2020). A machine-learning based model to identify phd-level skills in job ads. In *Proceedings of the 18th Annual Workshop of the Australasian Language Technology Association*, pages 72–80.

Cocos, A., Qian, T., Callison-Burch, C., and Masino, A. J. (2015). Crowd control: effectively utilizing unscreened crowd workers for biomedical data annotation. *Journal of biomedical informatics*, 69:86–92.

Cortes, C. and Vapnik, V. (1995). Support-vector networks. *Machine learning*, 20(3):273–297.

Da San Martino, G., Yu, S., Barron-Cedeno, A., Petrov, R., and Nakov, P. (2019). Fine-grained analysis of propaganda in news articles. In *Proceedings of the 2019 Conference on Empirical Methods in Natural Language Processing and the 9th International Joint Conference on Natural Language Processing*, pages 5636–5646.

Fort, K. (2016). *Collaborative Annotation for Reliable Natural Language Processing: Technical and Sociological Aspects*. John Wiley Sons, London, UK.

Hallgren, K. (2013). Computing inter-rater reliability for observational data: an overview and tutorial. *Tutorials in quantitative methods for psychology*, 8(1):23–24.

Heinisch, P. and Cimiano, P. (2021). A multi-task approach to argument frame classification at variable granularity levels. *Information Technology*, 63(1):59–72.

Hiissa, M., Pahikkala, T., Suominen, H., Lehtikunnas, T., Back, B., Karsten, H., Salantera, S., and Salakoski, T. (2006). Towards automated classification of intensive care nursing narratives. *Studies in health technology and informatics*, 124:789–794.

Hovy, E. and Lavid, J. (2010). Towards a 'science'of corpus annotation: a new methodological challenge for corpus linguistics. *International journal of translation*, 22(1):13–16.

Johnson, M., Anderson, P., Dras, M., and Steedman, M. (2018). Predicting accuracy on large datasets from smaller pilot data. In *Proceedings of the 56th Annual Meeting of the Association for Computational Linguistics*, pages 450–455.

Krippendorff, K. (2018). *Content analysis: An introduction to its methodology*. Sage publications., New York, USA.

Landis, R. and Koch, G. (1977). The measurement of observer agreement for categorical data. *Biometrics*, 33(1):159–174.

Maswana, S., Kanamaru, T., and Tajino, A. (2015). Move analysis of research articles across five engineering fields: What they share and what they do not. *Ampersand*, 2:1–11.

Mewburn, I., Grant, W. J., Suominen, H., and Kizimchuk, S. (2020). A machine learning analysis of the non-academic employment opportunities for phd graduates in australia. *Higher Education Policy*, 33(4):799–813.

Miller, C. (1984). Genre as social action. *Quarterly journal of speech*, 70(2):151–167.

Moreno, A. I. and Swales, J. M. (2018). Gstrengthening move analysis methodology towards bridging the function-form gap. *English for Specific Purposes*, 50:40–63.

Muller, A. C. and Guido, S. (2016). *Introduction to machine learning with Python: a guide for data scientists*. O'Reilly, Newton, US.

Munro, R., Bethard, S., Kuperman, V., Lai, V. T., Melnick, R., Potts, C., Schnoebelen, T., and Tily, H. (2010). Crowdsourcing and language studies: the new generation of linguistic data. In *NAACL Workshop on Creating Speech and Language Data with Amazon's Mechanical Turk*, pages 122–130.

Narkhede, S. (2018). Understanding auc-roc curve. *Towards Data Science*, 26:220–227.

Ng, A. (2020). Coursera: Machine learning by stanford university. Accessed: 2021-07-23.

Pavlick, E., Post, M., Irvine, A., Kachaev, D., and Callison-Burch, C. (2014). The language demographics of amazon mechanical turk. *Transactions of the Association for Computational Linguistics*, 2:79–92.

Qin, Y. P. and Wang, X. K. (2009). Study on multilabel text classification based on svm. In *Proceedings of the Sixth International Conference on Fuzzy Systems and Knowledge Discovery*, pages 333–304.

Racz, A., Bajusz, D., and Heberger, K. (2021). Effect of dataset size and train/test split ratios in qsar/qspr multiclass classification. *Molecules*, 26(4):1111.

Song, H., Tolochko, P., Eberl, J., Eisele, O., Greussing, E., Heidenreich, T., Lind, F., Galyga, S., and Boomgaarden, H. (2020). In validations we trust? the impact of imperfect human annotations as a gold standard on the quality of validation of automated content analysis. *Political Communication*, 37(4):550–572.

Suominen, H., Pyysalo, S., Hiissa, M., Ginter, F., Liu, S., Marghescu, D., Pahikkala, T., Back, B., Karsten, H., and Salakoski, T. (2008). Performance evaluation measures for text mining. In Song, M. and Wu, Y., editors, *Handbook of Research on Text and Web Mining Technologies*, pages 724–747. IGI Global, Hershey, USA.

Swales, J. M. (1990). *Genre analysis: English in academic and research setting*. Cambridge University Press, Cambridge, UK.

Tange, H. J., Schouten, H. C., Kester, A. D., and Hasman, A. (1998). The granularity of medical narratives and its effect on the speed and completeness of information retrieval. *Journal of the American Medical Informatics Association*, 5(6):571–582.

Vijayan, V. K., Bindu, K. R., and Parameswaran, L.-h. (2017). A comprehensive study of text classification algorithms. In *Proceedings of the 2017 International Conference on Advances in Computing, Communications and Informatics (ICACCI)*, pages 1109–1113.

Wang, T. Y. and Chiang, H. M. (2011). multi-label text categorization problem using support vector machine approach with membership function. *Neurocomputing*, 74(17):3682–3689.

Yang, B., Sun, J. T., Wang, T., and Chen, Z. (2009). Effective multi-label active learning for text classification. In *Proceedings of the 15th ACM SIGKDD international conference on Knowledge discovery and data mining*, pages 916–926.

Zhang, K., Lan, L., Wang, Z., and Moerchen, F. (2012). Scaling up kernel svm on limited resources: A low-rank linearization approach. *Artificial intelligence and statistics*, 22:1425–1434.

Curriculum Learning Effectively Improves Low Data VQA

Narjes Askarian
Dept. of Data Science and AI
Monash University

Ehsan Abbasnejad
Australian Institute for Machine Learning
The Univ. of Adelaide

Ingrid Zukerman and **Wray Buntine** and **Gholamreza Haffari**
Dept. of Data Science and AI
Monash University

Abstract

Visual question answering (VQA) models, in particular modular ones, are commonly trained on large-scale datasets to achieve state of the art performance. However, such datasets are sometimes not available. Further, it has been shown that training these models on small datasets significantly reduces their accuracy. In this paper, we propose a curriculum-based learning (CL) regime to increase the accuracy of VQA models trained on small datasets. Specifically, we offer three criteria to rank the samples in these datasets, and propose a training strategy for each criterion. Our results show that, for small datasets, our CL approach yields more accurate results than those obtained when training with no curriculum.

1 Introduction

Visual question answering (VQA) models are commonly trained on large-scale datasets to achieve the state of the art performance (Johnson et al., 2017a; Antol et al., 2015; Hudson and Manning, 2019). Modular VQA models, in particular, require large data sets for training. These models dynamically combine a number of neural networks according to a pre-specified layout (Andreas et al., 2016; Johnson et al., 2017b; Yu et al., 2018) to form a new larger network that produces an answer to an input question. The layout, or program, is generated for each question on the fly. As a consequence, the architecture of the resulting network varies according to the program.

Combining neural networks often leads to a wide and deep network. Training such a large-sized network with a varying architecture calls for a massive amount of labeled data, which is either expensive or very limited in many realistic settings. With insufficient data, a large and complex network can perform unsuccessfully. An example of this is our experience in training the VQA model by Johnson et al. (2017b) with only 20% of the CLEVR dataset (Johnson et al., 2017a). Our results showed only 54.24% accuracy compared to the accuracy of 96.90% on the full dataset according to the authors' report (Johnson et al., 2017b). Motivated by this experience, the work presented in this paper studies VQA in low data scenarios, and sheds light on the performance of current modular VQA models under data scarcity conditions. To the best of our knowledge, this is the first study to investigate VQA models in low-data regime.

Many approaches have been investigated to improve the performance of deep learning models when training on limited data, ranging from data augmentations (Zhang et al., 2019) and pre-training (Erhan et al., 2010) to semi-supervised learning (Kingma et al., 2014) and transfer learning (Raina et al., 2007). However, these works mostly deal with the scarcity of labeled data by assuming help from available unlabeled data, or by transferring knowledge from similar domains. Unlike them, our goal is to train a modular VQA model from scratch by using only a small amount of labeled data without using any other resources.

Specifically, we take the CL approach to tackle the problem of VQA models' low performance under low data conditions. Curriculum learning (Bengio et al., 2009) was introduced as a method to supervise the order in which data examples are exposed to the model. Our hope is to maximize the usage of training samples by performing supervision on the order of training data that are fed into the model.

The underlying idea of CL is to start learning from easy examples, and gradually consider harder ones, rather than using examples in a random sequence. To rank training examples from easy to hard, CL must define the concepts of easy and hard examples. Such a ranking is a key challenge in CL.

Many of the ranking criteria introduced in the CL literature are problem-specific heuristics (Liu et al., 2018) or automated measures based on model performance (Hacohen and Weinshall, 2019). In this paper, we propose and analyze the performance of three ranking criteria: (1) a length-based criterion, which considers longer questions as more complex than shorter questions, and ranks the examples in increasing order of their program length; (2) a criterion based on an answer hierarchy, which organizes all possible answers from coarse to fine; and (3) a criterion that relies on model loss for deciding about the hardness level of the examples and ranking them accordingly.

In addition to the ranking heuristics, in §5, we propose a CL training strategy for each criterion. We also argue that under CL training in low data regimes, a model is very susceptible to overfitting and poor generalization. Employing a regularizer is crucially important to prevent the model from becoming over-confident on the training data. We demonstrate that the proposed training strategies, when coupled with *L2-norm* regularization, lead to a significant improvement in performance, in some cases over 30% increase in accuracy.

We apply our approach to the model proposed by Johnson et al. (2017b) as a modular VQA model. The model originally consists of two main components: (1) a *program generator* that takes a question and generates a program; and (2) an *execution engine* that combines neural modules according to the program in order to create a network to produce an answer from the input image. Johnson et al. (2017b) demonstrate that the *program generator* can produce acceptable programs by training only on a small fraction of all possible programs ($\leq 4\%$). Thus, we focus on training the *execution engine* in a low-data setting and use ground-truth programs as input to the *execution engine*. To simulate a low data regime, we use four randomly chosen small subsets of the CLEVR dataset (Johnson et al., 2017a) for training. Our results show that our CL approach yields more accurate results than those obtained when training with no curriculum.

2 Background

Visual question answering is the task of inferring the answer by reasoning on the input question and image. Most of the current approaches map question-image pairs into a cross-modal common embedding space. A question is usually treated holistically in such approaches, thus the reasoning process is hard to explain (Tan and Bansal, 2019; Lu et al., 2019; Selvaraju et al., 2020).

In contrast, modular approaches perform visual reasoning by semantically parsing the question and generating a reasoning chain called a *program* (Andreas et al., 2016; Johnson et al., 2017b). The program shows the reasoning steps required for answering the question as a layout for the *modules*. The algorithm then combines the modules according to the program. Modules are small neural networks treated as single-task functions that are combined into a larger network to accomplish a complex job. The resulting network is *executed* on the input image to predict the answer.

Modular approaches naturally have a strong potential for interpretability. Hu et al. (2018) showed human evaluators can more clearly understand their modular VQA model compared to a non-modular model (Hudson and Manning, 2018). Thus, we are interested in studying modular models.

Similar to other VQA models, modular approaches call for a large amount of annotated data for both the semantic parser (program generator) and the executor. This issue has led to recent studies on sample efficient training strategies, ranging from multi-task learning (Hu et al., 2018) and active learning (Misra et al., 2018) to disentangling reasoning from vision and language understanding (Yi et al., 2018). For instance, Misra et al. (2018) propose an agent that, instead of operating on the training set, interactively learns by asking questions. Regarding the simulated low data setting in our work, efficient use of training data becomes extremely important. We employ curriculum learning in §4 and §5 as a method of making the best use of limited available data where a model can establish its understanding on simple concepts and gradually develop it by seeing harder examples over training.

3 VQA Model

In a VQA task, a model receives as input a pair $(\mathbf{x}, q)$ of image $\mathbf{x}$ and a question q about the image. The model learns to select an answer $a \in \mathcal{A}$ to the questions from a set $\mathcal{A}$ of possible answers.

The VQA model (Johnson et al., 2017b) includes two main components: a *program generator* $\mathcal{G}$ and an *execution engine* $\mathcal{E}$. The *program generator* predicts a program p to address a question q. The *execution engine* combines the modules according

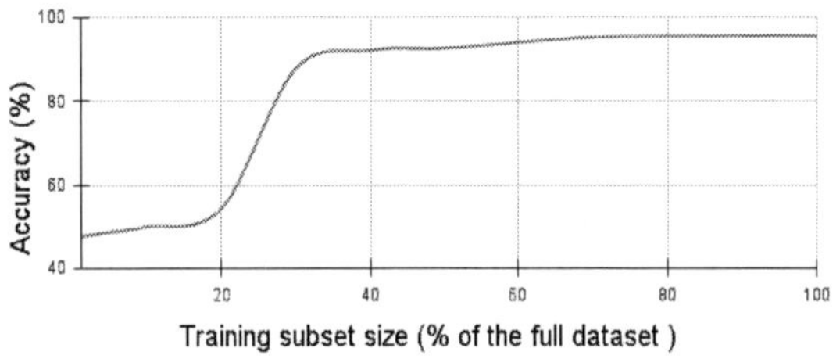

Figure 1: Accuracy of vanilla training of the *execution engine* on CLEVR `val` where trained on different-sized random subsets of the CLEVR `train` set.

to the program, and executes the obtained network on the image to produce an answer.

Johnson et al. (2017b) train the model using a semi-supervised learning approach. They demonstrate that the *program generator* can produce acceptable programs while training on only a small fraction of possible programs ($\leq 4\%$). To evaluate $\mathcal{E}$'s performance in a low data regime, we conducted a number of vanilla supervised training experiments with decreasing sized training sets. Note that we use ground truth program and image pairs as the input to $\mathcal{E}$ in all experiments. Figure 1 shows the best accuracy of each experiment on CLEVR's validation set while the *execution engine* is trained on a subset of the CLEVR's train set *e.g.,* 50% (See Figure 2 for some examples of the CLEVR dataset). The results verify *execution engine*'s poor performance on the small sized training subsets.

4 Curriculum Heuristics for VQA

Studies introduce various heuristics for measuring the hardness of examples. Some heuristics define hardness based on human judgment, in the sense that an example can be challenging for a machine if a human finds it difficult. Such criteria take features of examples into consideration such as *word frequency* and *sentence length* for texts (Spitkovsky et al., 2010; Platanios et al., 2019; Liu et al., 2018) and *shape complexity* for images (Bengio et al., 2009; Duan et al., 2020). The ordering of examples provided by these heuristics is task-dependent and does not change during training. In contrast, more general criteria determine the ordering of examples by incorporating the machine's response, *e.g.,* a teacher network supervises the learning process (Hacohen and Weinshall, 2019) or the progress of a model is taken into account (Kumar et al., 2010; Sachan and Xing, 2016; Zhou et al., 2021). In this study, we explore the heuristics described in the rest of this section.

4.1 Curriculum by program length

An intuitive measure of hardness for a VQA task is based on question length *i.e.,* longer questions are more complex to be understood and answered than shorter ones. This assumption has its root in the observation that a longer question generally involves understanding a larger number of objects and relations. We consider the length of the program corresponding to a question as an indicator of question length.

Under the program length curriculum, the network is fed with easy-to-hard ranked examples starting from shorter programs and gradually increasing programs' length.

4.2 Curriculum by answer hierarchy

Investigating the learning process of $\mathcal{E}$ while training with IID data batching, we hypothesized the model implicit curriculum to be as follows: the model quickly learns to correctly predict the type of the answers, *e.g.,* color, size or digit. However, the more distinct values each type includes, the longer it takes for the model to distinguish them. For instance, the model needs a longer time to distinguish between eight different color values compared to *large* and *small* as the values of size. We also assume that the model struggles to identify visual features that are hard to detect, regardless of the number of distinct values, *e.g.,* whether the material of an object is *metal* or *rubber*.

Motivated by the above observations, we define another measure based on a hand-crafted answer hierarchy in order to shift the focus from questions to answers. The higher level in the hierarchy includes a coarser categorization of each answer type, and the answer types are vertically extended downward to finer classes of types. In other words, the direct link between an answer type and its values is interleaved with intermediate levels of abstraction, *e.g.,* digit at a lower level is divided into three groups, such as *'0'*, *'1'* and *many*. This classification splits into finer groups toward the bottom of the path. The details of the hierarchy are given in Appendix A of the supplementary material.

4.3 Curriculum by hard examples

The intuition of this heuristic is to focus training on the hard examples where the learner does not perform well and consequently the loss is high. The notion of hardness is considered dynamic, as a hard problem tends to be deemed easier while it is be-

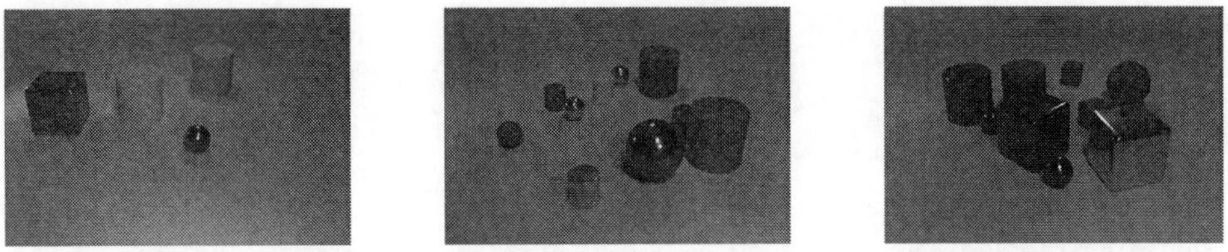

Easy Q: There is an object that is both right of the yellow rubber object and behind the large brown thing; what is its color? **A:** cyan

(A) Easy Question

Medium Q: What number of large objects are cyan metallic spheres or yellow spheres? **A:** 0

(B) Medium Question

Hard Q: What size is the metal block right of the brown metal thing right of the blue thing in front of the small blue rubber thing? **A:** large

(C) Hard Question

Figure 2: Examples of easy, medium and hard questions according to their H scores. The proposed heuristics do not always agree. According to the length-based heuristic, example A is harder than example B.

Hardness	Epoch					
	1	10	25	50	75	98
Easy	0.90	0.81	1.16	0.93	1.16	1.12
Medium	5.49	1.87	2.31	1.40	1.33	1.27
Hard	11.78	3.57	1.74	1.10	0.94	1.40

Table 1: Hardness scores at different epochs. The hardness scores decrease as training progresses.

ing understood. Following Zhou et al. (2020), we employ a dynamic hardness criterion based on the running average of *instantaneous hardness*, which is defined as the loss difference between two consecutive training iterations.

Let $(\mathbf{x}_i, p_i)$ be the ith image-program pair as a training example with the ground truth answer a_i. The instantaneous hardness $r_t(i)$ of $(\mathbf{x}_i, p_i)$ at time-step t is defined as follows:

$$r_t(i) = |\ell_t(a_i - \mathcal{E}(\mathbf{x}_i, p_i; w_t)) - \ell_{t-1}(a_i - \mathcal{E}(\mathbf{x}_i, p_i; w_{t-1}))| \quad (1)$$

where t represents training epochs.

The hardness score of an example is obtained by recursively computing a running average over instantaneous hardness, which reflects the dynamics of hardness,

$$H_{t+1}(i) = \begin{cases} \gamma \times r_t(i) + (1-\gamma) \times H_t(i) & \text{if } i \in S_t \\ H_t(i) & \text{else} \end{cases} \quad (2)$$

where $\gamma \in [0, 1]$ is a discount factor, and $S_t \subseteq \{(\mathbf{x}_1, p_1), ..., (\mathbf{x}_N, p_N)\}$ is a subset of the training set selected at each training step according to a sampling strategy. We employ the strategy of Johnson et al. (2017b), which uses a probability function based on the hardness score H. This function favors harder examples so long as the probability of selecting easy examples is not zero.

Once a sample is used to train the model, its H score becomes small and it stays low relative to the other samples. Thus samples' H score converges during training and remains consistent. This gives the unselected samples a higher chance to be selected by the sampling function in the future steps. Figure 2 shows three samples with low, medium and high H scores (denoted as easy, medium and hard questions) at the first iteration and Table 1 lists their corresponding H scores during training. It is clear that the H score is decreasing over training until convergence.

5 Curriculum Learning for VQA

We describe now our training procedure. A generic curriculum learning requires a model M and a training dataset D as inputs. It also requires the existence of a hardness criterion N, a curriculum scheduler E, a selection function L, and a performance measure P.

According to traditional curriculum learning, at every training iteration, the scheduler E decides when to update the curriculum. Curriculum learning is applied on top of the conventional training loop in machine learning. The output of each training loop is usually the model's performance measure, which may be used by the scheduling function L to specify the appropriate moment for modifying the curriculum. The scheduler can also decide merely based on the number of training iterations. A curriculum update typically includes re-ranking training examples according to the hardness criterion N. In the next step, the algorithm selects

Algorithm 1 Scheduled Training with Curriculum

1: $\mathcal{E}$: *execution engine*
2: $\{(\mathbf{x}_i, p_i, a_i)\}_{i=1}^{n}$: training examples
3: γ: $\in [0, 1]$, discount factor for reducing subset size
4: T: number of iterations
5: T_0: number of warm-starting iterations
6: **procedure** HEMTRAINING
7: **for** $t \in \{1, ..., T\}$ **do**
8: **if** $t \leq T_0$ **then** ▷ Phase1: Warm-starting
9: $S_t = [n]$
10: **else** ▷ Phase2: Hard example mining
11: **for** $i \in \{1, ..., n\}$ **do**
12: $p_i = H_t(i) + C_t(i)$
13: **end for**
14: Normalise(p_i)
15: $S_t \leftarrow$ sample k_t district elements from $Categorical(\vec{p})$
16: $w_t \leftarrow w_{t-1} + \pi\left(\nabla_w \sum_{i \in S_t} \ell(a_i, \mathcal{E}(p_i, x_i; w_{t-1}))\right)$
17: **end if**
18: Compute $r_t(i)$ for $i \in S_t$ using Eq. (1)
19: Update $H_{t+1}(i)$ using Eq.(2)
20: $k_{t+1} \leftarrow \gamma_k \times k_t$
21: **end for**
22: **end procedure**

a subset D^* of the training set D, which will be used by the model in the next round of training. The selection function SF can utilize different approaches, *e.g.,* weighting (Liang et al., 2016; Zhou et al., 2020), sampling (Zhou et al., 2021) or batching (Yong Jae Lee and Grauman, 2011).

Training by length-based curriculum. We design a CL training strategy for the length-based curriculum by equipping the CL training with a batching method as the selection function and a linear paced scheduler. The scheduler controls the curriculum update at a linear pace, *i.e.,* a hyper-parameter specifies the number of iterations for learning a curriculum.

Training by answer hierarchy curriculum. Our proposed training algorithm for the answer hierarchy curriculum takes advantage of a simple self-paced scheduler based on the model performance. Specifically, the scheduler updates the curriculum where the normalized difference of accuracy between two consecutive iterations goes higher than a predefined threshold.

Training by hard examples curriculum. This training strategy suggests training the model in two phases. The first phase is a warm-up phase, where the model sweeps all training examples. The next phase is curriculum training, where the model ranks the examples according to their hardness and learns a selected subset of them.

Algorithm 1 summarizes our training approach. To encourage diversity, we add a submodular optimization C to the hardness score in line 12, which is inspired by Zhou and Bilmes (2018). Since this can be any submodular function, we choose a function based on the similarity between examples,

$$\max_{S_t} \sum_{i \in S_t} H_t(i) + \lambda_t C(S_t) \tag{3}$$

where $C(S_t) = \sum_{i,j \in S_t} w_{i,j}$ and $w_{i,j}$ represents the similarity between example i and j. The preference for diversity can be controlled by λ_t. We gradually reduce it during training to further focus learning on hard examples. The input to C is a representation of a data point that can be a fusion of both text and image modalities. For this, we use the output of the model's penultimate layer as the representations of the examples.

Instead of deterministically choosing the top k samples based on H, we randomly select the examples for the next round of training with the probability $p_{t,i} \propto f(H_{t-1}(i))$ where $f(.)$ is a non-decreasing function, similar to Zhou et al. (2020). This probability function favors hard examples, yet selecting easy ones is possible. At early training, when the H scores are poorly estimated, $f(.)$ should encourage exploration, and move toward more exploitation as training progresses and H estimation is becoming more accurate. We balanced the trade off between exploration and exploitation using the upper confidence bandit (UCB) algorithm, similar to Auer et al. (2003) and Zhou et al. (2020),

$$f(i, t) = Normalized\left[H_t(i) + c\sqrt{\log T / N_t(i)}\right]$$

where T is the number of iterations, and $N_t(i)$ is the number of times that the ith sample has been selected prior to time step t. UCB controls the degree of exploration by the hyper-parameter c which we set as 0.001 in our implementation.

5.1 Improved Curriculum Learning

The idea of learning the answers in a non-random ordering as what happens in CL has been shown to be helpful for the learning process in many cases. However, this idea has one essential deficiency. It focuses on a particular subset of questions early and is not exposed to a diverse set of questions. When a new question arrives, the algorithm struggles to adjust to it, as the learned representations fit the previous questions. This problem exacerbates in low data settings. Many studies highlight the importance of selecting a diverse set of examples as a solution to this issue (Sachan and Xing, 2016; Zhou and Bilmes, 2018), and the CL algorithm generally benefits from diversity in training examples. However, as confirmed by our experiments (§6.4), it does not prevent the model from overfitting. We, therefore, explore the effect of other techniques of regularizing such as dropout and L2-norm.

6 Experiment

We use our implementation of the *execution engine* model (Johnson et al., 2017b). A vanilla training of the model posts the lowest threshold of the performance in our setting. We also implemented and compared the three heuristics for the hardness criterion: *program* length (§4.1), *answer hierarchy* (§4.2) and *hard example* (§4.3). The *length-based* curriculum can be seen as a baseline to the *answer hierarchy* criterion, while both of them play the role of baseline for the *hard example* curriculum. We do not compare with the state of the art, because the goal of our paper is to study VQA in a low-data regime, and to the best of our knowledge, there is no other work that conducts similar research. Thus, we focus on improving the performance of our baseline models.

We assessed our baselines under the following conditions: $i)$ **No-Reg** when no regularizer is applied. $ii)$ **Dropout** when we apply dropout technique to the final linear layer (classification layer) in $\mathcal{E}$. $iii)$ **L2-norm** when *L2-norm* regularizer is applied as a weight decay to the optimizer.

6.1 Dataset

We evaluate our approach on the CLEVR dataset (Johnson et al., 2017a), which provides a training set with $70k$ images, $\sim 700k$ $(\mathbf{x}, q, a)$ tuples and 32 answer classes. To simulate a low-data regime, we randomly sample four subsets of different sizes from CLEVR `train`. The size of the subsets are 5%, 10%, 15% and 20% of the full `train`set, which contain $35k$, $70k$, $105k$, and $140k$ $(\mathbf{x}, q, a)$ tuples respectively. We call these subsets s-CLEVR$_p$, where p denotes the percentage of the subset size wrt `train`, *e.g.*, s-CLEVR$_{15}$ refers to the subset of size 15% of `train`. As CLEVR `train` and CLEVR `val`(the evaluation set) have similar answer distributions, to perform a fair comparison, it is important that the sampled subsets also have similar answer distributions. Our evaluation is conducted on the `val`split, which contains $\sim 150k$ questions and $15k$ unique images.

6.2 Baselines

No-CL is used as the vanilla baseline where the *execution engine* is trained with an IID sampling on s-CLEVR subsets without any curriculum. In other words, the model sees all examples in the training set at every iteration.

Length-CL follows a linear paced scheduler when training the *execution engine*under the length-based curriculum (4.1).

AnswerH-CL makes use of a self-paced scheduler based performance measurement and the answer hierarchy curriculum (4.2). The curriculum updates if the changes in normalized accuracy between two consecutive iterations are higher than a pre-specified threshold. A batching function selects the sampled for every training iteration.

HardEx-CL uses the hard example heuristic 4.3 as the criterion of ranking data and follows the algorithm 1 for training. Unless stated otherwise, we use HEM-CL in all ablation analysis experiments.

6.3 Implementation Details

The *execution engine* uses the images features from $conv4$ of ResNet-101 (He et al., 2016) pretrained on ImageNet (Deng et al., 2009). We use Adam (Kingma, 2015) with a fixed learning rate of 1e-4 to optimize the first three baselines and a cyclic cosine annealing learning-rate schedule to optimize HEM-CL. In the case of the experiments that use *L2-norm*, a weight decay of $5e-4$ is added to the ADAM optimizer. We also use dropout $= 0.5$ for some experiments.

6.4 Results and Discussion

Curriculum heuristics' effect. We evaluate the impact of our proposed training strategies with the three heuristics by looking at their performance on CLEVR `val`in Table 2 while training on s-CLEVR subsets. As the table shows, using the **length-based curriculum** yields poor accuracy almost in all cases of s-CLEVR training subsets with and without regularization. An explanation for this could be overfitting. As mentioned, overfitting is a serious challenge in low data training.

According to our analysis, there is a high chance for the model to overfit some modules because they are more likely to appear in the first positions of a program. Figure 3 depicts the frequency of modules' appearance in various positions of programs in about $28k$ programs. These modules are commonly related to an *anchor object* in a question,

Method	No-Reg				Drop-out				L2-norm			
	5%	10%	15%	20%	5%	10%	15%	20%	5%	10%	15%	20%
No-CL	46.91	48.77	49.68	51.25	46.94	48.36	49.67	49.92	46.71	50.25	52.20	54.34
Length-CL	46.55	46.67	47.83	48.12	46.68	47.33	47.61	47.71	47.89	49.65	50.98	51.50
AnswerH-CL	47.42	48.59	49.73	51.65	47.43	47.73	48.60	50.24	48.62	49.03	48.70	48.95
HardEx-CL	47.93	50.04	51.97	53.14	48.80	49.94	51.69	56.29	48.95	51.49	53.27	**87.62**$\pm$1.3

Table 2: The *execution engine* accuracy (%) on CLEVR `val`when training on s-CLEVR$_5$, s-CLEVR$_{10}$, s-CLEVR$_{15}$ and s-CLEVR$_{20}$ with three different choices of curriculum. The length-based (**Length-CL**) and answer hierarchy (**AnswerH**) curriculum does not improve the performance while hard example (**HardEx-CL**) outperforms the vanilla baseline (**No-CL**) in all experiments.

where other objects are described by their relation to this object, *e.g., the yellow thing* is the anchor in the question *"What is the size of cube to the right of the yellow thing"*. To identify *the cube* and determine its *size*, one must find *the yellow thing*, and attend to the objects on its left side. Since objects are normally described by attributes such as color, size and material, attribute-related modules tend to appear at the beginning of a program.

Ranking programs by their length makes the model focus on a limited number of modules during early training, which increases the chance of overfitting. The model thus struggles with learning other modules when they appear later in longer programs. According to the results, dropout and L2 regularizations do not effectively prevent overfitting where the curriculum forces the model to over-concentrate on such structural biases in data.

Answer hierarchy curriculum makes a marginal improvement on some subsets particularly s-CLEVR$_5$. **Hard example curriculum** produces impressive results, improving the baselines in all cases. The result verifies the effectiveness of emphasizing hard examples in low data regimes where due to the limited size of data and its large capacity, a deep network tends to memorize easy data points without actually learning a pattern. Forcing the model to focus on hard examples induces a form of implicit regularization. Additionally, the self-pacing feature of the curriculum allows the algorithm to update the curriculum based on its progress.

Table 2 also shows that **HardEx-CL** method does not produce the best accuracy per se. Regarding that the table reports the average results, it is noteworthy to mention that the best accuracy we achieved in the case of **HardEx-CL** is 88.83 score in accuracy where the weights are uniformly initialized and L2-norm is used for regularization. In

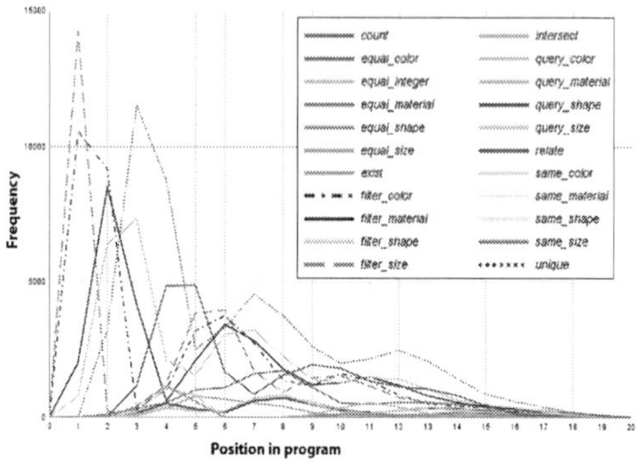

Figure 3: Frequency of modules appearance in different positions of programs. Some modules are more likely to appear at the first positions.

fact, the regularization causes a huge rise in accuracy. The next paragraphs look into the reasons that our regularization choice effectively boosts the **HardEx-CL** approach.

Regularization impact. To investigate the impact of different regularizers we conducted ablation studies by applying L1-norm in addition to L2 and drop-out regularization. Table 3 shows that in contrast to dropout and L1-norm, using L2 regularization results in improved performance in almost all experiments. To investigate the role of L2 regularization in CL training, we conducted an ablation experiment on the selected examples in **HardEx-CL** algorithm with and without L2-norm. First, we record the hardness measures of selected examples at every epoch $H_t(i)$ and split the range of measures into three categories, *easy*, *medium* and *hard*. The population distribution of examples by their hardness measure has a long tail. This long tail is excluded from the splitting and categorized as *very hard*. We then calculate the proportion of each category in the selected examples at 100 epochs as plotted in Figure 4.

These plots provide insight into the behavior of L2 regularization. Specifically, we observe that ex-

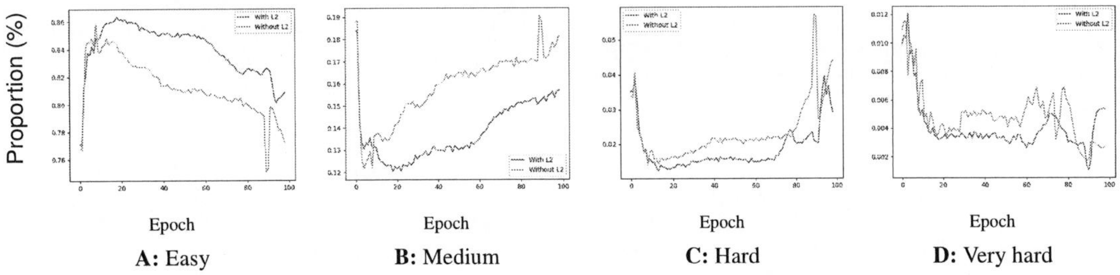

Figure 4: The proportion of different hardness categories in selected examples at 100 epoch in case of with and without L2 regularization. The regularization prevents forgetting by forcing the algorithm to incorporate more easy samples in the training set.

	No-Reg	Drop-out	L1-norm	L2-norm
No-CL	51.25	49.92	45.12	54.34
CL	53.14	56.29	46.79	86.65

Table 3: The impact of different regularizer on HardEX-CL accuracy when training on s-CLEVR$_{20}$.

cept for the easy category, the proportion of examples from other categories is higher for all epochs. It can be explained by the fact that **HardEx-CL** algorithm draws model attention to hard examples during training. As the model is learning the examples, their corresponding hardness measure is decreasing so that they finally are learned and considered as easy. Without using L2 regularization the model overly focuses on learning hard examples and as a consequence forgets the learned patterns of easy examples. L2-norm protects the model from forgetting such patterns by incorporating in loss and forcing the sampling function to also samples more from easy category.

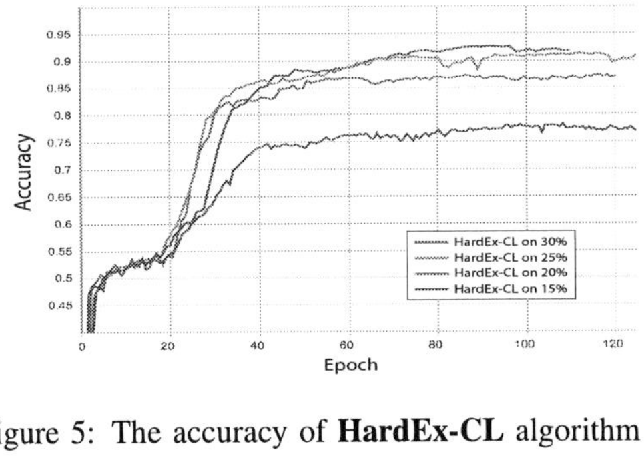

Figure 5: The accuracy of **HardEx-CL** algorithm on CLEVR `val`where *execution engine* weights is uniformly initialized and trained on s-CLEVR$_{15,20,25,30}$.

Why is there a jump in the accuracy of HardEx-CL with L2 regularization when training on s-CLEVR$_{20}$? Looking closely at the learning curve of *vanilla* training in Figure 1 reveals that the *execution engine* performance experiences a jump using training subsets larger than 20%. Different shapes of learning curves are defined in learning theory (Ebbinghaus, 1913; Bills, 1934). The S-curve that we can see here is the idealized general form of learning where the learner slowly accumulates small steps at first followed by a steep up stage with larger steps and the smaller steps successively occur to level off the curve. Due to lack of data, we do not see this performance gap when training on s-CLEVR$_{5-20}$. L2 regularization, however, stimulates the jump to happen earlier in **HardEx-CL.** To investigate it further, we run **HardEx-CL** with four training subsets of different sizes including 15%, 20%, 25% and 30% and report the accuracy on CLEVR `val`in Figure 5. All settings are similar to **HardEx-CL** with L2-norm in Table 2 except the weights are uniformly initialized. From these experiments, we observe the jump in the training set for even s-CLEVR$_{15}$ other than larger subsets. This shows the tipping point in the training can accrue earlier depending on the algorithm and settings.

7 Conclusion

This paper studied VQA in low data settings and shed light on the low performance of VQA models under the data scarcity condition. To improve the performance, we propose three curriculum learning approaches based on length, answer hierarchy, and hard examples. We also stressed the problem of overfitting and poor generalization that becomes crucially important in the absence of sufficient data. We explored the effect of using generalization techniques on a models' performance in low data regimes. Our results show that the proposed CL algorithms outperform the baseline in many cases while fail in some others. However, the algorithms when coupled with L2 regularization lead to improvements.

References

Jacob Andreas, Marcus Rohrbach, Trevor Darrell, and Dan Klein. 2016. Neural module networks. In *IEEE Conference on Computer Vision and Pattern Recognition (CVPR)*, pages 39–48.

Stanislaw Antol, Aishwarya Agrawal, Jiasen Lu, Margaret Mitchell, Dhruv Batra, C Lawrence Zitnick, and Devi Parikh. 2015. Vqa: Visual question answering. In *IEEE international conference on computer vision*, pages 2425–2433.

Peter Auer, Nicolò Cesa-Bianchi, Yoav Freund, and Robert E. Schapire. 2003. The Nonstochastic Multiarmed Bandit Problem. *SIAM Journal on Computing*, 32(1):48–77.

Yoshua Bengio, Jérôme Louradour, Ronan Collobert, and Jason Weston. 2009. Curriculum learning. In *International Conference on Machine Learning*, ICML '09, pages 41–48, Montreal, Quebec, Canada. Association for Computing Machinery.

Arthur Bills. 1934. *General experimental psychology*. Longmans Psychology. Longmans, Green and Co.

Jia Deng, Wei Dong, Richard Socher, Li-Jia Li, Kai Li, and Li Fei-Fei. 2009. ImageNet: A large-scale hierarchical image database. In *IEEE Conference on Computer Vision and Pattern Recognition (CVPR)*, pages 248–255. ISSN: 1063-6919.

Yueqi Duan, Haidong Zhu, He Wang, Li Yi, Ram Nevatia, and Leonidas J. Guibas. 2020. Curriculum DeepSDF. In *Computer Vision – ECCV*, Lecture Notes in Computer Science, pages 51–67, Cham. Springer International Publishing.

Hermann Ebbinghaus. 1913. *Memory: A Contribution to Experimental Psychology*. Annals of Neurosciences, Teachers College, Columbia University.

Dumitru Erhan, Aaron Courville, Yoshua Bengio, and Pascal Vincent. 2010. Why Does Unsupervised Pretraining Help Deep Learning? In *International Conference on Artificial Intelligence and Statistics*, pages 201–208. JMLR Workshop and Conference Proceedings.

Guy Hacohen and Daphna Weinshall. 2019. On The Power of Curriculum Learning in Training Deep Networks. In *International Conference on Machine Learning*, pages 2535–2544. PMLR.

Kaiming He, Xiangyu Zhang, Shaoqing Ren, and Jian Sun. 2016. Deep Residual Learning for Image Recognition. In *IEEE Conference on Computer Vision and Pattern Recognition (CVPR)*, pages 770–778. ISSN: 1063-6919.

Ronghang Hu, Jacob Andreas, Trevor Darrell, and Kate Saenko. 2018. Explainable neural computation via stack neural module networks. In *European conference on computer vision (ECCV)*, pages 53–69.

Drew A. Hudson and Christopher D. Manning. 2018. Compositional Attention Networks for Machine Reasoning. In *International Conference on Learning Representations*.

Drew A Hudson and Christopher D Manning. 2019. GQA: A New Dataset for Real-World Visual Reasoning and Compositional Question Answering. In *Conference on Computer Vision and Pattern Recognition (CVPR)*, pages 6700–6709.

Justin Johnson, Bharath Hariharan, Laurens van der Maaten, Li Fei-Fei, C Lawrence Zitnick, and Ross Girshick. 2017a. Clevr: A diagnostic dataset for compositional language and elementary visual reasoning. In *IEEE Conference on Computer Vision and Pattern Recognition (CVPR)*, pages 2901–2910.

Justin Johnson, Bharath Hariharan, Laurens van der Maaten, Judy Hoffman, Li Fei-Fei, C Lawrence Zitnick, and Ross Girshick. 2017b. Inferring and executing programs for visual reasoning. In *IEEE International Conference on Computer Vision (ICCV)*, pages 2989–2998.

Diederik P. Kingma. 2015. Adam: A Method for Stochastic Optimization. In *International Conference on Learning Representations (ICLR)*, San Diego, CA, USA. Conference Track Proceedings.

Diederik P. Kingma, Danilo J. Rezende, Shakir Mohamed, and Max Welling. 2014. Semi-supervised learning with deep generative models. In *International Conference on Neural Information Processing Systems - Volume 2*, NIPS'14, pages 3581–3589, Montreal, Canada. MIT Press.

M. Kumar, Benjamin Packer, and Daphne Koller. 2010. Self-Paced Learning for Latent Variable Models. In *Advances in Neural Information Processing Systems (NIPS)*, volume 23.

Junwei Liang, Lu Jiang, Deyu Meng, and Alexander Hauptmann. 2016. Learning to detect concepts from webly-labeled video data. In *International Joint Conference on Artificial Intelligence*, IJCAI'16, pages 1746–1752, New York, New York, USA. AAAI Press.

Cao Liu, Shizhu He, Kang Liu, and Jun Zhao. 2018. Curriculum learning for natural answer generation. In *International Joint Conference on Artificial Intelligence*, IJCAI'18, pages 4223–4229, Stockholm, Sweden. AAAI Press.

Jiasen Lu, Dhruv Batra, Devi Parikh, and Stefan Lee. 2019. Vilbert: Pretraining task-agnostic visiolinguistic representations for vision-and-language tasks. In *Neural Information Processing Systems (NeurIPS)*.

Ishan Misra, Ross Girshick, Rob Fergus, Martial Hebert, Abhinav Gupta, and Laurens van der Maaten. 2018. Learning by Asking Questions. In *IEEE/CVF Conference on Computer Vision and Pattern Recognition*, pages 11–20. ISSN: 2575-7075.

Emmanouil Antonios Platanios, Otilia Stretcu, Graham Neubig, Barnabas Poczos, and Tom Mitchell. 2019. Competence-based Curriculum Learning for Neural Machine Translation. In *Conference of the North American Chapter of the Association for Computational Linguistics: Human Language Technologies, Volume 1 (Long and Short Papers)*, pages 1162–1172, Minneapolis, Minnesota. Association for Computational Linguistics.

Rajat Raina, Alexis Battle, Honglak Lee, Benjamin Packer, and Andrew Y. Ng. 2007. Self-taught learning: transfer learning from unlabeled data. In *International conference on Machine learning (ICML)*, ICML '07, pages 759–766, New York, NY, USA. Association for Computing Machinery.

Mrinmaya Sachan and Eric Xing. 2016. Easy Questions First? A Case Study on Curriculum Learning for Question Answering. In *54th Annual Meeting of the Association for Computational Linguistics (Volume 1: Long Papers)*, pages 453–463, Berlin, Germany. Association for Computational Linguistics.

Ramprasaath R. Selvaraju, Purva Tendulkar, Devi Parikh, Eric Horvitz, Marco Tulio Ribeiro, Besmira Nushi, and Ece Kamar. 2020. SQuINTing at VQA Models: Introspecting VQA Models With Sub-Questions. In *IEEE/CVF Conference on Computer Vision and Pattern Recognition*, pages 10003–10011.

Valentin I. Spitkovsky, Hiyan Alshawi, and Daniel Jurafsky. 2010. From Baby Steps to Leapfrog: How "Less is More" in Unsupervised Dependency Parsing. In *Human Language Technologies: The 2010 Annual Conference of the North American Chapter of the Association for Computational Linguistics*, pages 751–759, Los Angeles, California. Association for Computational Linguistics.

Hao Tan and Mohit Bansal. 2019. LXMERT: Learning Cross-Modality Encoder Representations from Transformers. In *Conference on Empirical Methods in Natural Language Processing and the 9th International Joint Conference on Natural Language Processing (EMNLP-IJCNLP)*, pages 5100–5111, Hong Kong, China. Association for Computational Linguistics.

Kexin Yi, Jiajun Wu, Chuang Gan, Antonio Torralba, Pushmeet Kohli, and Josh Tenenbaum. 2018. Neural-Symbolic VQA: Disentangling Reasoning from Vision and Language Understanding. *Advances in Neural Information Processing Systems*, 31.

Yong Jae Lee and K. Grauman. 2011. Learning the easy things first: Self-paced visual category discovery. In *IEEE Conference on Computer Vision and Pattern Recognition*, CVPR '11, pages 1721–1728, USA. IEEE Computer Society.

Licheng Yu, Zhe Lin, Xiaohui Shen, Jimei Yang, Xin Lu, Mohit Bansal, and Tamara L Berg. 2018. Mattnet: Modular attention network for referring expression comprehension. In *IEEE Conference on Computer Vision and Pattern Recognition*, pages 1307–1315.

Xiaofeng Zhang, Zhangyang Wang, Dong Liu, and Qing Ling. 2019. DADA: Deep Adversarial Data Augmentation for Extremely Low Data Regime Classification. In *IEEE International Conference on Acoustics, Speech and Signal Processing (ICASSP)*, pages 2807–2811. ISSN: 2379-190X.

Tianyi Zhou and Jeff Bilmes. 2018. Minimax Curriculum Learning: Machine Teaching with Desirable Difficulties and Scheduled Diversity. In *International Conference on Learning Representations, (ICLR)*, Vancouver, BC, Canada.

Tianyi Zhou, Shengjie Wang, and Jeff Bilmes. 2021. Curriculum Learning by Optimizing Learning Dynamics. In *International Conference on Artificial Intelligence and Statistics*, pages 433–441. PMLR.

Tianyi Zhou, Shengjie Wang, and Jeffrey Bilmes. 2020. Curriculum Learning by Dynamic Instance Hardness. In *Advances in Neural Information Processing Systems*, volume 33, pages 8602–8613. Curran Associates, Inc.

Supplementary Material

We describe more key implementation details of our work in the ensuing sections.

Appendix A: Curriculum by answer hierarchy

As mentioned in §4.2, the answer hierarchy, shown in Figure 6, classifies the answers at different hierarchical levels. Specifically, we defined intermediate levels between answer types and their values. The intermediate levels are employed as the higher level pseudo answers to the questions. According to the curriculum, the algorithm maps the true answer to the higher levels pseudo answers in order to gradually guide the predicted answers from a coarse level to a more specific one. When the scheduler decides to update the curriculum, several nodes are expanded to the next level, *i.e.,* the model is exposed to the finer level of an answer type. We do not force the curriculum to simultaneously expand all of the nodes that are at a similar level of the hierarchy. Instead, we assign a number to every node that determines the expansion time in terms of curriculum update round. Specifically, a node is expanded when the count of the curriculum update is matched with its assigned number. For instance, the node **'size'** is expanded to its children **'small'** and **'large'** in the second round of curriculum update if number **2** is assigned to the node **'size'**. This provides a degree of freedom for the algorithm to gradually learn the answers. Although we statically specify these numbers in our algorithm, they can be implemented as learnable parameters, which we leave to future work. Learning expansion times helps the model move the curriculum further at its pace.

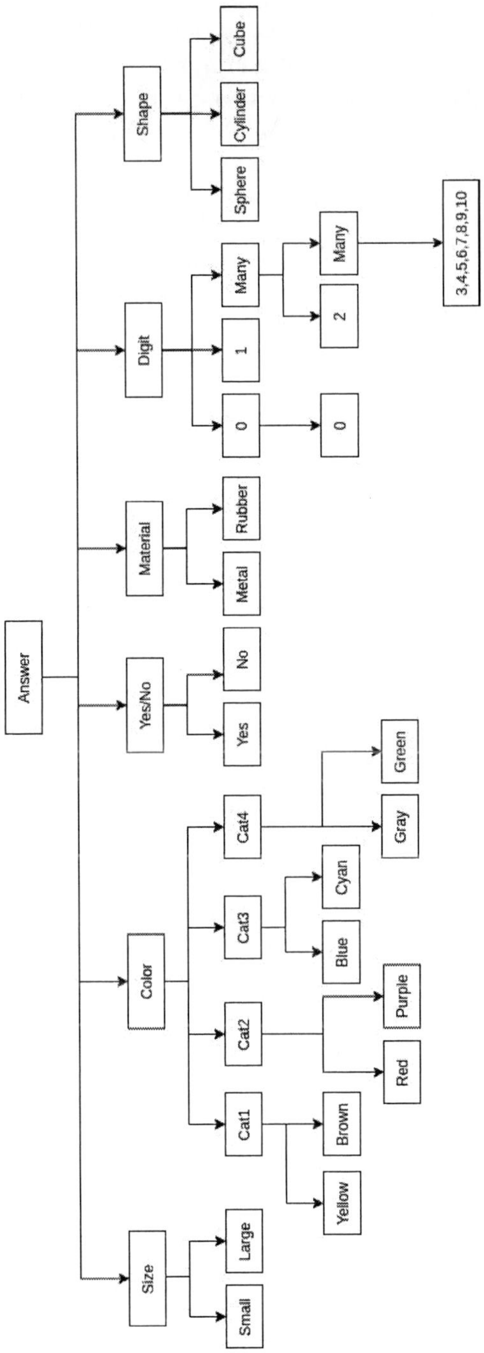

Figure 6: A schematic view of the answer hierarchy used as the base of a curriculum.

Using Word Embeddings to Quantify Ethnic Stereotypes in 12 years of Spanish News

Danielly Sorato
Universitat Pompeu Fabra
Barcelona, Spain
danielly.sorato@upf.edu

Diana Zavala-Rojas
European Social Survey ERIC
Universitat Pompeu Fabra
Barcelona, Spain
diana.zavala@upf.edu

Carme Colominas Ventura
Universitat Pompeu Fabra
Barcelona, Spain
carme.colominas@upf.edu

Abstract

The current study provides a diachronic analysis of the stereotypical portrayals concerning seven of the most prominent foreign nationalities living in Spain in a Spanish news outlet. We use 12 years (2007-2018) of news articles to train word embedding models to quantify the association of such outgroups with drug use, prostitution, crimes, and poverty concepts. Then, we investigate the effects of sociopolitical variables on the computed bias series, such as the outgroup size in the host country and the rate of the population receiving unemployment benefits. Our findings indicate that the texts exhibit bias against foreign-born people, especially in the case of outgroups for which the country of origin has a lower Gross Domestic Product per capita (PPP) than Spain.

1 Introduction

Languages are complex and systematic instruments of communication that reflect the culture of a given population. By studying language, it is possible to observe stereotypes, a type of social bias that is present when discourse about a given group overlooks the diversity of its members and focuses only on a small set of features (Sánchez-Junquera et al., 2021; Tajfel et al., 1964). As such, language analysis is a good way to depict, understand, and demonstrate stereotypes (Garg et al., 2018; Basow, 1992; Wetherell and Potter, 1993; Bonilla-Silva and Forman, 2000). Nonetheless, like society, languages are not static. Variations in lexical systems can be observed over time due to a myriad of intra- and extra-linguistic factors. By analyzing extra-linguistic aspects, it is possible to gain insights into the dynamics of social, cultural, and political phenomena reflected in texts (Marakasova and Neidhardt, 2020).

Efficient methods for performing diachronic analysis are crucial, as manually evaluating several years of text collections is unfeasible due to the large amount of data involved. As such, computational methods for diachronic linguistic analysis are of utmost importance, and ongoing research shows that word embeddings models are helpful tools to this end (Garg et al., 2018; Kroon et al., 2020; Hamilton et al., 2016; Kutuzov et al., 2018; Lauscher et al., 2020).

Word embeddings are powerful representations of language, that allow for the quantification of relationships between words through efficient numerical operations inside the vector space. In this context, previous works demonstrated that such models contain machine-learned biases in their geometry that closely depict societal stereotypes (Bolukbasi et al., 2016b; Gonen and Goldberg, 2019; Garg et al., 2018; Kroon et al., 2020), which is not surprising since stereotypes are massively present in texts used to train computational models (Sánchez-Junquera et al., 2021; Nadeem et al., 2020). Although such language models should be carefully tested for biases and not blindly applied to widely computational applications due to ethically concerning outcomes (Papakyriakopoulos et al., 2020; Brandon, 2021; Bender et al., 2021), they can be a valuable tool for enabling sociolinguistic analysis on large volumes of textual data. This topic establishes a collaboration between computer science, social sciences, and linguistics, as hypotheses about social phenomena can be tested on language using computational methods.

In this study, we analyze the dynamics of stereotypical associations with seven nationalities, in the period of 2007 to 2018. We train our word embedding models using 1,757,331 news articles published in the Spanish newspaper *20 Minutos*, for the aforementioned time span. We adopt a culturally diverse perspective by taking into account some of the most representative foreign nationalities that lived in Spain in the aforementioned period according to the Instituto Nacional de Estadística (INE)[1].

[1]"National institute of Statistics" https://www.ine.es/

Namely, British, Colombian, Ecuadorian, German, Italian, Moroccan, and Romanian are included in this study.

We conduct a fine-grained analysis, studying the association of such nationalities with drug use, prostitution, crimes, and poverty concepts. Then, we compare our findings with sociopolitical variables, such as survey items from the European Social Survey (ESS), number of residents by nationality living in Spain, the rate of the population receiving unemployment benefits from the Spanish government, and the number of offenses committed in Spain by outgroup background. Additionally, we investigate the effect of the outgroups' countries of origin having a lower Gross Domestic Product per capita (PPP) than the host country (Spain)[2]. To account for both group effects and error correlation, we use multilevel Random Effects (RE) models in our analysis.

This paper is organized as follows. In Section 2 we discuss related works. Subsequently, in Section 3 we state our research questions, present metrics, data, model training, and evaluation. Section 4 comprises the findings and discussion about results derived from this study. Finally, in Section 5 we present our conclusions, limitations, and future work.

2 Related Work

Word embeddings showed as a valuable tool, by means of enabling efficient methods for analyzing and quantifying linguistic and social phenomena in natural language. In the context of model stereotypical bias analysis, which is the focus of this paper, the first disseminated studies concern gender bias (Bolukbasi et al., 2016a,b; Zhao et al., 2018; Gonen and Goldberg, 2019; Park et al., 2018; Zhou et al., 2019). Nonetheless, biases can exist in many shapes and forms, which can lead to unfairness in subsequent downstream tasks (Mehrabi et al., 2019).

Garg et al., used both pre-trained models and models trained with the New York Times Annotated Corpus to quantify gender and ethnic stereotypes in 100 years of data for the English language. The reported bias series showed strong correlations with census data and demographic changes in the United States for gender and ethnic stereotypes. Similarly, Kozlowski et al. analyzed English embedding models, but focusing on social class biases.

Most works concerning the study of machine learned biases have English as target language, since there is more availability of linguistic resources that favors such analysis. Here we cite four relevant works conducted on non-English target languages. Wevers quantified gender biases in 40 years of Dutch newspapers categorized ideologically as liberal, social-democratic, neutral/conservative, Protestant, and Catholic. The results depict differences in gender bias and changes within and between newspapers over time. Tripodi et al. investigated the antisemitism in public discourse in France, by using diachronic word embeddings trained on a large corpus of French books and periodicals containing keywords related to Jews. Using the changes over time and embedding projections, they tracked the dynamics of antisemitic bias in the religious, economic, sociopolitical, racial, ethnic and conspiratorial domains. Sánchez-Junquera et al. detected stereotypes towards immigrants in political discourse by focusing in the narrative scenarios, i.e. the frames, used by political actors. They propose a taxonomy to capture immigrant stereotype dimensions and produced an annotated dataset with sentences that Spanish politicians have stated in the Congress of Deputies. Such dataset was used to train classifiers that detect and distinguish between stereotype categories.

More similar to ours, is the work of Kroon et al. In their study, the authors quantify the dynamics of stereotypical associations with different outgroups concerning low-status and high-threat concepts in 11 years of Dutch news data. The authors investigate both time invariant and time variant hypotheses, focusing on the difference of associations regarding the group membership (ingroup vs outgroups).

Our study distinguishes itself from the aforementioned studies by (i) the interdisciplinarity with social survey research, as the selected survey questions measure attitudes of Spanish people (the ingroup) towards immigrants (the outgroups) and can be interpreted as a proxy for cultural/economic threat perception; (ii) our choice of multilevel modeling (RE model), to combine types of phenomena (linguistic and social) and account for group effects; and (iii) the use of fine-grained lists representing crimes, drugs, poverty and prostitution concepts to investigate stereotypical portrayals. Additionally,

[2] According to the Data World Bank https://databank.worldbank.org

we contribute to the scarce literature on stereotypical bias analysis with non-English data sources by using Spanish from Spain as a target language.

3 Method

In this work, we aim to study the dynamics of the stereotypical portrayals of British, Colombian, Ecuadorian, German, Italian, Moroccan and Romanian nationalities with drugs, prostitution, crimes, and poverty concepts, which are some of the stereotypical frames associated to immigrants in the literature (Neyland, 2019; Kroon et al., 2020; Warner, 2005; Igartua et al., 2005; Light and Young, 2009). We investigate the effect that the Gross Domestic Product per capita (PPP) of the outgroup's country of origin has in the strength of stereotypical association. Namely, our hypothesis is that outgroups coming from countries with lower PPP than the host country (Spain), are more strongly associated with such concepts, due to posing a greater economic threat to the ingroup (Meuleman, 2011; Manevska and Achterberg, 2013)[3].

Then, we evaluate to what extent our findings can be explained by (i) the number of residents per nationality in Spain (i.e, the size of outgroup); (ii) rates of population receiving unemployment benefits; (iii) the number of offenses committed in the Spanish territory by outgroup background and; (iii) public opinion. In order to investigate such hypothesis, we adopt the following metrics, procedures and data.

3.1 Metrics

Distributional semantic models maintain the properties of vector spaces and adopt the hypothesis that meaning of a word is conveyed in its co-occurrences. Therefore, in order to measure the similarity between two given words represented by the vectors v_1 and v_2 we can apply the L_2 normalized cosine similarity, although as shown by Garg et al., one could apply the Euclidean distance interchangeably.

To quantify social stereotypes in the trained word embedding models, we used a metric referred throughout this paper as *bias score*, which is the same metric used in Garg et al.. Such metric has been specifically chosen because it has been externally validated by the authors through correlations with census data. The bias score captures the strength of the association of a given set of words S with respect to two groups v_1 and v_2. Hence, when we state that a word is biased toward a group, it is in the context of the bias score metric. The bias score equation is computed as in Equation 1, where S is a set of word vectors that represent a concept of interest (e.g., crimes), v_1 and v_2 are the averaged group vectors for word vectors in group one and two, respectively. An averaged group vector is computed by simply averaging the word vectors that compose a given group. The more negative that the bias score is, the more associated S is toward group two whereas the more positive, the more associated S is towards group one.

$$bias\ score = \sum_{v_s \in S} cos(v_s, v_1) - cos(v_s, v_2) \quad (1)$$

To refer to the representation of the outgroups inside of the context of the embedding model and the bias score metric throughout this paper, we will use the name of the nationality in italics (e.g., *Spanish*, *Moroccan*).

We compare the similarity of concepts (i.e., word lists) related to drugs, prostitution, crimes and poverty to the concepts that represent the ingroup and the outgroups. For instance, if the word vector that represents the adjective $\overrightarrow{delincuente}$ ("delinquent") is more strongly associated with the word vector $\overrightarrow{rumano}$ ("Romanian") than with the word vector $\overrightarrow{español}$ ("Spanish"), that suggests there is bias in the model. It is not the similarity between $\overrightarrow{delincuente}$ and $\overrightarrow{rumano}$ that determines the presence of bias, but the fact that the distances between $\overrightarrow{rumano}$ and $\overrightarrow{español}$ are not equal regarding the adjective $\overrightarrow{delincuente}$.

3.2 Corpus

We compiled the Corpus of Spanish news *20 Minutos* (Razgovorov et al., 2019). The corpus contains 14 years of articles written in Spanish from Spain, comprising 711.840.945 distinct words, that were web-scraped from the newspaper *20 Minutos*[4] website in JSON format. Due to the limited availability of data measuring the sociopolitical indicators of interest (stated in the next subsection), we consider the years 2007 up to 2018 in our analysis.

According to a survey made in 2017 by Cardenal et al., about 40% of the consulted experts in the areas of political science and information science in

[3]The PPP of the Italian outgroup for the 2007-2018 period is only slightly higher while it is considerably higher for the British and German nationalities

[4]https://www.20minutos.es/

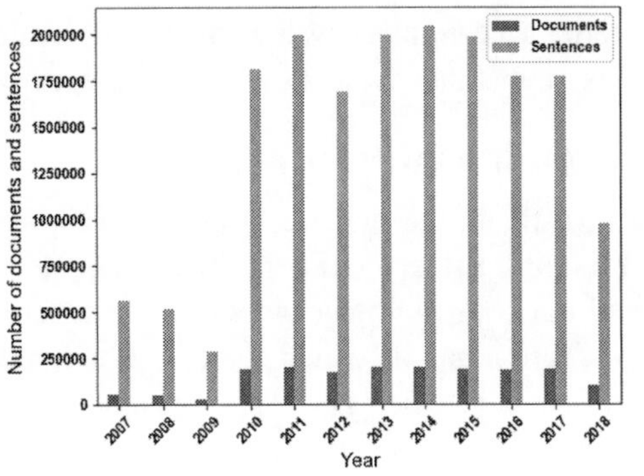

Figure 1: Number of documents and sentences per year in the *20 Minutos* data included in the analysis.

Spain consider *20 Minutos* is a neutral paper. The Figure 1 shows the number of articles and sentences per year in the corpus. Noticeably, for the years 2007 up to and including 2009 there is less data than for the subsequent years. We preprocessed the corpus, lower casing words, removing punctuation and numbers. Then, we filtered the data to create a dataset for each year of the corpus.

3.3 Sociopolitical variables

To build a sociopolitical indicator of ethnic threat perception, we use the mean score of three survey items from the European Social Survey (ESS) (NSD, 2020) studies (2006, 2008, 2010, 2012, 2014, 2016 and 2018). We used the Spanish respondent's answers (applying sample weights provided by ESS) of 11-point scales to the following questions: (i) "Is [country] made a worse or a better place to live by people coming to live here from other countries?"; (ii) "Would you say that [country]'s cultural life is generally undermined or enriched by people coming to live here from other countries?" and; (iii) "Would you say it is generally bad or good for [country]'s economy that people come to live here from other countries?". Missing data points for these time series were imputed using last observation carried forward (LOCF) strategy, which can be applied since the attitudes towards immigration tends to be stable from one year to another. Each survey was responded by at least 1500 people. The indicator of ethnic threat perception has the role of representing attitudinal data in the analysis, or in other words, identifying if the reported bias is somehow a reflection of the ingroup perceptions of these outgroups.

In addition, we use as indicators the number of foreign population by nationality residing in Spain[5], the rate of the population receiving unemployment social benefits (foreigners from the EU excluding Spain and foreigners from outside the EU)[6] and committed offenses by background, which can be countries from the EU excluding Spain (British, Germans, Italians and Romanians), America (Colombians and Ecuadorian), and Africa (Moroccans)[7]. Such datasets are publicly available and can be found in the INE database.

3.4 Word Embeddings Training and Evaluation

Using the datasets filtered by year, we trained skip-gram embedding models using the Fasttext implementation (Bojanowski et al., 2017). Since Spanish is a morphologically rich language, this model is a suitable choice as it takes into account the words' morphological structure. Due to the difference in the number of documents in the corpus across the years, we adopt a grid search strategy to define the optimal hyper-parameters of the models and favor embedding quality (see yearly hyper-parameters in Appendix). Only words that appeared at least 15 times in each yearly dataset were taken into account in the training phase. The resulting word vectors were L_2 normalized.

We evaluate our models using two Spanish word similarity benchmarks, namely *RG-65* (Camacho-Collados et al., 2015) and *MC-30* (Hassan and Mihalcea, 2009). The yearly models achieved an average of 0.72 and 0.70 Pearson correlation coefficient values in the *RG-65* and *MC-30* benchmarks for evaluating word similarity, respectively (variance $RG - 65 = 0.0003$ and variance $MC - 30 = 0.0011$). The evaluation results by year are shown in Appendix. In addition, we compute the average group vector for the ingroup and each of the outgroup nationalities and observe that, although some fluctuations can be observed for the *German* and *Spanish*, the variance is not significant. Therefore, our findings cannot be explained by the group vector variance.

3.5 Word lists

Here, we describe the process for selecting words that represent the crimes, drugs, poverty and prostitution concepts, as well as the ingroup and out-

[5]"Estadística del Padrón continuo. Población extranjera por Nacionalidad, provincias, Sexo y Año"

[6]"Tasa de paro por nacionalidad y periodo"

[7]"Estadística de condenados: Adultos. Condenados según número de delitos, nacionalidad y sexo"

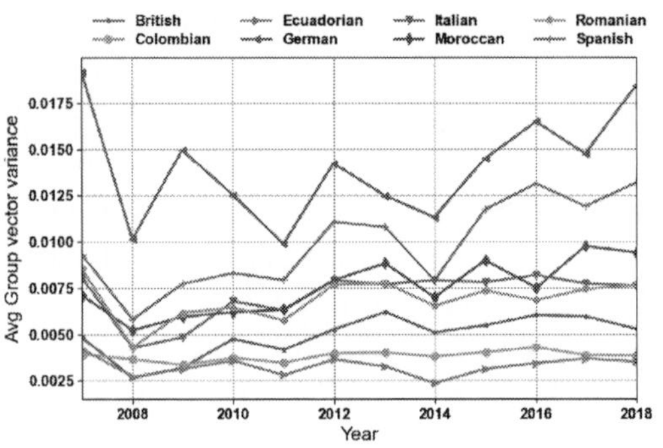

Figure 2: Average group vector variance.

groups. The word lists used for creating the vector representations of the ingroup and the outgroups were defined according to a simple rule: the nationality in masculine singular and plural form (e.g., Español, Españoles). The total frequencies per year for words that compose such lists are shown in the Appendix.

In order to identify words that represent crimes, drugs, poverty and prostitution categories, we start by fitting the high-treat and low-status words used by Kroon et al. in the aforementioned concepts[8]. Then, using an embedding model trained with the whole content of the corpus instead of the yearly slices, for each of the words in the initial list we retrieve the 20 most similar words in the vector space. Afterwards, the lists increased in the step described above were revised and updated again by the authors, excluding words that fall out of the desired concept category. We exclude feminine word inflections to favor lower group vector variances since the analyzed dataset is not very large. The lists of words for used each category of concepts are shown in the Appendix.

3.6 Panel Data

Due to the pooled structure of the data, i.e., yearly bias score measurements for each of the outgroups, we build a panel with $N = 84$ observations (12 years x 7 outgroups). The stationary behaviour of the panel was verified by applying the Levin–Lin–Chu test, which is equivalent to a pooled unit root test. The non-stationary hypothesis was rejected, meaning that the panel data series altogether is unaffected by changes in time. This same test was applied to test the panel data stationary behaviour in Kroon et al.. Additionally, we performed a careful analysis of the model residuals to ensure that there were no correlation patterns.

3.7 Random Effects model

To investigate the dependent series, we impose a Random Effects (RE) multilevel model for panel data. A multilevel model is an extension of a regression, in which data is structured in groups and coefficients can vary by group (Gelman and Hill, 2006). We consider the RE model an appropriate choice for this analysis, as we have pooled structured data and allows accounting for both group effects and error correlation. The following variables were used as predictors:
Year trend: the years from 2007 to 2018, treated as a categorical variable.
N Residents: size of outgroup residing in Spain, described in subsection 3.3.
Unemployment benefits: rate of population receiving unemployment benefits, described in subsection 3.3.
Perception: ingroup's perception of the outgroups, described in subsection 3.3.
Offenses number of offenses committed in the Spanish territory, described in subsection 3.3.
Lower PPP : dummy variable that indicates if the outgroups' country of origin has a *Lower PPP* than Spain. According to the Data World Bank[9], the countries with PPP lower than Spain for the period of analysis are Colombia, Ecuador, Morocco, and Romania ($LowerPPP = 1$). The countries with higher PPP are Germany, Italy and United Kingdom ($LowerPPP = 0$).

Analytical models should also be parsimonious, as fitting models with many random effects quickly multiplies the number of parameters to be estimated, particularly since random slopes are generally given covariances as well as variances (Bell et al., 2019; Matuschek et al., 2017). Hence, the chosen aforementioned indicators are the ones that, to the best of our knowledge, are most appropriated (both regarding data availability and purpose) to test our hypothesis.

4 Results and Discussion

In this section we discuss the findings and limitations of the present research. We analyse the dynamics of stereotypical associations comprised

[8]Excluding the words related to the police, terrorism and lack of intelligence, which do not suit the purposes of this work.

[9]Series named "GDP per capita, PPP (current international $)" available in the World Development Indicators series.

in 12 years (2007-2018) of Spanish local news published in the newspaper *20 Minutos*, comprising 1,757,331 news items, by training and analyzing yearly word embedding language models. Our objective is to quantify stereotypes in such items towards the aforementioned outgroups, taking into account a cultural dimension by studying seven of the most prominent foreign outgroups living in Spain considering the aforementioned period of analysis. We explore the hypothesis that outgroups coming from countries which have a *Lower PPP* than the host country (Spain), have stronger stereotypical associations with concepts related to crimes, drugs, poverty and prostitution, as a consequence of representing a greater social threat to the ingroup.

The yearly average bias scores concerning concepts related to crimes and drugs are depicted in Figures 3 and 4. The trends in Figure 3 show that, most of the outgroups are more strongly associated with the crimes concepts than the *Spanish* ingroup. The *Colombian* and the *Romanian* are the outgroups more strongly associated with crimes concepts, while the *German* and the *British* are the two outgroups less associated. In fact, for most years, the bias score values are negative for the *German* and the *British* outgroups. In contrast, for the *Colombian*, *Ecuadorian*, *Morrocan*, and *Romanian* outgroups, bias score values are always positive. A similar pattern can be observed in Figure 4, in the case of stereotypes concerning drugs.

The results of the Random effects model for the aforementioned series are presented in Table 1, and the main effects of the predictors are shown in the Model 1. In accordance to our expectations, the *Lower PPP* variable affects the bias significantly in both series. The positive coefficients indicate that the *Colombian*, the *Ecuadorian*, the *Moroccan* and the *Romanian* outgroups have higher stereotypical association with crimes and drugs concepts than the *German*, the *British* and the *Italian* outgroups. The year trend does have a significant effect, except for years 2009 and 2011 for crimes series, and years 2010 and 2011 for the drugs series. The positive coefficients indicate that the bias score for such years was higher than for the basis year, 2007.

To further inspect the effects of the *Lower PPP* variable, we add interaction terms in Model 2. For both series, there is a strongly significant relationship between *Lower PPP* and *Unemployment benefits*, such that when the rate of population receiving unemployment benefits increases, the stereotype association for *Colombian*, *Ecuadorian*, *Moroccan* and *Romanian* ($LowerPPP = 1$) also increases, but decreases for *German*, *British* and *Italian* outgroups. Similarly, the interaction with the number of committed offenses in the drugs series reveals that an increase in the offenses lead to stronger stereotypical associations for the first outgroups, but not for the latter. For the series concerning crimes concepts, it is also possible to observe that the public opinion threat perception decreases as stereotypical associations increases.

The yearly average bias scores for concepts related to poverty and prostitution are depicted in Figures 5 and 6. For poverty related concepts, *German*, *Italian*, and *British* bias score values are negative for most years, meaning that poverty concepts are actually more associated with the *Spanish* ingroup when compared to such outgroups. The same is not true for *Colombian*, *Ecuadorian*, *Moroccan*, and *Romanian* outgroups. Again, in Figure 6 it is possible to observe that same division between outgroups. The descriptive analysis show that, overall, outgroups in the *Lower PPP* classification exhibit stronger association with concepts related to prostitution and poverty.

The Table 2 shows the results of the Random Effects model for the aforementioned bias series. Consistently, for the two dependent series a strong effect regarding the *Lower PPP* variable can be observed meaning that again the *British*, the *German*, and the *Italian* are appreciably less associated with poverty and prostitution concepts than the *Colombian*, the *Ecuadorian*, the *Moroccan*, and the *Romanian* outgroups.

Concerning time effects, only the years 2009 and 2011 affect significantly the poverty series, while the year trend is not significant for the prostitution stereotypical associations. Comparably to the findings described for the crimes and drugs concepts, the *Unemployment benefits* predictor has a significant involvement with the dependent series, indicating discrepancy between lower and higher PPP groups. Aside from the interaction with the unemployment benefits predictor, which has the same pattern described above for the crimes and drugs series, no other predictor interacts significantly with the *Lower PPP* group.

The strong effect of the *Lower PPP* predictor on our analysis that news discourse emphasises the ethnicity of certain outgroups more than others. Furthermore, the interpretation of main effects and

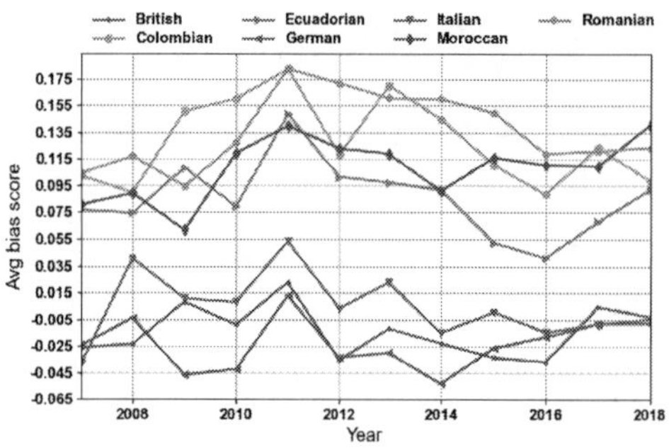

Figure 3: Average bias score for crimes concepts.

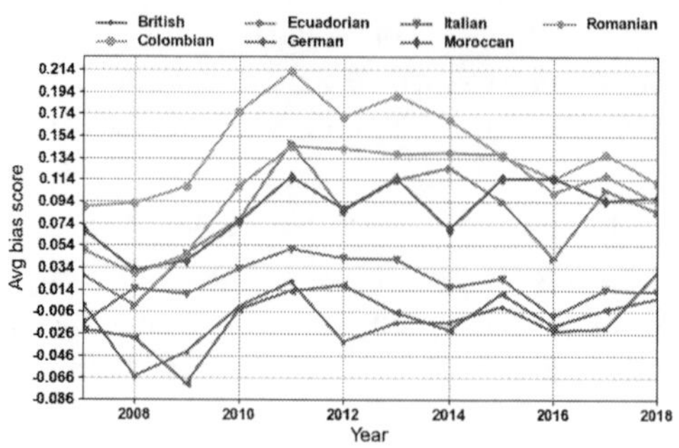

Figure 4: Average bias score for drugs concepts.

	Crimes		Drugs	
Predictors	**Model 1**	**Model 2**	**Model 1**	**Model 2**
Year.2008	0.0297 (0.0150)	0.0508** (0.0164)	-0.0047 (0.0219)	-0.0166 (0.0211)
Year.2009	0.0408* (0.0197)	0.0881*** (0.0217)	0.0139 (0.0269)	0.0440 (0.0294)
Year.2010	0.0306 (0.0264)	0.0731* (0.0327)	0.0508** (0.0351)	0.1314** (0.0393)
Year.2011	0.0753** (0.0303)	0.1232** (0.0376)	0.0868* (0.0400)	0.1786*** (0.0453)
Year.2012	0.0406 (0.0347)	0.0958* (0.0366)	0.0636 (0.0424)	0.1641*** (0.0470)
Year.2013	0.0551 (0.0325)	0.1118** (0.0394)	0.0736 (0.0423)	0.1750*** (0.0466)
Year.2014	0.0378 (0.0316)	0.0904* (0.0366)	0.0577 (0.0392)	0.1516*** (0.0425)
Year.2015	0.0292 (0.0252)	0.0689* (0.0294)	0.0581 (0.0319)	0.1321*** (0.0339)
Year.2016	0.0054 (0.0247)	0.0340 (0.0296)	0.0224 (0.0340)	0.0865* (0.0374)
Year.2017	0.0185 (0223)	0.0393 (0.0268)	0.0364 (0.0288)	0.0883* (0.0305)
Year.2018	0.0068 (0.0249)	0.0162 (0.0321)	0.0259 (0.0344)	0.0902 (0.0405)
Lower PPP	0.1207*** (0.0102)	0.2263*** (0.0637)	0.1186*** (0.0131)	0.0508 (0.0827)
N Residents	3.428e-05 (1.796e-05)	2.281e-05 (2.121e-05)	-3.799e-05 (2.239e-05)	-6.058e-05 (2.559e-05)
Unemployment benefits	-0.0013 (0.0012)	-0.0054** (0.0018)	-0.0009 (0.0015)	-0.0077*** (0.0021)
Offenses	2.842e-06 (1.953e-06)	4.621e-06 (2.465e-06)	1.543e-06 (2.396e-06)	-1.391e-06 (3.221e-06)
Perception	-0.0004 (0.0002)	-0.0002 (0.0003)	-0.0002 (0.0003)	0.0007 (0.0004)
Unemployment x Lower PPP	-	0.0023** (0.0008)	-	0.0040*** (0.0010)
Offenses x Lower PPP	-	-1.821e-06 (1.672e-06)	-	2.072e-06* (2.352e-06)
Perception x Lower PPP	-	-0.0007* (0.0003)	-	-0.0003 (0.0003)
N	84	84	84	84
Residual	0.000354	0.000292	0.000426	0.000342
R-squared	0.93	0.95	0.90	0.92

Table 1: Random Effects model predictions of bias scores for concepts related to crimes and drugs. $*p < .05$, $**p < .01$, $***p < .001$. Standard errors for each coefficient shown in parenthesis.

interactions with sociopolitical variables indicates that stereotypical portrayals seem to be dissociated from real demographic trends. Discourse is one of the everyday social practices that may be used for discriminatory purposes, for instance in intra-group discourse about resident minorities or immigrants frame these "others" negatively, thus leading to the reproduction of ethnic prejudices or ideologies (Van Dijk, 2000). Our findings go in line with frames described in other studies made with European newspapers, which indicate the semantic link between foreigners, prostitution, criminality and degeneracy (Neyland, 2019; Stenvoll, 2002; Light and Young, 2009; Igartua et al., 2005; Rancu, 2011), especially for Eastern European and Latin American backgrounds. We join previous studies pointing that media coverage can be stereotypical, associating ethnic outgroups with stigmatized attributes, and therefore having serious negative effects both on individuals and society, as news are powerful sources of the discursive demoralization of marginalised groups (Hamborg et al., 2018; Zilber and Niven, 2000; Angermeyer and Schulze, 2001; Sui and Paul, 2017; Kroon et al., 2020; Farris and Silber Mohamed, 2018; Milioni et al., 2015; Abrajano et al., 2017; Saiz de Lobado García et al., 2018; Neyland, 2019).

We cite the following limitations of our findings. The present analysis considers only one data source, therefore our conclusions cannot be generalized to other Spanish media outlets. Although the unavailability of other diachronic corpora for Spanish from Spain limits our conclusion to a single news outlet, we argue that this study is a valuable contribution to stereotype analysis in media discourse using a non-English target language.

Further, we acknowledge that by excluding gender inflected words, stereotypes about women that could be informative were left out. We do wish to explore gender inflected words in future work

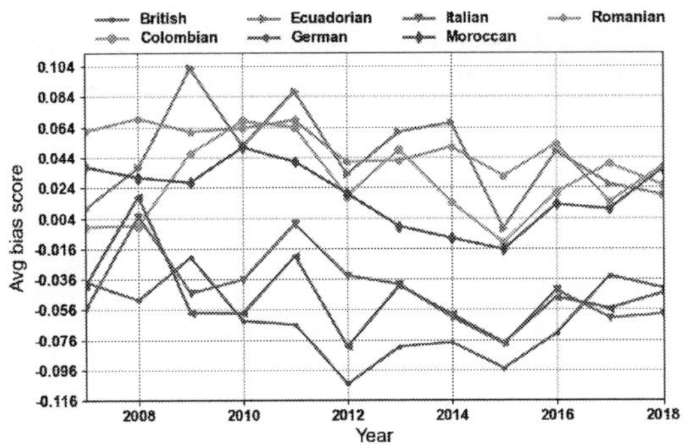

Figure 5: Average bias score for poverty concepts.

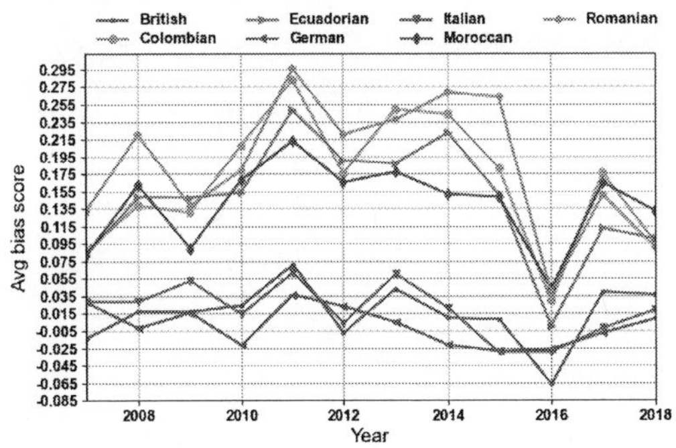

Figure 6: Average bias score for prostitution concepts.

	Poverty		Prostitution	
Predictors	**Model 1**	**Model 2**	**Model 1**	**Model 2**
Year.2008	0.0409 (0.0206)	0.0388* (0.0180)	0.0529 (0.0268)	0.0606* (0.0289)
Year.2009	0.0595** (0.0177)	0.0899*** (0.0202)	0.0397 (0.0387)	0.1230** (0.0377)
Year.2010	0.0429 (0.0253)	0.1036** (0.0328)	0.0350 (0.0446)	0.1720*** (0.0479)
Year.2011	0.0611* (0.0278)	0.1232** (0.0376)	0.1043 (0.0525)	0.2576*** (0.0550)
Year.2012	0.0270 (0.0316)	0.1027* (0.0389)	0.0487 (0.0551)	0.2184*** (0.0586)
Year.2013	0.0427 (0.0285)	0.1191** (0.0384)	0.0792 (0.0558)	0.2503*** (0.0597)
Year.2014	0.0302 (0.0270)	0.1008** (0.0352)	0.0736 (0.0563)	0.2305*** (0.0551)
Year.2015	-0.0033 (0.0229)	0.0516 (0.0291)	0.0425 (0.0507)	0.1627** (0.0504)
Year.2016	0.0197 (0.0219)	0.0656 (0.0296)	-0.0726 (0.0414)	0.0239 (0.0428)
Year.2017	0.0095 (0.0197)	0.0460 (0.0256)	0.0166 (0.0355)	0.0920* (0.0355)
Year.2018	0.0023 (0.0230)	0.0440 (0.0311)	-0.0233 (0.0380)	0.0565 (0.0445)
Lower PPP	0.0991*** (0.0108)	0.0821 (0.0767)	0.1399*** (0.0173)	0.1622 (0.1083)
N Residents	-1.664e-05 (1.549e-05)	-3.534e-05 (1.798e-05)	3.574e-05 (2.41e-05)	-1.492e-05 (2.731e-05)
Unemployment benefits	-0.0018 (0.0012)	-0.0070*** (0.0018)	-0.0007 (0.0021)	-0.0125*** (0.0029)
Offenses	1.004e-06 (1.708e-06)	1.084e-07 (2.227e-06)	4.065e-06 (2.168e-06)	5.893e-06 (3.789e-06)
Perception	-0.0003 (0.0002)	0.0003 (0.0003)	-0.0005 (0.0003)	0.0004 (0.0005)
Unemployment x Lower PPP	-	0.0031** (0.0009)	-	0.0070*** (0.0013)
Offenses x Lower PPP	-	-1.806e-08 (2.227e-06)	-	-5.458e-06 (3.336e-06)
Perception x Lower PPP	-	-0.0002 (0.0003)	-	-0.0003 (0.0004)
N	84	84	84	84
Residual	0.000366	0.000334	0.00118	0.000769
R-squared	0.84	0.87	0.93	0.96

Table 2: Random Effects model predictions of bias scores for concepts related to poverty and prostitution. $*p < .05$.$**p < .01$, $***p < .001$. Standard errors for each coefficient shown in parenthesis.

with a more suitable dataset. Lastly, we would like to point that all these nationalities have intricate and deep political relationships with Spain which certainly go beyond having a higher or lower GPD per capita.

5 Conclusion

In this work we analyzed the dynamics of stereotypical associations concerning seven of the most prominent ethnic outgroups living in Spain using language models trained with 12 years of news items from the Spanish newspaper *20 Minutos*. We investigated biases concerning concepts related to crimes, drugs poverty and prostitution, exploring the relation between the stereotypical associations and the GPD per capita (PPP) of the outgroups' countries of origin, public opinion, outgroup size, unemployment subsidy, and number of committed offenses in the Spanish territory.

Our results show that the texts exhibit stereotypical associations, especially for the Colombian, Ecuadorian, Moroccan and Romanian outgroups. We conclude that the examined news articles emphasize the nationality of certain ethnicities, which hinder the integration process of already marginalized outgroups. Moreover, these associations can be further propagated and amplified through computational algorithms if available data indiscriminately (Bolukbasi et al., 2016b; Nadeem et al., 2020), leading to concerning outcomes.

As future work, we aim to move to a multilingual perspective and compare outgroup stereotypes across different languages. Furthermore, we wish to examine stereotypes in political discourse, to inspect if patterns similar to the ones found in this work can be observed.

Acknowledgments

This work was partially supported by the Universitat Pompeu Fabra (UPF), through a PhD studentship grant and the use of Marvin Cluster[10] to train and analyse the language models.

References

Marisa A Abrajano, Zoltan Hajnal, and Hans JG Hassell. 2017. Media framing and partisan identity: The case of immigration coverage and white macropartisanship. *Journal of Race, Ethnicity and Politics*, 2(1):5.

Matthias C Angermeyer and Beate Schulze. 2001. Reinforcing stereotypes: how the focus on forensic cases in news reporting may influence public attitudes towards the mentally ill. *International Journal of Law and Psychiatry*.

Susan A Basow. 1992. *Gender: Stereotypes and roles*. Thomson Brooks/Cole Publishing Co.

Andrew Bell, Malcolm Fairbrother, and Kelvyn Jones. 2019. Fixed and random effects models: making an informed choice. *Quality & Quantity*, 53(2):1051–1074.

Emily M Bender, Timnit Gebru, Angelina McMillan-Major, and Shmargaret Shmitchell. 2021. On the dangers of stochastic parrots: Can language models be too big? In *Proceedings of the 2021 ACM Conference on Fairness, Accountability, and Transparency*, pages 610–623.

Piotr Bojanowski, Edouard Grave, Armand Joulin, and Tomas Mikolov. 2017. Enriching word vectors with subword information. *Transactions of the Association for Computational Linguistics*, 5:135–146.

Tolga Bolukbasi, Kai-Wei Chang, James Zou, Venkatesh Saligrama, and Adam Kalai. 2016a. Quantifying and reducing stereotypes in word embeddings. *arXiv preprint arXiv:1606.06121*.

Tolga Bolukbasi, Kai-Wei Chang, James Y Zou, Venkatesh Saligrama, and Adam T Kalai. 2016b. Man is to computer programmer as woman is to homemaker? debiasing word embeddings. In *Advances in neural information processing systems*, pages 4349–4357.

Eduardo Bonilla-Silva and Tyrone A Forman. 2000. "i am not a racist but...": Mapping white college students' racial ideology in the usa. *Discourse & society*, 11(1):50–85.

Jamie Brandon. 2021. Using unethical data to build a more ethical world. *AI and Ethics*, 1(2):101–108.

[10]https://www.upf.edu/web/sct-sit/marvin-cluster

José Camacho-Collados, Mohammad Taher Pilehvar, and Roberto Navigli. 2015. A framework for the construction of monolingual and cross-lingual word similarity datasets. In *Proceedings of ACL (2)*, pages 1–7.

Anas Cardenal, Carol Galais, and Joaquim Moré. 2018. El reto de medir el sesgo ideológico en los medios escritos digitales. *quaderns del cac*.

Emily M Farris and Heather Silber Mohamed. 2018. Picturing immigration: How the media criminalizes immigrants. *Politics, Groups, and Identities*, 6(4):814–824.

Nikhil Garg, Londa Schiebinger, Dan Jurafsky, and James Zou. 2018. Word embeddings quantify 100 years of gender and ethnic stereotypes. *Proceedings of the National Academy of Sciences*, 115(16):E3635–E3644.

Andrew Gelman and Jennifer Hill. 2006. *Data analysis using regression and multilevel/hierarchical models*. Cambridge university press.

Hila Gonen and Yoav Goldberg. 2019. Lipstick on a pig: Debiasing methods cover up systematic gender biases in word embeddings but do not remove them. *arXiv preprint arXiv:1903.03862*.

Felix Hamborg, Norman Meuschke, and Bela Gipp. 2018. Bias-aware news analysis using matrix-based news aggregation. *International Journal on Digital Libraries*, pages 1–19.

William L Hamilton, Jure Leskovec, and Dan Jurafsky. 2016. Diachronic word embeddings reveal statistical laws of semantic change. *arXiv preprint arXiv:1605.09096*.

Samer Hassan and Rada Mihalcea. 2009. Cross-lingual semantic relatedness using encyclopedic knowledge. In *Proceedings of the 2009 Conference on Empirical Methods in Natural Language Processing*, pages 1192–1201.

Juan José Igartua, Lifen Cheng, and Carlos Muñiz. 2005. Framing latin america in the spanish press: A cooled down friendship between two fraternal lands.

Austin C Kozlowski, Matt Taddy, and James A Evans. 2019. The geometry of culture: Analyzing the meanings of class through word embeddings. *American Sociological Review*, 84(5):905–949.

Anne C Kroon, Damian Trilling, and Tamara Raats. 2020. Guilty by association: Using word embeddings to measure ethnic stereotypes in news coverage. *Journalism & Mass Communication Quarterly*, page 1077699020932304.

Andrey Kutuzov, Lilja Øvrelid, Terrence Szymanski, and Erik Velldal. 2018. Diachronic word embeddings and semantic shifts: a survey. *arXiv preprint arXiv:1806.03537*.

Anne Lauscher, Rafik Takieddin, Simone Paolo Ponzetto, and Goran Glavaš. 2020. Araweat: Multidimensional analysis of biases in arabic word embeddings. *arXiv preprint arXiv:2011.01575.*

Duncan Light and Craig Young. 2009. European union enlargement, post-accession migration and imaginative geographies of the 'new europe': Media discourses in romania and the united kingdom. *Journal of Cultural Geography*, 26(3):281–303.

Katerina Manevska and Peter Achterberg. 2013. Immigration and perceived ethnic threat: Cultural capital and economic explanations. *European Sociological Review*, 29(3):437–449.

Anna Marakasova and Julia Neidhardt. 2020. Short-term semantic shifts and their relation to frequency change. In *Proceedings of the Probability and Meaning Conference (PaM 2020)*, pages 146–153.

Hannes Matuschek, Reinhold Kliegl, Shravan Vasishth, Harald Baayen, and Douglas Bates. 2017. Balancing type i error and power in linear mixed models. *Journal of memory and language*, 94:305–315.

Ninareh Mehrabi, Fred Morstatter, Nripsuta Saxena, Kristina Lerman, and Aram Galstyan. 2019. A survey on bias and fairness in machine learning. *arXiv preprint arXiv:1908.09635.*

Bart Meuleman. 2011. Perceived economic threat and anti-immigration attitudes: Effects of immigrant group size and economic conditions revisited. *Cross-cultural analysis: Methods and applications*, pages 281–310.

Dimitra L Milioni, Lia-Paschalia Spyridou, and Konstantinos Vadratsikas. 2015. Framing immigration in online media and television news in crisis-stricken cyprus. *The Cyprus Review*, 27(1):155–185.

Moin Nadeem, Anna Bethke, and Siva Reddy. 2020. Stereoset: Measuring stereotypical bias in pretrained language models. *arXiv preprint arXiv:2004.09456.*

Matilda FF Neyland. 2019. *The Sexual Other: Discursive constructions of migrant sex workers in New Zealand media.* Ph.D. thesis, Victoria University of Wellington.

NSD. 2020. European social survey cumulative file, ess 1-9 (2020). *Data file edition 1.0. NSD - Norwegian Centre for Research Data, Norway - Data Archive and distributor of ESS data for ESS ERIC.*

Orestis Papakyriakopoulos, Simon Hegelich, Juan Carlos Medina Serrano, and Fabienne Marco. 2020. Bias in word embeddings. In *Proceedings of the 2020 Conference on Fairness, Accountability, and Transparency*, pages 446–457.

Ji Ho Park, Jamin Shin, and Pascale Fung. 2018. Reducing gender bias in abusive language detection. *arXiv preprint arXiv:1808.07231.*

Raluca Oana Matu Rancu. 2011. Exclusion, marginalization and prejudice: The image of the romanian woman in spanish society. *International Journal of Diversity in Organisations, Communities & Nations*, 10(5).

Pavel Razgovorov, David Tomás, et al. 2019. Creación de un corpus de noticias de gran tamano en espanol para el análisis diacrónico y diatópico del uso del lenguaje.

María Ester Saiz de Lobado García et al. 2018. Metáfora y percepción: análisis de la ideología subyacente en el discurso jurídico sobre inmigración.

Javier Sánchez-Junquera, Berta Chulvi, Paolo Rosso, and Simone Paolo Ponzetto. 2021. How do you speak about immigrants? taxonomy and stereoimmigrants dataset for identifying stereotypes about immigrants. *Applied Sciences*, 11(8):3610.

Dag Stenvoll. 2002. From russia with love? newspaper coverage of cross-border prostitution in northern norway, 1990—2001. *European Journal of Women's Studies*, 9(2):143–162.

Mingxiao Sui and Newly Paul. 2017. Latino portrayals in local news media: Underrepresentation, negative stereotypes, and institutional predictors of coverage. *Journal of Intercultural Communication Research*, 46(3):273–294.

Henri Tajfel, Anees A Sheikh, and Robert Charles Gardner. 1964. Content of stereotypes and the inference of similarity between members of stereotyped groups. *Acta Psychologica.*

Rocco Tripodi, Massimo Warglien, Simon Levis Sullam, and Deborah Paci. 2019. Tracing antisemitic language through diachronic embedding projections: France 1789-1914. *arXiv preprint arXiv:1906.01440.*

Teun A Van Dijk. 2000. *On the analysis of parliamentary debates on immigration.* Citeseer.

Judith Ann Warner. 2005. The social construction of the criminal alien in immigration law, enforcement practice and statistical enumeration: Consequences for immigrant stereotyping. *Journal of Social and Ecological Boundaries*, 1(2):56–80.

Margaret Wetherell and Jonathan Potter. 1993. *Mapping the language of racism: Discourse and the legitimation of exploitation.* Columbia University Press.

Melvin Wevers. 2019. Using word embeddings to examine gender bias in dutch newspapers, 1950-1990. *arXiv preprint arXiv:1907.08922.*

Jieyu Zhao, Yichao Zhou, Zeyu Li, Wei Wang, and Kai-Wei Chang. 2018. Learning gender-neutral word embeddings. *arXiv preprint arXiv:1809.01496.*

Pei Zhou, Weijia Shi, Jieyu Zhao, Kuan-Hao Huang, Muhao Chen, Ryan Cotterell, and Kai-Wei Chang. 2019. Examining gender bias in languages with grammatical gender. *arXiv preprint arXiv:1909.02224*.

Jeremy Zilber and David Niven. 2000. Stereotypes in the news: Media coverage of african-americans in congress. *Harvard International Journal of Press/Politics*, 5(1):32–49.

A Word lists

In the next subsections we specify the word lists that were used to represent crimes, drugs, poverty and prostitution concepts, as well as the ingroup and outgroups. Please notice that some of the words in the lists are plural inflections that have no corresponding translation in English. We identify such words by adding '(plural)' next to the singular translation.

A.1 Ingroup and outgroups

Ingroup in Spanish: Español, Españoles'.
Ingroup translation: "Spanish", "Spanish (plural)".
British outgroup in Spanish: Británico, Británicos.
British outgroup translation: "British", "British (plural)".
Colombian outgroup in Spanish: Colombiano, Colombianos.
Colombian outgroup translation: "Colombian", "Colombians".
Ecuadorian outgroup in Spanish: Ecuatoriano, Ecuatorianos.
Ecuadorian outgroup translation: "Ecuadorian", "Ecuadorians".
German outgroup in Spanish: Alemán, Alemanes.
German outgroup translation: "German", "Germans".
Italian outgroup in Spanish: Italiano, Italianos.
Italian outgroup translation: "Italian", "Italians".
Moroccan outgroup in Spanish: Marroquí, Marroquíes.
Moroccan outgroup translation: "Moroccan", "Moroccans".
Romanian outgroup in Spanish: Rumano, Rumanos.
Romanian outgroup translation: "Romanian", "Romanians".

A.2 Frequency of Ingroup and outgroup words

The table 3 shows the frequencies by year of the words that were used to create the ingroup and outgroup vector representations in our study.

A.3 Crimes

Words in Spanish: Cabecilla, cabecillas, arrestado, arrestados, detenido, detenidos, sospecho, sospechos, sospechoso, sospechosos, ilegal, ilegales, ilegalidad, clandestino, clandestinos, clandestinidad, narcotráfico, narcotraficante, narcotraficantes, traficante, traficantes, contrabando, contrabandista, contrabandistas, aprehensión, aprehensiones, incautación, incautaciones, atraco, atracos, atracador, atracadores, asalto, asaltos, asaltante, asaltantes, crimen, criminalidad, criminal, criminales, delito, delitos, agresión, agresiones, delincuencia, delincuente, delincuentes, malhechor, malhechores, robo, robos, hurto,hurtos, sustracción, sustracciones, mafia, mafias, mafioso, mafiosos, violación, violaciones, violador, violadores, pedófilo, pedófilos, asesino, asesinos, asesinato,asesinatos, homicidio, homicidios, homicida, homicidas, violencia, violento, violentos,maltrato, maltratos, maltratador, maltratadores.

Translations: "faction leader", "faction leaders", "arrested", "arrested (plural)","detained", "detained (plural)", "suspect", "suspects", "shady", "shady (plural)", "illegal", "illegal (plural)", "illegality", "clandestine", "clandestine (plural)", "underground", "drug trafficking", "drug dealer", "drug traffickers", "trafficker", "traffickers", "smuggling", "smuggler", "smugglers", "apprehension", "apprehensions", "seizure", "seizures", "robbery", "robberies", "robber", "robbers", "assault", "assaults", "burglar", "burglars", "crime", "criminality", "criminal", "criminals", "felony", "felonies", "aggression", "aggressions", "delinquency", "delinquent", "delinquents", "malefactor", "malefactors", "stealing", "stealing (plural)", "theft", "theft (plural)", "thievery", "thievery (plural)", "mafia", "mafias", "gangster", "gangsters", "rape", "rapes", "rapist", "rapists", "pedophile", "pedophiles", "murderer", "murderers", "murder", "murders", "homicide", "homicides", "killer", "killers", "violence", "violent", "violent (plural)", "maltreatment", "maltreatments", "batterer", "batterers".

Year	British	Colombian	Ecuadorian	German	Italian	Moroccan	Romanian	Spanish
2007	340	199	226	433	411	679	472	3094
2008	338	312	172	362	273	981	457	3335
2009	190	124	93	271	167	539	171	2095
2010	1208	400	207	1927	954	2476	627	21158
2011	1294	387	165	2286	1171	1681	613	23566
2012	1240	288	122	1761	890	1738	443	18141
2013	1618	346	130	2212	905	2119	561	21183
2014	1519	357	104	2194	1154	2381	449	22082
2015	1366	286	88	1767	1051	1802	381	19123
2016	1526	206	141	1701	899	1087	287	15450
2017	1307	196	83	1518	947	1061	255	13986
2018	545	114	40	907	499	529	163	7556

Table 3: Frequency of the words that compose the ingroup and outgroup representations in the corpus *20 Minutos* by year.

A.4 Drugs

Words in Spanish: Droga, drogas, adicción, adicciones, adicto, adictos, drogadicción, drogadicto, drogadictos, estupefaciente, estupefacientes, drogodependencia, drogodependencias, drogodependiente, drogodependientes,alcohol, alcoholismo, borracho, borrachos, heroína, cocaína, papelina, papelinas, bolsita, bolsitas, hachís, marihuana, sustancia, sustancias, cannabis, metanfetamina, anfetamina, speed, éxtasis, mdma.

Translations: "drug", "drugs", "addiction", "addictions", "addict", "addicts","drug addiction", "drug addict", "drug addicts", "narcotic", "narcotics", drug addiction, drug addiction, "junkie", "junkies", "alcohol", "alcoholism", "drunk", "drunk (plural)", "heroin", "cocaine", " "drug paper"[11], "drug papers", "drug bag"[12], "drug bags" "hashish", "marijuana", "substance", "substances", "cannabis", "methamphetamine", "amphetamine", "speed", "ecstasy", "mdma".

A.5 Poverty

Words in Spanish: miseria, miserable, miserables, pobreza, pobre, pobres, empobrecimiento, empobrecido, empobrecidos, mendicidad, mendigo, mendigos, desfavorecido, desfavorecidos, necesitado, necesitados, desesperación, desesperados, desesperado, vulnerabilidad, vulnerables, vulnerable, chabola, chabolas, chabolista, chabolistas, infravivienda, infraviviendas, barriada, barriadas, vagabundo, vagabundos, marginalidad, marginal, marginales, marginación, marginado, marginados.

Translations: "misery", "miserable", "miserable (plural)", "poverty", "poor", "poor (plural)", "impoverishment", "impoverished", "impoverished (plural)", "begging", "beggar", "beggars", "disadvantaged", "disadvantaged (plural)", "people in need", "people in need (plural)", "desperation", "desperate", "desperate (plural)", "vulnerability", "vulnerable", "vulnerable (plural)", "shanty town", "shanty town (plural)", "person that lives in shanty town", "person that lives in shanty town (plural)", "slum", "slums", "poor neighborhood", "poor neighborhoods", "vagabond", "vagabonds", "marginality", "marginal", "marginal (plural)", "marginalization", "marginalized (plural)"," marginalized (plural)".

A.6 Prostitution

Words in Spanish: Prostitución, prostíbulo, prostíbulos, prostituta, prostitutas, proxenetismo, proxeneta, proxenetas.

Translations: "Prostitution"," brothel", "brothels", "prostitute", "prostitutes", "pimping", "pimp", "pimps".

B Word Embeddings

In the following subsections we show the hyper-parameters used to train the word embedding models and the yearly scores of the $RG-65$ and $MC-30$ semantic similarity benchmarks.

B.1 Hyper-parameters

All Fasttext skipgram models were trained with 250 dimensions, five epochs and minimum word frequency of 15 occurrences. The hyper-parameters selected by the grid-search are shown below in

[11]Papelina is a piece of paper to hold small amounts of drugs.

[12]Bolsita is a small plastic bag to hold small amounts of drugs.

the Table. Default values were used for hyper-parameters that are not mentioned here [13].

Year	Window size	N-grams	Min/max
2007	7	1	4/6
2008	8	2	2/6
2009	8	4	3/6
2010	7	3	default (0/0)
2011	6	1	2/6
2012	5	1	default (0/0)
2013	5	3	default (0/0)
2014	8	1	default (0/0)
2015	5	4	default (0/0)
2016	4	4	3/6
2017	4	1	default (0/0)
2018	5	1	4/6

Table 4: Embedding training hyper-parameters. Min/max means the minimum and maximum length of char ngram.

	RG-65 Pearson coefficient	RG-65 p-value	MC-30 Pearson coefficient	MC-30 p-value
2007	0.74	4.54e-08	0.67	2.99e-04
2008	0.75	2.51e-09	0.72	7.2e-04
2009	0.75	2.43e-07	0.78	9.56e-04
2010	0.70	5.66e-09	0.71	4.2e-04
2011	0.72	6.79e-09	0.66	1.6e-0.3
2012	0.70	7.75e-09	0.68	9.49e-04
2013	0.70	5.88-09	0.69	7.96e-04
2014	0.73	1.22e-09	0.71	4.35e-04
2015	0.71	3.35e-10	0.72	2.7e-04
2016	0.73	2.17e-09	0.69	7.76e-04
2017	0.73	5.16e-09	0.66	1.89e-03
2018	0.72	1.4e-08	0.72	5.27e-04

Table 5: Yearly semantic similarity evaluation results for RG-65 and MC-30 benchmarks.

B.2 Semantic similarity evaluation

The Table 5 shows the Pearson coefficients and p-values for the $RG-65$ and $MC-30$ Spanish word similarity scores, for each of the yearly trained embedding models.

[13] https://fasttext.cc/docs/en/options.html

Multi-modal Intent Classification for Assistive Robots with Large-scale Naturalistic Datasets

Karun Mathew [♣0] **Venkata S Aditya Tarigoppula** [♦♥] **Lea Frermann** [♠]

[♣]Newline Structures Pvt Ltd.

[♦]Department of Biomedical Engineering, The University of Melbourne

[♥]ARC Training Centre in Cognitive Computing for Medical Technologies

[♠]School of Computing and Information Systems, The University of Melbourne

karunmatthew@live.in aditya.tarigoppula@gmail.com lfrermann@unimelb.edu.au

Abstract

Recent years have brought a tremendous growth in assistive robots/prosthetics for people with partial or complete loss of upper limb control. These technologies aim to help the users with various reaching and grasping tasks in their daily lives such as picking up an object and transporting it to a desired location; and their utility critically depends on the ease and effectiveness of communication between the user and robot. One of the natural ways of communicating with assistive technologies is through verbal instructions. The meaning of natural language commands depends on the current configuration of the surrounding environment and needs to be interpreted in this multi-modal context, as accurate interpretation of the command is essential for a successful execution of the user's intent by an assistive device. The research presented in this paper demonstrates how large-scale situated natural language datasets can support the development of robust assistive technologies. We leveraged a navigational dataset comprising > 25k human-provided natural language commands covering diverse situations. We demonstrated a way to extend the dataset in a task-informed way and use it to develop multi-modal intent classifiers for pick and place tasks. Our best classifier reached > 98% accuracy in a 16-way multi-modal intent classification task, suggesting high robustness and flexibility.

1 Introduction

Paralysis is a loss of motor function to varying degrees of severity often resulting in severely reduced or complete loss of upper and/or lower limb control. Such impairments reduce the quality of life for millions of people affected by paralysis (Armour et al., 2016) and increase their dependence upon others to perform day-to-day activities including self- or

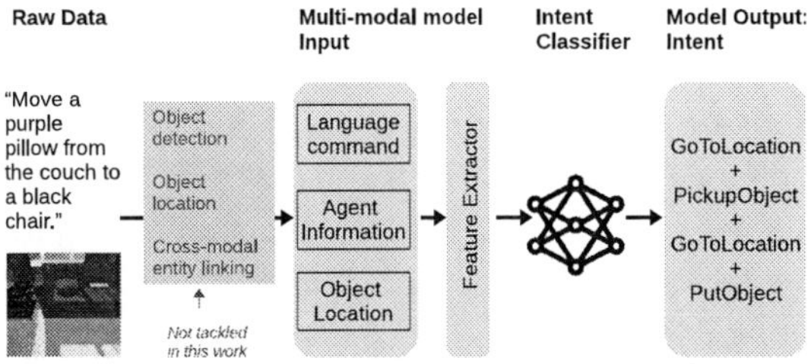

Figure 1: High-level overview of our intent classifier. The system receives visual information extracted from the environment together with a natural language task command as input; and uses this to predicts the *intent* as a suitable sequence of actions necessary to execute the command. Visual scene parsing and cross-modal entity linking are not tackled in this work.

object locomotion and object manipulation tasks like reaching, picking up an object and moving it to a desired location (pick and place). Assistive devices can compensate for some of the impairments provided that they can accurately infer and execute user intents. Most assistive devices currently in use rely on manual control (e.g., wheelchairs controlled with joysticks), and cannot understand natural language user commands or map them to potentially complex sequences of actions. Moreover, they do not perceptively account for the surrounding environment they are interacting with and as a consequence require a more detailed user input. Therefore, recent developments have focused on Intelligent Assistive Devices (IAD), that combine traditional assistive devices with advanced sensors and artificial intelligence, aiming for an accurate inference of a user's intent in the context of a multi-modal representation of the environment (Barry et al., 1994).

The utility of the IAD depends critically on the efficiency and effectiveness of the communication

[0]Work done while at Melbourne University.

with the user. One of the natural ways of instructing the IAD is through verbal communication. It is important to recognize that a majority of patients suffering a loss of limb control retain the ability to speak, albeit impaired in some cases. Modern voice controlled IADs such as wheelchairs (Hou et al., 2020; Umchid et al., 2018), smart home appliances and assistive anthropomorphic robots (Pulikottil et al., 2018a; John et al., 2020) are still limited to a pre-defined set of instructions that the user can choose from. This requires the user to explicitly dictate each individual action leading to the final goal rather than just stating the desired goal alone and off-loading the decision making to perform any required sequence of actions to accomplish the user's intent. Consider the example in Figure 1, where a robotic assistant situated in a complex and dynamic environment is given a verbal instruction "Pick up the book". While the need of a "pick" action is evident from the language command alone, possible additional actions (navigate to the book's location, or to turn around to face the book) depend on the agent and book's location, thus requiring an interpretation of the natural language command in the context of the surrounding environment.

In this paper, we present a step towards bridging this gap by drawing on large, data resources, state of the art language understanding and intent classification methods. We develop a classifier that takes a higher-order task command contextualized in the current environment as input and derives the necessary set of sub-actions (intents) required to achieve the goal intended by the user. We present a scalable framework to develop such flexible natural language interfaces for IAD that execute 'pick and place' tasks. Specifically, we leverage ALFRED (Shridhar et al., 2020), a large-scale naturalistic data set for developing indoor navigation systems, comprising diverse, crowd-sourced natural language commands and photo-realistic images, and adapt it to the pick-and-place task (Section 3). We augment the state-of-the-art natural language intent classifier DIET (Bunk et al., 2020) with a visual processing component (Section 4). Evaluation against simpler classifiers as well as exclusively text-based classification scenarios shows the advantage of joint processing of visual and language information, as well as the DIET architecture. The use of large-scale naturalistic data allows to build solutions that generalize beyond the confines of a laboratory, are easily adaptable and have the potential to improve the overall quality of life for the user. This framework is part of a larger project intended to develop a multi-modal (voice and brain signal) prosthetic limb control.

In short, our contributions are:

- We show that task-related large-scale data sets can effectively support the development assistive technology. We augmented the ALFRED data set with anticipated scenarios of human-assistive agent interaction, including noisy and partially observed scenarios.
- We contribute a multi-modal extension of a state-of-the-art natural language intent classifier (DIET) with a visual component, which lead to the overall best classification results.
- Our best performing model achieved 98% accuracy in a 16-way classification task over diverse user-generated commands, evidencing that our architecture supports flexible and reliable intent classification.

2 Related Work

Our work is cross-disciplinary, covering both medical robotics and (multi-modal) machine learning and NLP for intent classification.

Intent classification is the task of mapping a natural language input to a set of actions that when executed help achieve the underlying goals of the user. As an essential component of conversational systems, it has attracted much attention in the natural language understanding community with methods ranging from semantic parsing (Chen and Mooney, 2011) to more recent deep learning (Liu and Lane, 2016; Goo et al., 2018) and transfer learning approaches, with unsupervised pre-training (Liu et al., 2019; Henderson et al., 2020). The on-line interactive nature of dialogue applications makes model efficiency a central objective. We build on the recent DIET classifier (Dual Intent and Entity Transformer; (Bunk et al., 2020)) which achieves competitive performance in intent classification, while maintaining a lightweight architecture without the need for a large pre-trained language models. DIET was originally developed for language-based dialogue, and we extend the system with a vision understanding component and show that it generalizes to a multi-modal task setup.

Visually grounded language understanding addresses the analysis of verbal commands in the context of the visual environment. Prior work ranges from schematic representations of the environment avoiding the need for image analysis (Chen and Mooney, 2011) over simplistic visual environments ("block worlds" Bisk et al. (2016)) to complex outdoor navigation (Chen et al., 2019)). The advance of deep learning methods for joint visual and textual processing has lead to the development of large-scale datasets which feature both naturalisitic language as well as images (Bunk et al., 2020; Chen et al., 2019; Puig et al., 2018). We leverage a subset of the ALFRED dataset (Bunk et al., 2020) which is a benchmark dataset for learning a mapping from natural language instructions and egocentric (first person) vision to sequences of actions for performing household tasks. The commands in the ALFRED dataset are crowd-sourced from humans, and as such are diverse and resemble naturalistic language. The visual scenes are complex and photo-realistic, and the dataset contains tasks requiring the agent to execute complex sequences of multiple, context-dependent actions to manipulate objects in an environment that closely resembles the medical application scenario addressed in this paper. We note that we do not address the object recognition challenge in this work, but assume access to the object locations, and train intent classifiers to incorporate such information.

Interfacing medical assistive technologies Traditional interfaces to assistive technologies involved manipulating joysticks (House et al., 2009), or verbal commands which are restricted to simple templates. The latter include very simple templates ("up", "down", "left"; Pulikottil et al. (2018b)), or highly constrained training data sets based on command templates produced by five human annotators (Stepputtis et al., 2020). In this paper, we leverage natural commands produced by thousands of crowd workers with the aim to produce a robust intent classifier amenable to natural speech input.

3 Data

We leveraged and extended the ALFRED (Action Learning From Realistic Environments and Directives) dataset of visually grounded language commands (Shridhar et al., 2020), for training and testing our intent classifier. ALFRED consists of more than 8,000 sets of scenes with unique environmental layout with a fixed set of associated movable and static objects. Each scene is paired with an indoor navigation task, and contains three levels of information: (1) positional information of the agent and objects, (2) natural language descriptions of the high-level task and low-level instructions to achieve the goal, and (3) a sequence of discrete actions to be performed by the agent to achieve the goal. An example is shown in Figure 2.

The visual task information comprises the positional (x, y, z) co-ordinates of the agent (Agent Information), and the positional information of static and interactable objects in the environment (Scene Information). The natural language annotation includes a "high-level task" describing the overall goal, as well as detailed low-level instructions ("low-level subtasks") on how to achieve the goal. Low level instructions were provided by at least three human annotators through crowdsourcing. Finally, each ALFRED task in the train and validation set is augmented with an "action plan" listing the sequence of actions (or intents) such as `GoToLocation` or `PickUpObject` required to achieve the goal in the context of the scene configuration (Figure 2, bottom). Crowd workers were prompted by these action plans, so that a gold-standard utterance-intent alignment could be derived from the data set.

3.1 ALFRED for intent classification

We utilized a subset of the dataset corresponding to "pick and place" tasks, which is most relevant to our target application of humanoid arm control. We refer to the item that is to be picked up as "target object" and the item on which the picked-up object is to be placed as the "receptacle object". ALFRED contains around 3,000 different pick and place tasks, involving 58 unique target objects and 26 receptacle objects across 120 indoor scenes.

Leveraging the ALFRED action plans, we could map all "pick and place" language commands to a combination of three unique sub-actions: `GoToLocation`[1], `PickUpObject` and `PutObject`. `GoToLocation` actions referred to actions of the agent moving to a given location. `PickUpObject` and `PutObject` corresponded to the action of picking up the target object and placing the target object, respectively. Note that a single natural language directive can cover one or more atomic actions. We refer to com-

[1]in analogy to a lateral or vertical movement of the robotic arm

Agent Information	Agent	{x: -2.50, y: 0.92, z: 2.50, rotation=0}
Scene Information	FloorPlan:	FloorPlan214
	Plate,	{x: -0.31, y: 0.27, z: 5.99}
	WateringCan,	{x: -2.28, y: 0.45, z: 4.27}
	KeyChain,	{x: -4.31, y: 0.45, z: 6.73}
	Box,	{x: -2.40, y: 0.57, z: 4.57}
	Laptop,	{x: -2.49, y: 0.53, z: 0.79}
	Vase,	{x: -0.60, y: 1.46, z: 5.74}
	WateringCan,	{x: -2.40, y: 0.44, z: 3.83}
Language Information	High Level Task	"Move the purple pillow from the couch to the black chair."
	Low Level Subtask 1	"Turn right and walk up to the couch."
	Low Level Subtask 2	"Pick up the purple pillow off of the couch."
	Low Level Subtask 3	"Turn around and walk across the room, then hand a left and walk over to the black chair."
	Low Level Subtask 4	"Put the purple pillow on the black chair."
Action Plan	Discrete Action 1	`GoToLocation`
	Discrete Action 2	`PickUpObject`
	Discrete Action 3	`GoToLocation`
	Discrete Action 4	`PutObject`

Figure 2: Visual and Language information corresponding to a pick and place task in ALFRED, as well as the associated Action Plan, i.e., sequence of actions (or intents), as provided in the the data set.

mands describing a single task as "single intent" (*"Pick up the keys."*), and commands describing multiple tasks as "multi-intent" (*"Bring the keys from the chair to the table.""*). Table 1 illustrates the range of tasks and intents supported by the original ALFRED dataset and resulting training instances. In the original ALFRED data set, each low-level instruction was associated with a single intent (Table 1 middle).

We augmented high-level task descriptions with intents by concatenating the actions of its associated low-level tasks (Table1 top). In addition, we augmented the ALFRED tasks with additional diverse and relevant scenarios to our assistive agent use case. First, we created partial tasks where the agent was required to execute only parts of the complete pick and place action sequence (e.g., only move to, and pick up the object). We synthesized these instances by concatenating all possible ordered subsequences of the low- level sub-tasks for a scenario and concatenating their corresponding natural language commands. The resulting instances were then treated as a single "multi-intent" directive (Table 1, bottom). Second, we randomized the positions of the target and receptacle objects mentioned in the verbal commands to (1) far from the agent, (2) near the agent or (3) near the receptacle.

Finally, we imposed physical constraints onto the agent, resembling the characteristics of an assistive robotic arm. In the original ALFRED, all objects within a specific distance of the agent are considered 'pickable'. We introduced a threshold (60 degrees) beyond which an object is unreachable and requires the agent to turn to the object first. We introduced a corresponding new action called `RotateAgent` that needed to be performed before the `PickUpObject`. In addition, we reduced the maximum reach distance of the agent to 0.5 meters and updated ALFRED tasks accordingly with `GoToLocation` actions before `PickUpObject` where necessary. The resulting dataset more realistically represented the physical constraints faced by real world entities, and the actions to be taken to meet the necessary preconditions to perform a task. We also handled cases where visual features corresponding to a language command were missing or irrelevant. For example, the command "Take a step forward", has a single intent `GoToLocation` when considering the natural language command alone. For such commands, we generated multiple data instances with randomized visual features to encourage the model to be insensitive to an irrelevant input modality.

We divided our final dataset into non-overlapping training, testing and validation sets with no overlap in environments. We treated each unique action combination observed in the data as a distinct intent, leading to a total of 16 possible intents that could be selected in response to a spoken command.[2] Table 2 summarizes our data set, full

[2]In addition to the 9 unique intents in Table 1, these are {`PickUpObject`, `PutObject`}, {`RotateAgent`,

Intent type		Command	Intent
High-level single intent	1.	*"Move a red pillow from the couch to a black chair."*	{`GoToLocation`, `PickUpObject`, `GoToLocation`, `PutObject` }
Low-level single intent	2.	*"Turn right and walk up to the couch."*	{`GoToLocation` }
	3.	*"Pick up the red pillow off the couch."*	{`PickUpObject` }
	4.	*"Turn around and walk... to the chair."*	{`GoToLocation` }
	5.	*"Put the red pillow on the chair."*	{`PutObject` }
Low-level multi intent	6.	*"Turn right and walk up to the couch. Pick up the red pillow off the couch."*	{`GoToLocation`, `PickUpObject` }
	7.	*"Pick up the red pillow off the couch. Turn around and walk ... to the chair."*	{`PickUpObject`, `GoToLocation` }
	8.	*"Turn around and walk ... to the chair. Put the red pillow on the chair."*	{`GoToLocation`, `PutObject` }
	9.	*"Turn right and walk up to the couch. Pick up the red pillow off the couch. Turn around and walk ... to the chair."*	{`GoToLocation`, `PickUpObject`, `GoToLocation` }
	10.	*"Pick up the red pillow off the couch. Turn around and walk ... to the chair. Put the red pillow on the chair."*	{`PickUpObject`, `GoToLocation`, `PutObject` }
	11.	*"Turn right and walk up to the couch. Pick up the red pillow off the couch. Turn around and walk ... to the chair. Put the red pillow on the chair."*	{`GoToLocation`, `PickUpObject`, `GoToLocation`, `PutObject` }

Table 1: Example high level multi-intent (1.), low-level single-intent (2.–5.) and low-level multi-intent (6.–7.) tasks of type 'pick and place'. The model receives language commands (left col) together with relevant visual information, and predicts an intent (right col). Top/middle are from the original ALFRED dataset. Bottom instances from data augmentation.

	train	valid	test
# Commands	104,669	24,612	25,109
Percentage	70%	15%	15%

Table 2: Final data set statistics.

data set statistics are in Table 5 in the appendix.

4 Models

Our intent classification model took vector representations of the language command and visual context as input and predicted the underlying intent as one of 16 classes. We briefly describe the representation schemes for scene and language input. Afterwards, we present our proposed model, which extended a state-of-the-art language intent classifier to handle both visual and language input.

4.1 Visual Features

The visual data corresponding to a task instance in ALFRED dataset included the agent and object position information (Figure 2, Agent and Scene information). We represented the visual information of each task as a 4-dimensional vector with elements corresponding to (i) The L2 (Euclidean) distance between agent and target object, (ii) L2 distance between agent and receptacle object, (iii) L2 distance between target and receptacle object and (iv) the angle between the target object and the direction the agent is facing initially.

4.2 Language Features

We transformed the language command to pre-trained word embeddings (Pennington et al., 2014; Kenton and Toutanova, 2019; Peters et al., 2018). Specifically, we use Tok2Vec embeddings provided by SpaCy.[3] We mapped each word in an input command to its corresponding embedding and obtained a representation for the entire command by averaging the word embeddings. Following (Bunk et al., 2020) we augment the embeddings with word- and character-level n-grams.

4.3 The DIET Intent Classifier

DIET is a state of the art, natural language intent classification architecture developed for dialogue understanding tasks (Bunk et al., 2020). DIET classifiers are attractive for application to assistive technologies because they can be trained rapidly and work well even with small datasets. The DIET classifier represents natural language inputs as described above (Sec 4.2). This input representation is passed through a neural network transformer architecture (Vaswani et al., 2017) which is a state-of-the-art architecture for computing contextualized representations of input sequences. DIET is optimized to maximize the similarity between the final representation of the verbal command and an embedded representation of the true intent. We follow their optimization procedure, and at test time we predicted the intent with the closest predicted embedding to the gold label. We used the official implementation, with default parameters.[4]

4.4 Multi-modal DIET

We extended the DIET classifier to a multi-modal model (DIET-M) which predicted intents based on language and scene features. The language input was encoded exactly as in the original model. We then concatenated the output of the transformer along with the 4-dimensional numerical visual features and passed the result first through a 10% dropout layer, followed by two feed-forward layers of sizes 256 and 128 and finally through an output layer of size 40 to obtain a combined visual and language representation. ReLU was used as the activation function for all the feed-forward layers. This joint embedded representation was then used to identify the intents following DIET's original training objective, as described above.

5 Experiments

We present a series of experiments which assesses the impact of model complexity, multi-modal information as well as our data augmentation on final intent classification performance. This work focuses on robust multi-modal intent classification, and as such our experiments assume that the entity recognition and visual interpretation (such as object detection and location) have been solved externally. We discuss our contribution in the context of an end-to-end application Section 6.

PickUpObject}, {RotateAgent,PutObject}, {GoToLocation, PickUpObject, PutObject}, {RotateAgent, PickUpObject, PutObject}, {RotateAgent, PickUpObject, GoToLocation}, {RotateAgent, PickUpObject, GoToLocation, PutObject}

[3] https://spacy.io/usage/embeddings-transformers

[4] https://rasa.com/docs/rasa/reference/rasa/nlu/classifiers/diet_classifier/

5.1 Baselines

We compare DIET and DIET-M against a Multi-Layer Perceptron (MLP) with a single hidden layer. Two variations of the MLP were tested: (1) MLP which takes as input only the embedded language representations; and (2) MLP-M which is provided with the embedded language representations concatenated with the visual features, resulting in a multi-modal variant. Rectified linear unit (ReLU) was used as the activation function and stochastic gradient descent (Ruder, 2016) was used to minimize a cross-entropy loss. The output of the final layer was passed through a soft-max layer to get the probability distribution across all possible intents. At test time, the intent with the highest probability score was predicted as the true intent associated with a command.

We also report a simple majority class baseline, which labels all instances with the most prevalent class in the training set (`GoToLocation`).

5.2 Metrics

We report micro-averaged accuracy, acknowledging the class imbalance in our data set, as well as precision recall and F1 measure.

5.3 Results

Our experiments answered the following questions: (a) how important is the multi-modal (scene) input for accurate intent classification; (b) is a powerful contextual language encoding model necessary to achieve high intent classification performance; and (c) how does the training dataset augmentation impact performance with multi-intent commands? To answer the first question, we compared both machine learning models (DIET-M, MLP-M) against their unimodal language-only versions (DIET, MLP). To answer the second question, we compared the complex DIET classifier against the simpler MLP architecture, and a majority class baseline. Finally, the benefits of data augmentation were ascertained by testing DIET-M's performance on the same testing dataset after training on datasets with different levels of augmentation.

Powerful language encoders improve intent classification accuracy. Table 3 compares the performance of the majority class baseline (Majority), MLP and the DIET classifier. All models were trained and tested on the full, augmented data set. Unsurprisingly, we observed that all machine learning models outperformed the majority class baseline. Furthermore, the variants of the DIET classifier consistently achieved a higher score than the simpler MLP (improvement of 5.6% absolute accuracy). Even though both models achieve F1 measures > 90%, very high language understanding performance is essential for user satisfaction in dialogue systems in general, and in assistive technology settings in particular. In addition, our evaluation adopted "laboratory" conditions, assuming noise-free entity and vision processing. With these arguments in mind, and recalling the fact that DIET is by design fast and efficient, we conclude that state-of-the-art language understanding architectures are preferable for situated intent classification.

Method	Ac	Pr	Re	F1
Majority	0.142	0.142	1.0	0.248
MLP	0.451	0.379	0.374	0.333
DIET	0.591	0.409	0.508	0.429
MLP-M	0.929	0.931	0.929	0.930
DIET-M	**0.985**	**0.982**	**0.984**	**0.983**

Table 3: Intent classification performance of the majority class baseline, multi-layer perceptron (MLP) and our DIET classifier in a unimodal and multi-modal setup (-M). We report accuracy (Ac), precision (Pr), recall (Re) and F1-measure.

Grounding language in visual context information improved intent classification performance. Table 3 compares multi-modal model variants (DIET-M, MLP-M) – with access to visual *and* language information – against their unimodal variants, which classify intents based on language commands only and remain agnostic about the visual surroundings. For both the MLP and DIET we observed a substantial improvement with added visual information. This is unsurprising, given the fact that navigational language commands are often high-level and can only be fully disambiguated in the context of the environment. As evidenced by the large performance gain of our multi-modal models over their language-only counterparts, both systems successfully learned to leverage the additional visual context for accurate intent interpretation.

Data augmentation improved performance of DIET-M. We investigated the benefit of data augmentation on the best performing classifier (DIET-

Augmented	Ac	Pr	Re	F1
0%	0.630	0.529	0.607	0.545
10%	0.921	0.927	0.923	0.925
50%	0.952	0.947	0.944	0.945
100%	0.985	0.982	0.984	0.983
100% (multi)	0.981	0.974	0.976	0.973

Table 4: The performance of the DIET-M classifiers, trained on datasets with access to 0%, 10%, 50% or 100% of the augmented data. 100% (multi) tests only on the more challenging multi-intent subset of the test data.

M) by ablating the amount of augmented training data available to the classifier during training. Specifically, we augment 0%, 10%, 50% or 100% of the original ALFRED instances with multi-subtask variations (as described in Section 3) Rows 1-–4 in Table 4 show DIET-M performance trained on data sets with varying amounts of augmentation, and tested on the full, augmented test data. The model improved consistently with increased augmentation of the training data. Even a small amount of augmented data improved performance substantially, while more augmentation leads to diminishing returns. We finally analyzed specifically the benefit of data augmentation on understanding *multi-intent* commands, i.e., language commands which imply sequences of actions (bottom part of Table 1). To this end, we evaluated the classifier only on multi-intent commands. The result in the final row of Table 4 shows that the performance on these longer and more complex instances was practically on par with performance on the full test set, confirming that DIET-M successfully maps abstract comments to sequences of actions.

6 Discussion

We leveraged and extended a large-scale dataset of indoor navigation tasks to develop an intent classification component for robotic arm control to perform "pick and place" tasks. Our novel multimodal DIET classifier exceeded 98% in classification performance in an "in vitro" evaluation setup. We now discuss limitations of our work as well as future directions.

Toward end-to-end task completion. The intent classifier will be embedded in a larger system in order to enable end-to-end task completion. In our evaluation, we assumed that visual scene parsing (including object recognition and location) as well as entity recognition in the language had been solved perfectly and externally. In an ongoing project, the presented system is integrated with these components, leveraging the recent improvements and corresponding tools and frameworks powered by advances in machine learning, robotics and data sets (Liu et al., 2020; Zhu et al., 2020; Redmon and Farhadi, 2018). This paper presented a highly accurate system which provides a strong foundation and promising starting point for end-to-end integration as well as experiments under noisy conditions (e.g., malformed or ambiguous utterances, or speech recognition errors).

Diversity of tasks and inputs Our study was constrained to "pick-and-place" tasks which (a) are conceptually straightforward and (b) are typically expressed in a fairly regular, formulaic manner. Even though the underlying ALFRED data set was diverse and somewhat noisy due to its crowd-sourced nature, future work will extend our scenario to more complex tasks. ALFRED includes a variety of tasks beyond "pick-and-place" and can directly support this line of work. Our way of constructing multi-intent subtasks by concatenating low-level descriptions biased the data towards long descriptions and an underrepresentations of co-referential pronouns (e.g., "Pick up the keys and put *them* in the bowl"). Future work could leverage a mix of human data collection and natural language generation from language models to further augment the training data.

The accuracy-flexibility trade-off. This work developed a highly accurate intent classifier motivated by the fact that efficient and reliable language understanding is paramount to effective human-robot interaction. To achieve this, we limited the scenarios to a single task type as well as a simple but inflexible intent classification task: We exhaustively enumerated possible intents as 16 classes, thus preventing the model from meaningfully classifying an input that does not correspond to one of these categories. A more flexible system would predict a *sequence* of atomic intent labels of varying length. To this end, the task could be reframed as multi-label classification; or a sequence-to-sequence model could be developed to translate a natural language input into a sequence of intent labels. Analyzing the trade-off between reliability and flexibility in the context of robust multi-modal intent classification for assistive technologies is a fruitful direction for future research.

7 Conclusion

This paper presented a multi-modal intent classifier for "pick-and-place"-tasks which takes diverse natural language commands as input, and which will be incorporated into a natural language interface of an assistive robotic arm. Our work will help to improve the naturalness of human-robot communication, which to-date often consists of mechanical (joystick) control or formulaic and templated language input. We showed how a large-scale naturalistic data set for general indoor navigation can be adapted to support training of a specific, high-accuracy intent classifier. We extended a state-of-the-art natural language-based intent classifier to utilize both vision and language information. Our evaluation showed the effectiveness of our data augmentation, and the importance of *multi-modal* signal for our task. We hope that our work motivates a wider, cross-disciplinary use of large-scale naturalistic data sets – which are becoming more ubiquitous in the NLP and ML communities – as a valuable resource for developing flexible intelligent assistive technologies.

Acknowledgments

This research was supported by the ARC Industry Transformational Training Centre IC170100030 grant.

References

Brian S Armour, Elizabeth A Courtney-Long, Michael H Fox, Heidi Fredine, and Anthony Cahill. 2016. Prevalence and causes of paralysis—united states, 2013. *American journal of public health*, 106(10):1855–1857.

Philip Barry, John Dockery, David Littman, and Melanie Barry. 1994. Intelligent assistive technologies. *Presence: Teleoperators & Virtual Environments*, 3(3):208–215.

Yonatan Bisk, Deniz Yuret, and Daniel Marcu. 2016. Natural language communication with robots. In *Proceedings of the 2016 Conference of the North American Chapter of the Association for Computational Linguistics: Human Language Technologies*, pages 751–761.

Tanja Bunk, Daksh Varshneya, Vladimir Vlasov, and Alan Nichol. 2020. Diet: Lightweight language understanding for dialogue systems. *arXiv preprint arXiv:2004.09936*.

David Chen and Raymond Mooney. 2011. Learning to interpret natural language navigation instructions from observations. In *Proceedings of the AAAI Conference on Artificial Intelligence*, volume 25.

Howard Chen, Alane Suhr, Dipendra Misra, Noah Snavely, and Yoav Artzi. 2019. Touchdown: Natural language navigation and spatial reasoning in visual street environments. In *Proceedings of the IEEE/CVF Conference on Computer Vision and Pattern Recognition*, pages 12538–12547.

Chih-Wen Goo, Guang Gao, Yun-Kai Hsu, Chih-Li Huo, Tsung-Chieh Chen, Keng-Wei Hsu, and Yun-Nung Chen. 2018. Slot-gated modeling for joint slot filling and intent prediction. In *Proceedings of the 2018 Conference of the North American Chapter of the Association for Computational Linguistics: Human Language Technologies, Volume 2 (Short Papers)*, pages 753–757, New Orleans, Louisiana. Association for Computational Linguistics.

Matthew Henderson, Iñigo Casanueva, Nikola Mrkšić, Pei-Hao Su, Tsung-Hsien Wen, and Ivan Vulić. 2020. ConveRT: Efficient and accurate conversational representations from transformers. In *Findings of the Association for Computational Linguistics: EMNLP 2020*, pages 2161–2174, Online. Association for Computational Linguistics.

Tan Kian Hou et al. 2020. Arduino based voice controlled wheelchair. In *Journal of Physics: Conference Series*, volume 1432, page 012064. IOP Publishing.

Brandi House, Jonathan Malkin, and Jeff Bilmes. 2009. The voicebot: a voice controlled robot arm. In *Proceedings of the SIGCHI Conference on Human Factors in Computing Systems*, pages 183–192.

Ripcy Anna John, Sneha Varghese, Sneha Thankam Shaji, and K Martin Sagayam. 2020. Assistive device for physically challenged persons using voice controlled intelligent robotic arm. In *2020 6th International Conference on Advanced Computing and Communication Systems (ICACCS)*, pages 806–810. IEEE.

Jacob Devlin Ming-Wei Chang Kenton and Lee Kristina Toutanova. 2019. Bert: Pre-training of deep bidirectional transformers for language understanding. In *Proceedings of NAACL-HLT*, pages 4171–4186.

Bing Liu and Ian Lane. 2016. Attention-based recurrent neural network models for joint intent detection and slot filling. In *Interspeech 2016*, pages 685–689.

Li Liu, Wanli Ouyang, Xiaogang Wang, Paul Fieguth, Jie Chen, Xinwang Liu, and Matti Pietikäinen. 2020. Deep learning for generic object detection: A survey. *International journal of computer vision*, 128(2):261–318.

Xingkun Liu, Arash Eshghi, Pawel Swietojanski, and Verena Rieser. 2019. Benchmarking natural language understanding services for building conversational agents. In *10th International Workshop on Spoken Dialogue Systems Technology 2019*.

Jeffrey Pennington, Richard Socher, and Christopher D Manning. 2014. Glove: Global vectors for word representation. In *Proceedings of the 2014 conference on empirical methods in natural language processing (EMNLP)*, pages 1532–1543.

Matthew E Peters, Mark Neumann, Mohit Iyyer, Matt Gardner, Christopher Clark, Kenton Lee, and Luke Zettlemoyer. 2018. Deep contextualized word representations. In *Proceedings of NAACL-HLT*, pages 2227–2237.

Xavier Puig, Kevin Ra, Marko Boben, Jiaman Li, Tingwu Wang, Sanja Fidler, and Antonio Torralba. 2018. Virtualhome: Simulating household activities via programs. In *Proceedings of the IEEE Conference on Computer Vision and Pattern Recognition*, pages 8494–8502.

Terrin Babu Pulikottil, Marco Caimmi, Maria Grazia D'Angelo, Emilia Biffi, Stefania Pellegrinelli, and Lorenzo Molinari Tosatti. 2018a. A voice control system for assistive robotic arms: preliminary usability tests on patients. In *2018 7th IEEE International Conference on Biomedical Robotics and Biomechatronics (Biorob)*, pages 167–172. IEEE.

Terrin Babu Pulikottil, Marco Caimmi, Maria Grazia D'Angelo, Emilia Biffi, Stefania Pellegrinelli, and Lorenzo Molinari Tosatti. 2018b. A voice control system for assistive robotic arms: preliminary usability tests on patients. In *2018 7th IEEE International Conference on Biomedical Robotics and Biomechatronics (Biorob)*, pages 167–172. IEEE.

Joseph Redmon and Ali Farhadi. 2018. Yolov3: An incremental improvement. *arXiv preprint arXiv:1804.02767*.

Sebastian Ruder. 2016. An overview of gradient descent optimization algorithms. *arXiv preprint arXiv:1609.04747*.

Mohit Shridhar, Jesse Thomason, Daniel Gordon, Yonatan Bisk, Winson Han, Roozbeh Mottaghi, Luke Zettlemoyer, and Dieter Fox. 2020. Alfred: A benchmark for interpreting grounded instructions for everyday tasks. In *Proceedings of the IEEE/CVF conference on computer vision and pattern recognition*, pages 10740–10749.

Simon Stepputtis, Joseph Campbell, Mariano Phielipp, Stefan Lee, Chitta Baral, and Heni Ben Amor. 2020. Language-conditioned imitation learning for robot manipulation tasks. *Advances in Neural Information Processing Systems*, 33.

Sumet Umchid, Pitchaya Limhaprasert, Sitthichai Chumsoongnern, Tanun Petthong, and Theera Leeudomwong. 2018. Voice controlled automatic wheelchair. In *2018 11th Biomedical Engineering International Conference (BMEiCON)*, pages 1–5. IEEE.

Ashish Vaswani, Noam Shazeer, Niki Parmar, Jakob Uszkoreit, Llion Jones, Aidan N Gomez, Łukasz Kaiser, and Illia Polosukhin. 2017. Attention is all you need. In *Advances in neural information processing systems*, pages 5998–6008.

Haidi Zhu, Haoran Wei, Baoqing Li, Xiaobing Yuan, and Nasser Kehtarnavaz. 2020. A review of video object detection: Datasets, metrics and methods. *Applied Sciences*, 10(21):7834.

A Dataset Statistics

Intent	train	valid	test
{ GoToLocation }	14.3%	14.3%	14.3%
{ PickUpObject }	3.5%	3.7%	3.5%
{ PutObject }	3.5%	3.6%	3.5%
{ GoToLocation, PickUpObject }	7.2%	7.1%	7.2%
{ PickUpObject, GoToLocation }	3.5%	3.6%	3.6%
{ GoToLocation, PutObject }	7.1%	7.1%	7.1%
{ PickUpObject, PutObject }	3.5%	3.6%	3.6%
{ RotateAgent, PickUpObject }	3.6%	3.4%	3.7%
{ RotateAgent, PutObject }	3.6%	3.5%	3.6%
{ GoToLocation, PickUpObject, GoToLocation }	7.1%	7.1%	7.1%
{ PickUpObject, GoToLocation, PutObject }	7.0%	6.9%	7.2%
{ GoToLocation, PickUpObject, PutObject }	7.3%	7.1%	7.2%
{ RotateAgent, PickUpObject, PutObject }	3.6%	3.5%	3.5%
{ RotateAgent, PickUpObject, GoToLocation }	3.6%	3.6%	3.6%
{ GoToLocation, PickUpObject, GoToLocation, PutObject }	14.2%	14.3%	14.2%
{ RotateAgent, PickUpObject, GoToLocation, PutObject }	7.2%	7.4%	7.0%
Total Commands	104,669	24,612	25,109
Total Percentage	70%	15%	15%

Table 5: Full distribution of task instances by intent type in our final data set.

Harnessing Privileged Information for Hyperbole Detection

Rhys Biddle[♠♣] **Maciej Rybiński**[♣] **Qian Li**[♠] **Cécile Paris**[♣] **Guandong Xu**[♠]
[♠]Advanced Analytics Institute, University of Technology Sydney, Australia
[♣]CSIRO Data61, Sydney, Australia
rhys.biddle@student.uts.edu.au
{firstname.lastname}@uts.edu.au
{firstname.lastname}@csiro.au

Abstract

The detection of hyperbole is an important stepping stone to understanding the intentions of a hyperbolic utterance. We propose a model that combines pre-trained language models with privileged information for the task of hyperbole detection. We also introduce a suite of behavioural tests to probe the capabilities of hyperbole detection models across a range of hyperbole types. Our experiments show that our model improves upon baseline models on an existing hyperbole detection dataset. Probing experiments combined with analysis using local linear approximations (LIME) show that our model excels at detecting one particular type of hyperbole. Further, we discover that our experiments highlight annotation artifacts introduced through the process of literal paraphrasing of hyperbole. These annotation artifacts are likely to be a roadblock to further improvements in hyperbole detection.

1 Introduction

The analysis of figurative language by Natural Language Processing (NLP) systems is a challenge confronting researchers and practitioners (Reyes and Rosso, 2014; Rai and Chakraverty, 2020). Hyperbole is a common type of figurative language that is defined by an intentionally excessive contrast between utterance meaning and reality along a semantic scale to convey an evaluation (e.g., '*my bedroom is the size of a postage stamp*') (McCarthy and Carter, 2004; Mora, 2009; Claridge, 2010; Carston and Wearing, 2015; Burgers et al., 2016). The detection of hyperbole has proven to be a challenging problem for NLP systems, much like the detection of other figures of speech (Troiano et al., 2018; Kong et al., 2020; Abulaish et al., 2020). The evaluative nature of hyperbole motivates the importance of understanding hyperbole for affective computing applications (e.g., sentiment analysis).

Learning under Privileged Information (LUPI) is a learning paradigm that involves providing additional information during training to help teach a model to learn a particular phenomenon (Pechyony and Vapnik, 2010). The source and type of privileged information (PI) varies depending on application, such as a list of ingredients present in an image to help teach a computer vision model to detect food in images (Meng et al., 2019), or the human ratings of various aesthetic categories of images for automated assessment of aesthetic photo quality (Shu et al., 2020). We propose to use literal paraphrases of hyperbole as a source of PI for hyperbole detection. We hypothesise that this information will help a model to learn the excessive contrast within a particular hyperbole (e.g., '*my head is **exploding** right now*' $\rightarrow$ '*my head is **hurting** right now*').

Our contributions in this paper are as follows; (1) We propose a method for hyperbole detection based on the injection of PI; (2) We introduce **HyperProbe**, a suite of behavioural tests for hyperbole detection models; (3) We reveal that annotation artifacts are a potential roadblock for progress on hyperbole detection.

2 HYPO

The **HYPO** dataset is an annotated collection of hyperbole introduced by Troiano et al. (2018). The dataset consists of manually composed hyperbole and hyperbole sourced from various online sources including click-bait headlines, love letters, advertisements, and animated cartoons.

Annotation for **HYPO** was carried out by crowd workers who were given several tasks based on each example. The crowd workers had to assess whether they thought the utterance contained hyperbolic content. A follow up task was to highlight the specific words in the utterance they considered

Hyperbole Corpus	Paraphrase Corpus	Minimal Units Corpus
The principal is unhappy...we're **cooked.**	The principal is unhappy...we're *in trouble.*	Well **cooked** vegetables can be pureed easily.
Her morning jog turned into a **marathon**	Her morning jog turned into a *long run*	There was a **marathon** in the city today

Table 1: **HYPO examples. Hyperbole Corpus** contains original hyperbolic utterances. **Paraphrase Corpus** contains a literal paraphrase. **Minimal Units Corpus** contains examples that contain the hyperbolic words/phrases in a non-hyperbolic context.

Type	Keywords
ECF	absolute, complete, entire, pure, whole, impossible, never, no, nobody, nowhere, perfect, flawless, endless, eternal, infinite, all, always, every, everybody, everyone, everywhere, definite, exact, undeniable
Quantitative	small, big, slow, fast, thin, thick, tall, length, large, high
Qualitative	bad, corrupt, evil, fraud, wicked, chaos, confusion, disorder, garbage, riot, dead, hell, misery, murder, nightmare, alarm, fear, panic, scared, shock, anxiety, autism, blind, deaf, insomnia, bitter, pierce, sharp, spicy, toxic, cancer, fever, headache, pain, sad, suffer, attack, explode, fight, rape, ruin, wreck, dream, heaven, paradise, utopia, vital, attract, beauty, charm, grace, handsome, amaze, good, great, ideal, impress

Table 2: **Hyperbole term lists. Type** refers to the type of hyperbole as defined by Mora (Mora, 2009). **Keywords** is a list of the keywords in word list.

to be hyperbolic. Additionally, the workers were then asked to paraphrase the original hyperbolic sentence such that it was no longer hyperbolic.

The worker responses to the first task were used to filter out non-hyperbolic utterances resulting in 709 hyperbolic utterances in total, denoted as the Hyperbole Corpus. The list of hyperbolic tokens identified by the crowd workers was used to create a second corpus, denoted the Minimal Units Corpus (709 sentences). The literal paraphrases also made up another corpus, the Paraphrase Corpus (709 sentences). Combining these three corpora, every hyperbolic utterance in the Hyperbole Corpus has two non-hyperbolic counterparts from the Minimal Units Corpus and Paraphrase Corpus respectively, see Table 1. In total just over 2.1k sentences make up the final version of **HYPO**.

3 HyperProbe

Our **HyperProbe** suite consists of synthetic data generated to probe the ability of models to detect hyperbole[1]. The suite is created to target the three types of hyperbole identified by (Mora, 2009): **Extreme Case Formulations** (ECF), **Qualitative Hyperbole** and **Quantitative Hyperbole**. The creation of test sentences follows a general four step procedure:

1. **Word List Creation**: we create seed word lists containing words to be used in test sentences. These seed word lists are divided by part-of-speech class and are created based on the word lists curated by Mora (2009), see Table 2, for hyperbole-prone words.

2. **Sentence Template Creation**: we create syntactic templates to be filled by a sentence generator. The syntax for sentence templates is as follows; {TAG} indicates that a word is drawn from a user-defined seed word list (based on part-of-speech tags), **{TAG}** indicates that the word is drawn from a user-defined *hyperbole-prone* seed word list, {MASK} indicates that RoBERTa (Liu et al., 2019) will infill this token, a functionality provided by the CheckList framework (Ribeiro et al., 2020)[2].

3. **Test Sentence Generation**: consists of the generation of test sentences, via CheckList, using the word lists and templates generated in the previous steps.

4. **Manual Assessment and Annotation**: we assess the grammar and semantics of the generated test sentences and annotate the sentences. Our annotation consists of a binary label indicating the presence of hyperbolic content.

3.1 Extreme Case Formulation Tests

ECFs are semantic formulations that invoke extreme descriptions of events or objects (Whitehead, 2015; Pomerantz, 1986). A simple example of an ECF is a sentence that contains an extreme description via an adjective (*absolute*, *entire*, *infinite*, etc.), adverb (*always*, *never*, etc.), quantifier

[1]https://github.com/biddle-r/HyperProbe

[2]https://github.com/marcotcr/checklist

(*all*, *none*, etc.) or indefinite pronoun (*everybody*, *nobody*, etc.) (Edwards, 2000; Norrick, 2004). The intentionally non-literal use of ECFs has been identified as a rich source for hyperbolic expressions (McCarthy and Carter, 2004; Norrick, 2004; Mora, 2009; Whitehead, 2015; Carston and Wearing, 2015). The detection of ECFs is a fundamental requirement for a hyperbole detection model, and we design a set of test sentences to probe this ability. Given that ECF prone-words from Table 2 belong to various word classes and can appear in a myriad of grammatical patterns, we design several sentence templates, see Table 3. Upon completion of assessment and annotation there were 181 test sentences, 95 (52%) of which were labelled as hyperbolic, see Table 3.

3.2 Qualitative Hyperbole Tests

Qualitative hyperboles align with the subjective-emotional dimension of hyperbole (Mora, 2009). A subjective evaluation made to an excessive degree is the defining feature of qualitative hyperboles (e.g., '*this video is **cancer***', '*Sweet n sour chicken is **God Tier***'). The ability to detect and interpret qualitative hyperbole is a fundamental requirement of a hyperbole detection model. From the list of qualitative terms in Table 2, we compile a list containing 54 adjectives. We create six sentence templates to incorporate the adjectives into a sentence, see Table 4. Upon completion of assessment and annotation there were 306 test sentences, 87 (28%) of which were labelled as hyperbolic, see Table 4.

3.3 Quantitative Hyperbole Tests

Quantitative hyperboles align with the objective-gradational dimension of hyperbole (Mora, 2009). The defining feature of this type of hyperbole is the up-scaling of an *obvious* quantity or magnitude to an excessive degree (e.g., '*i have a **million** things left to do*', '*this year has felt like a **decade***'). We design a set of test sentences that allows us to probe the ability of models to detect hyperbolic expressions along quantitative dimensions. We use the list of quantitative terms in Table 2 and their comparative forms (e.g., *bigger*, *smaller*, *lighter*, etc.) as seed word lists for these sentences. We create two sentence templates to incorporate these into a sentence, see Table 5. Upon completion of assessment and annotation there were 43 test sentences, 21 (48%) of which were labelled as hyperbolic, see Table 5.

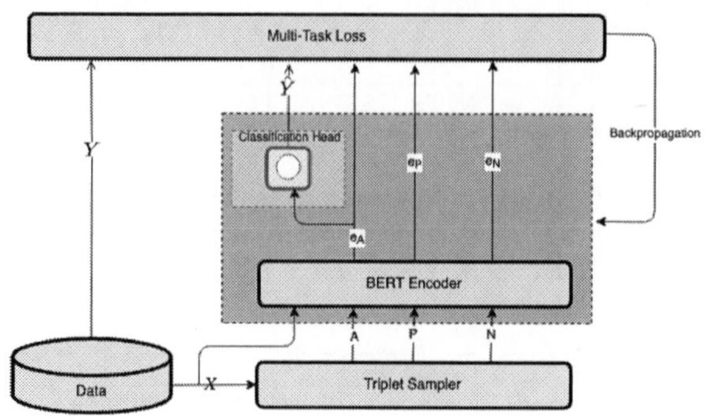

Figure 1: **BERT+PI**. Model contains a BERT encoder, a linear classification head and a Triplet Sampler. We incorporate PI via the triplet sampler.

4 Privileged Information for Hyperbole Detection

Our motivation for incorporating privileged information into a hyperbole detection model is based on observations from the foundational work of Troiano et al. (2018). The authors found that models trained on hyperboles and literal paraphrases performed marginally better on the task of hyperbole detection than models trained on hyperboles and non-literal sentences that used the hyperbolic words/phrases in a non-hyperbole context. We propose that treating literal paraphrases as privileged information and incorporating this information into a hyperbole detection model could improve the ability of a model to detect when a word or phrase was being used in an excessive hyperbolic manner.

In our proposed model, **BERT+PI**, we incorporate privileged information via triplet loss. We utilise a triplet loss because we want to force our model to differentiate between hyperbolic and non-hyperbolic usage of words and phrases, and we can strictly enforce this via triplet loss. Specifically, by specifying a hyperbolic sentence as an anchor sample, another hyperbole as a positive sample and a manually composed literal paraphrase (i.e., PI) as a negative sample, we are enforcing this difference in representation space.

4.1 BERT+PI

BERT+PI is based on a multi-task text classification framework. We use a triplet sampling module to sample negative and positive sentences for each sentence in the dataset. We use BERT (**?**) to encode a representation for each of these sentences and send the representation of the original sentence to a linear classification head. Representations of

Template	**Example**
{DT}{MASK}{MASK}{VB}{**JJ**}	the dishonest words are **endless**
{DT}{**JJ**}{MASK}{VB}{MASK}	the **endless** combinations are daunting
{DT}{MASK}{MASK}{**RB**}{VB$_a$}	the code was **never** cracked
{DT}{MASK}{MASK}{**RB**}{MASK}	the good times **always** roll
{DT}{MASK}{VB$_l$}{**RB**}{MASK}	the dog was **never** silent
{DT}{MASK}{MASK}{VB$_l$}{**RB**}	the drug problem is **everywhere**
{DT}{MASK}{MASK}{**DT**}{MASK}	The mother of **every** invention
{**DT**}{MASK}{MASK}{IN}{MASK}	**all** rights reserved in copyright
{**DT**}{MASK}{VB}{MASK}{MASK}	**every** child will be impacted
{DT}{MASK}{MASK}{MASK}{**PRON**}	The law applies to **everybody**
{**PRON**}{IN}{DT}{MASK}{VB}{MASK}	**nobody** on the street is home

Table 3: **Extreme Case Formulation Test Examples**. ***Template*** shows templates as provided to CheckList, ***Example*** is an example sentence as generated by CheckList.

Template	**Example**
{DT}{MASK}{MASK}{VB}{MASK}{**JJ**}	a world that is truly **wicked**
{DT}{MASK}{VB}{**JJ**}	The argument is **confusing**
{DT}{MASK}{VB}{MASK}{**JJ**}	The wine is very **bitter**
{DT}{MASK}{MASK}{VB}{**JJ**}	the oil residue is **toxic**
{DT}{**JJ**}{MASK}{VB}{MASK}	A **great** story was completed
{DT}{**JJ**}{MASK}{VB}{MASK}{MASK}	The **shocking** video was posted here

Table 4: **Qualitative Adjectives Test Examples**. ***Template*** shows templates as provided to CheckList, ***Example*** is an example sentence generated by CheckList.

Algorithm 1 Semi-Random Triplet Sampling

Require: $D = [t_0, t_1, ..., t_n]$
Require: $s \in \mathbb{Z}^+$ ▷ Sampling Factor
  $H \leftarrow t \forall t \in D \mid t.\text{label} == 1$ ▷ t.label contains annotated label for t
  $P \leftarrow t \forall t \in D \mid t.\text{label} == 2$ ▷ N consists of literal paraphrases (i.e., PI)
  $S \leftarrow \emptyset$
  for $i = 0, i < |D|, i++$ **do**
    $a \leftarrow D_i$
    $T \leftarrow \emptyset$
    for $j = 0, j < s, j++$ **do**
      if a.label $== 1$ **then**
        $p \leftarrow$ sample(H) ▷ sample(X) draws a random sample from X
        $n \leftarrow p$.par ▷ t.par is a literal paraphrase of t
      else if a.label $== 0$ **then**
        $p \leftarrow$ sample(P)
        $n \leftarrow p$.hyp ▷ t.hyp is a hyperbolic expression of t
      end if
      T.insert($[a, p, n]$)
    end for
    S.insert(T)
  end for
  return S

all three sentences are used in the computation of the triplet loss. An important aspect of models based on any type of contrastive loss, including triplet loss, is the sampling methodology (Wu et al., 2017). For **BERT+PI** our triplet sampling algorithm involves randomly sampling examples based on label and the relationship between a hyperbole and its literal paraphrase, see Algorithm 1 and see Table 6 for examples.

The logic in our sampling algorithm is that if the anchor is a hyperbole, then we randomly sample another hyperbole as a positive (i.e., same class) sample for that triplet. We then set the negative sample to be the literal paraphrase of the positive sample (note: This sample is PI). This ensures that optimisation of the triplet loss forces a hyperbole to be closer to another hyperbole than its literal paraphrase in representation space.

If the anchor is *not* a hyperbole, we randomly sample a literal paraphrase as a positive sample for that triplet (note: This sample is PI). We then set the negative sample to be the hyperbole of the positive. The motivation here is that optimisation of the triplet loss will result in a non-hyperbolic sentence and a literal paraphrase being closer in representation space than a non-hyperbolic text and a hyperbole.

Formally, the class probability for an individual

Template	Example
{MASK}{MASK} is as **{JJ}** as {MASK}{MASK}	my heart is as **heavy** as the world
{MASK}{MASK} is **{JJR}** than {MASK}{MASK}	this version is **longer** than I expected

Table 5: **Quantitative Dimensions Test Examples**. ***Template*** shows templates as provided to CheckList, ***Example*** is an example sentence generated by CheckList.

Anchor	Positive	Negative
Inviting my mother-in-law to stay here is a **recipe for disaster**.	He eats a **mountain** of junk food.	He eats a *lot* of junk food.*
This supersonic airliner breaks the sound barrier.	Football is *important to him.**	Football is **his oxygen**.

Table 6: **Semi-Random Triplet Sampling - Example Triplets**. ***Anchor*** indicates an anchor text. ***Positive*** indicates a positive text. ***Negative*** indicates negative text. Note: * indicates that the example is PI.

sentence is calculated by **BERT+PI** as follows:

$$\hat{y}_i = \sigma(e_i^a \mathbf{W} + b), \tag{1}$$

where e_i^a is the dense representation of anchor example i computed by BERT, $\mathbf{W}^Y$ and b^Y are learnable parameters and σ is a softmax function. The model is optimised via multi-task loss, see eq. 2.

$$\mathcal{L} = \mathcal{L}_c + \lambda \mathcal{L}_t \tag{2}$$

Where $\mathcal{L}_c$ is a binary cross entropy loss (eq 3), and $\mathcal{L}_t$ is a triplet loss (see eq. 4). λ is a parameter to weight the importance of the triplet loss and as a result the influence of the PI. In the cross-entropy loss, y_i is a binary indicator for class label, and $\hat{y}$ is the prediction output from eq. 1. In the triplet loss, D is the cosine distance, m is a hyperparamater indicating the margin, $e_i^a, e_{ij}^p, e_{ij}^n$ are the BERT representations for an anchor, positive and negative sample, and s is the sampling factor (i.e., how many positive and negative examples per anchor).

$$\mathcal{L}_c = -\frac{1}{N}\sum_{i=1}^{N}\left[y_i \log(\hat{y}_i) + (1 - y_i)\log(1 - \hat{y}_i)\right] \tag{3}$$

$$\mathcal{L}_t = \frac{1}{Ns}\sum_{i=1}^{N}\sum_{j=1}^{s}\left[\max(D(e_i^a, e_{ij}^p) - D(e_i^a, e_{ij}^n) + m, 0)\right] \tag{4}$$

5 Experiments

5.1 Baselines

We implement models presented in previous research on hyperbole as baseline methods for our experiments on hyperbole detection. Troiano et al. (2018) introduce an NLP pipeline style approach to detecting hyperbole in their foundational work on computational hyperbole detection. They introduce a number of hand-crafted features that are motivated by findings from cognitive linguistics on the mechanisms humans use for identifying and interpreting hyperbole. These features range from unexpectedness, imageability, polarity, subjectivity and intensity. These features are concatenated together and referred to as QQ (i.e., Qualitative and Quantitative) features by the authors, we adhere to that nomenclature and refer to our implementation of these features as QQ for the remainder of the paper. The authors experiment with several 'traditional' statistical learners for the classification layer of their pipeline. We use Logistic Regression and Naive Bayes, as those two methods were more accurate at the detection of hyperbole compared to the other methods in their experiments. We refer to these methods as **LR+QQ** and **NB+QQ** for the remainder of the paper.

Follow on from that work Kong et al. (2020) leverage the QQ features adjusting them slightly to compensate for differences in language and utilise pre-trained language models (i.e., BERT) for a hyperbole detection model. The authors combine the QQ features with the output from the BERT embeddings and pass the concatenated vector to a linear classification layer. We refer to this model as **BERT+QQ** in the remainder of the paper. We also include a simple vanilla BERT baseline that we refer to as **BERT** in the remainder of the paper.

5.2 Experiment Setup

We merge the Hyperbole Corpus and Minimal Units Corpus from **HYPO** and split into train-dev-test sets based on a 70:20:10 ratio. The Paraphrase Corpus is treated as a source of PI and thus only available at training time, also note that no sentences from **HyperProbe** were used for training,

Anchor	Positive	Negative
When the girl lost her puppy she cried an **ocean** of tears.	The little girl was **drowning in her** tears.	The little girl was crying a lot.*
I was crying for leaving my home.	My dad'll be very angry when he finds out that I wrecked his car.*	My dad'll **hit the roof** when he finds out that I wrecked his car.

Table 7: **Triplet Samples**. Examples of anchor, positive and negative samples generated by triplet sampler. Note: * indicates PI.

Hyperparameter	Values
Dropout	0.1, 0.2, 0.3
Learning Rate	1e-04, 1e-05, 1e-06
λ	0.25, 0.5, 1
s (Sampling Factor)	1, 3, 5
Encoder	BERT, RoBERTa

Table 8: **Hyperparameter search**. ***Hyperparameter*** indicates the hyperparameter. ***Values*** indicates the values used in search. Note: Not all parameters are applicable for all models (i.e., λ, s only required for **BERT+PI**)

Model	F1	Precision	Recall
LR+QQ	0.710(-)	0.679(-)	0.745(-)
NB+QQ	0.693(-)	0.689(-)	0.696(-)
BERT	0.709(.064)	0.711(.077)	0.735(.177)
BERT+QQ	0.671(.086)	0.650(.147)	0.765(.246)
BERT+PI	**0.781(.012)**	**0.754(.053)**	**0.814(.039)**

Table 9: **HYPO Results**. We provide the mean F1, precision and recall score as well as standard deviation across three runs for all models.

only testing. Overall we are left with four test datasets, HYPO, Extreme Case Formulations, Qualitative Hyperbole and Quantitative Hyperbole. We perform grid-search to find optimal hyperparameters for **BERT**, **BERT+QQ**, **BERT+PI**, see Table 8.

6 Results

6.1 HYPO

Results of our experiments on **HYPO** show that models that incorporate PI outperform the baselines, with respect to $F1$ score, see Table 9. We see a .071 (10%) increase in F1 for **BERT+PI** over the best performing baseline (**LR+QQ**). We use LIME (Ribeiro et al., 2016) to provide explanations for model predictions, see Figure 2. From this Figure we see examples that suggest that the increase in both precision and recall for **BERT+PI** seen in Table 9 is a result of a better contextual understanding of hyperbole-prone ECF terms. The first two examples in particular highlight the understanding of the word '*brainless*' in both a hyperbolic and non-hyperbolic context that are correctly classified by **BERT+PI**.

Model	F1	Precision	Recall
LR+QQ	0.678(-)	0.747(-)	0.621(-)
NB+QQ	0.523(-)	0.690(-)	0.421(-)
BERT	0.490(.340)	0.751(.158)	0.516(.453)
BERT+QQ	0.540(.337)	0.721(.184)	0.632(.484)
BERT+PI	**0.701(.014)**	**0.756(.033)**	**0.656(.047)**

Table 10: **Hyperprobe Results. Extreme Case Formulations**

Model	F1	Precision	Recall
BERT	0.407(-)	0.333(-)	0.522(-)
BERT	0.336(-)	0.400(-)	0.290(-)
BERT	0.278(.275)	0.240(.209)	0.401(.497)
BERT+QQ	0.352(.307)	0.255(.227)	0.599(.529)
BERT+PI	**0.527(.030)**	.486(.054)	0.590(.089)

Table 11: **Hyperprobe Results. Qualitative Hyperbole**

6.2 Extreme Case Formulations

From Table 10 we see models that incorporate PI provide improvements in detecting ECF hyperbole, .023 increase in F1, compared to **LR+QQ**. This aligns with results observed in Section 6.1 regarding the better understanding of hyperbole-prone ECF words in hyperbolic and non-hyperbolic contexts by **BERT+PI** compared to the baselines. We provide LIME explanations, (see Figure 3), and again observe examples that indicate a better contextual understanding of hyperbole-prone ECF terms by **BERT+PI**.

6.2.1 Qualitative Hyperbole

From Table 11 we observe that all models struggle to detect qualitative hyperbolic expressions, **BERT+PI** achieves the highest $F1$ of only 0.527 with a sub-0.5 precision of 0.486. With respect to variance we see many models with wild variances in recall, (.529, .497), suggesting that some of these runs are degenerating to outputting all positive class or all negative class predictions. These results suggest that qualitative hyperbole is harder to detect than ECF hyperbole.

BERT		BERT+PI	
LIME Word Weightings	P(*h*)	LIME Word Weightings	P(*h*)
Search engines are brainless entities.	.66	Search engines are brainless entities.	**.18**
Me, the wife of that boorish, brainless man.	**.78**	Me, the wife of that boorish, brainless man.	**.74**
This policy will plunge the country into a chaos.	.20	This policy will plunge the country into a chaos.	**.79**
Every flavor is dynamite.	.35	Every flavor is dynamite.	**.96**

Figure 2: **Model Explanation Comparisons - HYPO.** ***LIME Word Weightings*** indicate the importance of a word for a particular class, orange highlights indicate hyperbolic words, **blue** highlights indicate non-hyperbolic words. ***P(h)*** is the prediction probability that a sentence was hyperbolic with red indicating an incorrect classification (assuming a .5 decision threshold)

LR+QQ		BERT+PI	
LIME Word Weightings	P(*h*)	LIME Word Weightings	P(*h*)
the absolute majority was significant	.69	the absolute majority was significant	**.35**
the exam result was absolute	.70	the exam result was absolute	**.12**
the dead will never return	.53	the dead will never return	**.02**
nobody in the group looked interested	.51	nobody in the group looked interested	**.10**

Figure 3: **Model Explanation Comparisons ECF Tests.**

Model	F1	Precision	Recall
LR+QQ	**0.615(-)**	**0.5(-)**	**0.8(-)**
NB+QQ	0.565(-)	0.5(-)	0.65(-)
BERT	0.576(.048)	0.463(.001)	0.775(.177)
BERT+QQ	0.552(.183)	0.470(.073)	0.733(.379)
BERT+PI	0.590(.088)	0.492(.048)	0.750(.200)

Table 12: **Hyperprobe Results. Quantitative Dimensions**

BERT+PI	
LIME Word Weightings	P(*h*)
her brain is as small as a quarter	**.86**
Her hair is as thin as silk	**.84**
my heart is as heavy as the world	**.73**
his mouth is as big as a barn	**.87**
His beard is as thick as his mustache	.87
that bag is as heavy as a suitcase	.72
Her sister is as tall as her mother	.86
their hair is as long as a finger	.74

Figure 4: **LIME Explanations - Quantitative Dimensions**

6.2.2 Quantitative Hyperbole

From Table 12 we see that all models struggle to detect quantitative hyperbole and display a similar pattern of high recall (0.633 to 0.800) and low precision (0.463 to 0.5).

From an analysis of LIME explanations we identified one particular decision pattern as the source of many false positives. For sentences generated using the comparative sentence template (i.e., {*MASK*}{*MASK*} *is as* {*JJ*} *as* {*MASK*}{*MASK*}), the model always predicts a hyperbole irrespective of the comparison being made (see Figure 4). We observe that the first word of the sentence and the words and phrases '*is*', '*as*', '*is as*' and '*as a*' are the most influential words that lead to the decision to classify the sentence as a hyperbole. Our hypothesis for this error is that the literal paraphrases of hyperbolic expressions that take this form remove many tokens from the original sentence (e.g., '*He's* ***as*** *mad* ***as a*** *hippo with a hernia*' → '*He's* ***very*** *mad*'). We suspect this contributes to particular words and phrases (e.g., 'is as' and 'as a') being incorrectly considered hyperbolic because they were removed from the original sentence during the literal paraphrase. We also note, that this is a particularly common form of hyperbolic expression in the training data (e.g., '*There lived a man* ***as*** *big* ***as a*** *barge*' '*He has* ***as*** *many debts* ***as a*** *dog has fleas*', '*He's* ***as*** *mad* ***as a*** *hippo with a hernia*'. '*you look* ***as*** *white* ***as a*** *ghost*').

7 Related Work

Troiano et al. (2018) posed the hyperbole detection task as a binary sequence classification task and introduced a dataset of annotated hyperbole as a benchmark for this task. The existing methods for detecting hyperbole, albeit scant, share similarities to methodologies for solving the problem of detecting other figures of speech. Generally, features are hand-crafted based on linguistic insights of a particular phenomenon (e.g., hyperbole) then combined with general purpose representations of textual content (Barbieri and Saggion, 2014; Joshi et al., 2016; Troiano et al., 2018; Abulaish et al., 2020). We see this in sarcasm detection (Joshi et al., 2016), irony detection (Barbieri et al., 2014) and metaphor detection (Jang et al., 2015). With respect to hyperbole, we see this approach in the foundation work on hyperbole detection (Troiano et al., 2018). Approaches to figurative language detection based on deep learning models have been also developed, such as irony detection (Huang et al., 2017), sarcasm detection (Ghosh and Veale, 2016) and metaphor detection (Wu et al., 2018). With respect to hyperbole detection, research has shown that deep learning improves accuracy on the task of detection of hyperbole in Mandarin Chinese compared to the use of traditional statistical learners (Kong et al., 2020). We extend upon both of these works by introducing a new model for hyperbole detection and introducing new data to evaluate hyperbole detection models.

Recent research in NLP, and machine learning in general, has focused on the idea of explainability and interpretability. The problem of understanding the reasoning behind decisions made by increasingly complex models on increasingly complicated data is a core challenge and can be a roadblock to research progress (Ribeiro et al., 2016, 2020; Bhatt et al., 2020; Linardatos et al., 2021). We design a suite of synthetic test sentences to probe the capabilities of hyperbole detection models and utilise the LIME framework(Ribeiro et al., 2016) for local explainability to understand the reasoning behind the decisions made by hyperbole detection models. Our approaches to probing and explainability are based on existing efforts to uncover meaning in decisions made by NLP models (Ribeiro et al., 2016, 2020; Rogers et al., 2020; Liu et al., 2021).

8 Conclusion

In this paper we proposed a hyperbole detection model, **BERT+PI**, that incorporates PI via triplet loss with a pre-trained language model (BERT) into a multi-task text classification framework for hyperbole detection.

Experiment results showed improvements in detection using standard information retrieval metrics (i.e., F1, precision and recall), for models that incorporate PI on the **HYPO** test set. However, these results were not maintained across our synthetic test suite **HyperProbe**. In fact, only on the ECF test in **HyperProbe** did we observe similar results. On both the quantitative and qualitative hyperbole tests we observed poor performance.

Our hypothesis for this disparity is that the incorporation of PI into **BERT+PI** teaches the model to learn annotation artifacts introduced by the creation of literal paraphrases in the Paraphrase Corpus of **HYPO**. Specifically, ECF hyperbole can often be paraphrased quite simply by removing only a few tokens (e.g., *what an* ***absolute*** *idiot* $\rightarrow$ *what an idiot*). **BERT+PI** effectively incorporates this information well and as a result appears to be able to differentiate between hyperbolic and non-hyperbolic ECFs. However, for more complex hyperbole, unwanted annotation artifacts are introduced during the process of creating a literal paraphrase. For example, '*my heart is as heavy as the world*' could be paraphrased as '*i am sad*'. In this paraphrase, the contrast and the semantic scale of the hyperbole are lost in the paraphrase given the significant difference between the hyperbole and the paraphrase. In future work, exploring better annotation methods for complex hyperbole that encode the semantic scale and the source of excessive contrast will be an important focus to overcome the shortcomings caused by unwanted annotation artifacts.

References

Muhammad Abulaish, Ashraf Kamal, and Mohammed J Zaki. 2020. A survey of figurative language and its computational detection in online social networks. *ACM Transactions on the Web (TWEB)*, 14(1):1–52.

Francesco Barbieri and Horacio Saggion. 2014. Automatic detection of irony and humour in twitter. In *ICCC*, pages 155–162.

Francesco Barbieri, Horacio Saggion, and Francesco Ronzano. 2014. Modelling sarcasm in twitter, a novel approach. In *Proceedings of the 5th Workshop on Computational Approaches to Subjectivity, Sentiment and Social Media Analysis*, pages 50–58.

Umang Bhatt, Alice Xiang, Shubham Sharma, Adrian Weller, Ankur Taly, Yunhan Jia, Joydeep Ghosh, Ruchir Puri, José MF Moura, and Peter Eckersley. 2020. Explainable machine learning in deployment. In *Proceedings of the 2020 Conference on Fairness, Accountability, and Transparency*, pages 648–657.

Christian Burgers, Britta C Brugman, Kiki Y Renardel de Lavalette, and Gerard J Steen. 2016. Hip: A method for linguistic hyperbole identification in discourse. *Metaphor and Symbol*, 31(3):163–178.

Robyn Carston and Catherine Wearing. 2015. Hyperbolic language and its relation to metaphor and irony. *Journal of Pragmatics*, 79:79–92.

Claudia Claridge. 2010. *Hyperbole in English: A corpus-based study of exaggeration.* Cambridge University Press.

Derek Edwards. 2000. Extreme case formulations: Softeners, investment, and doing nonliteral. *Research on language and social interaction*, 33(4):347–373.

Aniruddha Ghosh and Tony Veale. 2016. Fracking sarcasm using neural network. In *Proceedings of the 7th workshop on computational approaches to subjectivity, sentiment and social media analysis*, pages 161–169.

Yu-Hsiang Huang, Hen-Hsen Huang, and Hsin-Hsi Chen. 2017. Irony detection with attentive recurrent neural networks. In *European Conference on Information Retrieval*, pages 534–540. Springer.

Hyeju Jang, Seungwhan Moon, Yohan Jo, and Carolyn Rose. 2015. Metaphor detection in discourse. In *Proceedings of the 16th Annual Meeting of the Special Interest Group on Discourse and Dialogue*, pages 384–392.

Aditya Joshi, Vaibhav Tripathi, Pushpak Bhattacharyya, and Mark Carman. 2016. Harnessing sequence labeling for sarcasm detection in dialogue from tv series 'friends'. In *Proceedings of The 20th SIGNLL Conference on Computational Natural Language Learning*, pages 146–155.

Li Kong, Chuanyi Li, Jidong Ge, Bin Luo, and Vincent Ng. 2020. An empirical study of hyperbole. In *Proceedings of the 2020 Conference on Empirical Methods in Natural Language Processing (EMNLP)*, pages 7024–7034.

Pantelis Linardatos, Vasilis Papastefanopoulos, and Sotiris Kotsiantis. 2021. Explainable ai: A review of machine learning interpretability methods. *Entropy*, 23(1):18.

Leo Z Liu, Yizhong Wang, Jungo Kasai, Hannaneh Hajishirzi, and Noah A Smith. 2021. Probing across time: What does roberta know and when? *arXiv preprint arXiv:2104.07885*.

Yinhan Liu, Myle Ott, Naman Goyal, Jingfei Du, Mandar Joshi, Danqi Chen, Omer Levy, Mike Lewis, Luke Zettlemoyer, and Veselin Stoyanov. 2019. Roberta: A robustly optimized bert pretraining approach. *arXiv preprint arXiv:1907.11692*.

Michael McCarthy and Ronald Carter. 2004. "there's millions of them": hyperbole in everyday conversation. *Journal of pragmatics*, 36(2):149–184.

Lei Meng, Long Chen, Xun Yang, Dacheng Tao, Hanwang Zhang, Chunyan Miao, and Tat-Seng Chua. 2019. Learning using privileged information for food recognition. In *Proceedings of the 27th ACM International Conference on Multimedia*, MM '19, page 557–565, New York, NY, USA. Association for Computing Machinery.

Laura Cano Mora. 2009. All or nothing: A semantic analysis of hyperbole. *Revista de Lingüística y lenguas Aplicadas*, 4(1):25–35.

Neal R Norrick. 2004. Hyperbole, extreme case formulation. *Journal of Pragmatics*, 36(9):1727–1739.

Dmitry Pechyony and Vladimir Vapnik. 2010. On the theory of learnining with privileged information. *Advances in neural information processing systems*, 23:1894–1902.

Anita Pomerantz. 1986. Extreme case formulations: A way of legitimizing claims. *Human studies*, 9(2-3):219–229.

Sunny Rai and Shampa Chakraverty. 2020. A survey on computational metaphor processing. *ACM Computing Surveys (CSUR)*, 53(2):1–37.

Antonio Reyes and Paolo Rosso. 2014. On the difficulty of automatically detecting irony: beyond a simple case of negation. *Knowledge and Information Systems*, 40(3):595–614.

Marco Tulio Ribeiro, Sameer Singh, and Carlos Guestrin. 2016. " why should i trust you?" explaining the predictions of any classifier. In *Proceedings of the 22nd ACM SIGKDD international conference on knowledge discovery and data mining*, pages 1135–1144.

Marco Tulio Ribeiro, Tongshuang Wu, Carlos Guestrin, and Sameer Singh. 2020. Beyond accuracy: Behavioral testing of NLP models with CheckList. In *Proceedings of the 58th Annual Meeting of the Association for Computational Linguistics*, pages 4902–4912, Online. Association for Computational Linguistics.

Anna Rogers, Olga Kovaleva, and Anna Rumshisky. 2020. A primer in bertology: What we know about how bert works. *Transactions of the Association for Computational Linguistics*, 8:842–866.

Yangyang Shu, Qian Li, Shaowu Liu, and Guandong Xu. 2020. Learning with privileged information for photo aesthetic assessment. *Neurocomputing*, 404:304–316.

Enrica Troiano, Carlo Strapparava, Gözde Özbal, and Serra Sinem Tekiroğlu. 2018. A computational exploration of exaggeration. In *Proceedings of the 2018 Conference on Empirical Methods in Natural Language Processing*, pages 3296–3304.

Kevin A Whitehead. 2015. Extreme-case formulations. *The international encyclopedia of language and social interaction*, pages 1–5.

Chao-Yuan Wu, R Manmatha, Alexander J Smola, and Philipp Krahenbuhl. 2017. Sampling matters in deep embedding learning. In *Proceedings of the IEEE International Conference on Computer Vision*, pages 2840–2848.

Chuhan Wu, Fangzhao Wu, Yubo Chen, Sixing Wu, Zhigang Yuan, and Yongfeng Huang. 2018. Neural metaphor detecting with cnn-lstm model. In *Proceedings of the Workshop on Figurative Language Processing*, pages 110–114.

Combining Shallow and Deep Representations for Text-Pair Classification

Vincent Nguyen[1,2] **Sarvnaz Karimi**[1] **Zhenchang Xing**[2]
[1]CSIRO Data61, Sydney, Australia
[2]The Australian National University, Canberra, Australia
{firstname.lastname}@csiro.au
{zhenchang.xing}@anu.edu.au

Abstract

Text-pair classification is the task of determining the class relationship between two sentences. It is embedded in several tasks such as paraphrase identification and duplicate question detection. Contemporary methods use fine-tuned transformer encoder semantic representations of the classification token in the text-pair sequence from the transformer's final layer for class prediction. However, research has shown that earlier parts of the network learn shallow features, such as syntax and structure, which existing methods do not directly exploit. We propose a novel convolution-based decoder for transformer-based architecture that maximizes the use of encoder hidden features for text-pair classification. Our model exploits hidden representations within transformer-based architecture. It outperforms a transformer encoder baseline on average by 50% (relative F1-score) on six datasets from the medical, software engineering, and open-domains. Our work shows that transformer-based models can improve text-pair classification by modifying the fine-tuning step to exploit shallow features while improving model generalization, with only a slight reduction in efficiency.[1]

1 Introduction

Text-pair classification determines the class relationship between two sentences; for example, it determines the inference class relationship (entailment, contradiction, or neutral) between a premise and a hypothesis (Bowman et al., 2015). Such classification requires interpreting the semantic content of sentences to determine their relationships. Applications of text-pair classification, which we experiment with here, are *natural language inference* (Bowman et al., 2015), *question answering candidate ranking* (Ben Abacha et al., 2019) and *duplicate question detection* (Wang et al., 2019a; Yang et al., 2019). For these tasks, we consider open, biomedical, and software engineering domains.

Contemporary methods in text-pair classification use transformer encoder networks, such as BERT (Devlin et al., 2019), which are popular in natural language processing (Wang et al., 2019b; Sun et al., 2019; Zhu et al., 2019). For these encoder models, there are several studies improving the model in different aspects. Liu et al. (2019b) and Yang et al. (2019) introduce improvements to the pretraining by removing Next Sentence Prediction (NSP) and using a larger batch-size with the LAMB optimizer (You et al., 2020). SciBERT (Beltagy et al., 2019) pretrains BERT over publications from SemanticScholar and adjusts the model's vocabulary to be domain-specific. ALBERT (Lan et al., 2020) increases model depth, adds layer parameter sharing, and includes the sentence coherence over NSP.

These studies primarily improve the transformer architecture by scaling up overall model capacity through dataset source (Lee et al., 2019; Alsentzer et al., 2019) and adjustment of the pretraining task (Lan et al., 2020; Joshi et al., 2019). They use only the *classification token* as the primary feature for classification. These improvements also require pretraining the architecture, which requires a high amount of computing resources.

Increasing model size and complexity is not the only approach to improve transformer-based models. Recent research shows that these models capture different levels of information at different layers in the network (Tenney et al., 2019). The information encoded in these levels are surface-level, structural and syntactic in the lower layers, and semantic in the upper layers (Jawahar et al., 2019). Shallow features are potentially useful because interpreting the semantic content of sentences may be difficult without additional knowledge. For instance, in software engineering

[1]Code and dataset will be released upon publication.

question-answering, structural knowledge and program syntax may aid in recognizing jargon in a programming question or the grammar of a program; a program does not work if the syntax is incorrect (e.g., func() vs. func{} only differ by bracketing in the *context* of the programming language). Likewise, in medical queries, the structural and syntactic information helps recognition of medical charts; for instance, blood pressure is written as BP 80/50 and understanding this structure and syntax (numbering order) aids in the semantic interpretation of *hypotension*.

We investigate the value of these structural, syntactic and semantic features in existing pretrained models for text-pair classification tasks in the medical and software engineering fields. Our model adjusts the decoder to use the *hidden representations* of the BERT transformer encoder model by combining shallow and deep feature representations of the input sentences. As our method involves adjusting the decoder, there is no requirement to pretrain the network, allowing it to be extended to all transformer-based encoders. Our main contributions are summarized as follows:

1. We design a decoder architecture to exploit shallow and deep representations from a transformer encoder-based architecture inspired by previous research on the learning capacity in BERT (Jawahar et al., 2019; Tenney et al., 2019). Our convolution-based decoder complements the parallel computation within transformers and ensures that computing features earlier in the network does not sacrifice overall efficiency.

2. We explore multi-gradient propagation in transformer architectures to adapt features from earlier layers in the network for more direct use in the downstream task. This propagation also improves generalization on tasks with fewer high-quality training samples.

3. We evaluate and analyze our methodology on natural language inference, question entailment and duplicate question detection task that use text-pair classification. Our experiments are in three domains: medical, software engineering, and open-domain. The diversity of domains tests the generalizability of our methods.

4. We *automatically* create and release a balanced duplicate question detection dataset of 1.6 million English question pairs from Stack-Overflow.

2 Related Work

Text-pair classification is a specialization of text classification. Early studies on text-pair classification used rule-based inference from a knowledge base of patterns and templates for textual entailment (Dagan and Glickman, 2004). This was superseded by supervised probabilistic models such as support vector machine (Malakasiotis and Androutsopoulos, 2007), naïve bayes, and decision trees (Newman et al., 2006), as well as unsupervised algorithms such as k-Nearest Neighbours (Inkpen et al., 2006).

Since 2014 (Kim, 2014), neural network-based techniques dominated the field. They are based on Convolutional Neural Network (CNN)-based encoders (Mou et al., 2016; Yin et al., 2016), Long Short-Term Memory (LSTM) and Recurrent Neural Network (RNN) sentence interaction encoder models (Liu and Huang, 2016; Lan and Xu, 2018a,b) which use shallow reasoning over sentences to capture semantics. These methods are limited by their model's receptive fields, as they cannot model deep semantic contextual knowledge and do not directly capture shallow information (Devlin et al., 2019).

Transformer-based methods The above mentioned limitations are contrasted by transformer-based models (Devlin et al., 2019). Although not strictly designed for text-pair classification, these models can take in pair sentence inputs for classification as well as a variety of other tasks (Wang et al., 2019a).

These models have subsequently seen a rise in the medical (Ben Abacha et al., 2019; Alsentzer et al., 2019; Lee et al., 2019) and software engineering fields (Zafar et al., 2019; Tabassum et al., 2020). In medical text-pair classification, there are model ensembles (Zhu et al., 2019; Ben Abacha et al., 2019) which exploit knowledge from multi-task learning. However, these models are computationally expensive, using several multi-task deep neural networks (Liu et al., 2019a) and SciBERT models for a single prediction, which prevents their use in applications where continual retraining is required. Several improvements to the transformer model in the medical domain involved using double transfer learning, where the model is further pretrained on the target domain before fine-tuning.

BlueBERT(Peng et al., 2019) and BioBERT (Lee et al., 2019) used additional pretraining data from PubMed whereas ClinicalBERT (Alsentzer et al., 2019) used a clinical dataset MIMIC-III (Johnson et al., 2016) for pretraining data. We note that these do not change the underlying architecture of encoders, and instead improved the model's effectiveness on downstream tasks via additional pretraining on the target domain or increasing ensemble size. Our work explores the feasibility of utilizing the underlying architecture instead.

CNN-based methods Our work is inspired by previous studies in *text classification* and *computer vision*. From text classification, Very Deep Convolutional Neural Network (VDCNN) (Conneau et al., 2017) is a deep convolutional neural network for text classification. VDCNN shows the importance of shortcut connections used heavily in Residual Networks (He et al., 2016) for effective gradient propagation when training deep networks, and k-max pooling for selecting the strongest signals for classification.

In computer vision, GoogleNet (Szegedy et al., 2015) introduced auxiliary multi-gradients during training to solve the vanishing gradient problem (Hochreiter, 1998). Solving the vanishing gradient problem is important as early layers in deep neural networks contain information that correlates more strongly with the input sequence. However, these layers receive less information from gradient propagation as the gradient is propagated from the output layer to the rest of the network—where each non-linearity the gradient passed through caused a sharp reduction in its magnitude. Auxiliary classifiers are added to the intermediate layers for increased gradient propagation to the early and intermediate layers while constraining the network to utilize early and intermediate features for image recognition. We experiment with auxiliary classifiers in our work.

3 Deeply Interconnected Convolutional Transformer Network

Transformer encoders learn different features of a language at different layers (Jawahar et al., 2019; Tenney et al., 2019). We explore if combining shallow features alongside deep features would improve the effectiveness of representation learning. We therefore design a new method that exploits all the hidden features within the transformer encoder. We use CNN-based decoders connected to each layer of the transformer encoder as a low-parameter fully-connected network (Lin et al., 2014) to combine hidden features in a highly parallelized manner. In doing so, multiple gradient flows (Szegedy et al., 2015) are subsequently introduced, allowing gradient propagation to shallower network layers and aiding the learning of downstream language features in earlier parts of the network.

However, the efficacy of multiple gradient flow is determined by convergence, which poses a significant challenge for our method as we use randomly initialized decoders together with a pretrained decoder. These two models expect different input distributions. To tackle this problem, we adopt convolutional components to help in dimensionality reduction and use larger batch-sizes with the LAMB optimizer (You et al., 2020) and One Cycle Policy (Smith, 2018) for hyper-convergence. We also include residual connections to ensure a stable gradient throughout the network.

We use convolutional components over LSTMs as the recurrent step is non-parallelizable (Vaswani et al., 2017) and slowdown the parallel computation in the transformer. We adopt two configurations similar to VDCNN and GoogleNet to test the generality of our method. We demonstrate that a stronger capability of learning is enabled by our method in text-pair classification tasks, especially for domains that require structural and syntactic knowledge such as the medical and software engineering domains.

3.1 Convolutional Transformer Encoder

Our first proposed network is a Convolutional transformer Encoder(TE_{conv}), where each encoder hidden layer is connected to a residual block in the decoder (Figure 1). We base this approach on past research, which shows that BERT learns surface-level, syntactic, and semantic features, but at different layers (Jawahar et al., 2019; Tenney et al., 2019). Thus, combining the final semantic output with earlier representations could aid downstream tasks. A possible approach is to concatenate all hidden states together. However, this approach is intractable at higher sequence lengths and dimensions, which causes overfitting. Another approach is to use a linear combination, scalar mix, or simple averaging (Tenney et al., 2019; Peters et al., 2018). However, this approach loses information from the summation (e.g., it may add to zero) which reduces generalization. Instead, as an intermediary, we use

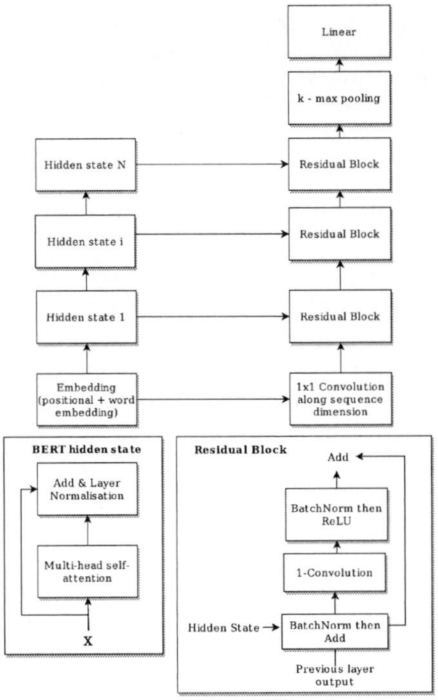

Figure 1: Network architecture of the Convolutional BERT Model.

1-convolutional filters as *information transformation gates* to transform *hidden representations*, H_i, and add it to the next hidden representation, H_{i+1}:

$$O_{i+1} = R_B(H_i) + H_{i+1}, \tag{1}$$

where R_B denotes a Residual Block, and O_{i+1} is the output for layer $i+1$ in the decoder network. Here, a residual block (Conneau et al., 2017) consists of a single 1-convolution operation along the sequence dimension. This 1-convolution acts as a fully connected linear layer across all channels with very few additional parameters (Lin et al., 2014).

Additionally, due to the use of ReLU activation function and convolutional operations, output of the CNN network must be non-negative. This output bound is in contrast with the transformer Encoder network with no bounds on the outputs. However, upon inspection, we find that the values were positive and negative and close to zero. To alleviate some of the distribution mismatch, we use batch normalization (Ioffe and Szegedy, 2015) on the hidden states inputted into the residual blocks.

3.2 Convolutional Transformer Encoder with Auxiliary Networks

Our second method, TE_{aux} uses auxiliary networks (Szegedy et al., 2015) to propagate gradients to different areas of the transformer network (see Figures 2 and 3).

An auxiliary network takes in J different hidden representations, $H_{i:i+j}$, from the transformer network. Each hidden representation undergoes dimensionality reduction using a 1-convolution to produce an output, C_i, with a feature dimension of $dim(H_i)/j$. These outputs, $C_{i:i+j}$, are concatenated and fed to a residual block, followed by k-max pooling and a fully connected layer. During inference, like GoogleNet, only the output of the final auxiliary network is used and the training loss function, ϕ_{final}, is given as a weighted sum of the auxiliary networks:

$$\phi_{final} = \phi_A^N + \alpha \sum_{i=1}^{N-1} (\phi_A^i), \tag{2}$$

where ϕ_A^i denotes the loss value of the ith auxiliary network, N denotes the number of auxiliary networks, and α denotes the weight of loss value of the non-terminal auxiliary networks. We set $\alpha = 0.3$, as this was the value used in the original GoogleNet (Szegedy et al., 2015). We do not connect the auxiliary networks to avoid gradient explosions due to the double-counting of auxiliary losses propagating in the network.

We use k-max pooling before the fully connected layer for both networks to select a subset of the strongest k-signals from the feature maps. We do this for two reasons: (1) it drastically reduces the parameters in the linear layer for reduced computation cost; and, (2) it adds a layer of interpretability as the k-signals may be converted back to tokens. However, due to the bidirectional nature of transformers and padding of input, interpretability may be lost as strong signals could be from the padded portion of the sequence, which is not interpretable. In this case, attention flow (Abnar and Zuidema, 2020) might be better.

We do not use dropout in our models as dropout is a hyperparameter that requires careful tuning, which adds additional complexity.

We use pretrained weights from BERT small; however, with the exclusion of dropout, results may deviate from the literature (Wang and Manning, 2013). To avoid confusion, we named this BERT variant as Transformer Encoder (TE).

4 Datasets

We use two datasets from medical and software engineering because these domains may benefit from

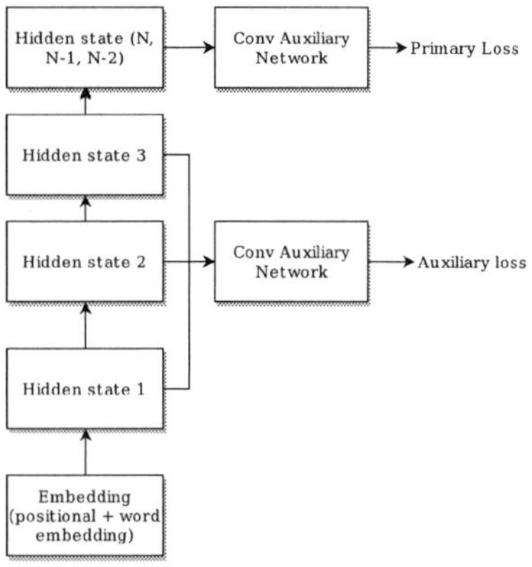

Figure 2: Network architecture of Convolutional Transformer Encoder with auxiliary networks.

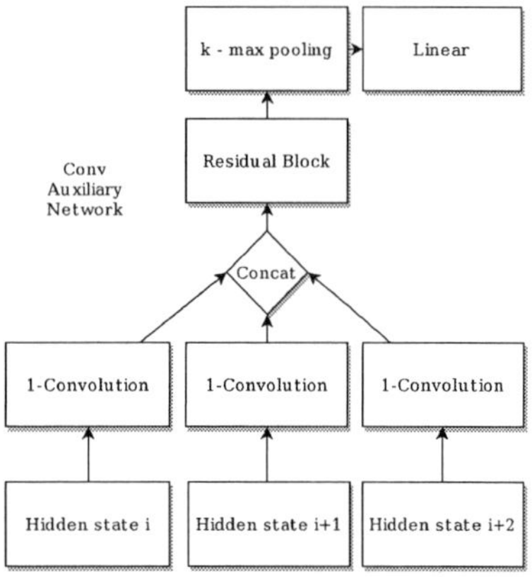

Figure 3: Architecture of the Convolutional auxiliary network.

the structural and syntactic knowledge for downstream tasks. We also use two datasets from the open-domain to test the generality of our method.

MEDIQA The MEDIQA challenge (Ben Abacha et al., 2019) was part of the BioNLP 2019 shared task. It features three separate tasks: (1) Recognizing Question Entailment (RQE), requiring binary entailment classification between text-pairs for 8,588 medical questions; (2) MEDical Natural Language (MEDNLI), a multi-label classification between premises and hypotheses for 14,049 clinical text-pairs; and, (3) Question Answering involving binary relevance classification and re-ranking between a query and retrieved answer for 476 medical questions. These datasets are smaller than those found in the open-domain because obtaining open medical data is difficult due to ethical, legal, and monetary concerns (Pampari et al., 2018; Nguyen, 2019; Ive et al., 2020). We use 5-fold cross-validation to

Original Question Conversion Error setting value for 'null Converter' - Why do I need a Converter in JSF?
Duplicate Question selectOneMenu with complex objects, is a converter necessary?
Negative Sample Conversion Error setting value '1' for 'null Converter'

Figure 4: Stack Overflow dataset examples.

generate non-overlapping training, validation, and testing splits as such, our results are not directly compared to the state-of-the-art (SOTA).

Stack Overflow Dataset To test our methods on a substantial, technical dataset, we create one in the Software Engineering field. Our Stack Overflow Duplicate Question dataset evaluates the performance of our methods and its ability to generalize on specialized technical domains. To create the dataset, we use Okapi BM25 scoring (Robertson et al., 1994) from ElasticSearch with default parameters and word embeddings. Specifically, we use question titles, which we expand with word embeddings trained on the Stack Overflow corpus (Efstathiou et al., 2018) for querying. For each word in the query, we found the three most similar words in the embedding space via cosine distance and added this to the original query, Q, as expansion terms, E. To promote diversity, we empirically set the weights of the E in to be 1.3 (multiplicative), which is higher than Q at 1.0. These expanded queries, (Q, E), were used to select candidates with the highest BM25 scores not already marked as a duplicate of Q. An example from the dataset is shown in Figure 4. This dataset consists of 1.6 million question pairs, with a balanced label distribution. To our knowledge, this is the first dataset created from StackOverflow with difficult examples for text-pair classification before this work.

Open-domain We also benchmark our model against two open-domain datasets: (1) the Stanford Natural Language Inference (SNLI) (Bowman et al., 2015) benchmark containing a collection of 570,000 text-pairs, a multi-label inference classification task; and, (2) Quora (Wang et al., 2019a), a duplicate question detection dataset of 404,000 text-pairs.

5 Experimental Setup

We use FastAI (Howard and Gugger, 2020), a PyTorch-based library. We use a one cycle policy learning rate scheduler over a cycle length of

		Method	A	P	R	F1
Open-Domain	SNLI	TE	0.798	0.599	0.609	0.604
		TE_{conv}	**0.869**†	**0.653**‡	**0.657**†	**0.657**
		TE_{aux}	0.830	0.624	0.633	0.627
		SOTA	0.923 (Liu et al., 2019b)			
	Quora	TE	0.811	0.739	0.755	0.747
		TE_{conv}	**0.880**‡	**0.842**‡	0.832‡	0.836‡
		TE_{aux}	0.879‡	0.811‡	**0.878**‡	**0.843**‡
		SOTA	0.923 (Yang et al., 2019)			
MediQA	NLI	TE	0.335	0.112	0.333	0.170
		TE_{conv}	**0.797**‡	**0.797**‡	**0.797**‡	**0.797**‡
		TE_{aux}	0.728‡	0.761‡	0.727‡	0.723‡
		SOTA	0.980 (Ben Abacha et al., 2019)			
	RQE	TE	0.557	0.278	0.500	0.358
		TE_{conv}	0.536	0.567‡	0.535	0.490‡
		TE_{aux}	**0.911**†	**0.9416**‡	**0.925**‡	**0.908**‡
		SOTA	0.749 (Ben Abacha et al., 2019)			
	QA	TE	0.575	0.287	0.500	0.365
		TE_{conv}	0.718	0.714‡	0.713‡	0.709‡
		TE_{aux}	**0.947**‡	**0.944**‡	**0.947**‡	**0.945**‡
		SOTA	0.783 (Ben Abacha et al., 2019)			
Stack Overflow	DQD	TE	0.919	0.929	0.907	0.918
		TE_{conv}	**0.943**	**0.960**	**0.926**	**0.942**
		TE_{aux}	0.939	0.952	0.924	0.938‡
Average		TE	0.667	0.502	0.592	0.529
		TE_{conv}	0.779	0.743	0.729	0.724
		TE_{aux}	**0.846**	**0.809**	**0.810**	**0.798**

Table 1: Accuracy (A), Precision (P), Recall (R) and F1-Score of different datasets. Note: † denotes a statistical significance of $p < 0.05$ and ‡ for $p < 0.001$.

15 epochs with a Label Smoothing Cross-Entropy loss and the LAMB optimizer. The peak learning rate was found using the learning rate exploration tool in FastAI. We use a batch size of 255 and a maximum sequence length of 64 for all tasks. For all other settings, we use defaults from the PyTorch transformer library (Wolf et al., 2019). We choose the best model over the 15 epochs based on the validation accuracy for test set inference. For reproducibility, we use the same seed for each experiment.

We train our models on a single GPU, V100 Tesla 16 GB. Training is repeated five times for each configuration to collect reliable statistics for paired t-test significance testing.

6 Results and Discussion

Effectiveness of the model under different dataset constraints We compare our model in differing constraints. We select the domain type (open or closed), and dataset size as constraints. We first discuss the main results.

On the SNLI dataset, a large open-domain dataset, the TE_{conv} model performs the best across all metrics. A similar observation is made for the stack overflow dataset, a large technical domain dataset, where the TE_{conv} model performs the best. On both datasets, the TE_{conv} model with auxiliary networks also performs better than the baseline. This suggests that the model performs well in data-rich environments.

This result contrasts with results from the smaller specialized datasets such as the MediQA collection. In these datasets, we see that the TE model overfits on all three medical tasks; this is apparent as the training and validation loss is lower on the TE model than the convolutional-based models. This means the model failed to generalize as test set performance was low despite performing well on the validation/training sets. This performance may be from vocabulary disparity between the train/test sets and the additional gradients which allowed convolutional models to reach a better optimum through regularization (Szegedy et al., 2015). On the NLI dataset, TE_{conv} significantly improves over TE and is stronger than TE_{aux}, suggesting that usage of all twelve layers of TE is useful for inference tasks. By contrast, TE_{aux} performed better on RQE and QA as TE_{conv} overfit on RQE and performed worse on QA.

Finally, on the Quora dataset, both TE_{conv} models performed significantly better ($p < 0.05$) with the TE_{aux} performing better in recall and F1-score while TE_{conv} performed better in terms of accuracy and precision. We note that our models do not match the state-of-the-art performance due to lack of large model ensembling and much lower total parameter count (Yang et al., 2019; Ben Abacha et al., 2019; Zhu et al., 2019) as our study is focused on investigating the usefulness of shallow features. However, our framework could potentially be applied to the current state-of-the-art models to improve their performance.

To summarize, the TE model performs poorly in the low-resource technical setting as reflected by the MediQA dataset results, MediQA has fewer training examples compared to the open-domain which made it challenging to train due to overfitting. However, we found that increased gradients allowed for better generalization. Therefore, in this low-resource setting, the convolutional TE model seems more suitable. Additionally, in more data-rich environments such as the Quora, Stack Overflow and SNLI datasets, we found the models performed better. However, on the Stack Overflow dataset, where the model performs better than the baseline, it was not statistically significant due to large variance between runs ($\sigma = 0.02$ for F1-

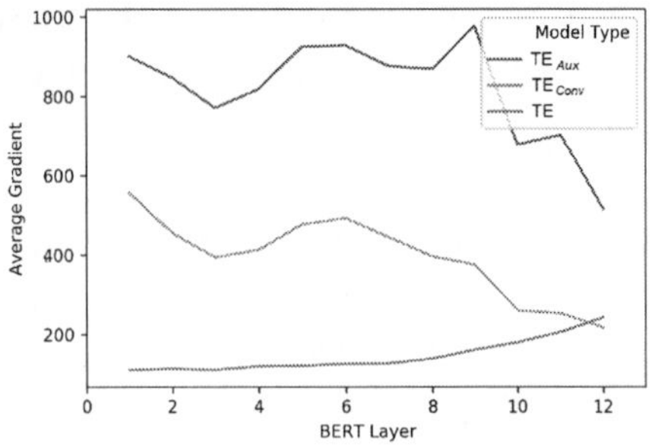

Figure 5: Average gradient over three epochs for all models on the SNLI dataset.

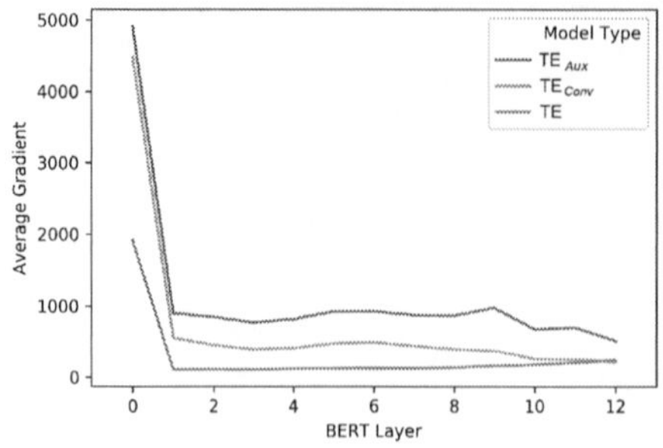

Figure 6: Average gradient over three epochs for all models on the SNLI dataset with Embedding Layer.

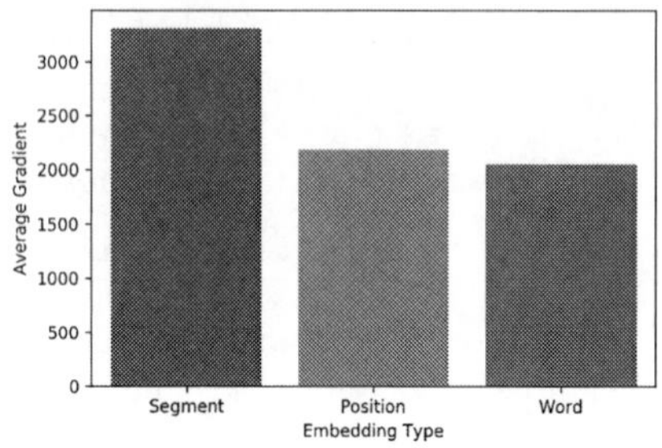

Figure 7: Average gradient over three epochs for all models on the SNLI dataset for the embedding Layer.

score).

Does including additional features from the lower layers of the network help prediction? For each domain, we select a dataset, and we analyze text-pairs to see situations where TE_{conv} benefits from additional features over the baseline. From Table 2, on the StackOverflow dataset, we see benefits from understanding using structural features and program syntax to differentiate between programming languages (e.g., angular and PHP). Similarly, on the MedNLI dataset, the model better understands medical numerical chart structure and syntax which guided better semantic understanding; which transformer encoders have been known to struggle with (Nguyen et al., 2019). Open-domain interpretation is more difficult, for instance, on the SNLI dataset, it seems additional training gradient, rather than shallow features, helped the model to learn co-reference resolution. Co-reference resolution may have helped guide the semantic understanding between sentence pairs, as this task is typically learned in deeper layers of the network (Tenney et al., 2019).

Furthermore, the model allows for improved gradient flow in the network, as shown in Figure 5, where the average gradient over three epochs on the SNLI is depicted. To illustrate each layer, we average all the gradients at that particular level. Specifically, the query, value, key attention weights gradients' are all averaged together in each hidden encoder layer. For the TE network, there is a diminishing gradient flow, a downwards slope, throughout the network. This slope contrasts with the TE_{conv} networks, which show a general increase in gradient flow (positive slope) throughout the network, allowing for learning in shallower layers of the network; which is useful because the shallower features, which are more correlated with the input, are now used for final layer prediction.

As the models exhibited similar trends in the embedding layer, we report a singular figure (Figure 7). A side effect of removing the NSP layer, we observe a large gradient flow in the segment(ation) embeddings, as the model learned sentence segmentation between the two text-pairs. This may explain the capacity of the network to better differentiate between the text-pairs during classification. The magnitude of this segmentation gradient is larger in both TE_{conv} models than the TE model (Figure 5), allowing for better modeling of pair semantics.

Encoder comparisons: efficiency and effectiveness Earlier, we hypothesize that using convolutional components should not hinder training speed. From Table 3, we found that TE_{conv} being a larger model, sharing the same number of layers as the original TE model, increases the training time by 13.8%, while the TE_{aux} with only three layers increases only by 7.44% in training time. TE_{aux} offers a trade-off between effectiveness and training time.

Our results indicate that both models are significantly better than the TE baseline in most settings.

Dataset	Sentence A	Sentence B	Gold Label	Baseline Prediction
StackOverflow	why does this setTimeout() call work in the console but not as a greasemonkey script?	setinterval() and .click() in a Greasemonkey script	Duplicate	Not Duplicate
	how to resolve Error: [$rootScope:inprog] http://errors.angularjs.org/1.5.8/$rootScope/inprog?p0=%24digest in dhtmlxTree	php parse/syntax errors; and how to solve them?	Not Duplicate	Duplicate
MedNLI	In the ED, initial VS were: 8 98 64 131/113	in the ED initial respiratory rate was low	Entailment	Not Entailment
	Received ASA 325mg and Nitro 0.4mg x3.	The patient has not had any vasodilator drugs.	Not Entailment	Entailment
SNLI	A young child dressed in a scarf, hat, jacket, gloves, pants, and boots, outside playing in the snow.	A child plays with a sled in the snow while dressed warmly.	Neutral	Contradiction
	A girl with a blue shirt and a girl with a striped shirt stand next to a girl with a green shirt sitting in a chair.	Two girls are standing next to a girl who is sitting.	Entailment	Contradiction

Table 2: Examples where shallow features lead to the correct prediction by our models.

The TE_{aux} model propagates higher level gradients to lower layers, takes less time to train, and is more consistent between runs as it has fewer parameters. However, the TE_{conv} model can achieve strong performance, provided the dataset is large enough.

We conduct additional experiments to verify if (1) convolutional components in the TE_{conv} network improve effectiveness; and, (2) including more layer representations (shallow and deep) to the decoder shows improvement over the baseline. These results are shown in Table 4. We conclude that the decoders can better use the encoder's features than a linear decoder from the frozen encoder experiments. Moreover, by comparing TE_{conv} with and without convolutional sub-networks, we see that convolutional components allow for better utilization of the additional features in the encoder for data-rich tasks as accuracy and F1-score increases for those tasks. Residual connections and additional features (summation of hidden states+k-max pooling-convolution) benefit medical tasks, giving an average 0.05 (absolute) boost in F1-score for each task, meaning that additional shallow features still help smaller datasets. However, we find that removing all additional parameters and utilizing only additional features provides an increase in effectiveness over the baseline. Our results are consistent with (Dong et al., 2021) which shows that skip connections are important for transformer model effectiveness. Our models exploit skip connections to combine shallow and deep representations.

Model	Total Training Time (hours)	% Slower
TE	16.75	–
TE_{conv}	19.50	13.8
TE_{aux}	18.25	7.44

Table 3: Comparison of average training time in hours between the models over a total of 15 epochs on the Stack Overflow dataset.

Model	A	F1
TE^{frozen}	0.583	0.505
${TE_{conv}}^{frozen}$	0.608	0.571
${TE_{aux}}^{frozen}$	0.584	0.544
TE_{conv} w/o Residual Block (no additional parameters)	0.700	0.668
TE_{conv}	0.711	0.636
TE	0.676	0.544

Table 4: Ablation comparisons between transformer encoders. Metrics are averaged over all tasks. Experiments encoder layers are frozen during training as denoted by *frozen*. We use mean pooling for the tasks as the classification feature token is not fine-tuned. We also include a baseline TE_{conv} model where additional parameters (such as convolution) are removed. The original splits for the MediQA datasets are used for these experiments and as such do not relate to experiments in Table 1.

Overall, we find that utilizing more layers in the TE architecture, and propagating gradient to multiple network layers allows for increased effectiveness and generalizability through regularization (Szegedy et al., 2015), especially on smaller specialized medical datasets.

7 Conclusions

We investigate whether using shallow hidden representations—which encode syntactic and structural information in the transformer encoder architecture—aids text-pair classification in the medical, software engineering and open-domains. To exploit these representations, we use deep convolutional neural networks as low-parameter networks to increase gradient propagation to the earlier layers of the network with a minimal decrease in efficiency. We find that including these representations, even as a simple summation over all hidden states, leads to increased system effectiveness. Validating if this holds for other variants of transformer encoder architecture is a suitable avenue for future research.

Acknowledgements

Vincent is supported by the Australian Research Training Program and the CSIRO Research Office Postgraduate Scholarship. This work is funded by the CSIRO Precision Health Future Science Platform (FSP).

References

Samira Abnar and Willem Zuidema. 2020. Quantifying attention flow in transformers. In *Proceedings of the 58th Annual Meeting of the Association for Computational Linguistics*, pages 4190–4197, Online.

Emily Alsentzer, John Murphy, William Boag, Wei-Hung Weng, Di Jindi, Tristan Naumann, and Matthew McDermott. 2019. Publicly available clinical BERT embeddings. In *Proceedings of the 2nd Clinical Natural Language Processing Workshop*, pages 72–78, Minneapolis, MN.

Iz Beltagy, Kyle Lo, and Arman Cohan. 2019. SciBERT: A pretrained language model for scientific text. In *Proceedings of the 2019 Conference on Empirical Methods in Natural Language Processing and the 9th International Joint Conference on Natural Language Processing*, pages 3606–3611, Hong Kong, China.

Asma Ben Abacha, Chaitanya Shivade, and Dina Demner-Fushman. 2019. Overview of the MEDIQA 2019 shared task on textual inference, question entailment and question answering. In *Proceedings of the 18th BioNLP Workshop and Shared Task*, pages 370–379, Florence, Italy.

Samuel Bowman, Gabor Angeli, Christopher Potts, and Christopher Manning. 2015. A large annotated corpus for learning natural language inference. In *Proceedings of the 2015 Conference on Empirical Methods in Natural Language Processing*, Lisbon, Portugal. Association for Computational Linguistics.

Alexis Conneau, Holger Schwenk, Loïc Barrault, and Yann Lecun. 2017. Very deep convolutional networks for text classification. In *Proceedings of the 15th Conference of the European Chapter of the Association for Computational Linguistics*, pages 1107–1116, Valencia, Spain.

I. Dagan and Oren Glickman. 2004. Probabilistic textual entailment: Generic applied modeling of language variability. In *PASCAL Workshop on Learning Methods for Text Understanding and Mining*, Grenoble, France.

Jacob Devlin, Ming-Wei Chang, Kenton Lee, and Kristina Toutanova. 2019. BERT: Pre-training of deep bidirectional transformers for language understanding. In *Proceedings of the Conference of the North American Chapter of the Association for Computational Linguistics: Human Language Technologies*, pages 4171–4186, Minneapolis, MN.

Yihe Dong, Jean-Baptiste Cordonnier, and Andreas Loukas. 2021. In *Proceedings of the 38th International Conference on Machine Learning*. [link].

V. Efstathiou, C. Chatzilenas, and D. Spinellis. 2018. Word embeddings for the software engineering domain. In *IEEE/ACM 15th International Conference on Mining Software Repositories*, pages 38–41, Gothenburg, Sweden.

K. He, X. Zhang, S. Ren, and J. Sun. 2016. Deep residual learning for image recognition. In *IEEE Conference on Computer Vision and Pattern Recognition*, pages 770–778, Las Vegas, NV.

Sepp Hochreiter. 1998. The vanishing gradient problem during learning recurrent neural nets and problem solutions. *International Journal of Uncertainty, Fuzziness and Knowledge-Based Systems*, 6(2):107–116.

Jeremy Howard and Sylvain Gugger. 2020. Fastai: A layered API for deep learning. *Information*, 11:108.

Diana Inkpen, Darren Kipp, and Vivi Nastase. 2006. Machine learning experiments for textual entailment. In *Proceedings of the second RTE Challenge*, Venice, Italy.

Sergey Ioffe and Christian Szegedy. 2015. Batch Normalization: Accelerating Deep Network Training by Reducing Internal Covariate Shift. In *Proceedings of the 32nd International Conference on Machine Learning*, volume 37, Lille, France.

Julia Ive, Natalia Viani, Joyce Kam, Lucia Yin, Somain Verma, Stephen Puntis, Rudolf N. Cardinal, Angus Roberts, Robert Stewart, and Sumithra Velupillai. 2020. Generation and evaluation of artificial mental health records for natural language processing. *Nature Partner Journal Digital Medicine*, 3(1):69.

Ganesh Jawahar, Benoît Sagot, and Djamé Seddah. 2019. What does BERT learn about the structure of language? In *Proceedings of the 57th Annual Meeting of the Association for Computational Linguistics*, pages 3651–3657, Florence, Italy.

Alistair E.W. Johnson, Tom J. Pollard, Lu Shen, Liwei H. Lehman, Mengling Feng, Mohammad Ghassemi, Benjamin Moody, Peter Szolovits, Leo Anthony Celi, and Roger G. Mark. 2016. Mimic-iii, a freely accessible critical care database. *Scientific Data*, 3(1):160035.

Mandar Joshi, Danqi Chen, Yinhan Liu, Daniel S. Weld, Luke Zettlemoyer, and Omer Levy. 2019. Spanbert: Improving pre-training by representing and predicting spans. *Computing Research Repository*, abs/1907.10529.

Yoon Kim. 2014. Convolutional neural networks for sentence classification. In *Proceedings of the 2014 Conference on Empirical Methods in Natural Language Processing*, pages 1746–1751, Doha, Qatar.

Wuwei Lan and Wei Xu. 2018a. Character-based neural networks for sentence pair modeling. In *Proceedings of the 2018 Conference of the North American Chapter of the Association for Computational Linguistics: Human Language Technologies, Volume 2 (Short Papers)*, pages 157–163, New Orleans, Louisiana.

Wuwei Lan and Wei Xu. 2018b. Neural network models for paraphrase identification, semantic textual similarity, natural language inference, and question answering. In *Proceedings of the 27th International Conference on Computational Linguistics*, pages 3890–3902, Santa Fe, New Mexico. Association for Computational Linguistics.

Zhenzhong Lan, Mingda Chen, Sebastian Goodman, Kevin Gimpel, Piyush Sharma, and Radu Soricut. 2020. ALBERT: A Lite BERT for Self-supervised Learning of Language Representations. In *Proceedings of the 8th International Conference on Learning Representations*.

Jinhyuk Lee, Wonjin Yoon, Sungdong Kim, Donghyeon Kim, Sunkyu Kim, Chan Ho So, and Jaewoo Kang. 2019. BioBERT: A pre-trained biomedical language representation model for biomedical text mining. *Bioinformatics*.

Min Lin, Qiang Chen, and Shuicheng Yan. 2014. Network In Network. In *Proceedings of 2nd International Conference on Learning Representations*, Banff National Park, Canada.

Biao Liu and Minlie Huang. 2016. A sentence interaction network for modeling dependence between sentences. In *Proceedings of the 54th Annual Meeting of the Association for Computational Linguistics*, pages 558–567, Berlin, Germany.

Xiaodong Liu, Pengcheng He, Weizhu Chen, and Jianfeng Gao. 2019a. Multi-task deep neural networks for natural language understanding. In *Proceedings of the 57th Annual Meeting of the Association for Computational Linguistics*, pages 4487–4496, Florence, Italy.

Yinhan Liu, Myle Ott, Naman Goyal, Jingfei Du, Mandar Joshi, Danqi Chen, Omer Levy, Mike Lewis, Luke Zettlemoyer, and Veselin Stoyanov. 2019b. RoBERTa: A robustly optimized BERT pretraining approach. *Computing Research Repository*, abs/1907.11692.

Prodromos Malakasiotis and Ion Androutsopoulos. 2007. *Learning Textual Entailment Using SVMs and String Similarity Measures*, page 42–47. Association for Computational Linguistics, USA.

Lili Mou, Rui Men, Ge Li, Yan Xu, Lu Zhang, Rui Yan, and Zhi Jin. 2016. Natural language inference by tree-based convolution and heuristic matching. In *Proceedings of the 54th Annual Meeting of the Association for Computational Linguistics*, pages 130–136, Berlin, Germany.

Eamonn Newman, Nicola Stokes, John Dunnion, and Joe Carthy. 2006. *Textual Entailment Recognition Using a Linguistically–Motivated Decision Tree Classifier*, volume 3944, pages 372–384.

Vincent Nguyen. 2019. Question answering in the biomedical domain. In *Proceedings of the 57th Annual Meeting of the Association for Computational Linguistics: Student Research Workshop*, pages 54–63, Florence, Italy.

Vincent Nguyen, Sarvnaz Karimi, and Zhenchang Xing. 2019. ANU-CSIRO at MEDIQA 2019: Question answering using deep contextual knowledge. In *Proceedings of the 18th BioNLP Workshop and Shared Task*, pages 478–487, Florence, Italy.

Anusri Pampari, Preethi Raghavan, Jennifer Liang, and Jian Peng. 2018. emrqa: A large corpus for question answering on electronic medical records. *Computing Research Repository*, abs/1809.00732.

Yifan Peng, Shankai Yan, and Zhiyong Lu. 2019. Transfer learning in biomedical natural language processing: An evaluation of BERT and ELMo on ten benchmarking datasets. In *Proceedings of the Workshop on Biomedical Natural Language Processing*, pages 58–65, Florence, Italy.

Matthew Peters, Mark Neumann, Mohit Iyyer, Matt Gardner, Christopher Clark, Kenton Lee, and Luke Zettlemoyer. 2018. Deep contextualized word representations. *Computing Research Repository*, abs/1802.05365.

Stephen Robertson, Steve Walker, Susan Jones, Micheline Hancock-Beaulieu, and Mike Gatford. 1994. Okapi at trec-3. In *Proceedings of the Third Text REtrieval Conference (TREC 1994)*, Gaithersburg, MD.

Leslie N. Smith. 2018. A disciplined approach to neural network hyper-parameters: Part 1 – learning rate, batch size, momentum, and weight decay. *Computing Research Repository*, page arXiv:1803.09820.

Chi Sun, Luyao Huang, and Xipeng Qiu. 2019. Utilizing BERT for aspect-based sentiment analysis via constructing auxiliary sentence. In *Proceedings of the 2019 Conference of the North American Chapter of the Association for Computational Linguistics: Human Language Technologies*, pages 380–385, Minneapolis, MN.

Christian Szegedy, Wei Liu, Yangqing Jia, Pierre Sermanet, Scott Reed, Dragomir Anguelov, Dumitru Erhan, Vincent Vanhoucke, and Andrew Rabinovich. 2015. Going deeper with convolutions. In *IEEE Conference on Computer Vision and Pattern Recognition*, pages 1–9, Boston, MA.

Jeniya Tabassum, Mounica Maddela, Wei Xu, and Alan Ritter. 2020. Code and named entity recognition in stackoverflow. In *Proceedings of the 58th Annual Meeting of the Association for Computational Linguistics*, pages 4913–4926.

Ian Tenney, Dipanjan Das, and Ellie Pavlick. 2019. BERT rediscovers the classical NLP pipeline. In *Proceedings of the 57th Annual Meeting of the Association for Computational Linguistics*, pages 4593–4601, Florence, Italy.

Ashish Vaswani, Noam Shazeer, Niki Parmar, Jakob Uszkoreit, Llion Jones, Aidan Gomez, Lukasz Kaiser, and Illia Polosukhin. 2017. Attention is all you need. *Computing Research Repository*, abs/1706.03762.

Alex Wang, Amanpreet Singh, Julian Michael, Felix Hill, Omer Levy, and Samuel R. Bowman. 2019a. GLUE: A multi-task benchmark and analysis platform for natural language understanding. In *In the Proceedings of International Conference on Learning Representations*, pages 353–355, Brussels, Belgium.

Haoyu Wang, Mo Yu, Xiaoxiao Guo, Rajarshi Das, Wenhan Xiong, and Tian Gao. 2019b. Do multi-hop readers dream of reasoning chains? In *Proceedings of the 2nd Workshop on Machine Reading for Question Answering*, pages 91–97, Hong Kong, China.

Sida Wang and Christopher Manning. 2013. Fast dropout training. In *Proceedings of the 30th International Conference on Machine Learning*, volume 28 of *Proceedings of Machine Learning Research*, pages 118–126, Atlanta, GA.

Thomas Wolf, Lysandre Debut, Victor Sanh, Julien Chaumond, Clement Delangue, Anthony Moi, Pierric Cistac, Tim Rault, Rémi Louf, Morgan Funtowicz, and Jamie Brew. 2019. HuggingFace's Transformers: State-of-the-art Natural Language Processing. *Computing Research Repository*, page arXiv:1910.03771.

Zhilin Yang, Zihang Dai, Yiming Yang, Jaime Carbonell, Ruslan Salakhutdinov, and Quoc V. Le. 2019. XLNet: Generalized Autoregressive Pretraining for Language Understanding. *Computing Research Repository*, page arXiv:1906.08237.

Wenpeng Yin, Hinrich Schütze, Bing Xiang, and Bowen Zhou. 2016. ABCNN: Attention-based convolutional neural network for modeling sentence pairs. *Transactions of the Association for Computational Linguistics*, 4:259–272.

Yang You, Jing Li, Sashank Reddi, Jonathan Hseu, Sanjiv Kumar, Srinadh Bhojanapalli, Xiaodan Song, James Demmel, Kurt Keutzer, and Cho-Jui Hsieh. 2020. Large Batch Optimization for Deep Learning: Training BERT in 76 minutes.

Sarim Zafar, Muhammad Zubair Malik, and Gursimran Singh Walia. 2019. Towards standardizing and improving classification of bug-fix commits. In *2019 ACM/IEEE International Symposium on Empirical Software Engineering and Measurement*, pages 1–6.

Wei Zhu, Xiaofeng Zhou, Keqiang Wang, Xun Luo, Xiepeng Li, Yuan Ni, and Guotong Xie. 2019. PANLP at MEDIQA 2019: Pre-trained language models, transfer learning and knowledge distillation. In *Proceedings of the 18th BioNLP Workshop and Shared Task*, pages 380–388, Florence, Italy.

Phone Based Keyword Spotting for Transcribing Very Low Resource Languages

Éric Le Ferrand,[1,2] Steven Bird,[1] and Laurent Besacier[2]
[1]Northern Institute, Charles Darwin University, Australia
[2]Laboratoire Informatique de Grenoble, Université Grenobles Alpes, France

Abstract

We investigate the efficiency of two very different spoken term detection approaches for transcription when the available data is insufficient to train a robust speech recognition system. This work is grounded in a very low-resource language documentation scenario where only a few minutes of recording have been transcribed for a given language so far. Experiments on two oral languages show that a pretrained universal phone recognizer, fine-tuned with only a few minutes of target language speech, can be used for spoken term detection through searches in phone confusion networks with a lexicon expressed as a finite state automaton. Experimental results show that a phone recognition based approach provides better overall performances than Dynamic Time Warping when working with clean data, and highlight the benefits of each methods for two types of speech corpus.

1 Introduction

Efforts are made across Australia to preserve, document and revitalize Aboriginal languages. These languages exist primarily in spoken form, and even if there often is an official orthography available, it is not widely used by local people. Making recordings of speakers has been a widespread practice for documenting traditional knowledge. However, such recordings are often not transcribed, making them hard to access.

Manual transcription is time consuming and is often described as a bottleneck (Brinckmann, 2009). While automatic speech recognition (ASR) has seen great improvements in recent years (Povey et al., 2011; Watanabe et al., 2018), it relies on a large amount of annotated data. Attempts to build ASR systems for low-resource languages end up with high word error rate or single-speaker models making them of limited use in Indigenous contexts (Gupta and Boulianne, 2020a,b).

Such methods assume that everything should be transcribed. Bird (2020) describes a sparse transcription model where we only transcribe the words we can confidently recognize, using word-spotting, while leaving the transcription of more difficult sections for later, perhaps when a speaker is available (Bird, 2020). Based on this model, Le Ferrand et al. (2020) proposed a workflow which combines spoken term detection and a human-in-the-loop to support transcription in under-resourced settings. Such a workflow avoids the use of a language model which requires too much textual data, data that we cannot find in most Aboriginal contexts, and which only needs a few spoken terms to be annotated. While they show through their simulation the capability of iterative transcription in remote communities, the precision of their method depends on the quality of the spoken queries, and the density of the resulting transcription is limited by the size of the lexicon.

Automatic phone recognition has seen progress with minimal data (Gupta and Boulianne, 2020b; Li et al., 2020). While Bird (2020) argues that phonetic transcriptions do not stand in for the speech data and cannot be segmented to generate the required higher-level word units, we can nevertheless view phone transcriptions as a speech encoding, retaining our commitment to the sparse transcription model. Such an approach has an advantage over traditional query-by-example methods in that a simple word list can be used instead of a spoken lexicon which can be challenging to collect. In this paper we show how this can be done, and compare it with dynamic time warping (DTW) (Sakoe and Chiba, 1978) commonly used for keyword spotting for Indigenous languages. We consider both methods as applied to two very low-resource languages, Kunwinjku (gup) spoken in the far north of Australia and Mboshi (mdw) spoken in Congo Brazzaville.

2 Background

Traditional ASR systems are not well suited to Aboriginal languages. The lack of data for such languages does not allow us to train an acoustic model or a language model. Additionally, the type of data usually recorded is often spontaneous and noisy which makes it difficult to transcribe, regardless of the amount of annotated data available.

Bird (2020) describes the sparse transcription model, which combines spoken term detection with a human-in-the-loop, in an iterative process. Using spoken term detection as a transcription method allows us to avoid traditional components of an ASR system, specifically the language model, to focus only on the recognition of isolated words.

Traditional Spoken Term Detection systems rely on text-based search in lattices extracted from ASR systems (Lleida et al., 2019; Saraclar and Sproat, 2004). Attempts to train ASR systems in low-resource contexts have so far provided poor results for single speaker systems (Gupta and Boulianne, 2020a,b). This makes traditional spoken term detection approaches questionable in very low-resource settings. A few papers linked to the Babel Project have explored lattice search using ASR systems trained in low-resource settings (Gales et al., 2014; Rosenberg et al., 2017). However, they work with much larger data collections than what is available in Indigenous contexts.

Query-by-Example methods have been preferred in very low-resource contexts since they only rely on acoustic comparison between spoken queries and utterances. Le Ferrand et al. (2020) explore feature representation using DTW in an iterative pipeline following the sparse transcription model (Bird, 2020), and have been able to transcribe up to 42% of a lexicon in their speech collections. This method, however, has shown limitations in terms of robustness in the face of speaker variability. Research around speech features for spoken term detection has explored the use of bottleneck features, or the hidden representation of an auto-encoder (Menon et al., 2019; Kamper et al., 2015, 2020). Such research highlights the benefits of multilingual approaches for spoken term detection when transcribed data are limited in the target language. Others have exploited neural approaches to train word classifiers from word pairs using a Siamese loss (Settle and Livescu, 2016; Settle et al., 2017), however pairs of words are required, limiting the selection to words that can be searched.

Query-by-example relies on a spoken lexicon and, by extension, a comparison between two acoustic vectors. A difference of speakers or recording channel between the query term and the speech collection has an influence on the likelihood of a given term to be retrieved. Moreover, a spoken lexicon is not simple to gather and this therefore limits the amount of terms we can retrieve. Using a lexicon made of terms recorded in isolation for spoken term detection purposes will lead to poor precision. Another solution would be to manually extract the terms of the lexicon from a speech collection which is time-consuming. Phone recognizers, like ASR systems, also need a few hours of annotated speech to provide acceptable performance (Gupta and Boulianne, 2020b; Adams et al., 2018). However, recent work has shown how multilingual phone recognizers can be fine-tuned with minimal data to work on a new language (Li et al., 2020). Raw phone transcriptions are hard to obtain as they require the skills of a trained linguist, and they cannot help directly for retrieving higher level-units (Bird, 2020). However, the orthography of most Indigenous languages is based on their phonology and there is usually a simple mapping from graphemes to phonemes can be obtained to train a phone recognizer, even with a shallow knowledge of the phonology. A spoken term detection method based on a phone recognizer could allow us to rely only on written queries following a traditional lattice-search method.

3 Methods

We begin with a lexicon of size s consisting of audio clips of spoken words, along with orthographic transcriptions, plus a speech collection in which more instances of those words may be found.

Two spoken term detection approaches, involving a multilingual component, are investigated here: (a) a baseline method based on DTW applied on multilingual BottleNeck Features (mBNF); and (b) a method based on a textual search in phone confusion networks extracted from a universal phone recognizer (P2W).

3.1 Baseline: Sparse Transcription using DTW

We first extract acoustic features from both the corpora and lexicons. Based on general performance scores reported in the literature, and in order to compare our method with another multilingual approach, we have chosen multilingual bottleneck features. These are extracted from a model trained on the Babel corpus and consist of 80 dimension acoustic vectors. They have been extracted with the Shennong library.[1] We slide each term of the lexicon along the utterances of the corpus with a step size of 30 milliseconds. We then select the best matches for each utterance-word pair based on DTW distance and retain all matches above a threshold m for evaluation.

3.2 Sparse Transcription using Phone Recognition (P2W)

Li et al. (2020) introduced *Allosaurus*, a universal phone recognition system which combines a language independent encoder and phone predictor, and a language dependent allophone layer with a loss function, associated with each language (Fig. 1). Allosaurus models are trained using standard phonetic transcriptions and the *allovera* database (Mortensen et al., 2020), a multilingual allophone database that can be used to map allophones to phonemes. The model first encodes speech with a standard ASR encoder which computes the universal phone distribution. Then an allophone layer is initialized with the allophone matrix and maps the universal phone distribution into the phoneme distribution for the given target language. The resulting model can be fine-tuned and applied to unseen languages.

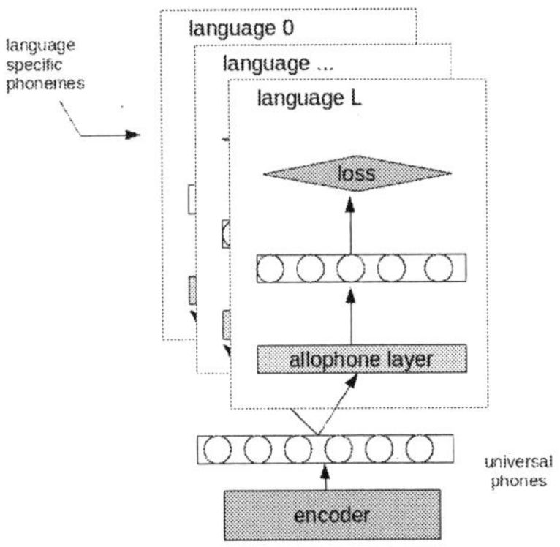

Figure 1: Allosaurus model (Li et al., 2020)

In the current context, since we only have an orthographic transcription for Kunwinjku, we transliterate it into IPA with the mapping shown in Table 1. The transcription contains some English words which will be mapped as if they were Kunwinjku words (e.g., school is written /sʔkool/ instead of /skʊl/). For Mboshi, the orthographic transcription already mostly matches the corresponding phonetic transcription.[2]

graphs	a	b	d	h	e	i	ch	y	o	k	dj	s	r	rr
phones	ɑ	b	d	ʔ	ɛ	i	ʃ	j	ɔ	k	ɟ	s	ɻ	r
graphs	ng	rd	rl	nj	rn	u	f	l	m	n	w	p	t	
phones	ŋ	ɖ	ɭ	ɲ	ɳ	u	f	l	m	n	w	p	t	

Table 1: Grapheme to phoneme mapping for Kunwinjku

We fine-tuned the original pretrained model with the training and validation subsets described in Section 4 following the mapping described above, resulting in one new phone recognition model per language. We used the resulting models to automatically extract phones in confusion networks from the validation and test sets of the two languages (Mboshi and Kunwinjku) (Fig. 3).

The graph extracted is a confusion network (confnet) and consists of a size s sequence of phones and the top k likely alternatives for each phone (see Fig. 3). For each phone in the graph a probability score between 0 and 1 is assigned. We also map the lexicons into phones and convert them into a finite state automaton (FSA) in which each final state corresponds to the end of a given word (Fig.2). We explore, in the confusion networks related to our collection, every path which corresponds to a valid transition in the FSA and has a probability strictly greater than zero. If a path reaches a terminal state in the FSA, we extract the word and a score corresponding to the mean of the accumulated likelihood scores. Like the baseline with DTW, we then select the best match for each pair utterance/word pairs based on the likelihood score and keep for evaluation the matches above a threshold n. For both systems, we do not keep for evaluation the pairs which correspond to the query instances used to build the lexicons.

4 Data

We are using a corpus of spontaneous speech in Kunwinjku built from several sources. The training, validation and test set are described in Table 2. The training and validation sets are built from transcribed recordings made for language descrip-

[1] https://docs.cognitive-ml.fr/shennong/

[2] The tones are marked in the orthographic transcription but this feature is not taken into account in the Allosaurus model. We thus decided to treat the orthographic transcription as a phonetic transcription so the accentuated vowels are considered as new phones.

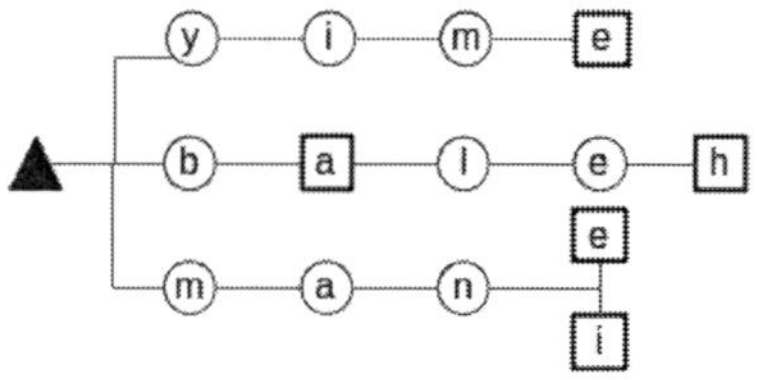

Figure 2: Example of lexicon converted into a FSA

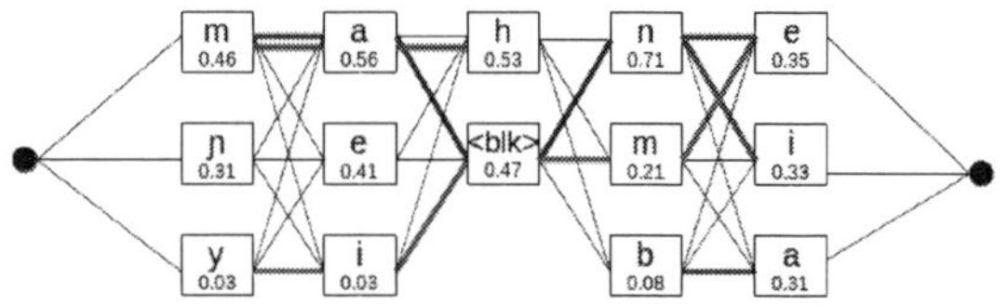

Figure 3: Example of search in a graph confusion network

tion purposes around language and emotion. They also contain some recording of guided tours of an Aboriginal town. The test set contains exclusively guided tour recordings. The orthographic transcription has been force-aligned using the MAUS forced aligner (Kisler et al., 2017). The train and validation sets contain the same 5 speakers and the test set has a non-overlapping set of 5 speakers.

We are also using a corpus of Mboshi speech which consists of 4.5 hours of speech elicited from text with orthographic transcription and a forced alignment at the word level (Godard et al., 2017). Training, validation and test sets have been extracted from the corpus and are described in Table 2. The same three speakers are represented among the three partitions.

The lexicon queries (for spoken term detection) are made of 100 words for Mboshi and 60 words for Kunwinjku. We randomly selected in the test set words which occur at least 3 times in the corresponding corpus. For each word, we manually selected examples clearly pronounced, respecting the speaker distribution of the test set (Table 3 and 4), and clipped them out.

Partitions	train	valid	test
Kunwinjku	35min45	7min39	19min43
Mboshi	21min10	10min03	3h56min

Table 2: Partition duration

Speaker	RB	TG	GN	SG	MM
Distribution	10%	25%	15%	38%	12%

Table 3: Speaker distribution across Kunwinjku lexicon

Speaker	AB	KO	MA
Distribution	63%	33%	4%

Table 4: Speaker distribution across Mboshi lexicon

5 Results

5.1 Phone Error Rate (PER)

We first evaluate the PER for both languages on the validation set. For Kunwinjku the PER started at 55.45%, and we obtained 38.82% after the system early stopped at the 24th epoch. For Mboshi the PER started at 59% and reached 38.72% at the 29th epoch. Although the PER is low considering the small amount of data used for fine-tuning Allosaurus, we would expect a bigger difference between Kunwinjku and Mboshi considering that Mboshi is read speech without foreign words and Kunwinjku is spontaneous speech containing English words. To estimate the performances for each language, we computed the PER on the test set between the top 1 phones generated by Allosaurus and the gold standard. For Kunwinjku the PER is at 39% and for Mboshi at 44%.

5.2 System performances

We evaluate the proposed methods using precision, recall and F-score.

We provide for each language the scores based on a threshold that is optimized on the respective validation sets. For the P2W method, the optimized threshold is set at 0.77 for Kunwinjku and 0.631 for Mboshi. For the DTW baseline, it is set at 0.217 for Kunwinjku and 0.174 for Mboshi. The results are detailed in Table 5. In Mboshi, the method outperforms the baseline with DTW with recall and precision. In Kunwinjku, the method does not outperform the baseline in terms of F-scores. We can see that while the baseline brings more candidates than P2W, our method is more precise. While it is clear that a phone recognition based method provides better overall performance on clean speech, the gap between the F-scores of each method in Kunwinjku is small which can make them both beneficial.

The Kunwinjku corpus contains spontaneous speech. We can observe elision phenomenon and fast speech which are not well supported by an approach based on recognition of canonical, lexical phone sequences. Figures 4 and 5 show that, while our approach seems to be more consistent across

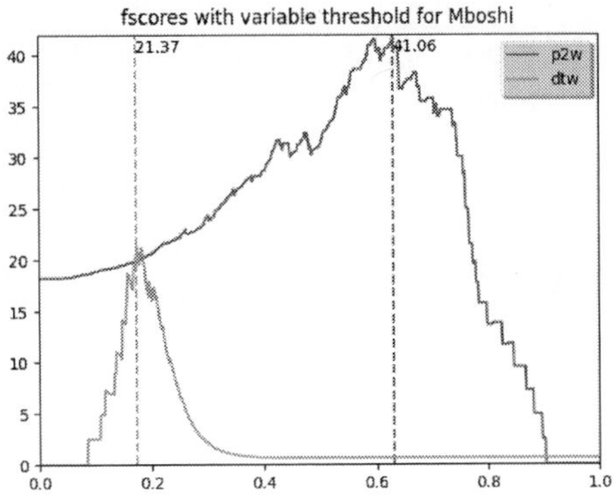

Figure 4: F-scores for Mboshi with variable thresholds on validation set

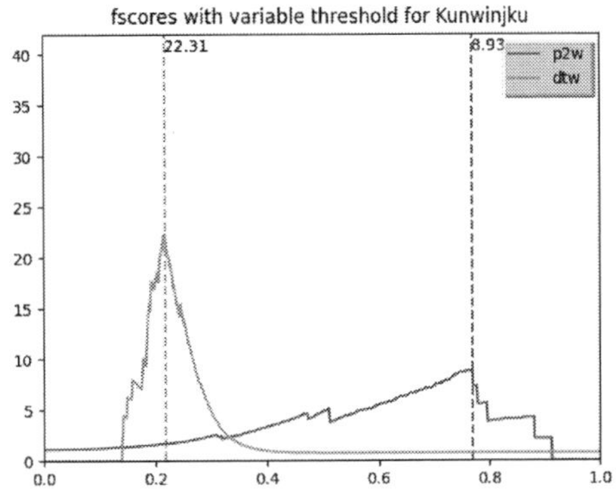

Figure 5: F-scores for Kunwinjku with variable thresholds on the validation set

	recall	precision	F-score
DTW_mb	14.55%	20.46%	17.01%
P2W_mb	22.61%	45.97%	30.31%
DTW_kun	42.09%	22.81%	29.59%
P2W_kun	17.41%	62.50%	27.23%

Table 5: Performance of spoken term detection on the test set with the optimized threshold

thresholds, it is less efficient than DTW for noisy and spontaneous speech corpora.

We present in Table 6 the top 5 false positives across methods and languages. We could only report the top 4 for P2W in Kunwinjku since most of the errors were isolated cases. We can see for P2W that the errors are made between very similar words. For Mboshi, the top 5 only includes tonal differences between the query and the hit. For Kunwinjku, the errors are made between similar words, some of which are morphologically related (balanda (man), balandaken (of the man); karrire (we-INCL go), ngarrire (we-EXCL go)). For DTW, the errors are not as consistent and the hits seem to only match subparts of the query terms (wa, **wáre**; marn**bolh**, bonj).

5.3 Speaker analysis

Le Ferrand et al. (2020) pointed out the limitation of their method in terms of cross speaker spoken term detection. To compare the two approaches on this aspect, we analyze each true positive that is output by each system: we check if the word matched is pronounced by a same or different speaker that the query term. Even if we only use the written forms of the queries for P2W, we also make the same analysis.

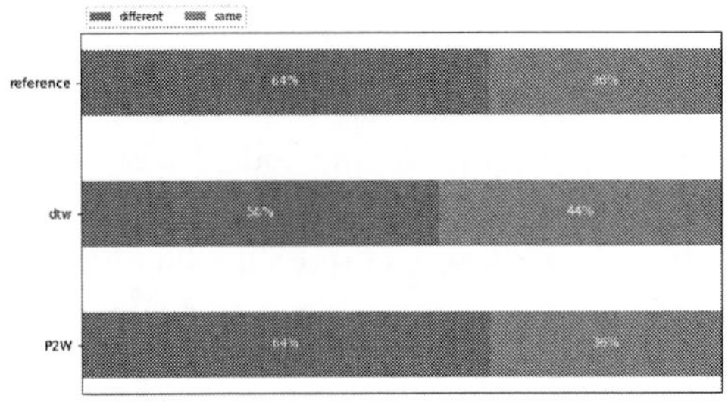

Figure 6: Proportion of same-speaker/different-speaker retrieval in Kunwinjku

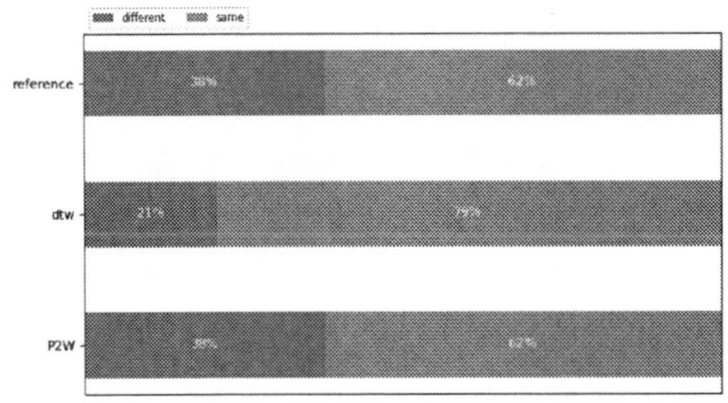

Figure 7: Proportion of same-speaker/different-speaker retrieval in Mboshi

Figures 6 and 7 present the proportion of spoken terms retrieved from same-speaker or different-speaker For a fair comparison, we also compute the distribution of same/different speaker between the lexicons and all the words to be retrieved in the corpora (reference). We can see that P2W method follows the general distribution in the corpora while the baseline DTW retrieves mostly terms pronounced by the same speaker.

Mboshi P2W		Kunwinjku P2W		Mboshi DTW		Kunwinjku DTW	
Query	Hit	Query	Hit	Query	Hit	Query	Hit
ádzá	ádza	balanda	balandaken	abvúa	wa	munguyh	bonj
ádzá	adzá	birrimarnbom	birrimanbun	mwána	wa	kahdi	konhda
ngala	ngalá	mani	yiman	mvúá	wa	kunak	konhda
ngaa	ngáa	karrire	ngarrire	wáre	wa	kunred	konhda
okándá	ɷkándá			ngaa	ngá	marnbolh	bonj

Table 6: Top 5 false positives

6 Combining the methods

We mentioned in Section 2 that DTW and P2W each have their own strengths. As we know, DTW will cope more easily with spontaneous speech and co-articulation effects such as assimilation and elision. Phone recognition allows us to avoid gathering spoken queries and retrieving terms with exact matching between written forms. To highlight the complementarity of the methods, we analyse the intersection of their true positives in Figure 8. We show that across both corpora the intersection of the true positives is small, and so combining the two methods can help us increase the coverage of the transcription to reach up to 49.99% for Kunwinjku and 32.16% for Mboshi.

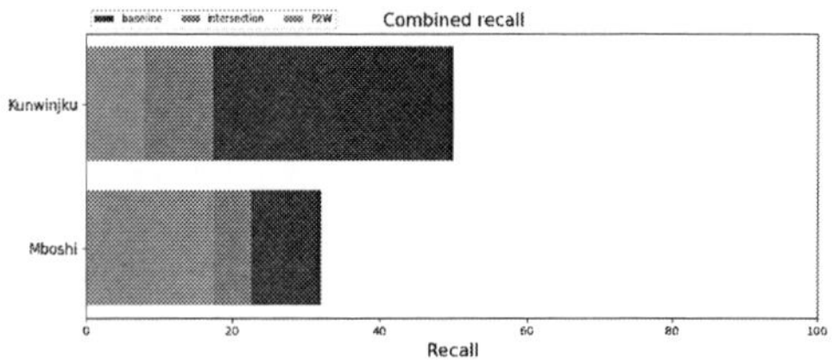

Figure 8: Relative coverage of the combined methods

We analysed the most common terms retrieved by DTW which have been ignored by P2W. For Kunwinjku, the glottal stop and doubled consonant are the phones the least properly recognized (*wanjh* written *wanj kunwardde* written *kunwarde* for example). More generally, since the data used in Kunwinjku is spontaneous speech, most of the missed hits by P2W are due to highly mistaken phone transcriptions by allosaurus. For Mboshi, beyond the main easily-confusable phones (*o* / *ω*, *e* / *ϵ* for instance) the main missed hits are due to tones or long vowels not being correctly recognized.

The baseline provides a match for every utterance/query pair if no threshold is applied. However, since P2W is restricted by the phones output by the phone recognizer, we have a limited amount of candidates regardless of the threshold. As mentioned before, this has the advantage of being more precise, but can easily miss a match if the phone lattices contain many mistakes. In view of this, we combine the two methods as follows. For each utterance/query pair brought by P2W, we first keep for evaluation the candidates which have a score greater than the P2W threshold. Then we send to evaluation every pair having a distance less than the DTW threshold. We provide in Table 7 the results for the same optimized thresholds mentioned before.

	recall	precision	F-score
comb_mb	24.89%	45.54%	32.19%
P2W_mb	22.61%	45.97%	30.31%
comb_kun	35.76%	31.48%	33.48%
P2W_kun	17.41%	62.50%	27.23%

Table 7: Performance of the combined methods

The described way of combining the methods outperforms both P2W and DTW approaches in terms of F-score. For Mboshi, we can observe a small increase of the recall with a precision barely affected. For Kunwinjku, the results are less clear. While the F-score outperforms both the baseline and P2W, combining the methods double the recall but decreases by half the precision.

7 Conclusion

This paper compares two methods of spoken term detection, one based on DTW with bottleneck features, and one based on on phone recognition. Both methods have been applied on two very low-resource languages, namely, a corpus in Mboshi recorded in a controlled environment, and a corpus of spontaneous speech in Kunwinjku recorded in remote communities. Experimental results shown that a few minutes of transcribed speech can be used to fine-tune a universal phone recognizer. Then searching terms in a confusion network with a lexicon expressed as a FSA outperforms the baseline for Mboshi but not for Kunwinjku.

A text-based approach has the advantage over traditional Query-by-example that a set of written queries is easier to gather than spoken queries. Further analysis has shown that the proposed phone recognition approach is more robust to speaker variability and tends to be more accurate than DTW overall. However, the baseline seems to have a better coverage over the corpora and to be more suitable with noisy data.

One method relies on canonical orthography while the other relies on acoustic comparison. Both methods have their own benefits depending on the type of data they are applied to. Experimental results have shown that it is possible to take advantage of both methods to increase the overall recall while maintaining precision at an acceptable rate.

References

Oliver Adams, Trevor Cohn, Graham Neubig, Hilaria Cruz, Steven Bird, and Alexis Michaud. 2018. Evaluating phonemic transcription of low-resource tonal languages for language documentation. In *LREC 2018 (Language Resources and Evaluation Conference)*, pages 3356–3365.

Steven Bird. 2020. Sparse transcription. *Computational Linguistics*, 46:713–744.

Caren Brinckmann. 2009. Transcription bottleneck of speech corpus exploitation. *Proceedings of the 2nd Colloquium on Lesser Used Languages and Computer Linguistics*, pages 165 – 179.

Mark JF Gales, Kate M Knill, Anton Ragni, and Shakti P Rath. 2014. Speech recognition and keyword spotting for low-resource languages: Babel project research at cued. In *Fourth International workshop on spoken language technologies for under-resourced languages (SLTU-2014)*, pages 16–23. International Speech Communication Association (ISCA).

Pierre Godard, Gilles Adda, Martine Adda-Decker, Juan Benjumea, Laurent Besacier, Jamison Cooper-Leavitt, Guy-Noël Kouarata, Lori Lamel, Hélène Maynard, Markus Müller, et al. 2017. A very low resource language speech corpus for computational language documentation experiments. *arXiv preprint arXiv:1710.03501*.

Vishwa Gupta and Gilles Boulianne. 2020a. Automatic transcription challenges for Inuktitut, a low-resource polysynthetic language. In *Proceedings of the 12th Language Resources and Evaluation Conference*, pages 2521–27.

Vishwa Gupta and Gilles Boulianne. 2020b. Speech transcription challenges for resource constrained indigenous language Cree. In *Proceedings of the 1st Joint Workshop on Spoken Language Technologies for Under-Resourced Languages and Collaboration and Computing for Under-Resourced Languages (CCURL)*, pages 362–367.

Herman Kamper, Micha Elsner, Aren Jansen, and Sharon Goldwater. 2015. Unsupervised neural network based feature extraction using weak top-down constraints. In *2015 IEEE International Conference on Acoustics, Speech and Signal Processing (ICASSP)*, pages 5818–22. IEEE.

Herman Kamper, Yevgen Matusevych, and Sharon Goldwater. 2020. Multilingual acoustic word embedding models for processing zero-resource languages. In *ICASSP 2020-2020 IEEE International Conference on Acoustics, Speech and Signal Processing (ICASSP)*, pages 6414–6418. IEEE.

Thomas Kisler, Uwe Reichel, and Florian Schiel. 2017. Multilingual processing of speech via web services. *Computer Speech and Language*, 45:326–347.

Eric Le Ferrand, Steven Bird, and Laurent Besacier. 2020. Enabling interactive transcription in an indigenous community. In *COLING 2020*.

Xinjian Li, Siddharth Dalmia, Juncheng Li, Matthew Lee, Patrick Littell, Jiali Yao, Antonios Anastasopoulos, David R Mortensen, Graham Neubig, Alan W Black, et al. 2020. Universal phone recognition with a multilingual allophone system. In *ICASSP 2020-2020 IEEE International Conference on Acoustics, Speech and Signal Processing (ICASSP)*, pages 8249–8253. IEEE.

Eduardo Lleida, Alfonso Ortega, Antonio Miguel, Virginia Bazán-Gil, Carmen Pérez, Manuel Gómez, and Alberto De Prada. 2019. Albayzin 2018 evaluation: the iberspeech-rtve challenge on speech technologies for spanish broadcast media. *Applied Sciences*, 9(24):5412.

Raghav Menon, Herman Kamper, Ewald van der Westhuizen, John Quinn, and Thomas Niesler. 2019. Feature exploration for almost zero-resource ASR-free keyword spotting using a multilingual bottleneck extractor and correspondence autoencoders. *Proceedings of Interspeech 2019*, pages 3475–3479.

David Mortensen, Xinjian Li, Patrick Littell, Alexis Michaud, Shruti Rijhwani, Antonios Anastasopoulos, Alan Black, Florian Metze, and Graham Neubig. 2020. Allovera: a multilingual allophone database. In *LREC 2020: 12th Language Resources and Evaluation Conference*.

Daniel Povey, Arnab Ghoshal, Gilles Boulianne, Lukas Burget, Ondrej Glembek, Nagendra Goel, Mirko Hannemann, Petr Motlicek, Yanmin Qian, Petr Schwarz, Jan Silovsky, Georg Stemmer, and Karel Vesely. 2011. The kaldi speech recognition toolkit.

In *IEEE 2011 Workshop on Automatic Speech Recognition and Understanding*. IEEE Signal Processing Society. IEEE Catalog No.: CFP11SRW-USB.

Andrew Rosenberg, Kartik Audhkhasi, Abhinav Sethy, Bhuvana Ramabhadran, and Michael Picheny. 2017. End-to-end speech recognition and keyword search on low-resource languages. In *2017 IEEE International Conference on Acoustics, Speech and Signal Processing (ICASSP)*, pages 5280–5284. IEEE.

Hiroaki Sakoe and Seibi Chiba. 1978. Dynamic programming algorithm optimization for spoken word recognition. *IEEE Transactions on Acoustics, Speech, and Signal Processing*, 26:43–49.

Murat Saraclar and Richard Sproat. 2004. Lattice-based search for spoken utterance retrieval. In *Proceedings of the Human Language Technology Conference of the North American Chapter of the Association for Computational Linguistics: HLT-NAACL 2004*, pages 129–136.

Shane Settle, Keith Levin, Herman Kamper, and Karen Livescu. 2017. Query-by-example search with discriminative neural acoustic word embeddings. *Proc. Interspeech 2017*, pages 2874–2878.

Shane Settle and Karen Livescu. 2016. Discriminative acoustic word embeddings: Tecurrent neural network-based approaches. In *2016 IEEE Spoken Language Technology Workshop (SLT)*, pages 503–510. IEEE.

Shinji Watanabe, Takaaki Hori, Shigeki Karita, Tomoki Hayashi, Jiro Nishitoba, Yuya Unno, Nelson-Enrique Yalta Soplin, Jahn Heymann, Matthew Wiesner, Nanxin Chen, et al. 2018. Espnet: End-to-end speech processing toolkit. *Proc. Interspeech 2018*, pages 2207–2211.

Evaluation of Review Summaries via Question-Answering

Nannan Huang
RMIT University, Australia
s3754491@student.rmit.edu.au

Xiuzhen Zhang
RMIT University, Australia
xiuzhen.zhang@rmit.edu.au

Abstract

Summarisation of reviews aims at compressing opinions expressed in multiple review documents into a concise form while still covering the key opinions. Despite the advancement in summarisation models, evaluation metrics for opinionated text summaries lag behind and still rely on lexical-matching metrics such as ROUGE. In this paper, we propose using the question-answering(QA) approach to evaluate summaries of opinions in reviews. We propose to identify opinion-bearing text spans in the reference summary to generate QA pairs so as to capture salient opinions. A QA model is then employed to probe the candidate summary to evaluate information overlap between the candidate and reference summaries. We show that our metric RunQA, Review Summary Evaluation via Question Answering, correlates well with human judgments in terms of coverage and focus of information.

1 Introduction

Opinion summarisation takes input documents like online reviews or social media posts where users express their opinions on topics and condense them into a single piece of text. The summary should reflect the core opinions expressed in the source documents. Recent studies in opinion summarisation have shown an advancement moving from extractive (Meng et al., 2012; Ku et al., 2006; *i.a*), i.e. copying sections from the original reviews to produce a summary, to abstractive (Chu and Liu, 2019; Bražinskas et al., 2020a; Bražinskas et al., 2020b; *i.a*), i.e. generating new phrases that reflect the information covered in the original text.

Despite the advancement in summarisation models, evaluation metrics for opinionated text summaries lag behind. For evaluation of review summaries, traditional token-matching ROUGE (Lin, 2004) is still widely used, supplemented with human evaluation on the relative ranking of system-generated summaries in terms of quality dimensions such as Fluency, Coherence, Non-redundancy, Informativeness, and Sentiment (Chu and Liu, 2019; Bražinskas et al., 2020a; Bražinskas et al., 2020b). It is well understood that ROUGE cannot capture the same meaning expressed in different token sequences.

Neural model-based metrics have been proposed for general text summarisation evaluation. Especially QAEval (Deutsch et al., 2021) has been proposed for evaluating the information quality of abstractive summaries with respect to the reference summaries. A key step for the success of QAEval for summarisation evaluation is extracting answers and generating questions covering a significant amount of important Summarisation Content Units (SCUs). Generally, noun phrases(NP) and named entities(NER) are used to generate question-answer pairs in QA models (Durmus et al., 2020; Wang et al., 2020; Deutsch et al., 2021), but their applicability for review summary evaluation is yet to be examined.

In this paper, we propose to evaluate review summaries with question answering (QA) based on neural models, with a focus on evaluating the information quality of review summaries. Modern abstractive summarisation systems can generate sentences of high linguistic quality – grammatically correct, easy to read and understand– but it is more important to evaluate the *information quality* of summaries. Specifically system summaries of high quality information should express opinions consistent with those in the reference summary.

We propose to evaluate the information quality of review summaries, in terms of coverage(recall) and focus(precision) (Koto et al., 2020), where coverage is the amount (proportion) of salient information of the reference summary that the system summary contains, and focus is the amount (proportion) of salient information in the system summary. To improve the QA framework for more effective review summary evaluation, we propose to identify opinion-bearing text spans to generate QA pairs rather than relying on NPs and NERs. In addition to the evaluation of the information quality of summaries, we further propose evaluating the robustness of evaluation metrics for ranking summaries through an adversarial task.

Our evaluation metric RunQA, namely Review Summaries Evaluation via Question Answering, was evaluated against QAEval and other metrics on an Amazon review summarisation dataset (Bražinskas et al., 2020b) We found that RunQA significantly outperforms QAEval and other metrics for evaluating the information quality of summaries, especially in terms of precision. We also found that RunQA is the most robust for ranking summaries.

2 Related Work

We first discuss automatic metrics for general text summarisation evaluation and then especially discuss the QA-based metrics.

2.1 Evaluation Metrics for Text Summarisation

Automatic metrics for summarisation evaluation can be broadly divided into three groups – traditional token matching-based metrics, embedding-based metrics and model-based metrics.

Token matching-based metrics: When evaluating the performance of a summarisation system, researchers introduced metrics by comparing n-gram token matching such as ROUGE (Lin, 2004), BLEU (Papineni et al., 2002) and METEOR (Banerjee and Lavie, 2005) over a decade ago. Owing to simplicity and ease of use, ROUGE is one of the most widely used automatic metrics. It is designed to capture the similarity between text sequences based on lexical overlaps.

Embedding-based metrics: The significant improvement in the summarisation domain moving from extractive to abstractive makes using lexical overlap metrics for evaluation inadequate. In abstractive summarisation, the summary does not necessarily use the exact word when contextual embeddings like BERT (Devlin et al., 2019) and ELMo (Peters et al., 2018) are used. ROUGE becomes less suitable in this setting, as it performs a surface-level comparison between texts, and it fails to compare words that express the same meaning expressed in different forms.

To overcome the problem of exact word matching, researchers introduced metrics using contextual embeddings, such as BERTScore (Zhang et al., 2019) and MoverScore (Zhao et al., 2019). Both of these metrics have proven to better correlate with human judgments than ROUGE.

Although the embedding-based metrics overcome problems with exact word matching, they are still comparing two pieces of text by capturing context similarity, but not evaluating whether they express the same information (Deutsch and Roth, 2020).

ROUGE is still the most widely used and the default metric for evaluating opinion summarisation. In recent opinion summarisation papers (Chu and Liu, 2019; Bražinskas et al., 2020a; Bražinskas et al., 2020b), the ROUGE family is still the only automatic metric used for evaluating their systems.

Researchers have shown ROUGE is weakly correlated with human judgments (Novikova et al., 2017), and it is not suitable to be used for opinion summarisation evaluation (Tay et al., 2019) or abstractive summarisation (Ng and Abrecht, 2015). It is calculated based on token overlap rather than looking at whether summaries express the same opinion. This makes ROUGE not an ideal metric for evaluating opinionated text summaries.

Both the token overlap-based and embedding-based metrics have the drawback of weakly penalising information or opinion inconsistency (Tay, 2019). For example, for documents expressing opposite opinions like 'I like sushi' and 'I hate sushi'. ROUGE will penalise it weakly by putting equal weight on each token. Whereas embedding-based metrics will treat 'like' and 'hate' similarly because of the similar context.

Model-based metrics: Recent studies have introduced different model-based metrics. For example, SUPERT (Gao et al., 2020) and LS-Score (Wu et al., 2020) target to evaluate text summarisation without references. SUPERT achieved this by generating pseudo references using the top sentences in the source documents, and LS-Score by generating different negative samples and applying unsupervised contrastive learning to learn the metric.

Model-based metrics include QA-based metrics. Following that, we go into metrics based on QA models in further depth.

2.2 QA-based Metrics

There are two types of QA-based metrics targeting evaluation in different dimensions. One type is reference-free models such as FEQA (Durmus et al., 2020) and QAGS (Wang et al., 2020), where questions are generated using the candidate summary, and asked against the source document to measure the faithfulness of the candidate summary. The other type is reference-based models such as QAEval (Deutsch et al., 2021), where questions are generated using a reference summary and asked against the candidate summary to evaluate content and information overlap between the summaries.

QAEval is proven to generate question-answer pairs that cover a significant amount of information expressed in summaries. It also correlates well with human judgments when used as a reference-based metric. Our work builds on QAEval for opinion summarisation evaluation. The original QAEval model generates questions by extracting noun phrases only. In this work, we use a different answer selection strategy to capture and evaluate the information and opinions expressed in summaries.

3 RunQA: Review Summary Evaluation via Question Answering

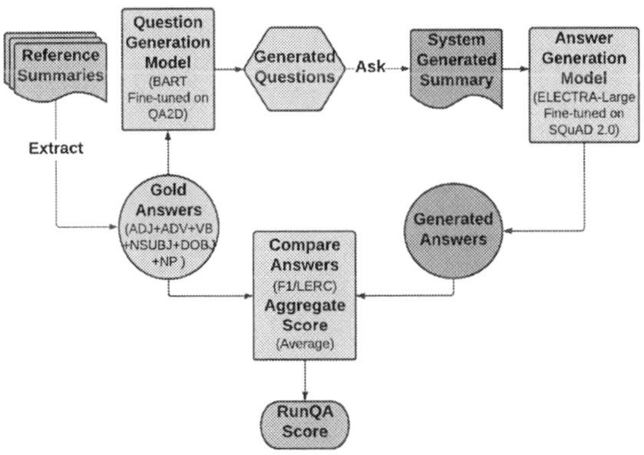

Figure 1: The RunQA model architecture. The answer selection strategy changed from noun phrases(NP) only to the combination of adjectives, adverbs, verbs with their subject child and object child and NP.

The overall architecture of the RunQA model is shown in Figure 1. Like the original model, it consists of a question generation model using a pre-trained BART language model (Lewis et al., 2020) and fine-tuned on QA data provided by Demszky et al. (2018). QAEval uses a pre-trained ELECTRA-Large language model (Clark et al., 2020) and fine-tuned it on the SQuAD 2.0 (Rajpurkar et al., 2018) dataset for question answering.

RunQA has several key differences from QAEval (Deutsch et al., 2021). We modified the answer selection strategy to make it better suited for opinion summarisation evaluation. We also use different variants of answer verification strategies.

3.1 Answer Selection

In general text summarisation, the datasets used are mostly articles from the news domain, like CNN/DailyMail (Nallapati et al., 2016) and Newsroom (Grusky et al., 2018). Where these articles contain a significant number of named entities(NER) and noun phrases(NP). Different from general text summarisation datasets where the information is contributed heavily by NERs and NPs. For opinion summarisation, there is a limited number of NERs and NPs in reviews. This suggests using NPs alone may not be sufficient to capture opinionated information.

Deutsch and Roth (2020) showed that in addition to the NP, information is expressed in the combination of the verb and its subject child (NSUBJ) and object child (DOBJ). Subrahmanian and Reforgiato (2008) suggested that opinions can also be captured by the combination of adjectives with verbs and adverbs. Our answer selection strategy therefore includes opinion-bearing text spans – adjectives, adverbs, and verbs with their object child and subject child, in addition to NPs. Our experiments evaluating (Section 5) the quality of answers showed that our answer selection strategy can effectively capture the Summarisation Content Units (SCUs) (Nenkova and Passonneau, 2004) in reference summaries. Our further evaluation of the QA pairs shows that the generated QA pairs are of high quality, covering a significant amount of information expressed in SCUs.

3.2 Answer Verification

Previous QA methods (Durmus et al., 2020; Wang et al., 2020; Deutsch et al., 2021) reported the shortcoming of using the F_1 score for answer verification. F_1 score is calculated by using an exact matching of tokens between the answer spans. It works well in an extractive setting but not necessarily in an abstractive scenario. It has the risk of incorrectly penalising a correct answer due to token mismatch.

To overcome the shortcoming of using the F_1 score for answer verification. We propose to leverage LERC (Chen et al., 2020) to verify answers. It is a learned evaluation metric for reading comprehension to verify the correctness of answers. It was shown to better correlate with human judgements for answer verification by using a more flexible way to evaluate answers. It is achieved by not only comparing the answer spans when generating a score, but also the provided summary and the question.

4 Dataset and Baselines

We conducted experiments to evaluate the QA model and benchmark RunQA against QAEval and other metrics. The dataset we use in our experiments is from Bražinskas et al. (2020b). It was obtained from Amazon product reviews, where 60 products from 4 different categories (15 for each category) were randomly selected. For each product there are 8 source reviews, 1 system generated summary using the Copycat model (Bražinskas et al., 2020b), and 3 reference summaries obtained from Amazon Mechanical Turk [1].

The summary of the dataset is in Table 1. The average number of sentences and words in the reference summaries and reviews is similar. This is because the annotators were instructed to generate summaries of a similar length as the reviews. The candidate summaries have a relatively smaller number of words and sentences generated compared to them.

Document	Avg. No. Words	Avg. No. Sents
Reviews	49.58	3.74
Candidates	34.02	3.13
References	54.54	4.07

Table 1: Statistics of the Amazon review dataset.

Baseline metrics include the lexical overlap-based ROUGE family of metrics (Lin, 2004), embedding-based metrics BERTScore (Zhang et al., 2019) and MoverScore (Zhao et al., 2019), as well as the QA model-based metric QAEval (Deutsch et al., 2021).

5 Evaluation of the QA Model

We conducted experiments to evaluate the effectiveness of our answer selection strategy and the quality of the generated question-answer pairs. To ensure product diversity, we randomly selected two products from each product category. One of the authors manually annotated the SCUs using the reference summaries following the guidelines and using the annotation tool provided by the Pyramid method (Nenkova and Passonneau, 2004) [2].

Token categories in SCUs: The same author applied spaCy[3] to tag tokens in each SCU as categories (e.g. Noun, Verb), and check whether the token is part of a noun phrase(NP). This step aims to examine whether tokens that express information can be successfully captured using NPs only. We put words that do not express information into a separate category and excluded them from our analysis.

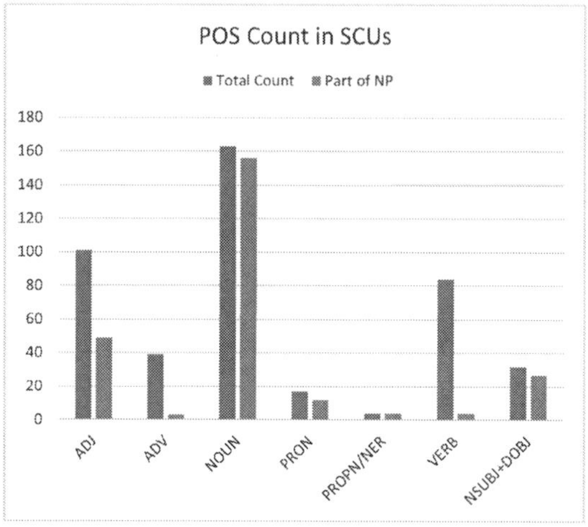

Figure 2: Nouns are a great contributor to NP. There are a significant number of verbs, adverbs, and adjectives presented in the SCUs but not captured by NPs. The number of NSUBJs and DOBJs is not significant due to the structure of SCUs. A limited number of NER suggest that using NP together with NER is not sufficient for review summaries evaluation.

The final result can be found in Figure 2. Not surprisingly, nouns are a great contributor to NPs. Note that there are a significant number of verbs, adverbs, and adjectives presented in the SCUs but not in the NPs. However, since an SCU is similar to a clause but not a full sentence, it is common for an SCU to not contain the subject child (NSUBJ) or the object child (DOBJ) of a verb. The very limited number of proper nouns (NERs) suggests that they do not capture significant information in review summaries. Figure 2 clearly shows that NPs alone cannot capture information in summaries and justifies our proposed approach of selecting answers

[1] https://www.mturk.com/.

[2] http://www1.cs.columbia.edu/~ani/DUC2005/AnnotationGuide.htm.

[3] https://spacy.io/.

based on adjectives, adverbs, and verbs with their subject and objective children as well.

Quality of Generated Question-Answer Pairs: A boxplot of the number of question-answer pairs generated using different answer selection strategies can be found in Figure 3. It is not surprising that our answer selection strategy generates the largest number of QA pairs since we select text spans based on more diverse categories, while using other selection strategies alone generates a limited number of QA pairs. The number of QA pairs generated using NPs only is rather limited, and NERs with NPs do not generate more either, which again suggests that there is a limited number of NERs in review summaries.

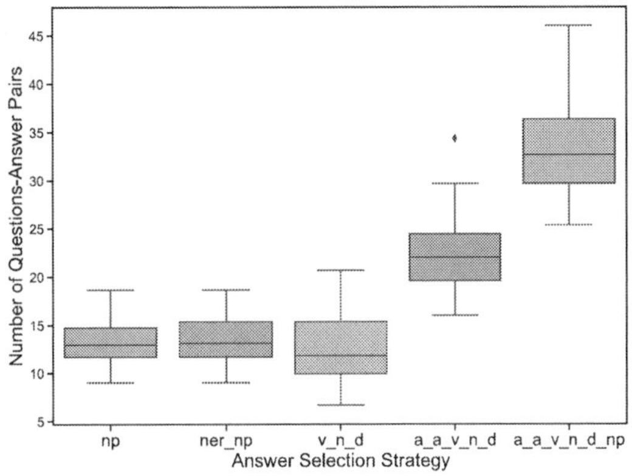

Figure 3: The number of QA pairs generated using different answer selection strategies. Abbreviations: "np" for "noun phrase", "ner_np" for "NER and noun phrase", "v_n_d" for "verb with object and subject child", "a_a_v_n_d" for "adjective, adverb, verb with object and subject child", and "a_a_v_n_d_np" for "adjective, adverb, verb with object and subject child, and noun phrase".

We further evaluated the quality of the generated question-answer pairs. A total of 715 QA pairs were generated for the 8 products in 4 categories. Similar to Deutsch et al. (2021) we calculate the SCU coverage and precision for the QA pairs. QA precision captures the amount of information expressed in the QA pairs that are also in the SCUs. SCU coverage measures the amount of information captured by the SCUs that can also be found in the QA pairs. The results can be found in Table 2. By adopting our answer selection strategy, a significant amount of the information expressed by the SCUs is captured by the generated QA pairs, with 95% coverage and 82% precision. The drop in QA precision is not surprising since we are generating questions more diversely, including information in addition to SCUs.

Strategy	QA Precision	SCUs Coverage
NP	88%	92%
Ours	82%	95%

Table 2: QA precision and SCU coverage by the generated QA pairs for 8 products in 4 categories. Our selection strategy generates QA pairs that have high information overlap with the SCUs.

In summary, we further investigated the quality of the question-answer pairs generated using our proposed strategy. We show that it generates QA pairs that are high quality by covering a significant amount of information expressed in SCUs.

Example questions and answers generated by RunQA can be found in Table 3. In the first example, the first two questions are generated based on NPs. The third question is generated using an adjective. In the first example, the reference answer and the candidate answer do not match for the first two questions, while they match for the third question, which indicates that some information of the reference summary is not captured in the candidate summary.

6 Experiments for Summary Information Quality

Introduced by Koto et al. (2020), coverage and focus are metrics designed to evaluate information in summaries. Coverage(recall) measures the amount of key information expressed in the reference summary that is also captured by the candidate summary. Focus(precision) measures the amount of primary information expressed in the candidate summary that is also true in the reference summary. To compute coverage and focus, we need to gather gold-standard scores by recruiting human annotators. Then calculate the correlation between the human annotations and the scores generated by the metrics.

We followed Koto et al. (2020) and Graham et al. (2017), and used the customised Direct Assessment method to collect human scoring annotations using the Amazon Mechanical Turk. The annotation interface is shown in Figure 4. To control possible bias in annotation, each HIT contained a balanced number of annotations for both coverage and focus using different products (30 different products). On top of the 30 required annotations, each HIT also contained 6 quality control questions. Where 3 are

Reference Summary: This purse is well-designed in terms of appearance, but not in terms of usability and reliability. It is smaller than advertised...
Candidate Summary: I love this purse! It is a bit smaller than I thought it would be, but I love it! It's a perfect size for me.
Question 1: This purse is well-designed in terms of what?
Reference Answer: appearance **Candidate Answer**: perfect size
Question 2: This purse is well-designed in terms of appearance, but not in terms of what else?
Reference Answer: usability **Candidate Answer**: NA
Question 3: How big is it than advertised?
Reference Answer: smaller **Candidate Answer**: smaller

Reference Summary: This camera bag, constructed as a backpack with padded straps and back is functional and comfortable to wear as well... It is well designed and made of durable materials...
Candidate Summary: This is the best backpack I have ever owned. It's very comfortable and holds a lot of stuff...
Question 1: What is this camera bag constructed as with padded straps and back?
Reference Answer: a backpack **Candidate Answer**: backpack
Question 2: This camera bag, constructed as a backpack with what type of straps and back is functional and comfortable to wear as well?
Reference Answer: padded **Candidate Answer**: backpack
Question 3: What type of material is it well designed and made of?
Reference Answer: durable **Candidate Answer**: NA

Table 3: Example question and answer pairs generated by RunQA.

exact match summaries that should score 100, and 3 are from random product pair summaries that should score 0.

HITs were restricted to workers from English-speaking countries, with over 10,000 approved HITs and a 98% approval rate. We first collected more than required, then filtered out annotations that failed the quality control tests. It leaves us with an uneven number of annotations per HIT (ranging between 3 and 7). For quality control, we implemented several tests. First, work is only considered if a worker passed 4 of the quality control questions. On top of the distractor questions in each HIT, we further examine workers' time spent on the task and its variation of scores similar to Graham et al. (2017). If the amount of time spent or the variation between the scores is suspiciously low, we disregard all of the worker's annotations. Lastly, the annotations are removed for workers with a Pearson Correlation to other workers(agreement score) of less than 0.2.

After quality control, a mean Pearson Correlation of 0.41 is achieved, with a reasonable average time spent (16.35 minutes) and a quality score (94.74%). Like Koto et al. (2020) and Graham et al. (2017), for annotations pass quality controls we standardise the annotation scores to a z-score of each worker before averaging. This helps remove personal bias introduced by different annotators. Then take an average among workers who completed the same HIT and use the score as the final score for that HIT. We collected both the coverage and focus scores for 180 (60×3) summary pairs.

We use various automatic metrics to generate scores for the candidate summaries based on the reference summaries, and then calculate their correlation with human annotations. Each product has 3 reference summaries, we average both the human and metric scores to one final score for each product. The original BERTScore suggested when comparing against multiple references, the maximum score should be used as the final score. We calculated both the maximum and average BERTScore and found that the average score better correlates with human judgements. Therefore, we use average BERTScore instead of maximum in this paper.

We present the Pearson, Spearman, and Kendall correlations between human annotations for coverage and focus, with various metrics. Results are shown in Tables 4 and 5, all results are significant with p-value <0.01.

The token overlap-based metrics have the weakest correlation with human judgements in both coverage and focus. Context embedding-based met-

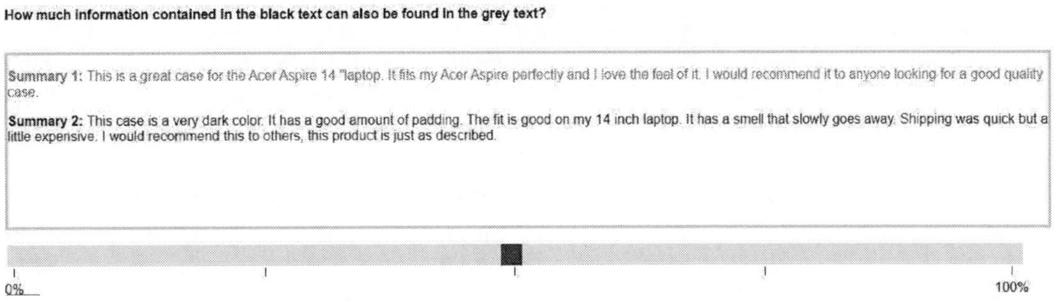

Figure 4: The interface for annotators on the Amazon Mechanical Turk platform.

Metric	r	ρ	τ
ROUGE-1	0.479	0.472	0.310
ROUGE-2	0.413	0.387	0.265
ROUGE-L	0.439	0.403	0.266
MoverScore	0.535	0.471	0.334
BERTScore	**0.599**	**0.549**	**0.398**
QAEval	0.409	0.416	0.290
RunQA (F_1)	0.460	0.484	0.344
RunQA (LERC)	**0.597**	**0.575**	**0.400**

Table 4: Pearson, Spearman and Kendall correlation coefficients of metrics (Coverage)

Metric	r	ρ	τ
ROUGE-1	0.496	0.494	0.339
ROUGE-2	0.525	0.543	0.374
ROUGE-L	0.436	0.388	0.254
MoverScore	0.609	0.597	0.432
BERTScore	**0.651**	**0.645**	**0.470**
QAEval	0.555	0.555	0.409
RunQA (F_1)	0.551	0.654	0.475
RunQA (LERC)	**0.714**	**0.712**	**0.542**

Table 5: Pearson, Spearman and Kendall correlation coefficients for metrics (Focus)

rics show a stronger correlation, especially with BERTScore. Using F_1 to evaluate answers in the QA-based models has a similar performance as the ROUGE family, where we suspect this may be due to the exact match of answers with no consideration of the questions or summaries. Compared with QAEval, correlation improves significantly for RunQA when the answer selection strategy changes to our proposed strategy. RunQA (LERC) has the strongest correlation with human judgements, performs on-par with BERTScore in coverage, and shows the strongest performance in focus.

We further calculated the Pearson correlation for the metrics. The correlation heatmap is shown in

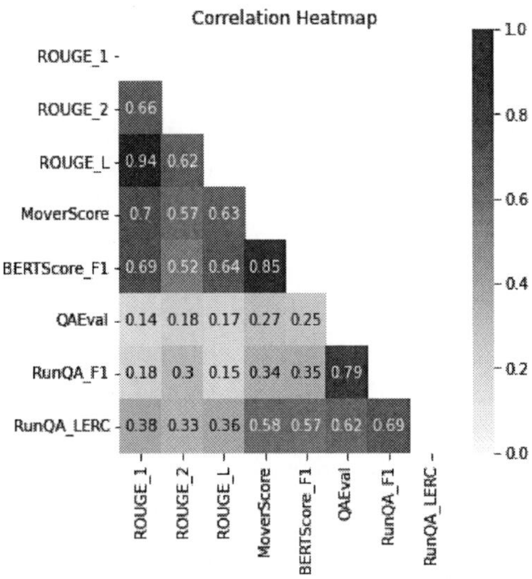

Figure 5: Pearson correlation between metrics.

Figure 5. Similar to Eyal et al. (2019) and Deutsch et al. (2021), we observe that the ROUGE family correlates well with its variants. MoverScore and BERTScore are highly correlated with each other, this is not surprising since BERTScore is a special form of MoverScore. They also have a moderate correlation with the ROUGE variants. Whereas the QA variants have a weak correlation with the ROUGE family. This result suggests that RunQA and QAEval are more likely to evaluate the information expressed in summaries, which is distinct from the lexical overlap in the ROUGE family.

7 Experiments for Ranking Summaries

One of the fundamental requirements for a summarisation metric is to rank summaries and compare the performance of summarisation systems. To simulate the scenario of system summaries with varying quality, we designed a task for ranking summaries generated using the Copycat system (Bražinskas et al., 2020b) and summaries gen-

Metric	Accuracy(%)
ROUGE-1	68.33
ROUGE-2	52.78
ROUGE-L	63.89
BERTScore	54.44
MoverScore	80.56
QAEval	77.78
RunQA (F_1)	82.22
RunQA (LERC)	**91.67**

Table 6: The percentage of each metric that successfully assigns a higher score for the ground-truth summary(human system).

erated by human annotators. We then apply the metrics to calculate the metric scores for human and system summaries. The accuracy that a metric correctly gives human summaries a score higher than that for the Copycat system indicates the reliability of the metric for comparing the human (as an ideal system) and the Copycat system.

Generally, human-generated summaries are of high quality. It is shown in Bražinskas et al. (2020b) that while human ground truth has a relatively close score in fluency compared against the Copycat model, it outperforms all other models significantly in all other dimensions, including Opinion Consensus (measuring whether the summary reflects the common opinions expressed in reviews). Therefore, we would expect the human summary to have better overall quality and should receive a higher score than the system summary.

Previous work (Nenkova and Passonneau, 2004) suggests that individuals tend to both write and pick up information in different ways. For a fair comparison, we compare the summary against different references using each metric. Then pick the higher score because it means the two summaries are closer in terms of information agreement. The same reference is then used in the comparison with the system summary.

We compare the scores generated using different metrics for the human and the Copycat system (Bražinskas et al., 2020b), and count the number of times the human system receives a higher score. Accuracy is calculated by dividing the count by the total number of references (180). The metric with higher accuracy for rating a human summary over a system summary is deemed to be more reliable with a better ability to distinguish between better summaries.

The result is presented in Table 6, BERTScore performs as poorly as the ROUGE family with only 54.44% of correct rankings. RunQA (LERC) performs the best to rank systems, and can distinguish the better quality human summary from the system-generated summary over 90% of the time. We suspect this is because RunQA ranks summaries based on answerable questions hence evaluating the information quality. The embedding-based metrics examine distance between tokens. If the layout of the summaries is similar but express opposite opinions, scores will be similar, which makes it hard to rank summaries based on information quality. As discussed in (Tay et al., 2019), ROUGE is not sensitive to opinion mismatch, which explains its poor performance.

8 Limitations

While our study has shown that RunQA is a better metric for opinion summarisation evaluation. There are some limitations with our research. First, we did the experiments using only one summarisation system. It would be more assuring if we explored other summarisation models.

The dataset (Bražinskas et al., 2020b) in our experiments is the only publicly available dataset with a significant number of products and multiple ground-truth summaries. The dataset is from the product review domain and is not representative of the other domains, such as restaurant or movie reviews. Using multiple datasets and summarisation models would give a better picture in terms of human correlation in different domains.

9 Conclusion

We proposed RunQA, which uses the Question-Answering model to evaluate review summarisation. We proposed to identify answers based on opinion-bearing token categories to generate QA pairs. Experiments on a public Amazon review summary dataset show that RunQA correlates well with human judgements for evaluating the amount of salient opinion captured in the candidate summary against the reference summary. RunQA is also more reliable than existing metrics in the literature for ranking summaries.

RunQA has shown high potential when used for opinion summarisation evaluation for opinion quality. Our future work will explore applying RunQA for review summarisation evaluation in other domains.

References

Satanjeev Banerjee and Alon Lavie. 2005. Meteor: An automatic metric for mt evaluation with improved correlation with human judgments. In *Proceedings of the acl workshop on intrinsic and extrinsic evaluation measures for machine translation and/or summarization*, pages 65–72.

Arthur Bražinskas, Mirella Lapata, and Ivan Titov. 2020a. Few-shot learning for opinion summarization. In *Proceedings of the 2020 Conference on Empirical Methods in Natural Language Processing (EMNLP)*, pages 4119–4135.

Arthur Bražinskas, Mirella Lapata, and Ivan Titov. 2020b. Unsupervised opinion summarization as copycat-review generation. In *Proceedings of the 58th Annual Meeting of the Association for Computational Linguistics*, pages 5151–5169, Online. Association for Computational Linguistics.

Anthony Chen, Gabriel Stanovsky, Sameer Singh, and Matt Gardner. 2020. MOCHA: A dataset for training and evaluating generative reading comprehension metrics. In *Proceedings of the 2020 Conference on Empirical Methods in Natural Language Processing (EMNLP)*, pages 6521–6532, Online. Association for Computational Linguistics.

Eric Chu and Peter Liu. 2019. Meansum: a neural model for unsupervised multi-document abstractive summarization. In *International Conference on Machine Learning*, pages 1223–1232. PMLR.

Kevin Clark, Minh-Thang Luong, Quoc V. Le, and Christopher D. Manning. 2020. ELECTRA: Pre-training text encoders as discriminators rather than generators. In *ICLR*.

Dorottya Demszky, Kelvin Guu, and Percy Liang. 2018. Transforming question answering datasets into natural language inference datasets. *arXiv preprint arXiv:1809.02922*.

Daniel Deutsch, Tania Bedrax-Weiss, and Dan Roth. 2021. Towards question-answering as an automatic metric for evaluating the content quality of a summary. *Transactions of the Association for Computational Linguistics*, 9:774–789.

Daniel Deutsch and Dan Roth. 2020. Understanding the extent to which summarization evaluation metrics measure the information quality of summaries. *arXiv preprint arXiv:2010.12495*.

Jacob Devlin, Ming-Wei Chang, Kenton Lee, and Kristina Toutanova. 2019. Bert: Pre-training of deep bidirectional transformers for language understanding. In *Proceedings of the 2019 Conference of the North American Chapter of the Association for Computational Linguistics: Human Language Technologies, Volume 1 (Long and Short Papers)*, pages 4171–4186.

Esin Durmus, He He, and Mona Diab. 2020. FEQA: A question answering evaluation framework for faithfulness assessment in abstractive summarization. In *Proceedings of the 58th Annual Meeting of the Association for Computational Linguistics*, pages 5055–5070, Online. Association for Computational Linguistics.

Matan Eyal, Tal Baumel, and Michael Elhadad. 2019. Question answering as an automatic evaluation metric for news article summarization. In *Proceedings of the 2019 Conference of the North American Chapter of the Association for Computational Linguistics: Human Language Technologies, Volume 1 (Long and Short Papers)*, pages 3938–3948, Minneapolis, Minnesota. Association for Computational Linguistics.

Yang Gao, Wei Zhao, and Steffen Eger. 2020. Supert: Towards new frontiers in unsupervised evaluation metrics for multi-document summarization. In *Proceedings of the 58th Annual Meeting of the Association for Computational Linguistics*, pages 1347–1354.

Yvette Graham, Timothy Baldwin, Alistair Moffat, and Justin Zobel. 2017. Can machine translation systems be evaluated by the crowd alone. *Natural Language Engineering*, 23(1):3–30.

Max Grusky, Mor Naaman, and Yoav Artzi. 2018. Newsroom: A dataset of 1.3 million summaries with diverse extractive strategies. In *Proceedings of the 2018 Conference of the North American Chapter of the Association for Computational Linguistics: Human Language Technologies, Volume 1 (Long Papers)*, pages 708–719, New Orleans, Louisiana. Association for Computational Linguistics.

Fajri Koto, Jey Han Lau, and Timothy Baldwin. 2020. Ffci: A framework for interpretable automatic evaluation of summarization. *arXiv preprint arXiv:2011.13662*.

Lun-Wei Ku, Yu-Ting Liang, Hsin-Hsi Chen, et al. 2006. Opinion extraction, summarization and tracking in news and blog corpora. In *AAAI spring symposium: Computational approaches to analyzing weblogs*, volume 100107, pages 1–167.

Mike Lewis, Yinhan Liu, Naman Goyal, Marjan Ghazvininejad, Abdelrahman Mohamed, Omer Levy, Veselin Stoyanov, and Luke Zettlemoyer. 2020. BART: Denoising sequence-to-sequence pre-training for natural language generation, translation, and comprehension. In *Proceedings of the 58th Annual Meeting of the Association for Computational Linguistics*, pages 7871–7880, Online. Association for Computational Linguistics.

Chin-Yew Lin. 2004. Rouge: A package for automatic evaluation of summaries. In *Text summarization branches out*, pages 74–81.

Xinfan Meng, Furu Wei, Xiaohua Liu, Ming Zhou, Sujian Li, and Houfeng Wang. 2012. Entity-centric topic-oriented opinion summarization in twitter. In *Proceedings of the 18th ACM SIGKDD international conference on Knowledge discovery and data mining*, pages 379–387.

Ramesh Nallapati, Bowen Zhou, Cicero dos Santos, Ça glar Gulçehre, and Bing Xiang. 2016. Abstractive text summarization using sequence-to-sequence rnns and beyond. *CoNLL 2016*, page 280.

Ani Nenkova and Rebecca J Passonneau. 2004. Evaluating content selection in summarization: The pyramid method. In *Proceedings of the human language technology conference of the north american chapter of the association for computational linguistics: Hlt-naacl 2004*, pages 145–152.

Jun Ping Ng and Viktoria Abrecht. 2015. Better summarization evaluation with word embeddings for rouge. In *Proceedings of the 2015 Conference on Empirical Methods in Natural Language Processing*, pages 1925–1930.

Jekaterina Novikova, Ondřej Dušek, Amanda Cercas Curry, and Verena Rieser. 2017. Why we need new evaluation metrics for NLG. In *Proceedings of the 2017 Conference on Empirical Methods in Natural Language Processing*, pages 2241–2252, Copenhagen, Denmark. Association for Computational Linguistics.

Kishore Papineni, Salim Roukos, Todd Ward, and Wei-Jing Zhu. 2002. Bleu: a method for automatic evaluation of machine translation. In *Proceedings of the 40th annual meeting of the Association for Computational Linguistics*, pages 311–318.

Matthew E. Peters, Mark Neumann, Mohit Iyyer, Matt Gardner, Christopher Clark, Kenton Lee, and Luke Zettlemoyer. 2018. Deep contextualized word representations. In *Proc. of NAACL*.

Pranav Rajpurkar, Robin Jia, and Percy Liang. 2018. Know what you don't know: Unanswerable questions for squad. In *Proceedings of the 56th Annual Meeting of the Association for Computational Linguistics (Volume 2: Short Papers)*, pages 784–789.

Venkatramana S Subrahmanian and Diego Reforgiato. 2008. Ava: Adjective-verb-adverb combinations for sentiment analysis. *IEEE Intelligent Systems*, 23(4):43–50.

Wenyi Tay. 2019. Not all reviews are equal: Towards addressing reviewer biases for opinion summarization. In *Proceedings of the 57th Annual Meeting of the Association for Computational Linguistics: Student Research Workshop*, pages 34–42, Florence, Italy. Association for Computational Linguistics.

Wenyi Tay, Aditya Joshi, Xiuzhen Jenny Zhang, Sarvnaz Karimi, and Stephen Wan. 2019. Red-faced rouge: Examining the suitability of rouge for opinion summary evaluation. In *Proceedings of the The 17th Annual Workshop of the Australasian Language Technology Association*, pages 52–60.

Alex Wang, Kyunghyun Cho, and Mike Lewis. 2020. Asking and answering questions to evaluate the factual consistency of summaries. In *Proceedings of the 58th Annual Meeting of the Association for Computational Linguistics*, pages 5008–5020.

Hanlu Wu, Tengfei Ma, Lingfei Wu, Tariro Manyumwa, and Shouling Ji. 2020. Unsupervised reference-free summary quality evaluation via contrastive learning. In *Proceedings of the 2020 Conference on Empirical Methods in Natural Language Processing (EMNLP)*, pages 3612–3621.

Tianyi Zhang, Varsha Kishore, Felix Wu, Kilian Q Weinberger, and Yoav Artzi. 2019. Bertscore: Evaluating text generation with bert. *arXiv preprint arXiv:1904.09675*.

Wei Zhao, Maxime Peyrard, Fei Liu, Yang Gao, Christian M. Meyer, and Steffen Eger. 2019. MoverScore: Text generation evaluating with contextualized embeddings and earth mover distance. In *Proceedings of the 2019 Conference on Empirical Methods in Natural Language Processing and the 9th International Joint Conference on Natural Language Processing (EMNLP-IJCNLP)*, pages 563–578, Hong Kong, China. Association for Computational Linguistics.

Exploring Story Generation with Multi-task Objectives in Variational Autoencoders

Zhuohan Xie **Trevor Cohn** **Jey Han Lau**
School of Computing and Information Systems
The University of Melbourne
zhuohanx@student.unimelb.edu.au, t.cohn@unimelb.edu.au, jeyhan.lau@gmail.com

Abstract

GPT-2 has been frequently adapted in story generation models as it provides powerful generative capability. However, it still fails to generate consistent stories and lacks diversity. Current story generation models leverage additional information such as plots or commonsense into GPT-2 to guide the generation process. These approaches focus on improving generation quality of stories while our work look at both quality and diversity. We explore combining BERT and GPT-2 to build a variational autoencoder (VAE), and extend it by adding additional objectives to learn global features such as story topic and discourse relations. Our evaluations show our enhanced VAE can provide better quality and diversity trade off, generate less repetitive story content and learn a more informative latent variable.

1 Introduction

Autoregressive pretrained models such as GPT-2 (Radford et al., 2019) have been frequently applied to story generation. While GPT-2 can generate coherent single sentences, it suffers from inconsistencies in the storylines and lacks *generation diversity*, i.e. the storylines tend to use "bland" language and multiple generation produces similar plot lines (Guan et al., 2021). Current story generation models add more controllability into language models for story generation, such as story plan (Yao et al., 2019) or commonsense (Guan et al., 2020). These approaches focus on improving generation quality but does not address the diversity issue.

Variational autoencoder (VAE) is an extension of autoencoder (AE) (Rumelhart et al., 1986). It defines a prior distribution and the encoder learns an approximate posterior distribution that is optimised close to the prior distribution. In doing so, the VAE is able to learn a more tractable latent space than AE and it is easier to sample meaningful latent variables to guide the generation process to generate diverse meaningful sequences.

In order to leverage pretrained models for VAE, Li et al. (2020) propose OPTIMUS, a large-scale VAE that combines BERT (Devlin et al., 2019) and GPT-2 (Radford et al., 2019) and further pretrain it on large corpus to create an off-the-shelf pretrained VAE. We follow a similar approach to build our VAE in this paper, but our aim is to develop a VAE for domain-specific story generation (rather than creating a domain-general large-scale pretrained VAE) and as such our evaluation focuses on assessing generation capability.

Our core innovation in this paper is the introduction of multi-task learning objectives to the VAE to enhance the latent variables, as Bosc and Vincent (2020) found that they tend to learn local features such as the first few words or the length of input sequences. Our first auxiliary objective uses the latent variable to learn story topics, and our second objective seeks to distinguish between original stories and "negative samples", created by altering the stories to simulate common machine generation errors. We conduct experiments on several datasets to show our proposed VAE has better quality-diversity trade off than GPT-2 and learn better latent representations than vanilla VAE.

To summarise: (1) we combine BERT and GPT-2 to build domain-specific VAE for story generation; (2) we propose an alternative approach to incorporate the latent variable into the VAE's decoder; (3) we introduce two auxiliary objectives to encourage the latent variable to capture topic information and discourse relations; and (4) we experiment with several story datasets and show that our enhanced VAE produces higher quality latent variables and generates stories with better quality-diversity trade off compared to GPT-2.

2 Related Work

Conventional approaches of automatic story generation typically contain two parts: (1) learn a language model from the training dataset with the objective of minimising KL divergence between probability distribution of training dataset and language model; and (2) find the most suitable way to decode the story from a given starting point (usually a title or the leading context) with the trained language model. Autoregressive transformers such as GPT-2 (Radford et al., 2019) and its scaled-up GPT-3 (Brown et al., 2020) mask the attention heads after the current word during training so that they can serve as language models to predict the next token. However, even large pretrained language models suffer from issues such as self-repetition, conflicting logic and incoherence (Guan and Huang, 2020).

Therefore, recent approaches resort to two main strategies to alleviate above issues, by adding more controllability into the story generation model and incorporating commonsense knowledge. One of the most influential strategies of controllability is "plan and write" (Yao et al., 2019) where they first use a RAKE algorithm to extract the most important word from each sentence and train a storyline planner based on such dataset. The language model is trained conditional on both the previous context and the keywords. During generation, the keywords are generated from the given title and can be used to guide generation of each sentence. Commonsense contains shared knowledge about the world (Alabdulkarim et al., 2021). Guan et al. (2020) fine-tune a pretrained GPT-2 with knowledge triples from commonsense datasets. They first use pre-defined rules to turn triples into sentences (e.g. `(eiffel tower, AtLocation, paris)` $\rightarrow$ "eiffel tower is at paris") and train on the knowledge sentences with conventional maximum likelihood estimation objective. Xu et al. (2020) combine these two approaches by first training a keyword planner with GPT-2 and use the keywords to search a knowledgebase to retrieve the top ranked sentences to guide the generation process.

The aforementioned approaches add complementary information in training the language model, but does not address the diversity issue in language generation. VAE can generate content with more diversity (Kingma and Welling, 2019; Yu et al., 2020), and has been variously explored in story generation. For example, Jhamtani and Berg-Kirkpatrick (2020) treat the latent variables as story plots to guide story generation and Yu et al. (2020) build a hiererchical conditional VAE draft and edit stories.

To incorporate pretrained models for building VAEs, Li et al. (2020) propose OPTIMUS, a VAE that uses BERT (Devlin et al., 2019) as the encoder and GPT-2 (Radford et al., 2019) as the decoder. They further pretrain OPTIMUS on English Wikipedia using standard VAE objectives to create an off-the-shelf pretrained VAE, and demonstrate its benefits as a pretrained model for downstream tasks. We follow their approach of using BERT and GPT-2 for building a VAE, although with a different goal: here we are interested in developing domain-specific story generators, and as such our evaluation metrics focus on assessing story generation capabilities.

Story evaluation is a challenging problem, BLEU (Papineni et al., 2002) and ROUGE (Lin, 2004) are commonly used to assess the quality of generated stories. Diversity of generated stories is another important evaluation aspect and Caccia et al. (2020) propose temperature sweep to evaluate the trade off between quality and diversity for story generation models.

3 Framework

Denoting the text sequence as x and the latent variable as z, a VAE uses the inference model (i.e. the stochastic encoder) $q_\phi(z|x)$ to approximate the posterior distribution, $p_\theta(z|x)$, since the true posterior density $p_\theta(z|x) = p_\theta(x|z)p_\theta(z)/p_\theta(x)$ is intractable (Kingma and Welling, 2014). The prior over z is set as a multivariate Gaussian $p_\theta(z) = N(z; 0, I)$. VAE is trained with the evidence lower bound (ELBO) loss:

$$\mathbb{E}_{q_\phi(z|x)}[\log p_\theta(x|z)] - D_{KL}(q_\phi(z|x)||p(z)) \quad (1)$$

The left part of equation can be interpreted as the reconstruction loss (L^R) and the right part as the KL loss (L^{KL}) that pushes the latent space close to the pre-defined prior so as to obtain a regular latent space.

We use BERT as the encoder and GPT-2 as the decoder to build a VAE language model. BERT naturally handles multiple sentences (delimited by [SEP]) and we use the [CLS] token to represent the whole story and add two linear layers on top to compute the mean (μ) and standard deviation

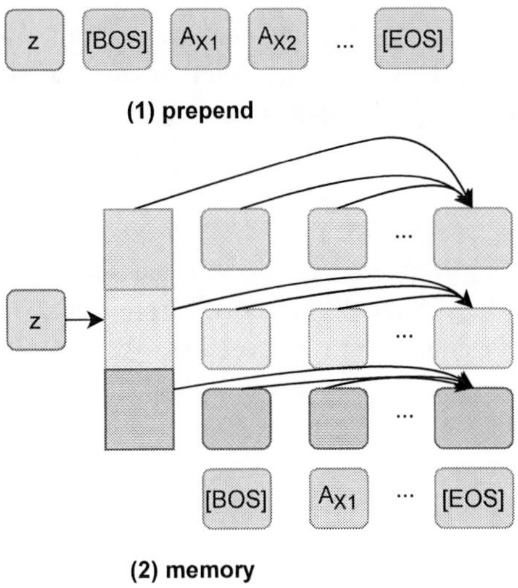

Figure 1: Illustration of three approaches of interacting the latent variable with decoder input. Both [BOS] and [EOS] are <|endoftext|> token in GPT-2. "A" denotes the first sentence of the story, x1 and x2 represent tokens of the first sentence. For the "memory" approach, different colors indicate different layers in GPT-2.

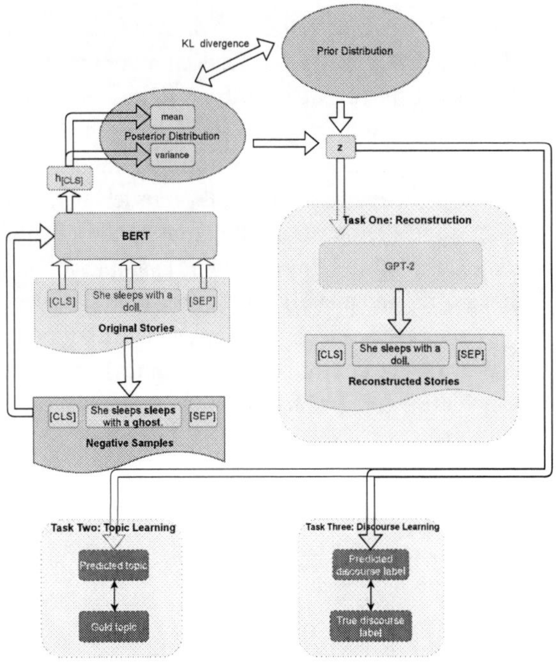

Figure 2: Our proposed multi-task VAE model with pretrained BERT and GPT-2. In additional to the original objective of reconstructing the original story, the latent variable is also used to predict the story topic and distinguish between original and negative samples. Here we show a simple one sentence story and the negative sample is constructed using repetition and substitution. Our training dataset contains stories of multiple sentences, separated by [SEP].

(σ) of the latent variable z. To incorporate the latent variable z into the GPT-2 decoder, we explore two approaches: (1) "prepend", where we append the latent variable as prefix token at the beginning of input sequence. (2) "memory", where we apply an MLP to the latent variable to generate key and values in each layer (proposed by Li et al. (2020)); and Figure 1 presents an illustration of these two approaches.

3.1 Global Feature Learning

To encourage the VAE to learn global features, we propose a multi-task learning framework. Figure 2 presents an overall architecture of our model. The first objective is the reconstruction objective (L^R, the left part of Equation 1). The two additional objectives train latent variable to: (1) predict the story topic; and (2) distinguish between negative samples vs. original stories. These auxiliary objectives are designed to encourage the latent variable to capture topic and discourse information.

Story Topic Learning We add additional MLP layers to learn the topic distribution of the story and calculate the topic loss with the ground truth topic distribution of the document based on KL divergence. While this is straightforward for topic-annotated dataset which contains ground truth topic labels, most story datasets do not have such label. To this end, we train a latent Dirichlet allocation topic model (Blei et al., 2003) to extract the topics. We use the topic model-inferred topic distribution $Q(T)$ of each document as ground truth and compute KL divergence as the loss. Note that we use the full topic distribution instead of selecting one topic with the highest probability as the representative topic as the full distribution is more informative and that most documents have multiple topics.

Given z, we predict the topic distribution $P(T)$ as follows:

$$P(T) = \text{softmax}(W_t z + b_t) \tag{2}$$

We calculate the topic loss L^T with KL divergence over the predicted and topic model-inferred topic distribution as follows:

$$L^T = \sum_{t \in T} P(t) \log \left(\frac{P(t)}{Q(t)} \right) \tag{3}$$

Story Discourse Learning For discourse relation learning, we first construct negative samples from the original stories. Following Guan and Huang (2020), we use a random combination of four heuristic rules to construct the common machine generation issues in story: (1) repeat of n-grams or sentences, (2) substitution of random keywords or the entire sentence, (3) reordering of sentences and (4) negation alteration of the original sentences. Table 1 presents some examples of original stories and altered stories (negative samples).

Given a story and its discourse label (1.0 for original stories or 0.0 for negative samples) and z, we apply a linear layer on z to compute the discourse score $\hat{y}_n$:

$$\hat{y}_n = \text{sigmoid}(W_d z + b_d) \tag{4}$$

We then compute the discourse loss L^D using standard binary cross entropy:

$$L^D = -y_n \text{log}\hat{y}_n - (1 - y_n)\text{log}(1 - \hat{y}_n) \tag{5}$$

For each original story, we create one negative sample.

Given the topic and discourse losses, we add them with weights to the original reconstruction loss and KL loss function to train the VAE and perform grid search to find the suitable weights. During training, to alleviate posterior collapse — the issue where both the variational posterior distribution obtained from the encoder and the true posterior for the real dataset collapse to the prior, resulting in zero KL loss (He et al., 2019) — we use β-VAE (Burgess et al., 2018) that sets an additional target C to the KL loss (by computing an absolute difference between KL loss and C) to optimise it close to C. The full objective our model is thus given as follows:

$$L = L^R + \beta \left|L^{KL} - C\right| + \alpha\, L^T + \gamma\, L^D \tag{6}$$

where β, α and γ are hyper-parameters to control the weights of different objetives.

4 Dataset

We use four datasets in our experiments: ROCStories, APNEWS, Reuters and WritingPrompts. APNEWS is a collection of Associated Press news (Bhatia et al., 2017) from 2009 to 2016. Reuters[1] is the Reuters-21578 "ApteMod" corpus for text categorization from the Reuters financial newswire service. ROCStories (ROC) contains commonsense stories of five sentences (Mostafazadeh et al., 2016). To obtain more generalization as all sentences are rather short in the dataset, we follow the delexicalization approach from prior studies (Guan et al., 2020; Xu et al., 2020) where male/female/unknown names are replaced by tokens [MALE]/[FEMALE]/[NEUTRAL]. The WritingPrompts (WP) dataset consists of 303,358 human generated long stories from Reddit's Writing Prompts forum[2]. Fan et al. (2018) collect them by scraping three years of prompts and their associated stories. We use 10% of the stories in our experiments. Table 2 presents some statistics of the four datasets.

In terms of preprocessing, we add [SEP] token at the end of each sentence and use WordPiece tokenizer for BERT and Byte-Pair-Encoding (BPE) for GPT-2. We set the maximum length of a story as 100 subwords for short story datasets (ROC and Reuters) and 200 for long story datasets (APNEWS and WritingPrompts).

5 Experiments

We use implementations of BERT and GPT-2 from HuggingFace (Wolf et al., 2019). We set learning rate at 10^{-4} and use Adam (Kingma and Ba, 2014) as optimiser. The dimension of latent variable is set as 256. All models are trained using 20 epochs on single NVIDIA V100 GPU node per model.

5.1 Topic Extraction

We use MALLET LDA[3] to extract the topics. We filter out tokens that appear more than half of the dataset and keep the most frequent 50K tokens as the vocabulary for the LDA models. We select the best topic number based on topic coherence (Röder et al., 2015).

5.2 Evaluation Metrics

We evaluate our system using intrinsic metrics where we compute perplexity, number of active units of language model training and the extent to which the latent variable captures topic and discourse information. To evaluate story generation capability, we look at self-repetition metrics and measure the quality-diversity trade off using Corpus-BLEU.

Perplexity (PPL) Perplexity of test data is widely used to evaluate language models. However, exact PPL is unavailable so ELBO is often

[1] https://www.kaggle.com/nltkdata/reuters

[2] https://www.reddit.com/r/WritingPrompts/

[3] http://mallet.cs.umass.edu

Rule	Original Story	Negative Sample
repeat, substitution and negation alteration	[NEUTRAL] knew the solution to a problem . he told people the solution . the people thought [NEUTRAL] was smart . [NEUTRAL] agreed with them . [NEUTRAL] went on to achieve .	[NEUTRAL] knew the solution to a problem . he told **animals** the solution . *[NEUTRAL] did not go on to achieve . he told animals the solution . he told animals the solution .*
reordering and substitution	[FEMALE] really loved the sun . she would play in it all day . one day the dark clouds came and shooed the sun away . [FEMALE] was very sad to see it go . she was happy though when she saw it back the next morning !	[FEMALE] really loved the sun . *she was happy though when she saw it back the next morning !* she would play in it all day . [FEMALE] was very sad to see it go . one day the dark clouds came and shooed the **moon** away .

Table 1: Examples of negative story samples generated from a combination of heuristic rules of repeat, substitution, reordering and negation alteration.

Collection	Average Length	Training		Development		Test	
		#Docs	#Tokens	#Docs	#Tokens	#Docs	#Tokens
APNEWS	138	46.4K	4.68M	1.9K	187K	1.8K	187K
Reuters	88	7.8K	695K	2K	180K	1K	93.6K
ROC	60	88K	5.28M	5K	0.3M	2K	0.12M
WritingPrompts	110	26.8K	2.95M	2K	0.22M	2K	0.22M

Table 2: Statistics of APNEWS, Reuters, ROC and WritingPrompts Dataset.

used to approximate the probability. But as Li et al. (2019) found, such approximation is not appropriate since the gap between ELBO and log marginal likelihood might be large when the true posterior did not converge with the approximate posterior. Burda et al. (2016) propose using k-sample importance weighting estimate, which provides a tighter lower bound for the log marginal likelihood with Jensen's inequality. Our results therefore use this approach for computing PPL.

Number of Active Units (AU) Burda et al. (2016) propose a way to evaluate if each dimension of the latent variable is active over the posterior distribution as follows:

$$A_u = \text{Cov}_x(\mathbb{E}_{u \sim q(u|x)}[u]) \quad (7)$$

and set the bar that the dimension u of the latent variable is active if $A_u > 0.01$. Intuitively, more active units means a more informative latent variable is learned from the input.

Sequence Repetition As neural generation models are prone to generate repetitive content with high probabilities (Yao et al., 2018), we evaluate sequence-level repetition evaluation by computing the portion of duplicate n-grams for a continuation $x_{k+1:k+N}$:

$$1.0 - \frac{|\text{unique n-grams}(\mathbf{x}_{k+1:k+N})|}{|\text{n-grams}|} \quad (8)$$

Corpus-BLEU and Self-BLEU Corpus-BLEU uses the test dataset as reference and compute BLEU score for each generated story and use average result as a measurement of quality. Zhu et al. (2018) propose Self-BLEU, that regards one generated story as the hypothesis and all other generated stories as the references and calculates the BLEU score for each story and use the average score to measure diversity. A lower Self-BLEU score means the story is less similar to the other generated stories, and thus, higher diversity.

5.3 Evaluation Results

5.3.1 Intrinsic Results

We first show evaluation results where we explore two methods ("memory" and "prepend") of injecting z to the decoder on ROC in Table 3. Here the models are vanilla VAE models without the auxiliary losses (as our objective here is to evaluate the

Method	C	Recon. loss	KL loss	AU	PPL
prepend	6.0	123.89	5.96	209	9.53
prepend	8.0	122.61	7.99	206	9.58
prepend	10.0	121.64	9.96	197	9.61
memory	6.0	127.67	5.94	0	9.69
memory	8.0	127.49	7.93	0	9.80
memory	10.0	127.46	9.84	0	9.96

Table 3: Intrinsic results of training with different C in beta-VAE (Equation 6) and with "prepend" and "memory" (Section 3) for incorporating the latent variable to the decoder on the ROC dataset. PPL is computed by 500 samples of importance weighting estimate.

best way to incorporate the latent variable to the VAE's decoder). Note that perplexity is estimated using 500 samples with importance weighting and it captures both reconstruction and KL loss. We found that "prepend" generally outperforms "memory", as it can keep more dimensions of the latent variable active while "memory" has no active dimensions. It also has a KL divergence marginally closer to the target (C in Equation 6), and has better reconstruction and overall better perplexity. "prepend" is in a way similar to memory where all tokens in the GPT-2 input have the extra vector to attend to, but instead of transforming it using extra MLP layers, "prepend" relies on the inherent self-attention mechanism to produce a more natural key/value representations in each layer, which might explain the improved performance.

By increasing C for the KL target, more information is encoded into the latent variable, and so the model achieves a better performance in terms of reconstruction loss. But this also means it becomes harder to sample a latent variable from the prior, as the posterior no longer matches the prior, and as such we see an increase of perplexity. Our results highlight the importance of controlling C to find a reasonable trade off between reconstruction and KL loss.

Given these results, we next train the VAE with the topic and discourse objectives (Section 3.1), using $C = 6.0$ and the "prepend" method. We now assess the extent to which the encoder can identify the topics or distinguish between the original stories and stories with flaws (negative samples).

Topic Learning Evaluation We evaluate the extent to which the BERT encoder can learn story topics in the latent space and how much the GPT-2 decoder can make use of it. We use the Reuters

Model	μ	z
AE	0.702	0.699
VAE	0.446	0.436
VAE+t	0.691	0.583

Table 4: Topic classification accuracy using mean of the posterior distribution μ and the latent variable z on Reuters.

dataset here since the documents/stories are annotated with ground truth topics.

We follow Bosc and Vincent (2020) and freeze the parameters of BERT and add one MLP layer on top of the mean of the posterior distribution μ and the latent variable z and train a classifier to predict the ground truth topics and report test accuracy results in Table 4. The baseline "AE" is a VAE model without using the KL loss (L^{KL} in Equation 1), and so functions like an autoencoder (since the posterior is no longer constrained to be close to the prior).

Looking at the results, we see that using μ as input for the classifier yields much better results compared to using the latent variable z. But as pointed out in Bosc and Vincent (2020), z is ultimately the latent variable that goes into the decoder, and so the performance using z is the more important number. There is no surprise that AE achieves better test accuracy scores with both μ and z than vanilla VAE since the VAE's encoder is forced to discard some information in the posterior distribution so as to match the prior distribution. Encouragingly, we see that our topic-enhanced VAE is indeed able to capture much of the topic information, producing a better topic classification accuracy compared to vanilla VAE.

Discourse Learning Evaluation One advantage of our discourse-enhanced VAE is that after training we can obtain a discourse score using the output of the additional layer (Equation 4), which tells us the quality of a story. Table 5 presents the predicted discourse scores on a set of generated stories. Note that all stories are generated from randomly sampled latent variables. Looking at the generated stories, we found that stories with high discourse scores are generally coherent, while stories with low scores often have logical or repetition problems. To quantify this, we compute the average discourse score on test stories and their negative samples, and the average scores are 0.75 and 0.25

Score	Story	Issue
0.83	[MALE] went fishing . he was excited about the trip . he saw a big fish . he was excited to get it . he caught a huge fish .	
0.81	[FEMALE] was nervous for her first day of school . she was nervous because she was so new to school . [FEMALE] was scared to be in the classroom . the teacher introduced her to other students . [FEMALE] was very excited to learn about her new class .	
0.56	[FEMALE] was hungry for some cookies . she decided to make some chocolate chip cookies . she mixed the ingredients together . **then she mixed them together .** [FEMALE] was happy to have some cookies .	repeat
0.48	**[FEMALE] was a lesbian . she was in love with [MALE] .** [MALE] was jealous of her . [FEMALE] 's boyfriend cheated on her . [FEMALE] was dumped .	conflict logic
0.40	[MALE] received a call from his boss . he had a promotion . **he took it . he took it anyway . he got it .**	repeat and incoherent
0.32	[MALE] grew up on a farm . [MALE] wanted to grow vegetables . **he was tired of them . [MALE] bought carrots .** he then grew vegetables .	incoherent

Table 5: Predicted discourse scores using the discourse-enhanced VAE.

respectively, showing that our discourse-enhanced VAE is able to distinguish between original stories and negative samples.

5.3.2 Extrinsic Results

Quality and Diversity Trade-off Quality and diversity of generated stories from a model can be affected by decoding strategies. Therefore, it is difficult to determine which model is superior based on a single performance since models that achieve high quality score tend to lack diversity (Caccia et al., 2020). Temperature sweep uses a set of quality and diversity results generated by altering values of temperature in temperature sampling, and the best model is one that produces the best trade off between these two aspects (Caccia et al., 2020; Hashimoto et al., 2019; Alihosseini et al., 2019). We follow this evaluation approach and use top-p sampling with varying p values as Holtzman et al. (2019) demonstrate that top-p sampling has a better control over sampling and produce sequences that have a more similar nature with human text than temperature sampling.

We use a range of different p values from 0.4 to 1.0 with an increment of 0.02, creating stories for 31 different p values to assess the quality and diversity trade off. For each p value, we sample 500 latent variables from the prior distribution to generate 500 stories. The results are shown in Figure 3. Note that we use *negative* Corpus-BLEU here (by flipping the sign), so that a lower score indicates better performance for both scores. The best model is one that produces a trade off curve closest to the axes. The figure shows that the VAEs generally achieve a better trade off than fine-tuned GPT-2 in all domains. Encouragingly, our enhanced VAEs ("VAE+t", "VAE+d" and "VAE+td") also perform generally better than the vanilla VAE (with the exception of the WP dataset). Curiously, AE is not able to generate high quality stories under our tested p values and it produces a short curve near the bottom right corner.

Sequence Repetition Self-BLEU measures the diversity of a set of generated stories, revealing whether they tend to use similar plots or share similar words. Here we assess the extent of self repetition *within a story*. We compute 4-grams repetition ("seq-rep-4"; Equation 8) and present the results in Table 6 for the ROC dataset.[4] Note that a lower score means less repetition (better performance).

We can see that higher p values produce less repetitive texts (lower scores) since at each timestep more word types are included in the sampling process. For comparison, we also compute the "human" repetition score using the test data and its result is 0.021. At lower p values, the VAE models tend to have much lower repetition than the fine-tuned GPT-2. However, if we do not constrain much on the token probabilities and use a higher p values, most models produce similar repetition scores. At the extreme when we set $p = 1.0$, all models are able to generate stories with little self-repetition like the human-written stories. AE seems to be able to repeat less, however the generated stories tend to be incoherent (recall in Figure

[4]Other domains produce similar trends and for brevity we present only the ROC results.

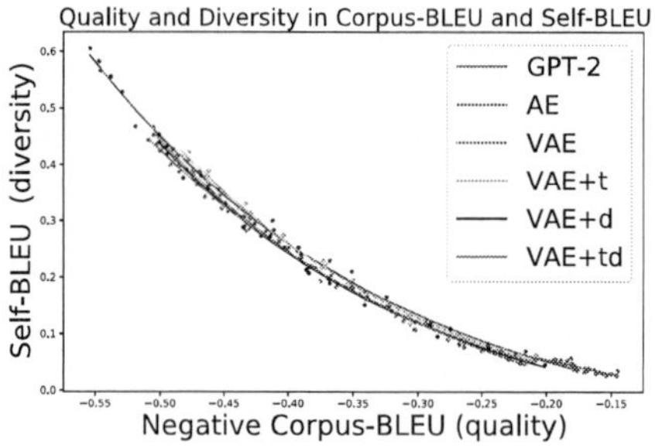

(a) ROC

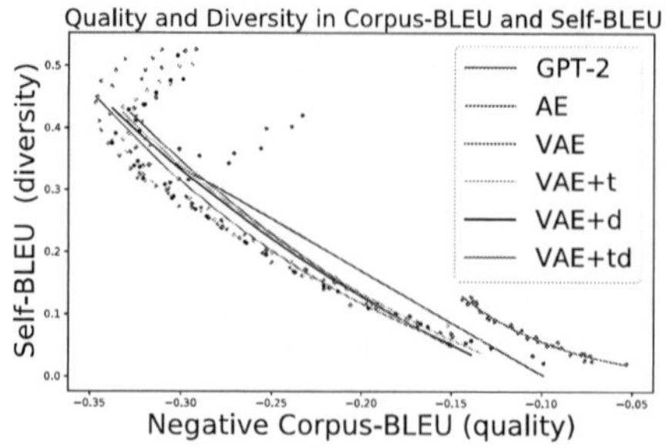

(b) WP

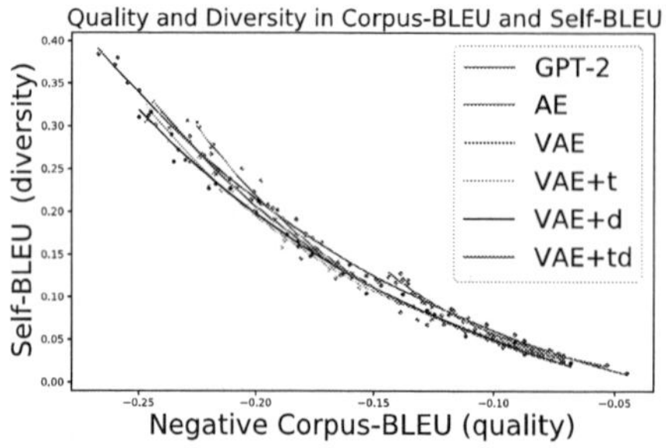

(c) APNEWS

Figure 3: Quality and diversity trade-offs of generated sentences on three dataset. For both quality and diversity metrics, lower score means better performance and the curve that is closest to the axes have the best overall performance.

Model	**p value**						
	0.4	0.5	0.6	0.7	0.8	0.9	1.0
GPT-2	0.0594	0.0300	0.0196	0.0125	0.0081	0.0043	0.0021
AE	0.0009	0.0006	0.0009	0.0004	0.0004	0.0005	0.0002
VAE	0.0297	0.0191	0.0153	0.0109	0.0070	0.0042	0.0021
VAE+t	0.0272	0.0235	0.0185	0.0124	0.0077	0.0045	0.0028
VAE+d	0.0257	0.0173	0.0143	0.0114	0.0086	0.0049	0.0031
VAE+td	0.0237	0.0218	0.0168	0.014	0.0078	0.0054	0.0031

Table 6: Sequence repetition of 4-grams of generated stories under different p values with top-p sampling on ROC.

3 we saw it has poor Corpus-BLEU scores generally).

6 Conclusion

We explore using pretrained models such as BERT and GPT-2 to build a VAE for story generation. We additionally propose enhancing the VAE by introducing two auxiliary objectives to encourage it to learn topical and discourse information in the stories. Our experiments show that the latent variable of our enhanced VAE is more informative, in that it captures the story topics and good vs. poor quality stories. In terms of story generation, we also demonstrate that our enhanced VAE produce generally a better quality-diversity trade off compared to vanilla VAE and GPT-2.

References

Amal Alabdulkarim, Siyan Li, and Xiangyu Peng. 2021. Automatic story generation: Challenges and attempts. In *Proceedings of the Third Workshop on Narrative Understanding*, pages 72–83, Virtual. Association for Computational Linguistics.

Danial Alihosseini, Ehsan Montahaei, and Mahdieh Soleymani Baghshah. 2019. Jointly measuring diversity and quality in text generation models. In *Proceedings of the Workshop on Methods for Optimizing and Evaluating Neural Language Generation*, pages 90–98, Minneapolis, Minnesota. Association for Computational Linguistics.

Shraey Bhatia, Jey Han Lau, and Timothy Baldwin. 2017. An automatic approach for document-level topic model evaluation. In *Proceedings of the 21st Conference on Computational Natural Language Learning (CoNLL 2017)*, pages 206–215, Vancouver, Canada. Association for Computational Linguistics.

David M. Blei, Andrew Y. Ng, and Michael I. Jordan. 2003. Latent dirichlet allocation. *J. Mach. Learn. Res.*, 3(null):9931022.

Tom Bosc and Pascal Vincent. 2020. Do sequence-to-sequence VAEs learn global features of sentences? In *Proceedings of the 2020 Conference on Empirical Methods in Natural Language Processing (EMNLP)*, pages 4296–4318, Online. Association for Computational Linguistics.

Tom B. Brown, Benjamin Mann, Nick Ryder, Melanie Subbiah, Jared Kaplan, Prafulla Dhariwal, Arvind Neelakantan, Pranav Shyam, Girish Sastry, Amanda Askell, Sandhini Agarwal, Ariel Herbert-Voss, Gretchen Krueger, Tom Henighan, Rewon Child, Aditya Ramesh, Daniel M. Ziegler, Jeffrey Wu, Clemens Winter, Christopher Hesse, Mark Chen, Eric Sigler, Mateusz Litwin, Scott Gray, Benjamin Chess, Jack Clark, Christopher Berner, Sam McCandlish, Alec Radford, Ilya Sutskever, and Dario Amodei. 2020. Language models are few-shot learners. *arXiv*.

Yuri Burda, Roger Grosse, and Ruslan Salakhutdinov. 2016. Importance weighted autoencoders. In *ICLR*.

Christopher P Burgess, Irina Higgins, Arka Pal, Loic Matthey, Nick Watters, Guillaume Desjardins, and Alexander Lerchner. 2018. Understanding disentangling in β-vae. *arXiv preprint arXiv:1804.03599*.

Massimo Caccia, Lucas Caccia, William Fedus, Hugo Larochelle, Joelle Pineau, and Laurent Charlin. 2020. Language gans falling short. In *8th International Conference on Learning Representations, ICLR 2020, Addis Ababa, Ethiopia, April 26-30, 2020*. OpenReview.net.

Jacob Devlin, Ming-Wei Chang, Kenton Lee, and Kristina Toutanova. 2019. BERT: Pre-training of deep bidirectional transformers for language understanding. In *Proceedings of the 2019 Conference of the North American Chapter of the Association for Computational Linguistics: Human Language Technologies, Volume 1 (Long and Short Papers)*, pages 4171–4186, Minneapolis, Minnesota. Association for Computational Linguistics.

Angela Fan, Mike Lewis, and Yann Dauphin. 2018. Hierarchical neural story generation. In *Proceedings of the 56th Annual Meeting of the Association for Computational Linguistics (Volume 1: Long Papers)*, pages 889–898, Melbourne, Australia. Association for Computational Linguistics.

Jian Guan, Fei Huang, Zhihao Zhao, Xiaoyan Zhu, and Minlie Huang. 2020. A knowledge-enhanced pretraining model for commonsense story generation. *Transactions of the Association for Computational Linguistics*, 8:93–108.

Jian Guan and Minlie Huang. 2020. UNION: An Unreferenced Metric for Evaluating Open-ended Story Generation. In *Proceedings of the 2020 Conference on Empirical Methods in Natural Language Processing (EMNLP)*, pages 9157–9166, Online. Association for Computational Linguistics.

Jian Guan, Xiaoxi Mao, Changjie Fan, Zitao Liu, Wenbiao Ding, and Minlie Huang. 2021. Long text generation by modeling sentence-level and discourse-level coherence. In *Proceedings of the 59th Annual Meeting of the Association for Computational Linguistics and the 11th International Joint Conference on Natural Language Processing (Volume 1: Long Papers)*, pages 6379–6393, Online. Association for Computational Linguistics.

Tatsunori B. Hashimoto, Hugh Zhang, and Percy Liang. 2019. Unifying human and statistical evaluation for natural language generation. In *Proceedings of the 2019 Conference of the North American Chapter of the Association for Computational Linguistics: Human Language Technologies, Volume 1 (Long and Short Papers)*, pages 1689–1701, Minneapolis, Minnesota.

Junxian He, Daniel Spokoyny, Graham Neubig, and Taylor Berg-Kirkpatrick. 2019. Lagging inference networks and posterior collapse in variational autoencoders. *CoRR*, abs/1901.05534.

Ari Holtzman, Jan Buys, Maxwell Forbes, and Yejin Choi. 2019. The curious case of neural text degeneration. *CoRR*, abs/1904.09751.

Harsh Jhamtani and Taylor Berg-Kirkpatrick. 2020. Narrative text generation with a latent discrete plan. In *Findings of the Association for Computational Linguistics: EMNLP 2020*, pages 3637–3650, Online. Association for Computational Linguistics.

Diederik Kingma and Jimmy Ba. 2014. Adam: A method for stochastic optimization. *International Conference on Learning Representations*.

Diederik P. Kingma and Max Welling. 2014. Auto-Encoding Variational Bayes. In *2nd International Conference on Learning Representations, ICLR 2014, Banff, AB, Canada, April 14-16, 2014, Conference Track Proceedings*.

Diederik P Kingma and Max Welling. 2019. An introduction to variational autoencoders. *arXiv preprint arXiv:1906.02691*.

Bohan Li, Junxian He, Graham Neubig, Taylor Berg-Kirkpatrick, and Yiming Yang. 2019. A surprisingly effective fix for deep latent variable modeling of text. In *Proceedings of the 2019 Conference on Empirical Methods in Natural Language Processing and the 9th International Joint Conference on Natural Language Processing (EMNLP-IJCNLP)*, pages 3603–3614, Hong Kong, China. Association for Computational Linguistics.

Chunyuan Li, Xiang Gao, Yuan Li, Baolin Peng, Xiujun Li, Yizhe Zhang, and Jianfeng Gao. 2020. Optimus: Organizing sentences via pre-trained modeling of a latent space. In *Proceedings of the 2020 Conference on Empirical Methods in Natural Language Processing (EMNLP)*, pages 4678–4699, Online. Association for Computational Linguistics.

Chin-Yew Lin. 2004. ROUGE: A package for automatic evaluation of summaries. In *Text Summarization Branches Out*, pages 74–81, Barcelona, Spain. Association for Computational Linguistics.

Nasrin Mostafazadeh, Lucy Vanderwende, Wen-tau Yih, Pushmeet Kohli, and James Allen. 2016. Story cloze evaluator: Vector space representation evaluation by predicting what happens next. In *Proceedings of the 1st Workshop on Evaluating Vector-Space Representations for NLP*, pages 24–29, Berlin, Germany. Association for Computational Linguistics.

Kishore Papineni, Salim Roukos, Todd Ward, and Wei-Jing Zhu. 2002. Bleu: a method for automatic evaluation of machine translation. In *Proceedings of the 40th Annual Meeting of the Association for Computational Linguistics*, pages 311–318, Philadelphia, Pennsylvania, USA. Association for Computational Linguistics.

Alec Radford, Jeffrey Wu, Rewon Child, David Luan, Dario Amodei, and Ilya Sutskever. 2019. Language models are unsupervised multitask learners. *OpenAI blog*, 1(8):9.

M. Röder, A. Both, and A. Hinneburg. 2015. Exploring the space of topic coherence measures. *Proceedings of the Eighth ACM International Conference on Web Search and Data Mining*.

David E. Rumelhart, James L. McClelland, and CORPORATE PDP Research Group, editors. 1986. *Parallel Distributed Processing: Explorations in the Microstructure of Cognition, Vol. 1: Foundations*. MIT Press, Cambridge, MA, USA.

Thomas Wolf, Lysandre Debut, Victor Sanh, Julien Chaumond, Clement Delangue, Anthony Moi, Pierric Cistac, Tim Rault, Rémi Louf, Morgan Funtowicz, and Jamie Brew. 2019. Huggingface's transformers: State-of-the-art natural language processing. *CoRR*, abs/1910.03771.

Peng Xu, Mostofa Patwary, Mohammad Shoeybi, Raul Puri, Pascale Fung, Anima Anandkumar, and Bryan Catanzaro. 2020. MEGATRON-CNTRL: Controllable story generation with external knowledge using large-scale language models. In *Proceedings of the 2020 Conference on Empirical Methods in Natural Language Processing (EMNLP)*, pages 2831–2845, Online. Association for Computational Linguistics.

Lili Yao, Nanyun Peng, Weischedel Ralph, Kevin Knight, Dongyan Zhao, and Rui Yan. 2019. Plan-and-write: Towards better automatic storytelling. In *The Thirty-Third AAAI Conference on Artificial Intelligence (AAAI-19)*.

Lili Yao, Nanyun Peng, Ralph M. Weischedel, Kevin Knight, Dongyan Zhao, and Rui Yan. 2018. Plan-and-write: Towards better automatic storytelling. *CoRR*, abs/1811.05701.

Meng-Hsuan Yu, Juntao Li, Danyang Liu, Dongyan Zhao, Rui Yan, Bo Tang, and Haisong Zhang. 2020. Draft and edit: Automatic storytelling through multi-pass hierarchical conditional variational autoencoder. *Proceedings of the AAAI Conference on Artificial Intelligence*, 34(02):1741–1748.

Yaoming Zhu, Sidi Lu, Lei Zheng, Jiaxian Guo, Weinan Zhang, Jun Wang, and Yong Yu. 2018. Texygen: A benchmarking platform for text generation models. In *The 41st International ACM SIGIR Conference on Research & Development in Information Retrieval*, pages 1097–1100.

Principled Analysis of Energy Discourse across Domains with Thesaurus-based Automatic Topic Labeling

Thomas Scelsi[1] **Alfonso Martínez Arranz**[2] **Lea Frermann**[1]
[1] School of Computing and Information Systems, The University of Melbourne
[2] Department of Chemical Engineering, The University of Melbourne
tscelsi@student.unimelb.edu.au {alfonso.arranz,lfrermann}@unimelb.edu.au

Abstract

With the increasing impact of Natural Language Processing tools like topic models in social science research, the experimental rigor and comparability of models and datasets has come under scrutiny. Especially when contributing to research on topics with worldwide impacts like energy policy, objective analyses and reliable datasets are necessary. We contribute toward this goal in two ways: first, we release two diachronic corpora covering 23 years of energy discussions in the U.S. Energy Information Administration. Secondly, we propose a simple method for automatic topic labelling drawing on domain knowledge via political thesauri. We empirically evaluate the quality of our labels, and apply our labelling to topics induced by diachronic topic models on our energy corpora, and present a detailed analysis.

1 Introduction

Policy-making in highly technical areas such as energy is deemed to require neutral input from specialised government agencies, e.g. the US's Energy Information Administration (EIA) or the International Energy Agency (IEA). Their publications are known as"grey literature", given that they are expertly produced but not peer-reviewed. In contrast to academic literature, grey literature is often freely available online and aims to be more accessible to lay readers.

Energy grey literature has been shown to display biases towards incumbent fossil fuel technologies (Martínez Arranz, 2016; Mohn, 2020), but no thorough exploration exists of the disconnect between grey and academic literature in their coverage of energy issues. In this paper, we provide a reproducible and automated assessment of topics across both literatures.

We analyse and make available two diachronic corpora derived covering 23 years of energy discussions from two EIA publications: the International Energy Outlook (IEO) and the more nationally focused Annual Energy Outlook (AEO). Parsing reports of government agencies is non-trivial due to their diverse layouts (changing over time), and text frequently disrupted with tables and graphs. We release a clean text corpus as a basis for future research on energy communication. We also make available a software tool-set for the creation and analysis of these corpora, easily generalisable to diachronic datasets in general.

We analyse the corpora using dynamic topic models (Blei and Lafferty, 2006). We compare their discussion of various facets of energy politics against the discourse in the scientific community over the same period, drawing on a corpus of abstracts of articles published in established energy journals.

By releasing our grey literature corpus, we address the reproducibility challenge of large-scale text analyses with unsupervised models like topic models in the social sciences (Müller-Hansen et al., 2020). Studies are often difficult to reproduce, compare against or build upon due to a lack of public resources, as well as ad-hoc subjective choices of the researchers. We address the latter problem by proposing a conceptually simple and theoretically sound method for automatic topic labelling, drawing from thesauri over the political domain. In summary, our contributions are:

- A diachronic dataset of grey literature from the EIA, supporting research into (a) the discussion of energy policies and technologies over time; and (b) the discussion of energy policies across outlets. We release scripts to reproduce our data set at at: `https://github.com/tscelsi/eia-diachronic-analysis`
- A topic labelling framework for policy is-

sues, leveraging the publicly available and exhaustive EuroVoc thesaurus. Publicly available at `https://github.com/tscelsi/dtm-toolkit`

- A comparison of the dynamics of energy-related topics within and between grey and academic literature with a focus on electricity generation technologies, sustainability, and geopolitics & economy.

2 Background

Topic modeling Topic models are statistical models which aim to uncover latent semantic structure of texts through a small set of distinctive topics, each of which is represented through a coherent set of words. Latent Dirichlet Allocation (LDA; Blei et al. (2003)) is probably the most widely used topic model, where each document d is modelled as a mixture of topics k, $p(k|d)$, and each topic is represented as a probability distribution over words w, $p(k|w)$. LDA is an *exchangeable* model, it is agnostic about the order of words and documents. Applications of topic models to social science questions (including our own), however, have a specific interest in the temporal development of topics.

The dynamic topic model (DTM; Blei and Lafferty (2006)) extends LDA to time series data, capturing the subtle changes of the *same* topic over time, with the intuition that over extended periods of time, discussions, themes and words surrounding the same topic change. The DTM accounts for this evolution by inducing topic proportions as well as topic representations sensitive to time t as $p(k|d,t)$ and $p(w|k,t)$, respectively. The time-specific parameters are tied through a random walk process in order to encourage a smooth change from time t to $t+1$.

Topic models and their dynamic counterparts have been extended to leverage the power of deep learning (Card et al., 2017; Dieng et al., 2020, 2019) leading to a better data fit at the cost of substantial increase in compute cost and technical expertise. In this work we will leverage the DTM as introduced above to explore the discussion of energy technologies in scientific and government publications over the past 30 years.

Topic labelling Topics as induced by the DTM are probability distributions over the vocabulary. While they are often visualized through the top N words with highest probability, a principled interpretation of their content remains a challenge. Various methods have been proposed for labelling a topic, ranging from single best word selection (Lau et al., 2010) over involved methods leveraging domain-general external resources like Wikipedia (Lau et al., 2011; Bhatia et al., 2016) by retrieving relevant phrases, which requires substantial IR and NLP overhead to process the potential label inventory. Other work has employed graph-based methods over the structured DBPedia (Hulpus et al., 2013) , generated candidate labels using WordNet (Poostchi and Piccardi, 2018) or created descriptive labels as text summaries by extracting and aggregating candidate sentences from documents highly relevant to a topic (Wan and Wang, 2016). We propose a simpler solution by leveraging structured, and broadly domain-relevant Thesauri as our label inventory. Specifically, we use the EuroVoc thesaurus, compiled by the European Union which covers all areas of European Parliament discussion (including energy policy), noting that our methods extend to any thesaurus. We propose methods for filtering the resource to a focused set of labels (§ 4.1); and mapping induced topics to one or more thesaurus labels (§ 4.3).

2.1 The EuroVoc Thesaurus

EuroVoc[1] is a multilingual thesaurus (Steinberger et al., 2014), originally developed as a framework to support hierarchical search and indexing of documents produced in the European Union (EU). It covers a wide range of political terminology, and consists of 127 general "topics", each associated with a list of phrases (cf., Table 1). EuroVoc has been used in the NLP community predominantly in the context of multi-label classification (Steinberger et al., 2012) and as a multi-lingual lexical resource (Fišer and Sagot, 2008). To the best of our knowledge, this paper is the first to leverage this openly available, expert-created resource for principled labelling of automatically learnt topics. We use the English EuroVoc in this work, leaving multi-lingual topic labelling for future work.

3 Data

3.1 Grey Literature: The EIA Corpus

We focus on publicly available documents by the US Energy Information Administration (EIA). The EIA is the longest extant energy agency and the US is the world's second energy consumer and

[1] `https://op.europa.eu/s/sCG9`

Renewable Energy: bioenergy, biogas, geothermal energy, marine energy, renewable energy, soft energy, solar energy, wind energy
Prices: reduced price, price index, price reduction, farm prices, world market price, target price, producer price, price list, price increase
Environmental Policy: nature reserve, waste recycling, industrial hazard, environmental tax, emission allowance, environmental impact

Table 1: Selected EuroVoc labels (bold) and some of their associated keyphrases.

producer of energy, being recently overtaken by China. Its *Annual Energy Outlook* (AEO) and *International Energy Outlook* (IEO) are mandated to provide US citizens and lawmakers with future-oriented evaluations of, respectively, domestic and international energy trends.[2]

We obtained all IEO and AEO releases between 1997–2020.[3] Python package `pdfminer`[4] was used to convert the PDFs to text, adjusting parser parameters to ensure adequate parsing of single- and multi-column documents.

3.2 Scientific Literature: The Journals corpus

In order to obtain a reliable corpus of academic literature to contrast against EIA publications, we select two top-ranked energy policy journals in the Scimago Journal rankings in both 1999 and 2019: *Applied Energy* and *Energy Policy*. Both are open to submissions on any technology, and deal with policy and applied engineering questions that should be closest to the concerns of the EIA. Through the Scopus Search API complete view,[5] we download all article abstracts published in these two journals for the period 1997-2020. The format is already machine-readable and contains metadata on publication date requiring only minimal data cleaning.

We assume that abstracts synthesize the main points of each paper succinctly. Future research could include analysing the entire textual content of the papers.

3.3 Corpus Analysis

We automatically split each parsed EIA report into header-paragraph pairs, which are then used as documents to train our topic models. Paragraphs and headers were identified based on font size. As mentioned previously, for the Journals corpus we focus only on the abstract paragraphs of each paper and use these as documents to train our Journals topic models. We tokenize all corpora using spaCy.

Table 2 lists various statistics for our three corpora. Given that we train topic models over documents corresponding to paragraphs in the grey literature, we verify that paragraphs are of sufficient length to support topic modelling. From the average sentence per paragraph aggregations we can see that the EIA paragraphs are longer than the Journals paragraphs, however, the Journals corpus is significantly larger than the EIA corpora.

4 Topic Labeling with Thesauri

In this section we propose a new way of assigning automatic labels to DTM topics. Even though a variety of methods for automatic topic labeling exist (Lau et al., 2010, 2011; Sorodoc et al., 2017; Hulpus et al., 2013), case studies in the social sciences have largely resorted to qualitative analysis and manual labeling (Martínez Arranz, 2015; Müller-Hansen et al., 2020), resulting in a bottleneck for analysis as well as the potential for introduction of human bias.

We introduce a general and conceptually simple method, drawing on established domain-specific thesauri as a label inventory, and propose two methods for mapping topics to a small set of labels that reflect its content. We use the EuroVoc thesaurus in our study (§ 2.1), however, our method generalizes to any domain-specific thesaurus which organizes related keyphrases into succinct labels. Formally, we describe the set of EuroVoc labels as L. Each label $l \in L$ represents a set of keyphrases[6] v in the EuroVoc thesaurus that fall under that label (Table 1).

Our method consists of two steps: (1) thesaurus filtering, in order to retain only domain-relevant labels; and (2) an algorithm to map a topic (represented as a weighted list of words) to one or more

[2] https://www.eia.gov/

[3] IE0 and AEO have been released since 1985 and 1979, respectively. Parsing earlier documents would have involved OCR, which we rejected in the interest of producing a high-quality dataset. The 2021 reports have not been released at the time of research.

[4] https://pypi.org/project/pdfminer

[5] https://dev.elsevier.com/sc_search_views.html

[6] Keyphrases can consist of one or more tokens. e.g. *mining industry*

Source	Corpus	# Paragraphs	#Token (thousands)	Avg. #sentences / paragraph	Years
EIA	AEO	2,909	1,919	18.1	1997-2020
EIA	IEO	1,411	1,475	51.42	1997-2020
Scopus	Journals	24,353	5,483	7.87	1997-2020

Table 2: Corpus statistics.

labels (each represented as an unweighted set of associated phrases). Below we describe both steps, and propose two concrete mapping algorithms.

4.1 Label Filtering

The EuroVoc thesaurus was designed to cover all policy areas within the context of the EU. However, we are often interested in a subset of policy discussions and we can increase the relevance of our label selection by constraining the choice. We first remove all EU-specific entries (coded 10XX in the EuroVoc system; e.g. "EU finance"), remove near-duplicates (e.g., "economic geography" and "political geography" consist of country names), and merge highly similar labels whose phrases' mean GloVe embeddings value have a cosine similarity greater than 0.95 (e.g. "trade" and "trade policy").

From the remaining set, we filter irrelevant labels using log-odds ratios with informative Dirichlet prior (Monroe et al., 2008; Lucy et al., 2020), a widely used method to identify words that are statistically over-represented in a focus corpus of interest C_f as those words that have a higher chance of occurrence compared to a suitably chosen reference corpus C_r. Raw log-odds have a bias toward low-frequency words, which is alleviated by the Dirichlet prior which forces high-odds terms to significantly deviate from word-specific expected value of counts (as estimated from the joint $C_f \cup C_r$). We take as our focus corpus the concatenated three energy corpora described in § 3, while our reference corpus a representative sample of discussions in the Australian parliament, reflecting general political discourse as covered in EuroVoc.[7]

We calculate the log odds scores for all the terms in the EuroVoc dictionary, and associate each EuroVoc label l with a relevance score s_l as the median log-odds score of its associated terms in EuroVoc,

$$s_l = \text{median}(\{LO(v)\} : v \in V^{C_f} \cap V^l), \quad (1)$$

[7]See https://www.aph.gov.au/Parliamentary_Business/Hansard

where V^{C_f} and V^l is the corpus vocabulary and the set of keyphrases under label l, respectively, and $LO(v)$ is the log-odds score of term v. We finally retain the top 40 labels with highest s_l as our energy topic label inventory.

4.2 DTM Topic Representation

The DTM learns one topic representation per time period, however, we want to assign EurVoc labels to topics as a whole. We obtain a single, global representation for each topic k as its aggregate weighted sum over all time steps t, where the terms at each timestep are weighted by that topic's probability of occurrence at that time. We then retain the 10 terms with highest score, and re-normalize the resulting scores to a valid probability distribution. The resulting topic representation is a 10-dimensional unit vector, which we denote as $\hat{k}$, and we refer to a word w's probability under this representation as $\hat{k}[w]$.

4.3 Topic Labeling

Given a DTM topic k represented as $\hat{k}$, we want to assign the top N EuroVoc labels that best match the topics content. We approach the automatic labelling task in two ways. The first is a match-based approach and the second uses word embeddings to label topics.

4.3.1 Importance-Based Topic Labeling

Intuitively, a label is relevant to a learnt topic if (a) it contains the topic's most relevant terms; and (b) these keyphrases are unique to the label, and do not occur widely across EuroVoc labels ("keyphrase uniqueness"). If a term occurs in many labels, it is often less informative as it loses the ability to distinguish labels. We quantify term-topic relevance as $\hat{k}[w]$ the probability of w in the re-normalized topic representation; and keyphrase uniqueness as $TFIDF[w, l]$, the TFIDF value of w under l, where the documents are all EuroVoc labels. The final topic-label score $\sigma_{k,l}^{imp}$ is

$$\sigma_{k,l}^{imp} = \sum_{w \in \hat{k} \cap l} \hat{k}[w] \times TFIDF[w, l]. \quad (2)$$

We define the intersection in the summation based on either a full or a sub-token match between topic term and label keyphrase (e.g., topic term *solar* would match label keyphrase *solar energy*).

The proposed method is fast and simple to implement, and requires no resources beyond the trained topics and thesaurus labels. A disadvantage is its string-matching approach, which is oblivious to synonyms, or thematically related words. Our second labeling approach addresses this weakness.

4.3.2 Embedding-based Topic Labeling

The second approach makes use of pre-trained word embeddings. At a high level we produce an aggregated representation of our top word vector $\hat{k}$ as well as each EuroVoc label l in word vector space. We obtain a similarity score as the cosine similarity between the topic and label embeddings.

We use 50-dimensional pre-trained GloVe embeddings (Pennington et al., 2014).[8] We convert our top word vector $\hat{k}$ into an embedding-based vector emb_k, by taking a *weighted* average of the GloVe embedding representations of each word in it, where each word embedding is weighted by the words topic relevance $\hat{k}[w]$. An embedding for label l, emb_l, is computed as an unweighted average over its keyphrases. Multi-token topic terms (or keyphrases in EuroVoc) are represented as an unweighted average over their token embeddings.

The relevance score σ_k^l for DTM topic k and EuroVoc label l is then defined as the cosine similarity between their representations,

$$\sigma_{k,l}^{emb} = \text{cosine\_sim}(emb_k, emb_l). \quad (3)$$

We finally associate each topic with its top $I \geq 1$ associated labels as measured by either $\sigma_{k,l}^{imp}$ or $\sigma_{k,l}^{emb}$.

5 Experiment Settings

Our experiments consist of two parts. The first empirically evaluates the effectiveness of our proposed topic labelling method (§ 6) and the second leverages these labels to support a large-scale diachronic investigation of the discussion of energy technologies in the grey- and scientific literature (§ 7). We use the official DTM implementation.[9] Automatic model selection for topic models is an open research problem, where automatic methods such as normalized pointwise mutual information (NPMI) do not always correlate well with human judgment. As a consequence, especially in non-technical fields, researchers resort to their domain knowledge when selecting a parameterization. We selected a DTM parameterization based on a combination of NPMI scores and modelers' expectation in terms of topic variation over time. As a result, we set the number of topics K=30, and the topic variance parameter σ=0.05, and use default values for all other parameters. We applied the DTM with the above parameters independently to the three corpora described in § 3. All experiments below are based on the induced topics.

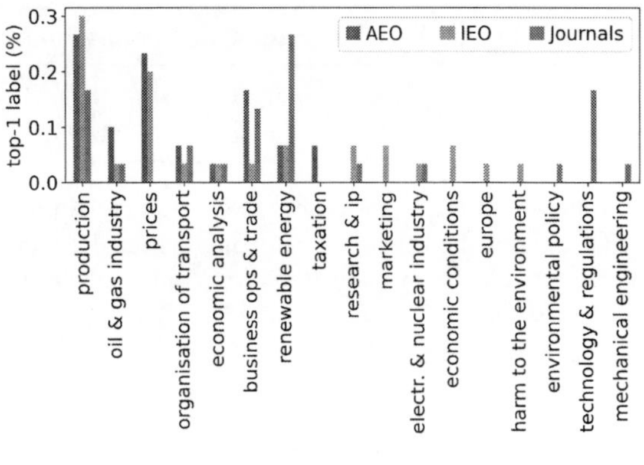

Figure 1: Proportion (%) of topics assigned a particular EuroVoc entry as top-1 topic label for our three corpora, using the embedding-based approach.

6 Topic Labeling Evaluation

6.1 Qualitative Analysis

We applied our topic labelling methods to the three corpora introduced in § 3, and inspected the distribution of top-1 (i.e., most highly associated) labels. The results for the Embedding method are shown in Figure 1. We can see that (a) the labels are varied and cover intuitively relevant aspects of energy-related discussions in government and academia; and (b) that the label distribution differs across corpora in meaningful ways. For example, *Renewable energy* is much more prevalent in the Journals dataset. Table 4 shows examples of induced topics represented as their 10 most highly associated terms with Embedding- and TFIDF-based top-2

[8] *'glove-wiki-gigaword-50'* obtained through https://radimrehurek.com/gensim/downloader.html.

[9] https://github.com/blei-lab/dtm

Strategy	TFIDF	Embedding	Baseline
Top-1	0.46	0.47	0.07
Top-4	0.45	0.47	0.08

Table 3: Human preferences (%) of automatic topic labeling methods when considering the top-1 or top-4 predicted labels by our methods or a random baseline.

labels.

6.2 Quantitative Evaluation

We evaluated our thesaurus-based topic labeling approach through human judgements. We obtained annotations from a group of 36 annotators who are proficient English speakers. All but one annotator were not domain experts. We presented annotators with DTM-induced topics, together with three label options: one based on the TFIDF mapping, one based on the Embedding-based mapping, and a randomly selected label. Annotators were asked to select the most appropriate label in a forced-choice paradigm. Given that we want to compare what label best represents a topic when our strategies differ, we do not include topics in the task where the embedding and TFIDF labels are automatically assigned the same label. Over our three models, this occurs for 23 topics. We evaluated two versions of our strategy: one where we paired each topic k with the single most highly associated label l in terms of labeling score $\sigma^*_{l,k}$ (top-1); and a second where we associate topics with their four most associated labels, capturing a mixture of information (top-4). Each annotation task consisted of a random sample of 30 out of a total of 90 induced topics (30 per corpus). We collected 20 sets of annotations for the top-4 strategy, and 16 sets for the top-1. Table 3 summarizes the human preferences. We can see that both our strategies significantly outperform the random baseline from filtered topics. In both the top-1 and top-4 strategy we see no difference between annotator preference toward either the TFIDF or embedding labelling strategy. The same pattern holds for each individual corpus.

We acknowledge the simple setup of our human evaluation, and leave comparison against stronger models for future work. The user study shows that non-experts can discern meaningful labels from our method, and as such complements our intrinsic qualitative label evaluation (§ 6.1), and our label-based case study of diachronic energy discussion which we present next.

7 Energy Discussions in EIA and Journals over Time

We present a broad analysis of the discussion of energy technologies in the grey- and scientific literature, showcasing the utility of our labeling scheme. We cover the following overarching themes: Electricity Generation Technologies, Sustainability and Geopolitics & Economy. We provide representative selection of DTM-induced topics for each of our corpora, with their automatically assigned labels, in Tables 5–7 in the appendix.

7.1 Electricity Generation Technologies

The EIA discusses electricity generation in detail as part of both AEO and IEO. Figure 2 shows how selected terms change over time in a topic on electricity generation in the AEO (2a), labelled as *Production*. We see similar patterns of discussion surrounding various energy sources in the IEO (2b). In both outlets natural gas and renewables increase in prevalence over time while coal (AEO) and nuclear (IEO) decrease. 2c shows the actual changes in generation (U.S. Energy Information Administration, 2021). These depictions allow us to more objectively assess how these two outlets have forecast, or not, the evolution of the energy system. The contrast between 2a and 2c is particularly illustrative as we see that the AEO has a somewhat belated reaction to the increase in new renewables (wind & solar) generation. The spike in the IEO topic on renewable energy only towards the end of the last decade is also remarkable, given that the situation in Europe, China and other major producers was similar to the US depicted in Figure 2c.

We also leverage our automatic labelling to uncover change within a topic over time. We create a normalised representation for a topic through its top 10 most probable words at each timestep, renormalized to sum to one, which we call $\hat{k}_t$. We assign topic labels to each $\hat{k}_t$ using the Embedding-based labelling strategy. Taking again IEO's topic "Renewable energy" on electricity generation as an example, Figure 3 shows how the top-3 labels assigned to this topic change in prevalence over time. Initially, we observe *renewable energy* and *electrical and nuclear industries* being discussed in similar proportions while *oil and gas industry* is less prevalent. By 2020 *renewable energy* is the most prevalent label for this topic, while *Oil and gas industry* is discussed in the same proportion as *electrical and nuclear industries*. Our assigned

Corpus	Topic terms	Embedding	TFIDF
Journals	market; price; electricity; paper; competition; company; investment; risk; reform; industry	1 business ops & trade 2 production	1 prices 2 business ops & trade
AEO	resource; oil; production; natural_gas; tight; gas; shale_gas; drilling; estimate; technology	1 oil & gas industry 2 renewable energy	1 oil & gas industry 2 production
IEO	projection ; energy ; eia ; model ; international ; outlook ; include ; analysis ; world ; case	1 economic analysis 2 research & ip	1 renewable energy 2 world organisations

Table 4: One topic from each of our corpora, with its top-2 EuroVoc labels as assigned by the embedding and tfidf-strategy, respectively.

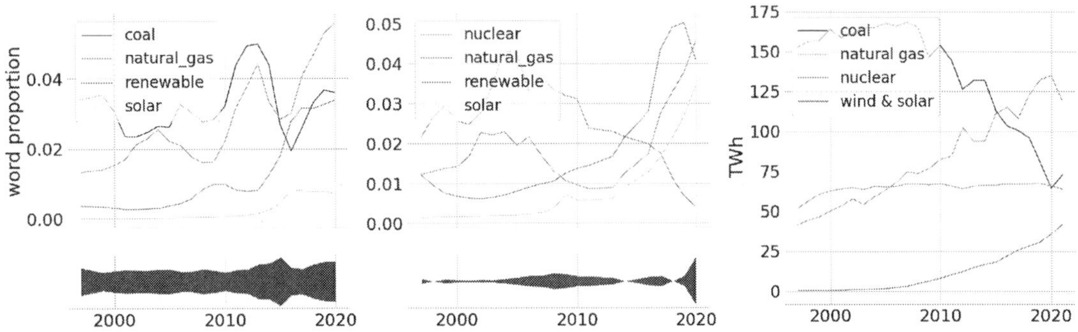

(a) AEO topic 0 (Production). (b) IEO topic 27 (Renewable Energy). (c) Real U.S. electricity generation

Figure 2: Change in word (top) and topic (bottom; blue bar) prevalence over time for two topics related to electricity generation (a) and (b). (c) shows real generation statistics for the U.S.

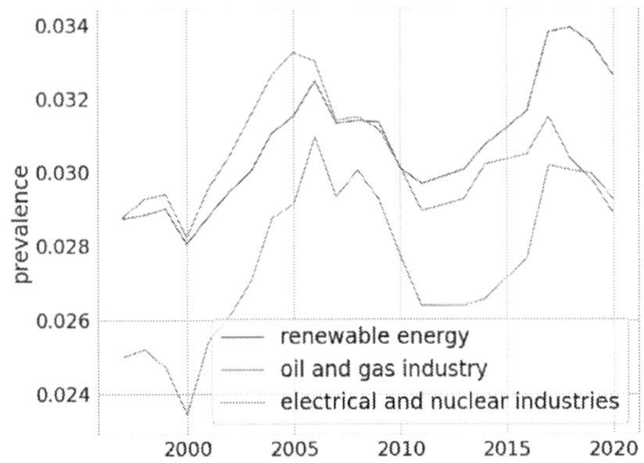

Figure 3: Label prevalence change over time for IEO topic 27 (Renewable Energy) (same as Figure 2b).

labels confirm the trends exhibited by topic-word prevalences in Figure 2.

7.2 Sustainability

Our automatic topic labels allow us to identify differences in discussion between publications. We combine topics from a model that have the same top-1 automatically assigned label by summing their proportions over time.[10] We sum again over all topics that have the same top-1 label assignment to achieve an overall proportion for the top-1 label at timestep t. We present the results in Figure 4.[11]

We can see that the Journals corpus has a larger focus on renewable energy and sustainability than AEO and IEO. The *renewable energy* and *environmental damage* top-1 label is much more prevalent in discussion in the Journals corpus. We confirm this by inspecting the learnt representations of topics in Journals by the DTM. Emissions are discussed from various perspectives including fuel sources (topic 29), China and coal (topic 22) and emission reduction (topic 4). The respective topics and their associated labels are shown in Table 5 in the appendix. We also see in topics not explicitly surrounding emissions mention of emission-reducing technologies such as 'chp' (combined heat and power) and 'ccs' (carbon capture and storage) and increase in 'energy_efficiency' and 'efficiency' terms over time in many topics, suggesting that even in non-explicit emission topics, sustainability and emission-reducing technologies are of increasing importance. This is exemplified

[10]For a topic k, it's topic proportion at a timestep t, $p(k|t)$, can be calculated by marginalising over the documents d at that timestep.

[11]We utilise the open-source plotting strategy implemented by Müller-Hansen (Müller-Hansen et al., 2021).

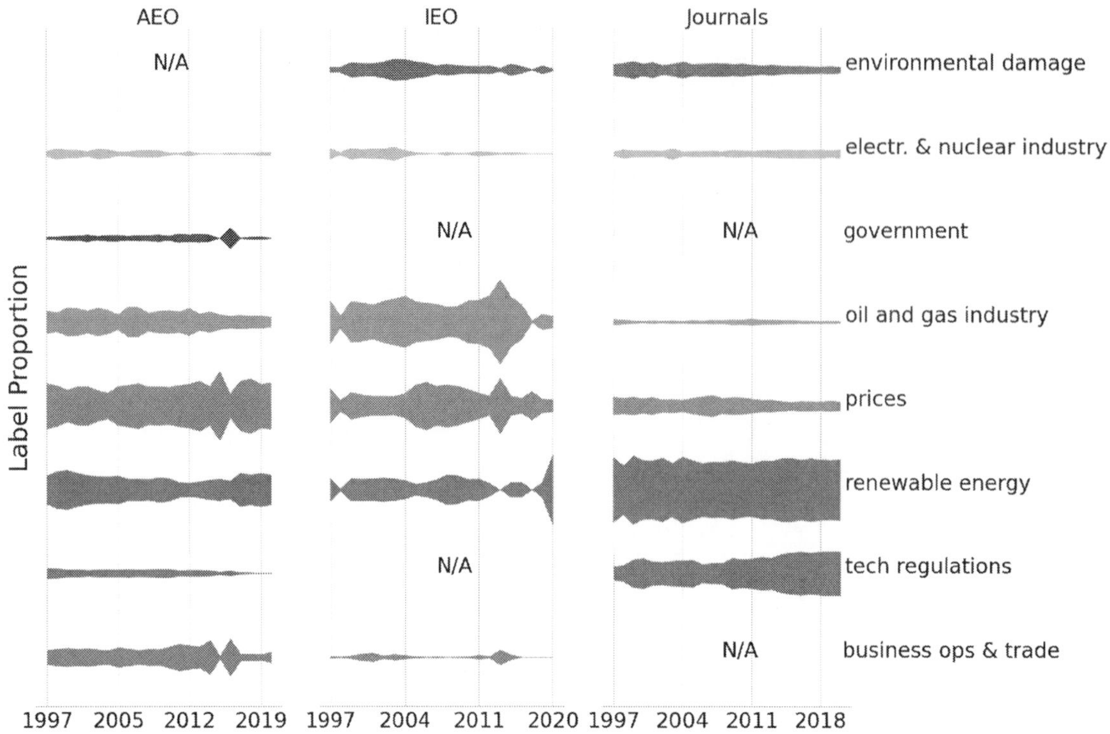

Figure 4: Comparison of discussions in the AEO, IEO and Journals. Topics were grouped by top-1 label.

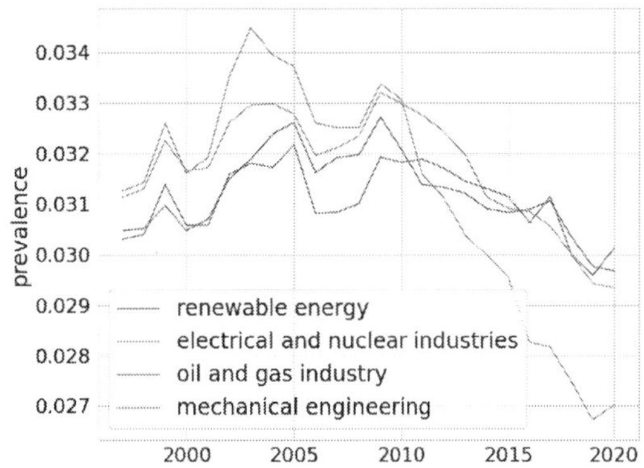

Figure 5: Label prevalence change over time for Journals topic 27 (Electric & nuclear industry).

in Figure 5, a topic on electricity generation with an early focus on electricity, oil and gas which is replaced in later years by renewables and mechanical engineering, indicating a shift toward sustainable technological development.

7.3 Economy and Geopolitics

Taking the same strategy we can analyse in Figure 4 the difference in discussion between the three outlets in terms of economic factors, see topics *prices* and *business ops & trade*. We see a large discrepancy between the proportion of discussion in the AEO and IEO corpora compared to the Journals corpus, and economic discussions are most prominent in the AEO corpus. This is expected as the AEO discusses prices and economy from a national perspective, while the IEO outlet instead discusses global markets and trade between countries. Surprisingly, the Journals dataset discusses *prices* very little proportional to other themes and does not discuss trade enough for it ever to be assigned as a top-1 label in any topic. We also note that most topics in AEO and IEO, particularly those related to economy and the oil industry, exhibit jumps in prevalence around the year 2015. This coincides with geopolitical events like the Paris Climate summit and follow-up policies like Obama's 2016 Clean Power Plan (CPP) in the U.S. Overall, our analysis again suggests a disconnect between corpora. Scientific journals show less concern for economic effects and more about regulatory aspects compared with the EIA.

8 Conclusions

We presented a novel method for topic labeling leveraging domain-relevant structured resources. We empirically showed the quality of our approach through human evaluation, and through its application in a detailed analysis of discussions on energy policy over the past 23 years. We highlighted differences in the discussions around electricity generation, sustainability and economy between nationally and internationally focused reports from the EIA and scientific publications over the same period. We release our grey literature corpora and software tool-set to support future research.

There are several areas of future work. In terms of down-stream analyses, our labelling framework can support additional comparisons for example across countries or other agencies such as non-governmental organizations; and can be extended to different thesauri, with different focus or level of detail. For example, EuroVoc captures all of *renewable energy* under a single label. Future work could also involve automatic splitting of assigned labels for example based on further hierarchical clustering of keyphrases associated with a label.

References

Shraey Bhatia, Jey Han Lau, and Timothy Baldwin. 2016. Automatic labelling of topics with neural embeddings. In *Proceedings of COLING 2016, the 26th International Conference on Computational Linguistics: Technical Papers*, pages 953–963, Osaka, Japan. The COLING 2016 Organizing Committee.

David M Blei and John D Lafferty. 2006. Dynamic topic models. In *Proceedings of the 23rd international conference on Machine learning*, pages 113–120.

David M Blei, Andrew Y Ng, and Michael I Jordan. 2003. Latent dirichlet allocation. *the Journal of machine Learning research*, 3:993–1022.

Dallas Card, Chenhao Tan, and Noah A Smith. 2017. Neural models for documents with metadata. *arXiv preprint arXiv:1705.09296*.

Adji B Dieng, Francisco JR Ruiz, and David M Blei. 2019. The dynamic embedded topic model. *arXiv preprint arXiv:1907.05545*.

Adji B Dieng, Francisco JR Ruiz, and David M Blei. 2020. Topic modeling in embedding spaces. *Transactions of the Association for Computational Linguistics*, 8:439–453.

Darja Fišer and Benoît Sagot. 2008. Combining multiple resources to build reliable wordnets. In *International Conference on Text, Speech and Dialogue*, pages 61–68. Springer.

Ioana Hulpus, Conor Hayes, Marcel Karnstedt, and Derek Greene. 2013. Unsupervised graph-based topic labelling using dbpedia. In *Proceedings of the sixth ACM international conference on Web search and data mining*, pages 465–474.

Jey Han Lau, Karl Grieser, David Newman, and Timothy Baldwin. 2011. Automatic labelling of topic models. In *Proceedings of the 49th Annual Meeting of the Association for Computational Linguistics: Human Language Technologies*, pages 1536–1545, Portland, Oregon, USA. Association for Computational Linguistics.

Jey Han Lau, David Newman, Sarvnaz Karimi, and Timothy Baldwin. 2010. Best topic word selection for topic labelling. In *Coling 2010: Posters*, pages 605–613, Beijing, China. Coling 2010 Organizing Committee.

Li Lucy, Dorottya Demszky, Patricia Bromley, and Dan Jurafsky. 2020. Content analysis of textbooks via natural language processing: Findings on gender, race, and ethnicity in texas us history textbooks. *AERA Open*, 6(3):2332858420940312.

Alfonso Martínez Arranz. 2015. Carbon capture and storage: Frames and blind spots. *Energy Policy*, 82(0):249–259.

Alfonso Martínez Arranz. 2016. Hype among low-carbon technologies: carbon capture and storage in comparison. *Global Environmental Change*, 41:124–141.

Klaus Mohn. 2020. The gravity of status quo: A review of iea's world energy outlook. *Economics of Energy & Environmental Policy*, 9(1).

Burt L Monroe, Michael P Colaresi, and Kevin M Quinn. 2008. Fightin'words: Lexical feature selection and evaluation for identifying the content of political conflict. *Political Analysis*, 16(4):372–403.

Finn Müller-Hansen, Max W Callaghan, Yuan Ting Lee, Anna Leipprand, Christian Flachsland, and Jan C Minx. 2021. Who cares about coal? analyzing 70 years of german parliamentary debates on coal with dynamic topic modeling. *Energy Research & Social Science*, 72:101869.

Finn Müller-Hansen, Max W. Callaghan, and Jan C. Minx. 2020. Text as big data: Develop codes of practice for rigorous computational text analysis in energy social science. *Energy Research & Social Science*, 70:101691.

Jeffrey Pennington, Richard Socher, and Christopher D Manning. 2014. Glove: Global vectors for word representation. In *Proceedings of the 2014 conference on empirical methods in natural language processing (EMNLP)*, pages 1532–1543.

Hanieh Poostchi and Massimo Piccardi. 2018. Cluster labeling by word embeddings and wordnet's hypernymy. In *Proceedings of the Australasian Language Technology Association Workshop 2018*, pages 66–70.

Ionut Sorodoc, Jey Han Lau, Nikolaos Aletras, and Timothy Baldwin. 2017. Multimodal topic labelling.

In *Proceedings of the 15th Conference of the European Chapter of the Association for Computational Linguistics: Volume 2, Short Papers*, pages 701–706, Valencia, Spain. Association for Computational Linguistics.

Ralf Steinberger, Mohamed Ebrahim, Alexandros Poulis, Manuel Carrasco-Benitez, Patrick Schlüter, Marek Przybyszewski, and Signe Gilbro. 2014. An overview of the european union's highly multilingual parallel corpora. *Language resources and evaluation*, 48(4):679–707.

Ralf Steinberger, Mohamed Ebrahim, and Marco Turchi. 2012. Jrc eurovoc indexer jex-a freely available multi-label categorisation tool. In *Proceedings of the Eighth International Conference on Language Resources and Evaluation (LREC'12)*, pages 798–805.

U.S. Energy Information Administration. 2021. Electricity generation, capacity, and sales in the United States - U.S. Energy Information Administration (EIA). [Online; accessed 1. Oct. 2021].

Xiaojun Wan and Tianming Wang. 2016. Automatic labeling of topic models using text summaries. In *Proceedings of the 54th Annual Meeting of the Association for Computational Linguistics (Volume 1: Long Papers)*, pages 2297–2305.

A Example DTM topics and labels

Tables 5–7 show for each of our corpora a set of induced topics. For each topic, we also provide the top-4 assigned EuroVoc by the Embedding and the TFIDF strategy, respectively. Topic 4, 22 and 29 of the Journals corpus are discussed in the results section. All other topics were chosen to be a representative sample of the discussion of the respective corpus to which they fall under.

ID	Top 10 Topic terms	Embedding	TFIDF
0	power; system; heat; generation;electricity; chp; energy; electric; district_heating; electrical	renewable energy (0.88); mechanical engineering (0.86); electronics and electrical engineering (0.84); technology and technical regulations (0.83)	electrical and nuclear industries (9.47); business operations and trade (4.88); renewable energy (3.67); organisation of transport (2.0)
4	emission; carbon; reduction; cost; ghg; greenhouse_gas; reduce; policy; result; country	deterioration of the environment (0.79); environmental policy (0.78); renewable energy (0.77); production (0.74)	environmental policy (15.19); accounting (2.61); deterioration of the environment (1.4); economic conditions (1.15)
22	china; carbon; reduction; sector; reduce; intensity; result; energy; increase	environmental policy (0.84); renewable energy (0.82); production (0.81); deterioration of the environment (0.81)	environmental policy (13.92); asia and oceania (3.85); renewable energy (2.15); economic conditions (1.71)
28	energy; energy_efficiency; building; system; paper; analysis; indicator; measure; present; energy_consumption	renewable energy (0.96); environmental policy (0.86); production (0.85); technology and technical regulations (0.85)	renewable energy (22.08); world organisations (5.76); electrical and nuclear industries (3.9); building and public works (1.86)
29	engine; fuel; emission; injection; diesel; co; combustion; high; low; increase	mechanical engineering (0.84); renewable energy (0.8); electrical and nuclear industries (0.8); oil and gas industry (0.8)	environmental policy (4.61); oil and gas industry (3.32); mechanical engineering (2.67); electrical and nuclear industries (1.28)

Table 5: Five example topics induced from the **Journals corpus**, with their top-4 EuroVoc labels (scores) as assigned by the Embedding and TFIDF-strategy, respectively.

ID	Top 10 Topic terms	Embedding	TFIDF
1	coal; ton; production; cost; percent; productivity; export; u.s; increase; region	oil and gas industry (0.89); coal and mining industries (0.88); production (0.81); renewable energy (0.77)	coal and mining industries (16.94); production (4.35); regions and regional policy (2.82); accounting (2.19)
17	gasoline; ethanol; gallon; fuel; mtbe; sulfur; blend; motor; percent; requirement	oil and gas industry (0.85); renewable energy (0.72); food technology (0.7); deterioration of the environment (0.69)	oil and gas industry (2.69); electrical and nu clear industries (0.81); taxation (0.35); organisation of transport (0.19)
19	vehicle; fuel; sale; percent; economy; new; increase; hybrid; car; standard	organisation of transport (0.88); production (0.88); prices (0.86); marketing (0.83)	economic conditions (8.02); organisation of transport (5.56); marketing (5.1); land transport (3.21)
21	emission; carbon; co; ton; metric; ghg; carbon_dioxide; energy; relate; percent	renewable energy (0.78); oil and gas industry (0.76); deterioration of the environment (0.74); electrical and nuclear industries (0.73)	environmental policy (11.52); renewable energy (2.28); deterioration of the environment (1.24); technology and technical regulations (1.21)
29	cost; market; electricity; price; competitive; customer; state; utility; transmission; power	prices (0.91); business operations and trade (0.91); production (0.9); accounting (0.9)	prices (26.58); business operations and trade (14.09); accounting (5.78); environmental policy (3.57)

Table 6: Five example topics induced from the **AEO corpus**, with their top-4 EuroVoc labels (scores) as assigned by the Embedding and TFIDF-strategy, respectively.

ID	Top 10 Topic terms	Embedding	TFIDF
5	coal; import; ton; export; increase; percent; world; project; trade; coke_coal	oil and gas industry (0.9); coal and mining industries (0.88); production (0.82); renewable energy (0.77)	coal and mining industries (15.34); business operations and trade (8.08); world organisations (1.28); deterioration of the environment (1.18)
6	natural_gas; cubic; foot; gas; lng; reserve; increase; percent; year; production	oil and gas industry (0.88); renewable energy (0.85); production (0.84); deterioration of the environment (0.82)	oil and gas industry (2.01); production (2.01); environmental policy (1.01); agricultural activity (0.99)
9	coal; china; world; percent; use; increase; consumption; share; total; btu	production (0.87); business operations and trade (0.83); oil and gas industry (0.83); prices (0.83)	coal and mining industries (11.93); business operations and trade (4.49); asia and oceania (2.47); world organisations (2.1)
25	emission; sulfur; reduce; reduction; standard; fuel; new; require; target; dioxide	deterioration of the environment (0.82); renewable energy (0.8); environmental policy (0.8); electrical and nuclear industries (0.78)	environmental policy (10.89); technology and technical regulations (2.3); oil and gas industry (1.43); asia and oceania (0.94)
27	generation; natural_gas; renewable; nuclear; capacity; electricity; cost; increase; coal; power	renewable energy (0.91); electrical and nuclear industries (0.88); production (0.87); oil and gas industry (0.84)	electrical and nuclear industries (8.21); coal and mining industries (2.97); accounting (2.36); demography and population (1.75)

Table 7: Five example topics induced from the **IEO corpus**, with their top-4 EuroVoc labels (scores) as assigned by the Embedding and TFIDF-strategy, respectively.

Robustness Analysis of Grover for Machine-Generated News Detection

Rinaldo Gagiano[1]
S3870806@student.rmit.edu.au
Xiuzhen Zhang[1]
xiuzhen.zhang@rmit.edu.au

Maria Myung-Hee Kim[2]
maria.kim@dst.defence.gov.au
Jennifer Biggs[2]
jennifer.biggs@dst.defence.gov.au

[1] School of Computing Technologies, RMIT University, Australia
[2] Defence Science and Technology Group, Australia

Abstract

Advancements in Natural Language Generation have raised concerns on its potential misuse for deep fake news. Grover is a model for both generation and detection of neural fake news. While its performance on automatically discriminating neural fake news surpassed GPT-2 and BERT, Grover could face a variety of adversarial attacks to deceive detection. In this work, we present an investigation of Grover's susceptibility to adversarial attacks such as character-level and word-level perturbations. The experiment results show that even a singular character alteration can cause Grover to fail, affecting up to 97% of target articles with unlimited attack attempts, exposing a lack of robustness. We further analyse these misclassified cases to highlight affected words, identify vulnerability within Grover's encoder, and perform a novel visualisation of cumulative classification scores to assist in interpreting model behaviour.

1 Introduction

Online disinformation has become a crucial issue in current society and has been the focus of extensive study in recent years (Buning, 2018; Fletcher, 2018; Zerback, 2020). Fake news, one form of online disinformation, can deceive people with intent of monetary gain, political slander, or entity discreditation (Quandt et al., 2019). While current sources of fake news are mainly derived from human hand, recent developments in Natural Language Generation (NLG) (Radford, 2018, 2019; Brown, 2020) have made it possible to produce neural fake news [1] at scale. The key problem with this technology is that it is harder for humans to distinguish machine-generated text from human-produced text (Heaven, 2020; Hao, 2020).

To counter the rising threat of neural fake news, an automatic discriminator has been developed that can serve as a defence mechanism. In 2019, Grover (Zellers et al., 2019) (**G**enerating a**R**ticles by **O**nly **V**iewing m**E**tadata **R**ecords), a neural fake news generator and discriminator, was released to the public. As a generator, it generates formal news articles, (including title, domain, authors, date) with given contextual metadata. As a discriminator, it detects the difference between machine and human-produced articles. By utilising articles produced by the generator, Grover's discriminator achieved 92% accuracy while detectors based deep contextual language models including GPT-2 and BERT achieved 73% (Zellers et al., 2019).

Grover can be misused to mass produce plausible disinformation by adversaries. For example, Grover generated propaganda articles were rated as more trustworthy than human-produced ones of the same context by human judges (Zellers et al., 2019). Given this alarming ability, the capability to auto-detect the differences between machine and human-produced articles can reduce the risk of neural fake news spreading online.

Following the establishment of text-based perturbations by Jia and Liang (2017), studies on robustness interpretability through adversarial examples have grown rapidly through the Natural Language Processing (NLP) community (Vadillo, 2021; Zafar, 2021; Yuan, 2021). Since then, there have been several attempts to manipulate NLP models by character-level alterations on its input text. For example, Belinkov and Bisk (2017) demonstrated that synthetic and natural noise can cause state-of-the-art language translation models

[1]From here on out, we will use 'neural fake news' and 'machine-generated fake news' interchangeably.

to fail. Gao (2018) also proposed DeepWord-Bug, a novel algorithm for small character perturbations causing drastic classification inaccuracies in tasks such as text classification, sentiment analysis, and spam detection. These studies conducted character-level perturbations to identify a lack of robustness within various mainstream language models.

In a similar manner, Grover, when acting as a defence mechanism against neural fake news, can face heavy adversarial scrutiny. Thus, following the direction of recent studies (Belinkov and Bisk, 2017; Gao, 2018), we conducted analyses through various adversarial attacks including character-level and token-level perturbations.

This paper presents an investigation of Grover to examine its performance change on various adversarial attacks. In our assessment, we find that Grover is highly susceptible to adversarial attacks with around 93% of target articles vulnerable to misclassification after alteration. Analysing the effects of successful perturbations, we identify a weakness within the model's encoding framework which influences Grover's classification scoring, with recorded score variations of 0.74 on average. In this work, we introduce our novel visualisation of cumulative classification score on various unaltered/altered articles and explore classification score polarity induced by adversarial attacks.

This paper is organised as follows. Section 2 accounts related work and section 3 reports a general summary of Grover. Section 4 presents the experiments of adversarial attacks. Section 5 conveys the results of the experiments along with error analysis. Section 6 presents cumulative classification score visualisation and analysis on extreme polarity change. Finally, section 7 presents our concluding discussion.

2 Related Work

Recent studies on adversarial attacks in NLP follow a white-box approach leveraging accessible information from within a model as surveyed by Zhang (2020). Many studies have utilised a white-box gradient-based approach for various attacks such as character-based alterations (Ebrahimi, 2017, 2018; Liang, 2017), word-based alterations (Cheng, 2020; Liang, 2017; Neekhara, 2018), and word-based concatenations (Wallace, 2019; Behjati, 2019). Blohm (2018) used white-box model attention to attack a reading comprehension model as well as a question answering model.

Contrary to the white-box approach, Wolff and Wolff (2020) adopted a black-box approach and performed homoglyph and misspelling attacks on a variety of neural text classifiers including GPT-2, GLTR, RoBERTa, and Grover. They conducted adversarial attacks on 20 samples of *Machine* articles to draw comparison between leading neural classifiers and Grover yet refrain from exploring the results of Grover's classification in detail. Our work includes the attack concepts from Wolff and Wolff's work (2020) but explore singular applications of the attacks, rather than multiple applications. We also focus our analysis solely on Grover, studying the effect of the attacks produced on Grover, and its potential fragile points within the framework.

Visualising a language model's outcome to increase a model's interpretability is another recent trend in NLP. Gehrmann (2019) introduced GLTR, a visualisation tool (using statistical methods) that can detect generation artifacts across a sample and display its findings through coloured annotation on the input to support a human's fake text detection. Stemming from this concept, we propose a novel visualisation approach through the plotting of cumulative classification scores. Our visualisation method aims to help a user to interpret how Grover is affected at each word vector and highlight key alteration artifacts within an article.

3 Grover

Grover consists of two components: a generator and a discriminator.

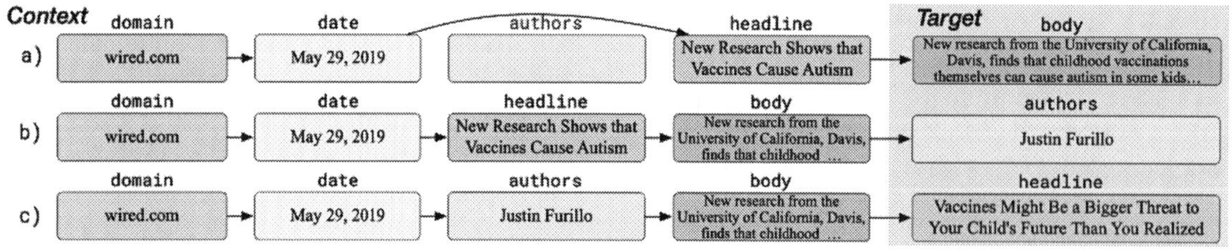

Figure 1: A diagram of Grover examples for article generation. Note ~ Fig 2 from 'Defending Against Neural Fake News' by Zellers et al., 2019.

3.1 Generator

The generator component of Grover comprises a novel architecture with adapted components of GPT-2. Grover, as shown in Figure 1, can generate the domain, date, headline, body, or author of a news article, given any subsetted combination of these fields. The generator comes in three versions – Grover-Base, consisting of 12 layers and 124 million parameters, Grover-Large, consisting of 24 layers and 355 million parameters, and Grover-Mega, with 48 layers and 1.5 billion parameters matching GPT-2's architecture; each trained on successively larger datasets (comprised of real news articles scraped from common crawl[2]).

3.2 Discriminator

The discriminator component of Grover acts as a detector of neurally generated articles. Utilising articles produced by the generator, the discriminator is trained to differentiate between machine-generated articles and human-produced articles. Articles can be classified on their own or with additional metadata such as domain, date, headline, and author, that aids prediction strength.

4 Experiments

The functionality of Grover's discriminator, given either machine-generated articles (labelled as *Machine*) or human-produced articles (labelled as *Human*), is to produce a classification label of '**Human**' or '**Machine**' on each article. Input articles contain the body of an article, with or without metadata (title, domain, date, or authors).

To assess Grover's robustness, we conducted experiments on the discriminator's classification accuracy when classifying altered (adversarial attacked) *Machine* articles. Minor alterations (altering only one character or one word in a whole news article) have been performed on a subset of *Machine* articles applying four methods of adversarial attacks including (1) upper/lower flip, (2) homoglyph, (3) whitespace, and (4) misspelling. After each attack, the altered articles were submitted to Grover's discriminator for reclassification and the classification results were investigated.

4.1 Discriminator Setup

For experiments, the publicly available pre-trained Grover Mega discriminator was used; the set-up contains Grover Mega config file and necessary checkpoints[3]. We ran the discriminator in its GPU configuration.

4.2 Dataset

Grover provides a dataset containing 12,000 articles with metadata[4]; it consists of 8,000 *Human* articles (RealNews dataset[5]), and 4,000 *Machine* articles, which were generated using Grover's generator (Grover-Mega). Submitting this dataset to Grover's discriminator, we gain the predictions seen in Table 1. From the prediction we obtain a total accuracy of 0.93, a precision score of 0.85, a recall score of 0.94, and a F1 score of 0.89.

		True Class	
		Machine n=4000	*Human* n=8000
Predicted Class	**Machine**	TP (3,751)	FP (649)
	Human	FN (249)	TN (7,351)

Table 1: Confusion Matrix of 12,000 articles classified by Grover Mega discriminator. True Positives (TP). False Positives (FP). False Negatives (FN). True Negatives (TN).

For our experiments, we sampled 100 articles with the highest true positive (TP) classification scores produced by the discriminator. This will be referenced as 100 *Machine* article subset. All articles selected have classification score over 0.49 where 0.5 is the maximum score an article could be assigned for a '**Machine**' classification.

[2]https://commoncrawl.org/

[3]https://github.com/rowanz/grover/tree/master/discrimination

[4]gs://grover-models/discrimination/generator=medium~discriminator=grover~discsize=medium~dataset=p=0.96/checkpoint

[5]https://github.com/rowanz/grover/tree/master/realnews

Original	"A Romanian hospital will face a fine for leaving a towel in a patient's stomach…"
Whitespace	"A Romanian hospital **willface** a fine for leaving a towel in a patient's stomach…"
Upper/Lower Flip	"A Romanian hospital will face a fine for leav**I**ng a towel in a patient's stomach…"
Misspelling	"A Romanian hospital will face a fine for leaving a towel in a patient's **stomache**…"
Homoglyph	"A Romanian hospital will face a **fine*** for leaving a towel in a patient's stomach…"

Table 2: Adversarial attacks and their respective change on an article. *The word 'Fine' in the homoglyph example contains Cyrillic 'e' ~ Unicode: U+x0435 compared to the regular Latin 'e' ~ Unicode: U+0065.

Attack	Alterations	Misclassifications (Proportion)	Affected Articles
U/L Flip	212,224	4,295 (2.02%)	96%
Homoglyph	157,532	6,914 (4.39%)	97%
Whitespace	46,036	1,447 (3.14%)	85%
Misspelling	43,789	4,281 (9.78%)	94%

Table 3: Classification results of all adversarial examples. **Alterations** indicate how many iterations of the specified attack was conducted across the dataset. **Affected Articles** indicate how many articles, from the 100 *Machine target* articles, had one or more misclassifications resulting from an alteration.

4.3 Adversarial Attack Parameters

As news articles are written to a high level of coherency with minimal punctual mistakes or grammatical errors, an adversary would want to limit article alteration to preserve readability and ensure a human reader does not question the article's credibility. To simulate this mindset, we limit the application of an attack to only a single change, such as one character or one-word alteration on an article, iterating the attack through the entirety of an article to assess all possible combinations for each attack's relative application. As demonstrated in Table 2, the following four types of adversarial attacks were applied for the experiments:

(1) **Upper/Lower Flip:** Uppercasing or lowercasing of a letter originally lowercased or uppercased respectively.

(2) **Homoglyph:** Replacement of certain characters with their homoglyph equivalent from either the Greek or Cyrillic alphabet[6].

(3) **Whitespace:** Removal of a space between adjacent words.

(4) **Misspelling:** Replacement of certain words coinciding with a list of commonly misspelled English words on Wikipedia[7].

4.4 Adversarial Attack Results

We present the results from our adversarial attack experiments on Grover.

As shown in Table 3, character-level attacks (U/L Flip and Homoglyph) create a higher number of altered articles compared to word-level attacks (Whitespace and Misspelling). Based on the number of alterations, the Misspelling attack achieved the highest misclassification rates (nearly 10%) compared to the other three attacks which got a relatively lower rate of 2-4%.

Surprisingly, across the 100 *Machine* article subset, Homoglyph, U/L Flip and Misspelling attacks affected 97%, 96% and 94% of the target articles, respectively. Even the simplest attack, Whitespace attack, could affect 85% of the 100 target *Machine* articles. This suggests that Grover is highly susceptible to adversarial efforts.

Table 4 shows the ten most common words that affected (flipped the classification from '**Machine**' to '**Human**') Grover's discriminator during adversarial attacks. Around 20% of

[6]We use 19 different Greek substitutions and 30 different Cyrillic substitutions. All substitutions can be found in the appendix.

[7]https://en.wikipedia.org/wiki/Wikipedia:Lists_of_common_misspellings/For_machines

Affected Word	Frequency	Proportion	POS
that	1639	8.92%	IN
the	1533	8.34%	DT
to	516	2.81%	TO
and	334	1.82%	CC
with	321	1.75%	IN
in	298	1.62%	IN
of	279	1.52%	IN
for	257	1.40%	IN
from	236	1.28%	IN
The	202	1.10%	DT

Table 4: Statistics of affected words from all misclassified inputs. **POS** is the part-of-speech tag for that respective word obtained from NLTK[5]. **IN** ~ Preposition, **DT** ~ Determiner, **TO** ~ To, **CC** ~ Coordinating Conjunction. Note we only take the top 10 most occurring words within the misclassified subset.

misclassifications were caused by altering the words 'that', 'the' and 'to'. Noticeably, the majority of the affected words are stop words.

4.5 Input Encoding

We observed in general which words were altered to elicit a misclassification. To assess how character-level perturbations affect Grover, we examined how the model interprets and scores a given input.

Grover uses a byte-pair encoder (BPE) to pre-process input data. BPE (Senrich et al., 2015) splits a given input into its largest subword units based on character co-occurrence frequency distribution and assigns each unit a pre-determined pairing ID. This turns a tokenised input into a vector of numbers.

Previously, BPEs have been found to be lacking in robustness when facing character-level perturbations (Heigold et al., 2017). In Table 5 we can see the effect that the upper/lower flip attack has on a particular sequence from one of the articles. The uppercasing of the letter 'i' in 'hospital' changes the subword unit allocation. Originally encoded as [4437], 'hospItal' gets broken down into 'hosp','It','al' then encoded into [10497, 1027, 283].

Original	Vector IDs		Altered
A	33		A
Romanian	34345		Romanian
		10497	**hosp**
hospital	**4437**	**1027**	**It**
		283	**al**
will	482		will
face	1987		face
a	258		a
fine	3735		fine
for	330		for

Table 5: An original encoding sequence compared to the same encoded sequence after a single character alteration.

5 Visual Analysis

Grover produces a classification score at each word vector, as it processes the input from left to right. If we successively and cumulatively feed Grover word vectors in sequential order, we can obtain a classification score at each step, allowing for a cumulative classification score to be recorded. Using the classification scores recorded at each increment as word vectors are appended to the accumulating input, we can visualise how these are perceived by Grover over the course of an entire input.

5.1 Cumulative Classification Score Visualisation

***Human* Articles:** Figure 2 illustrates the cumulative classification score of five randomly selected *Human* articles from the original 8,000 *Human* article dataset. At the initial processing of the sequence, all articles start at a strong '**Machine**' classification. As more of the respective input is processed, we see the articles' classification scores increase toward '**Human**' over time. It is observed that cumulative classification scores often plateau with greater encoded sequence lengths.

[5]https://www.nltk.org/

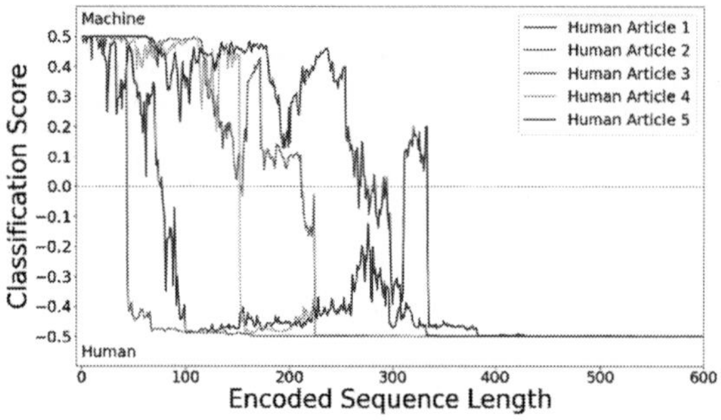

Figure 2: Comparison of cumulative classification scores between five *Human* articles.

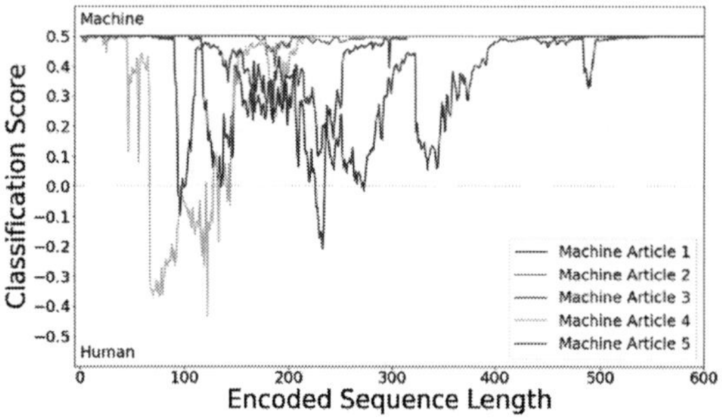

Figure 3: Comparison of cumulative classification scores between five *Machine* articles.

***Machine* Articles:** Figure 3 shows the cumulative classification scores of five randomly selected *Machine* articles from our target dataset. As seen in the visualisation of *Human* articles, the beginning of each sequence starts at a strong '**Machine**' classification. Over the early stages of the sequence, we see high classification score variance due to the limited word vectors processed. Over time, the selected *Machine* articles tend to return to a strong '**Machine**' classification, plateauing toward the end of the encoded sequence.

False Negative (FN) Case: Figure 4 presents the cumulative classification score of one of the misclassified articles from our experiments. The red line indicates the location of the adversarial attack within the encoded sequence. In this example, the input word 'that' was transformed into 'thaT' by U/L Flip attack which uppercased the second 't'. At the point where Grover processed the altered word vector, the classification score of the article dropped dramatically, falling a total of 0.98. This large variation in classification score due to alteration will be discussed in terms of 'Extreme Polarity Change' in section 5.2.

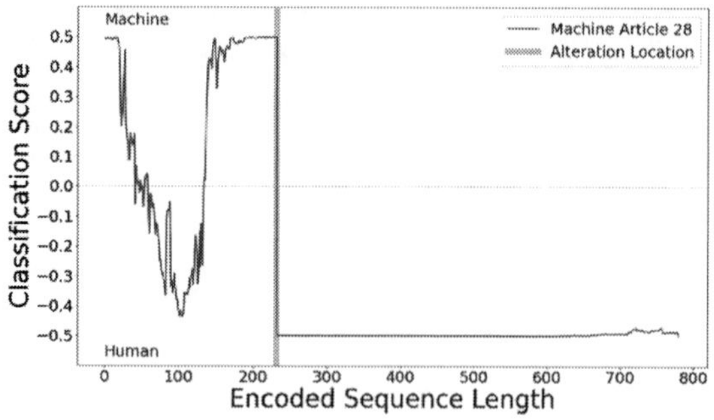

Figure 4: Cumulative classification scores of misclassified altered *Machine* article after the U/L Flip attack.

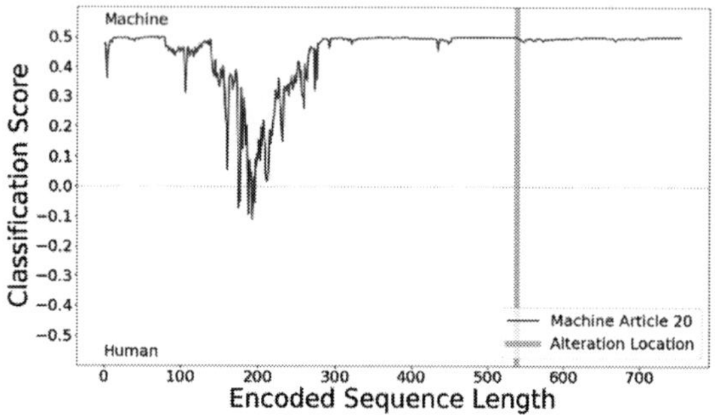

Figure 5: Cumulative classification scores of correctly classified altered *Machine* article after the U/L Flip attack.

True Positive (TP) Case: Figure 5 demonstrates the cumulative classification score of a *Machine* article that had its classification unaffected after an adversarial attack. Again, the red line indicates the location of the attack. In this example, the input word, 'These' was altered to 'these' by the U/L Flip attack which lowercased the first 'T'. This alteration causes a very minimal change in classification score at the site of alteration.

5.2 Extreme Polarity Change

From visualising a FN case's cumulative classification scores, we observed a large change in classification score at the point of an adversarial attack. To analyse whether all FN cases show a drastic variation in classification score, we took a random sample of 500 FN case articles and 500 TP case articles from each of the four adversarial attacks. In total, we examined the 4,000 articles' classification score at each point of the adversarial attack. The average score variation of each subset is shown in Table 6.

	Average Score Variation	
Attack	**TP Subset**	**FN Subset**
U/L Flip	0.12	0.76
Homoglyph	0.17	0.81
Whitespace	0.04	0.70
Misspelling	0.21	0.69
Average	0.14	0.74

Table 6: Average classification score variation at the point of an attack within an input.

The FN cases had a much higher average variation in classification score compared to the TP cases as shown in Table 7. This implies that particular alterations caused Grover's classification score to drop dramatically (at the site of an attack) ultimately affecting the final prediction produced by Grover.

6 Discussion

In this study, the robustness of Grover's discriminator was assessed through various adversarial attacks. We found that even a singular character change can cause the model to fail. Through analyses of successful perturbations, it was found that Grover's encoder is highly sensitive to selected perturbations, causing downstream effects in classification assignment.

We conducted a broad implementation of adversarial attacks and identified vulnerabilities in single alterations on certain types of words. These results outline potential dependencies within Grover's language modelling which could be potentially extorted by adversaries through implementation of multiple instances of an adversarial attack across an article or an adversary targeting and affecting more than one key word outlined in Table 4.

To the best of our knowledge, the proposed visualisation of cumulative classification scores are novel, allowing interpretation of model behaviour, as it gives a user the ability to visually understand the effects that each word vector has at its relative point of inference as well as the effects that alterations may produce on the classification prediction.

Our findings open various paths for further exploration. Our adversarial attacks' focus was exclusively directed onto the body of an article. One path for future work could consist of focussing adversarial attacks on the metadata of an article, further exploring Grover's robustness. Our visualisation of cumulative classification scores highlighted the effects some character-level alterations had on the classification score of an article. The large score variations noted could allow for work to be done in the field of adversarial attack detection. Finally, the nature of our assessment was broad and based on a black-box approach. Furthering our work, the undertaking of a white-box approach could be performed to explore model interpretability.

Acknowledgments

R. Gagiano is supported by Defence Science and Technology Group Graduate Industry Placement. X. Zhang is supported by the ARC Discovery Project DP200101441.

References

Melika Behjati, Seyed-Mohsen Moosavi-Dezfooli, Mahdieh Soleymani Baghshah, and Pascal Frossard. "Universal adversarial attacks on text classifiers." In ICASSP 2019-2019 IEEE International Conference on Acoustics, Speech and Signal Processing (ICASSP), pp. 7345-7349. IEEE, 2019.

Yonatan Belinkov, and Yonatan Bisk. "Synthetic and natural noise both break neural machine translation." arXiv preprint arXiv:1711.02173 (2017).

Matthias Blohm, Glorianna Jagfeld, Ekta Sood, Xiang Yu, and Ngoc Thang Vu. "Comparing attention-based convolutional and recurrent neural networks: Success and limitations in machine reading comprehension." arXiv preprint arXiv:1808.08744 (2018).

Tom B. Brown, Benjamin Mann, Nick Ryder, Melanie Subbiah, Jared Kaplan, Prafulla Dhariwal, Arvind Neelakantan et al. "Language models are few-shot learners." arXiv preprint arXiv:2005.14165 (2020).

Madeleine de Cock Buning. "A multi-dimensional approach to disinformation: Report of the independent High level Group on fake news and online disinformation." (2018).

Minhao Cheng, Jinfeng Yi, Pin-Yu Chen, Huan Zhang, and Cho-Jui Hsieh. "Seq2sick: Evaluating the robustness of sequence-to-sequence models with adversarial examples." In Proceedings of the AAAI Conference on Artificial Intelligence, vol. 34, no. 04, pp. 3601-3608. 2020.

Javid Ebrahimi, Anyi Rao, Daniel Lowd, and Dejing Dou. "Hotflip: White-box adversarial examples for text classification." arXiv preprint arXiv:1712.06751 (2017).

Javid Ebrahimi, Daniel Lowd, and Dejing Dou. "On adversarial examples for character-level neural machine translation." arXiv preprint arXiv:1806.09030 (2018).

Richard Fletcher, Alessio Cornia, Lucas Graves, and Rasmus Kleis Nielsen. "Measuring the reach of" fake news" and online disinformation in Europe." Australasian Policing 10, no. 2 (2018).

Ji Gao, Jack Lanchantin, Mary Lou Soffa, and Yanjun Qi. "Black-box generation of adversarial text sequences to evade deep learning classifiers." In 2018 IEEE Security and Privacy Workshops (SPW), pp. 50-56. IEEE, 2018.

Sebastian Gehrmann , Hendrik Strobelt, and Alexander M. Rush. "GLTR: Statistical detection and visualization of generated text." arXiv preprint arXiv:1906.04043 (2019).

Will Douglas Heaven. 2020. "A GPT-3 Bot Posted Comments on Reddit for a Week and No One Noticed." MIT TECHNOLOGY REVIEW (blog). October 8, 2020.

Georg Heigold, Günter Neumann, and Josef van Genabith. "How Robust Are Character-Based Word Embeddings in Tagging and MT Against Wrod Scramlbing or Randdm Nouse?." arXiv preprint arXiv:1704.04441 (2017).

Karen Hao. 2020. "A College Kid's Fake, AI-Generated Blog Fooled Tens of Thousands. This Is How He Made It." MIT TECHNOLOGY REVIEW (blog). August 14, 2020.

Robin Jia, and Percy Liang. "Adversarial examples for evaluating reading comprehension systems." arXiv preprint arXiv:1707.07328 (2017).

Bin Liang, Hongcheng Li, Miaoqiang Su, Pan Bian, Xirong Li, and Wenchang Shi. "Deep text classification can be fooled." arXiv preprint arXiv:1704.08006 (2017).

Paarth Neekhara, Shehzeen Hussain, Shlomo Dubnov, and Farinaz Koushanfar. "Adversarial reprogramming of text classification neural networks." arXiv preprint arXiv:1809.01829 (2018).

Thorsten Quandt, Lena Frischlich, Svenja Boberg andTim Schatto-Eckrodt. (2019). Fake News. 1-6. 10.1002/9781118841570.iejs0128.

Alec Radford, Karthik Narasimhan, Tim Salimans, and Ilya Sutskever. "Improving language understanding by generative pre-training." (2018).

Alec Radford, Jeffrey Wu, Rewon Child, David Luan, Dario Amodei, and Ilya Sutskever. "Language models are unsupervised multitask learners." OpenAI blog 1, no. 8 (2019): 9.

Rico Sennrich, Barry Haddow, and Alexandra Birch. "Neural machine translation of rare words with subword units." arXiv preprint arXiv:1508.07909 (2015).

Jon Vadillo, Roberto Santana, and Jose A. Lozano. "When and How to Fool Explainable Models (and Humans) with Adversarial Examples." arXiv preprint arXiv:2107.01943 (2021).

Eric Wallace, Shi Feng, Nikhil Kandpal, Matt Gardner, and Sameer Singh. "Universal adversarial triggers for attacking and analyzing NLP." arXiv preprint arXiv:1908.07125 (2019).

Max Wolff, and Stuart Wolff. "Attacking neural text detectors." arXiv preprint arXiv:2002.11768 (2020).

Chaoran Yuan, Xiaobin Liu and Zhengyuan Zhang, "The Current Status and progress of Adversarial Examples Attacks." 2021 International Conference on Communications, Information System and Computer Engineering (CISCE), 2021, pp. 707-711, doi: 10.1109/CISCE52179.2021.9445917. (2021)

Muhammad Bilal Zafar, Michele Donini, Dylan Slack, Cédric Archambeau, Sanjiv Das, and Krishnaram Kenthapadi. "On the Lack of Robust Interpretability of Neural Text Classifiers." arXiv preprint arXiv:2106.04631 (2021).

Rowan Zellers, Ari Holtzman, Hannah Rashkin, Yonatan Bisk, Ali Farhadi, Franziska Roesner, and Yejin Choi. "Defending against neural fake news." arXiv preprint arXiv:1905.12616 (2019).

Thomas Zerback, Florian Töpfl, and Maria Knöpfle. "The disconcerting potential of online disinformation: Persuasive effects of astroturfing comments and three strategies for inoculation against them." New Media & Society 23, no. 5 (2021): 1080-1098.

Wei Emma Zhang, Quan Z. Sheng, Ahoud Alhazmi, and Chenliang Li. "Adversarial attacks on deep-learning models in natural language processing: A survey." ACM Transactions on Intelligent Systems and Technology (TIST) 11, no. 3 (2020): 1-41.

Supplementary Material

Appendix A: Full list of Latin characters with their respective Greek and Cyrillic substitutions and all respective character Unicode.

Original (Basic Latin) Letter ~ Unicode		Greek Letter ~ Unicode		Cyrillic Letter ~ Unicode	
A ~ U+0041	a ~ U+0061	A ~ U+x0391		A ~ U+x0410	a ~ U+x0430
B ~U+0042	b ~ U+0062	B ~ U+x0392		B ~ U+x0412	Ь ~ U+x044C
C ~ U+0043	c ~ U+0063	C ~ U+x2CA3	c ~ U+x03C2	C ~ U+x0421	c ~ U+x0441
E ~ U+0045	e ~ U+0065	E ~ U+x0395		E ~ U+x0415	e ~ U+x0435
F ~ U+0046		F ~ U+x03DC			
H ~ U+0048	h ~ U+0068	H ~ U+x0397		H ~ U+x041D	h ~ U+x04BB
I ~ U+0049	i ~ U+0069	I ~ U+x0399		I ~ U+x0406	i ~ U+x0456
J ~ U+004a	j ~ U+006a			J ~ U+x0408	j ~ U+x0458
K ~ U+004b		K ~ U+x039A		K ~ U+x041A	
M ~ U+004d		M ~ U+x039C		M ~ U+x041C	
N ~ U+004e		N ~ U+x039D			
O ~ U+004f	o ~ U+006f	O ~ U+x039F	o ~ U+x03BF	O ~ U+x041E	o ~ U+x043E
P ~ U+0050	p ~ U+0070	P ~ U+x03A1		P ~ U+x0420	p ~ U+x0440
S ~ U+0053	s ~ U+0073			S ~ U+x0405	s ~ U+x0455
T ~ U+0054		T ~ U+x03A3		T ~ U+x0422	
V ~ U+0056	v ~ U+0076		v ~ U+x03BD	V ~ U+x0474	v ~ U+x0475
	w ~ U+0077				w ~ U+x0461
X ~ U+0058	x ~ U+0078	X ~ U+x03A7		X ~ U+x0425	x ~ U+x0445
Y ~ U+0059	y ~ U+0079	Y ~ U+x03A5		Y ~ U+x04AE	y ~ U+x0443
Z ~ U+005a	z ~ U+007a	Z ~ U+x036			

Document Level Hierarchical Transformer

Najam Zaidi
Monash University
syed.zaidi1@monash.edu

Trevor Cohn
University of Melbourne
trevor.cohn@unimelb.edu.au

Gholamreza Haffari
Monash University
gholamreza.haffari@monash.edu

Abstract

Generating long and coherent text is an important and challenging task encompassing many application areas such as summarization, document level machine translation and story generation. Despite the success in modeling intra-sentence coherence, existing long text generation models (e.g., BART and GPT-3) still struggle to maintain a coherent event sequence throughout the generated text. We conjecture that this is because of the difficulty for the model to revise, replace or revoke any part that has been generated by the model.

In this chapter, we present a novel semi-autoregressive document generation model capable of revising and editing the generated text. Building on recent models by (Gu et al., 2019; Xu and Carpuat, 2020), we propose document generation as a hierarchical Markov decision process with a two level hierarchy, where the high and low level editing programs generate and refine the document. We train our model using imitation learning and introduce roll-in policy such that each policy learns on the output of applying the previous action. Experiments applying the proposed approach convey various insights on the problems of long text generation using our model. We suggest various remedies such as using distilled dataset, designing better attention mechanisms and using autoregressive models as a low level program.

1 Introduction

Generating long and coherent text encompass various tasks such as summarization, story generation, document level machine translation and document level post editing. Each task is characterised by modelling long range dependencies to make the document coherent as well as modelling a high level plot to make the document thematically consistent (Fan et al., 2018). This is challenging as the models need to plan content, while producing local words consistent with the global context in a timely manner.

Recent work on autoregressive generation models, such as GPT-3 and BART (Lewis et al., 2019; Brown et al., 2020), have shown impressive performance in generating short fluent text with a maximum length ranging from 150 to 350 tokens (Bosselut et al., 2018; Shen et al., 2019; Zhao et al., 2020b). But applying the same model to generate longer passages of text (e.g., 1000 tokens) has resulted in syntactic and semantic errors throughout the document requiring extensive human curations (Tan et al., 2020). These massive language models are usually pre-trained using large corpora of generic text, and then fine-tuned with small domain-specific data. Most of the time, the models are not publicly available to adapt to arbitrary desired domains.

On the other hand, recent non-autoregressive approaches allow generation to be done within a much smaller number of decoding iterations (Gu et al., 2017; Wang et al., 2019; Kasai et al., 2020). But due to its problems with modelling dependencies among the tokens, the approach still lags behind its autoregressive counterparts and has not yet been applied to long text generation (Zhou et al., 2019; Gu and Kong, 2020). In both of these model families, the length of generated sequences is either fixed or monotonically increased as the decoding proceeds. This makes them incompatible with human-level intelligence where humans can revise and edit any part of their generated text.

In this paper, we present a novel semi-autoregressive document generation model capable of revising and editing the generated text. We build on recent models by (Gu et al., 2019; Xu and Carpuat, 2020), who framed generation as a Markov decision process (Garcia and Rachelson, 2013) and showed that iteratively refining output sequences via insertions and repositions yields a fast and flexible generation process for machine translation and automatic post editing task. We extend their model by proposing document generation as a hierarchical Markov decision (Liu et al., 2018) process with a two level hierarchy. The high level program produce actions $a_H \in$ *{reposition, insert, update}* which tries to capture global context and plan content while the low level program produce actions $a_L \in$ *{reposition, insert}* to generate local words in a consistent and timely manner. Due to unavailability of large-scale data to train our model, we propose a noising process to simulate the error patterns observed in document level tasks such as redundancy of words, key information omission and disordered sentences. The noising process can be reversed by applying a set of high and low level actions to get back the original document. This serve as an efficient oracle to train our model using imitation learning (Hussein et al., 2017). The roll-in policy is defined such that each policy learns on the output of applying the previous action.

2 Problem formulation

2.1 Hierarchical Markov decision process

We cast document generation and refinement as a hierarchical Markov decision process (HMDP) with a two level hierarchy. The high level program is defined by the tuple $(\mathscr{D}, \mathscr{A}_{\mathscr{H}}, \mathscr{E}, \mathscr{R}, \mathbf{d_0})$ where a state $\mathbf{d} \in \mathscr{D}$ corresponds to a set of sequences $\mathbf{d} = (\mathbf{s_1}, \mathbf{s_2}, ..., \mathbf{s_L})$ up to length L, and $\mathbf{d_0} \in \mathscr{D}$ is the initial document. The low level program corresponds to the tuple $(\mathscr{S}, \mathscr{A}_{\mathscr{L}}, \mathscr{E}, \mathscr{R}, \mathbf{s_0})$ where a state $\mathbf{s} \in \mathscr{S}$ corresponds to a sequence of tokens $\mathbf{s} = (w_1, w_2, ..., w_n)$ from the vocabulary V up to length n, and $\mathbf{s_0} \in \mathscr{S}$ is the initial sequence.

At any time step t, the model takes as input $\mathbf{d_{t-1}}$, the output from the previous iteration, chooses an action $a_H \in \mathscr{A}_{\mathscr{H}}$ to refine the sequence into $\mathbf{d_t} = \mathscr{E}(\mathbf{d_{t-1}}, a_H)$, and receives a reward $r_t = \mathscr{R}(\mathbf{d_t})$. The policy π_H maps the input sequence $\mathbf{d_{t-1}}$ to a probability distribution $P(A_H)$ over the action space $\mathscr{A}_{\mathscr{H}}$. A high level program may call a low level program with the initial input $\mathbf{s_0}$. It is similar to high level program with its set of actions $a_L \in \mathscr{A}_{\mathscr{L}}$, reward function $r_t = \mathscr{R}(\mathbf{s_t})$ and the policy π_L. Instead of sequences, the low level actions are applied to individual tokens. This results in a trajectory $\sigma := \{\mathbf{d_1}, a_H^1, \tau_1, r_1, \mathbf{d_2}, ..., \mathbf{d_N}, a_H^N, \tau_N, r_N, \mathbf{d_{N+1}}\}$ which is the concatenation of high-level trajectory $\tau_H := (\mathbf{d_1}, a_H^1, r_1, \mathbf{d_2}, a_H^2, r_2, ..., \mathbf{d}_{H+1})$ and the low level trajectory $\tau_L := (\mathbf{s_1}, a_L^1, \mathbf{s_2}, a_L^2, ..., \mathbf{s}_{T+1})$. We define a reward function $R = dist(\mathbf{D}, \mathbf{D}^*)$ which measures the distance between the generation and the ground-truth sequence. We use Levenstein distance (?) as our distance metric.

2.2 HMDP policies:

Following the formulation of HDMP, we define a high level policy $\pi_H : \mathbf{d} \rightarrow A_H$, as well as the low level policy $\pi_L : \mathbf{s} \rightarrow A_L$ as a mapping from state to actions. The high level actions consist of $a_H \in \{reposition, insert, update\}$ and the low level actions consist of $a_L \in \{reposition, insert\}$.

INSERT$_\mathbf{H}$: The insertion policy reads the input document $\mathbf{d}$ consisting of set of sequences $\{\mathbf{s_1}, \mathbf{s_2}, ...\mathbf{s_i}, \mathbf{s_{i+1}}, ...\mathbf{s_L}\}$, and for every possible slot $i, i+1$, the insertion policy $\pi_H^{ins}(x|i, \mathbf{d})$ makes a binary decision which is 1 (insert here) or 0 (do not insert). For each insertion position, low level MDP is called to generate the new sequence from scratch. This allows the model to generate a sentence conditioned on the surrounding context resulting in outputs that are consistent with the theme and plot of the document.

UPDATE$_\mathbf{H}$: The update policy reads the input document $\mathbf{d}$, consisting of set of sequences $\{\mathbf{s_1}, \mathbf{s_2}, ...\mathbf{s_i}, \mathbf{s_{i+1}}, ...\mathbf{s_L}\}$, and for every sequence position i, the update policy $\pi_H^{upd}(x|i, \mathbf{d})$ makes a binary decision which is 1 (update this sentence) or 0 (do not update). In order to make the update, the low level MDP is called to refine the given sequence. This allows the model to correct mistakes and improve the sentences generated by the insert policy.

REPOSITION$_\mathbf{H}$: The reposition policy reads in the document $\mathbf{d}$ consisting of set of sequences $\{\mathbf{s_1}, \mathbf{s_2}, ...\mathbf{s_i}, \mathbf{s_{i+1}}, ...\mathbf{s_L}\}$. For every sentence position i, the reposition policy $\pi_H^{rep}(x|i, \mathbf{d})$ makes a categorical decision between 0 and $L+1$ where L is the number of sequences in the document. The given sequence is repositioned to the output value. If x is 0 then the sequence is deleted. This policy allows the model to observe the complete document and make it more coherent by repositioning and deleteing sentences.

INSERT$_\mathbf{L}$, REPOSITION$_\mathbf{L}$: The Low level MDP is made up of actions reposition and insert. They work in a similar manner as defined in the paper (Gu et al., 2019; Xu and Carpuat, 2020) with the difference that the conditioning context contains document d along with the sentence s. Therefore the reposition policy at the word level is defined by $\pi_L^{rep}(x|i,\mathbf{y},\mathbf{d})$. The insertion policy is made up of a placeholder and token prediction policy as defined by $\pi_L^{plh}(x|i,\mathbf{y},\mathbf{d})$ and $\pi_L^{tok}(x|i,\mathbf{y},\mathbf{d})$ respectively. The placeholder policy first determines the number of words that need to be inserted at a given position. Special <*mask*> tokens are then inserted. These <*mask*> tokens are filled by the token prediction policy.

2.3 Generative process:

The generative process is outlined in algorithm 1. The combination of high and low level policies can either generate a document from scratch or edit a given initial document. The insertion and update policy calls the low level program in Lines 6 and 11. Line 2 in algorithm 2 builds the initial scaffolding which is later used by the algorithm for its set of actions. If the low level program is called by the high level update action the initial scaffolding is created by concatenating the sentences identified by the high level update policy. Otherwise in case of high level insert action, it is the concatenation of empty sentences. Although one iteration is made up of multiple stages, within each stage an action is performed in parallel.

3 Hierarchical Transformer

3.1 Architectures

Our model is based on the Transformer encoder-decoder architecture (Vaswani et al., 2017). We extract the hidden representations $(\mathbf{h_1},...,\mathbf{h_n})$ to make the policy predictions. We extract sentence representations by concatenating all sentences with a special <*sep*> token. The hidden states corresponding to these special tokens are then used as sentence representation by the policies. Along with position embeddings for individual tokens, we also introduce segment embeddings for sentences, which identify the position of a sentence in a document. We show the illustration of the proposed model in Figure 1.

3.2 Policy classifiers

We implement policies as classifiers whose prediction depends upon the hidden state representations generated by the transformer layers.

Reposition classifier: The reposition classifier gives a categorical distribution over the index of the input, where the input can be the representation of a sentence or a word. The input sequence is then repositioned accordingly. Along with reordering, this classifier can also perform deletion by predicting special delete token. This classifier is implemented as:

$$\pi_\theta^{rep}(r|\mathbf{s}_i,\mathbf{d}) = \text{softmax}(\mathbf{h}_i \cdot [\mathbf{b},\mathbf{e_1},...,\mathbf{e_n}])$$

for $i \in \{1..n\}$ where $\mathbf{e}$ can be the embedding of a sentence or token and $\mathbf{b} \in \mathbb{R}^{\mathbf{d}_{\text{model}}}$ is a special token to predict deletion. Note that in case of low level program, we also condition on the complete document. This is done by having cross-attention on the hidden representation of the sentences.

Insertion classifier: The high level insert classifer scans over the consecutive sentences and make a binary decision to insert or not.

$$\pi_\theta^{ins}(p|\mathbf{s}_i,\mathbf{d}) = \text{softmax}([\mathbf{h}_i;\mathbf{h}_{i+1}] \cdot \mathbf{A})$$

for $i \in \{1..n\}$ and $\mathbf{A} \in \mathbb{R}^{2\times\mathbf{d}_{\text{model}}}$ is a parameter to be learned. The low level insert classifier is made up of placeholder insertion followed by token insertion. The placeholder classifier predicts the number of tokens to be inserted at every consecutive position pairs, by casting the representation to a categorical distribution

$$\pi_\theta^{ins}(p|w_i,\mathbf{s},\mathbf{d}) = \text{softmax}([\mathbf{h}_i,\mathbf{h}_{i+1}] \cdot \mathbf{B})$$

for $i \in \{1..n\}$ and $\mathbf{B} \in \mathbb{R}^{(k_{max}+1)\times(2\mathbf{d}_{\text{model}})}$ is a parameter to be learned. Following (Gu et al., 2019), k_{max} is 255. Token classifier then fill the placeholders

$$\pi_\theta^{tok}(t|w_i,\mathbf{s},\mathbf{d}) = \text{softmax}(\mathbf{h_i} \cdot \mathbf{C})$$

for $i \in \{1..n\}$ where w_i is a placeholder and $\mathbf{C} \in \mathbb{R}^{|\mathcal{V}|\times\mathbf{d}_{\text{model}}}$ is a parameter to be learned.

Update classifier: The update classifier is only present in the high level program. It scans over the sentences and make a binary decision to update a given sentence

$$\pi_\theta^{upd}(u|\mathbf{s}_i,\mathbf{d}) = \text{softmax}(\mathbf{h}_i \cdot \mathbf{D})$$

for $i \in \{1..n\}$ and $\mathbf{D} \in \mathbb{R}^{2\times\mathbf{d}_{\text{model}}}$ is a parameter to be learned.

(a) Transformer blocks extract the sentence representations which are used by high level policy classifiers. Suppose that the update policy predicts to refine sentence 1 and 3

(b) The input to the low level transformer is the concatenated sentences identified by the high level update policy.

Figure 1: The illustration of the proposed model for the update iteration. The same architecture can be applied for different tasks with specific classifiers. We have omitted attention from transformer blocks for simplicity. p stands for position embedding wheras s is for segment embedding

3.3 Noise

There is no large-scale labeled training dataset for document-level rewriting. Accordingly we train on synthetic dataset. To generate artificial broken text, we apply transformation techniques both at the sentence and word level and then learn to reverse the transformation to recover the original document. The techniques we use at the sentence level include: i) *sentences reordering* where sentences are randomly shuffled and/or deleted; ii) *sentence insertion* that a totally independent sentence is inserted into the source. iii) *sentence update* the sentence is slightly modified. For the lower-level transformation, we apply: i) *word insertion* that we insert a random word from another pre-defined vocabulary into the source. ii) *shuffle and delete* that we shuffle and delete some words. Each transformation is applied with a uniform probability between 0 and 1 leads to different trajectories of noise.

3.4 Oracle

Expert policy actions $\mathbf{a}^*$ are created by reversing the noise in the data. This is done by keeping track of the noise actions that have been used to create a corrupted output. In order to get alignment among sentences, we create a bipartite graph where the nodes are the sentences and the edge weight is the Levenstein distance between those sentences. We use max-flow min-cut algorithm to get the alignment (Dantzig and Fulkerson, 2003).

3.5 Training

Training is done by imitating the expert policy. We design roll-in policy such that each classifier is trained on the output of the other classifier. This reduces exposure bias as the model is trained on conditions it will encounter at decoding. The algorithm for training is shown in algorithm 3. The objective function is the product of decisions made during the generation process. It is the loses incurred by both the high level and low level program and is shown on line 14.

4 Experiments and Analysis

4.1 Experimental Setup

Data sets. We conduct experiments on synthetically generated dataset consisting of sorted and unsorted sequence pairs. Each sequence contains 5 - 10 and each line has between 20 to 100 tokens. The document is sorted in numerical order with tens coming before hundreds. The numbers lie between 1 and 1000. We generated 300K such pairs for training consisting of unsorted sequence as input and sorted sequence as output.

We further use real world datasets including ROC stories (Mostafazadeh et al., 2016), consisting of multiple 5 lines stories to check the capabilities of our model. We also conducted experiemnts on Multi-news and DUC-2004 for multi-document summarization (MDS), which is a sub-task of summarization tasks. Multi-news (Lebanoff et al., 2018) is a large-scale dataset for MDS and DUC-2004 (Over and Yen, 2004) is a benchmark dataset in MDS and its source documents are truncated to 1,500 tokens. To generate our input and output pairs, we inserted noise in the output sequences as outlined in section 3.3.

Evaluation Metrics. Rouge (Hovy et al., 2006), an automatic evaluation metric, is commonly used in Summarization to evaluate the quality of summaries. We use Rouge-l, Rouge-2 and Rouge-L to measure unigram-overlap, bigram-overlap, and the longest common sequence between system and actual summaries. Synthetic and ROC stories are evaluated with BLEU score (Papineni et al., 2002).

Baselines. We compare three models: i) *Copy*: the original text is copied without any change, which establishes the lower bound for the task. ii) *Transformer*: a vanilla Transformer (Vaswani et al., 2017) is used to generate a sequence of text by reconstructing the source text. Without explicit editing guidance, we have little control over its generation process. iii) *Levenshtein Transformer (LevT)*: LevT is a semi autoregressive model for parallel sentence-level sequence generation (Gu et al., 2019). It refines a given sequence in an iterative manner with three operations, including *deletion*, *placeholder prediction* and *token prediction*. The iteration terminates when a certain stopping criterion is met. iv) *Editor transformer*: It is similar to the LevT, with the exception that it introduce a reposition operator instead of the deletion operator (Xu and Carpuat, 2020).

Implementation Details. To train the our models, we follow most of the hyper-parameter settings in (Gu et al., 2019). The only differences are that we use 3 Nvidia V100 GPUs and adopt fastbpe (**?**).

4.2 Results

The main results for summarization are shown in table 1. The best result is obtained by copy across both dataset indicating that post editing of long sequences may hurt its quality. Copy consist of output from SummPip system (Zhao et al., 2020a). SummPip uses graph clustering to find relevant sentences which are then used to generate the summary. Among other models, the Vanilla transformer performed better showing a strong bias present in the languages for autoregressive monotone generation. Levenshtein and the Editor transformer performed comparably whereas as our model showed no improvement over the baselines. We see similar performance in Synthetic and ROC-stories dataset in table 2 with Vanilla transformer performing better then the other models.

	Multi-News			DUC-2004		
	R-1	R-2	R-L	R-1	R-2	R-L
Copy	42.32	13.28	37.86	36.30	8.47	32.52
Transformer	40.62	12.42	36.37	35.4	7.78	31.71
LevT	25.93	8.59	28.95	23.45	4.89	25.12
Editor	25.56	8.13	28.33	23.17	4.21	25.01
Ours	21.67	5.89	24.03	18.22	2.17	20.87

Table 1: Experiment Results on Multi-News and DUC2004 dataset

	Synthetic	ROC-Stories
Copy	23.59	28.82
Transformer	30.17	35.72
LevT	22.42	25.29
Editor	22.78	25.89
Ours	20.63	23.10

Table 2: Experiment Results on Synthetic and ROC-stories dataset. We report the BLEU score in the table.

4.3 Analysis

We outlines various ways to improve the results of our model:

Evaluation metrics sensitivity towards document level ordering: We measure the sensitivity of our evaluation metrics towards capturing sentence reordering. We permuted sentences in a document and measure the metric's mean and standard deviation. The results in table 2 shows the inadequacy of using these metrics(BLEU, ROGUE) towards document level phenomenons. This suggest a training approach where a low level program is initially trained separately and then kept frozen while the high level program is trained.

	Mean	Standard Deviation
Synthetic	97.84	±0.05
ROC stories	98.94	±0.03
Multi-News	97.95	±0.05
DUC-2004	97.73	±0.05

Table 3: Sensitivity of metrics towards capturing sentence reordering. We synthetic and ROC stories we report the BLEU score. For Multi-news and DOC-2004 we report the R1 score. Mean and standard deviation is measured over 10 runs.

Distilled Dataset: Semi/non-autoregressive models struggle to achieve quality similar to autoregressive models. As the dependencies are broken, it become difficult for the model to generalise across multimodal dataset. The situation is further aggravated when the sequences are long. Distilled dataset has been found useful in dealing with multomodality problem in non-autoregressive modals (Zhou et al., 2019). Instead of using the actual output, the outputs generated from an autoregressive teacher modal are used with the input sequence. It is not directly clear as to how we can use distilled data in our model. One way is to insert the noise in distilled dataset to get input sequences. Another way is to use curriculum learning (Bengio et al., 2009), starting with distilled dataset and then moving to harder actual examples.

Better Training: Pre-training and fine-tuning approach has been found useful in various tasks. Our model consist of various components including classifiers at two levels. These classifiers can be individually pre-trained. Once the pre-training step is done, the whole model can be fine tuned for better model generalisation.

Use of Autoregressive model: The low level program is responsible for word generation. Due to the inherent left to right generation bias, autoregressive models have shown better results in our experiments. We can take advantage of this bias by using autoregressive model as a low level program but this can lead to longer decoding times.

Attention Mechanism: Wider context have been shown to improve results for various document level task (Kim et al., 2019). Designing an attention mechanism such that more attention is given to the sentences around the given sentence than those far away in the document can improve results. This can be done by having more attention heads for the near context then the far away context.

5 Related Work

Previous work on long text generation has mostly focused on generating tokens up to three hundred words. These method usually employ the idea of planning a document before generating it (Shen et al., 2019; Zhao et al., 2020b; Rashkin et al., 2020). Another line of work, focus on extending transformer architecture to model long sequences (Wang et al., 2020; Choromanski et al., 2020). Recent work by (Tan et al., 2020) used pre-train language models to progressively generate longer text greater than 300 tokens. Our work differs from previous approaches as it allows editing the generated text while it is being written. Previous work on non-monotonic generation and refinement (Welleck et al., 2019; Stern et al., 2019; Lee et al., 2018) has mostly focused on generating shorter text. Our proposed approach, differs from prior works by extending non-monotonic generation towards longer texts.

6 Conclusion

We present a hierarchical document generation model, that is capable of revising and editing its generated text thus bringing it closer to human-level intelligence. Although results showed that our approach lags behind the baselines, it did shed light into various problems present in semi-autoregressive models and long document generation. In the future, we will be incorporating these insights into our model to make it more robust.

Acknowledgments

References

Yoshua Bengio, Jérôme Louradour, Ronan Collobert, and Jason Weston. 2009. Curriculum learning. In *Proceedings of the 26th annual international conference on machine learning*, pages 41–48.

Antoine Bosselut, Asli Celikyilmaz, Xiaodong He, Jianfeng Gao, Po-Sen Huang, and Yejin Choi. 2018. Discourse-aware neural rewards for coherent text generation. *arXiv preprint arXiv:1805.03766.*

Tom B Brown, Benjamin Mann, Nick Ryder, Melanie Subbiah, Jared Kaplan, Prafulla Dhariwal, Arvind Neelakantan, Pranav Shyam, Girish Sastry, Amanda Askell, et al. 2020. Language models are few-shot learners. *arXiv preprint arXiv:2005.14165.*

Krzysztof Choromanski, Valerii Likhosherstov, David Dohan, Xingyou Song, Andreea Gane, Tamas Sarlos, Peter Hawkins, Jared Davis, Afroz Mohiuddin, Lukasz Kaiser, et al. 2020. Rethinking attention with performers. *arXiv preprint arXiv:2009.14794.*

G Dantzig and Delbert Ray Fulkerson. 2003. On the max flow min cut theorem of networks. *Linear inequalities and related systems*, 38:225–231.

Angela Fan, Mike Lewis, and Yann Dauphin. 2018. Hierarchical neural story generation. *arXiv preprint arXiv:1805.04833.*

Frédérick Garcia and Emmanuel Rachelson. 2013. Markov decision processes. *Markov Decision Processes in Artificial Intelligence*, pages 1–38.

Jiatao Gu, James Bradbury, Caiming Xiong, Victor OK Li, and Richard Socher. 2017. Non-autoregressive neural machine translation. *arXiv preprint arXiv:1711.02281*.

Jiatao Gu and Xiang Kong. 2020. Fully non-autoregressive neural machine translation: Tricks of the trade. *arXiv preprint arXiv:2012.15833*.

Jiatao Gu, Changhan Wang, and Jake Zhao. 2019. Levenshtein transformer. *arXiv preprint arXiv:1905.11006*.

Eduard H Hovy, Chin-Yew Lin, Liang Zhou, and Junichi Fukumoto. 2006. Automated summarization evaluation with basic elements. In *LREC*, volume 6, pages 604–611. Citeseer.

Ahmed Hussein, Mohamed Medhat Gaber, Eyad Elyan, and Chrisina Jayne. 2017. Imitation learning: A survey of learning methods. *ACM Computing Surveys (CSUR)*, 50(2):1–35.

Jungo Kasai, James Cross, Marjan Ghazvininejad, and Jiatao Gu. 2020. Non-autoregressive machine translation with disentangled context transformer. In *International Conference on Machine Learning*, pages 5144–5155. PMLR.

Yunsu Kim, Duc Thanh Tran, and Hermann Ney. 2019. When and why is document-level context useful in neural machine translation? *arXiv preprint arXiv:1910.00294*.

Logan Lebanoff, Kaiqiang Song, and Fei Liu. 2018. Adapting the neural encoder-decoder framework from single to multi-document summarization. *arXiv preprint arXiv:1808.06218*.

Jason Lee, Elman Mansimov, and Kyunghyun Cho. 2018. Deterministic non-autoregressive neural sequence modeling by iterative refinement. *arXiv preprint arXiv:1802.06901*.

Mike Lewis, Yinhan Liu, Naman Goyal, Marjan Ghazvininejad, Abdelrahman Mohamed, Omer Levy, Ves Stoyanov, and Luke Zettlemoyer. 2019. Bart: Denoising sequence-to-sequence pre-training for natural language generation, translation, and comprehension. *arXiv preprint arXiv:1910.13461*.

Ming Liu, Wray Buntine, and Gholamreza Haffari. 2018. Learning to actively learn neural machine translation. In *Proceedings of the 22nd Conference on Computational Natural Language Learning*, pages 334–344.

Nasrin Mostafazadeh, Nathanael Chambers, Xiaodong He, Devi Parikh, Dhruv Batra, Lucy Vanderwende, Pushmeet Kohli, and James Allen. 2016. A corpus and evaluation framework for deeper understanding of commonsense stories. *arXiv preprint arXiv:1604.01696*.

Paul Over and James Yen. 2004. An introduction to duc-2004. *National Institute of Standards and Technology*.

Kishore Papineni, Salim Roukos, Todd Ward, and Wei-Jing Zhu. 2002. Bleu: a method for automatic evaluation of machine translation. In *Proceedings of the 40th annual meeting of the Association for Computational Linguistics*, pages 311–318.

Hannah Rashkin, Asli Celikyilmaz, Yejin Choi, and Jianfeng Gao. 2020. Plotmachines: Outline-conditioned generation with dynamic plot state tracking. *arXiv preprint arXiv:2004.14967*.

Dinghan Shen, Asli Celikyilmaz, Yizhe Zhang, Liqun Chen, Xin Wang, Jianfeng Gao, and Lawrence Carin. 2019. Towards generating long and coherent text with multi-level latent variable models. *arXiv preprint arXiv:1902.00154*.

Mitchell Stern, William Chan, Jamie Kiros, and Jakob Uszkoreit. 2019. Insertion transformer: Flexible sequence generation via insertion operations. In *International Conference on Machine Learning*, pages 5976–5985. PMLR.

Bowen Tan, Zichao Yang, Maruan AI-Shedivat, Eric P Xing, and Zhiting Hu. 2020. Progressive generation of long text with pretrained language models. *arXiv preprint arXiv:2006.15720*.

Ashish Vaswani, Noam Shazeer, Niki Parmar, Jakob Uszkoreit, Llion Jones, Aidan N Gomez, Łukasz Kaiser, and Illia Polosukhin. 2017. Attention is all you need. In *Advances in neural information processing systems*, pages 5998–6008.

Sinong Wang, Belinda Z Li, Madian Khabsa, Han Fang, and Hao Ma. 2020. Linformer: Self-attention with linear complexity. *arXiv preprint arXiv:2006.04768*.

Yiren Wang, Fei Tian, Di He, Tao Qin, ChengXiang Zhai, and Tie-Yan Liu. 2019. Non-autoregressive machine translation with auxiliary regularization. In *Proceedings of the AAAI Conference on Artificial Intelligence*, pages 5377–5384.

Sean Welleck, Kianté Brantley, Hal Daumé III, and Kyunghyun Cho. 2019. Non-monotonic sequential text generation. *arXiv preprint arXiv:1902.02192*.

Weijia Xu and Marine Carpuat. 2020. Editor: an edit-based transformer with repositioning for neural machine translation with soft lexical constraints. *arXiv preprint arXiv:2011.06868*.

Jinming Zhao, Ming Liu, Longxiang Gao, Yuan Jin, Lan Du, He Zhao, He Zhang, and Gholamreza Haffari. 2020a. Summpip: Unsupervised multi-document summarization with sentence graph compression. In *Proceedings of the 43rd International ACM SIGIR Conference on Research and Development in Information Retrieval*, pages 1949–1952.

Liang Zhao, Jingjing Xu, Junyang Lin, Yichang Zhang, Hongxia Yang, and Xu Sun. 2020b. Graph-based multi-hop reasoning for long text generation. *arXiv preprint arXiv:2009.13282*.

Chunting Zhou, Graham Neubig, and Jiatao Gu. 2019. Understanding knowledge distillation in non-autoregressive machine translation. *arXiv preprint arXiv:1911.02727*.

A Appendices

A.1 Generation Algorithm

Algorithm 1 Generation in HMDP

Require: Initial document $\mathbf{d}_0$, policy: π_{θ_H}

$\mathbf{d} \leftarrow \mathbf{d}_0$
while Termination condition is not met **do**
  $\textbf{rep\_index} \leftarrow \arg\max_{\mathbf{r}} \sum_{\mathbf{s}_i \in \mathbf{d}} \log \pi_{\theta_H}^{rep}(r_i|\mathbf{s}_i, \mathbf{d})$ ▷ Do reposition
  $\mathbf{d} \leftarrow \mathscr{E}(\mathbf{d}, \textbf{rep\_index})$
  $\textbf{ins\_index} \leftarrow \arg\max_{\mathbf{p}} \sum_{\mathbf{s}_i, \mathbf{s}_{i+1} \in \mathbf{d}} \log \pi_{\theta_H}^{ins}(p_i|\mathbf{s}_i, \mathbf{s}_{i+1}, \mathbf{d})$ ▷ Do insertion
  $\mathbf{d} \leftarrow \mathscr{E}(\mathbf{d}, \textbf{ins\_index})$ ▷ Call to Low level MDP
  $\textbf{upd\_index} \leftarrow \arg\max_{\mathbf{u}} \sum_{\mathbf{s}_i \in \mathbf{d}} \log \pi_{\theta_H}^{upd}(u_i|\mathbf{s}_i, \mathbf{d})$ ▷ Do update
  $\mathbf{d} \leftarrow \mathscr{E}(\mathbf{d}, \textbf{upd\_index})$ ▷ Call to Low level MDP
end while

Algorithm 2 Low Level MDP

Require: Document $\mathbf{d}$, policy: π_{θ_L}, Hi Level MDP action: $\mathbf{H}$

while Termination condition is not met **do**
  $\mathbf{s}_0 \leftarrow \text{buildFrame}(\mathbf{d}, \mathbf{H})$
  if $\mathbf{s}_0$ is empty **then**
    $\mathbf{s} \leftarrow \mathbf{s}_0$ ▷ Skip reposition
  else
    $\textbf{rep\_index} \leftarrow \arg\max_{\mathbf{r}} \sum_{w_i \in \mathbf{s}} \log \pi_{\theta_L}^{rep}(r_i|w_i, \mathbf{s}, \mathbf{d})$ ▷ Do reposition
    $\mathbf{d} \leftarrow \mathscr{E}(\mathbf{s}, \textbf{rep\_index})$
  end if
  $\textbf{plh\_index} \leftarrow \arg\max_{\mathbf{p}} \sum_{w_i, w_{i+1} \in \mathbf{s}} \log \pi_{\theta_L}^{ins}(p_i|w_i, w_{i+1}, \mathbf{s}, \mathbf{d})$ ▷ Insert placeholders
  $\mathbf{s} \leftarrow \mathscr{E}(\mathbf{s}, \textbf{plh\_index})$
  $\textbf{tok\_index} \leftarrow \arg\max_{\mathbf{t}} \sum_{w_i \in \mathbf{s}, w_i == <mask>} \log \pi_{\theta_L}^{tok}(t_i|w_i, \mathbf{s}, \mathbf{d})$ ▷ Fill placeholders
  $\mathbf{s} \leftarrow \mathscr{E}(\mathbf{s}, \textbf{tok\_index})$
end while
$\mathbf{d} \leftarrow \text{documentUpdate}(\mathbf{d}, \mathbf{s})$

A.2 Training Algorithm

Algorithm 3 Training for Hierarchical Levenshtein Transformer

Require: Training data $\mathcal{T}$, Model policy: π_θ, Expert policy: π_*

while Maximum training steps reached **do**

$\quad (\mathbf{d}, \mathbf{d}_*) \sim \mathcal{T}$ ▷ Sample a training pair

$\quad \mathbf{repH}^*, \mathbf{insH}^*, \mathbf{updH}^* \leftarrow \pi_*^H(\mathbf{d}, \mathbf{d}_*)$ ▷ Get oracle actions

$\quad \mathbf{repL1}^*, \mathbf{insL1}^*, \mathbf{tokL1}^*, \mathbf{repL2}^*, \mathbf{insL2}^*, \mathbf{tokL2}^* \leftarrow \pi_*^L(\mathbf{d}, \mathbf{d}_*)$

$\quad \mathcal{L}_{\theta_H}^{rep} \leftarrow -\sum_{\mathbf{s}_i \in \mathbf{d}} \log \pi_{\theta_H}^{rep}(repH_i^* | \mathbf{s}_i, \mathbf{d})$

$\quad \mathbf{d} \leftarrow \text{applyAction}(\mathbf{d}, \mathbf{repH}^*)$

$\quad \mathcal{L}_{\theta_H}^{ins} \leftarrow -\sum_{\mathbf{s}_i, \mathbf{s}_{i+1} \in \mathbf{d}} \log \pi_{\theta_H}^{ins}(insH_i^* | \mathbf{s}_i, \mathbf{s}_{i+1}, \mathbf{d})$

$\quad \mathbf{s} \leftarrow \text{buildFrame}(\mathbf{insH}^*, \mathbf{d})$

$\quad \mathcal{L}_{\theta_L}^{rep1} \leftarrow -\sum_{w_i \in \mathbf{s}} \log \pi_{\theta_L}^{rep}(repL1_i^* | w_i, \mathbf{s}, \mathbf{d})$ ▷ Low Level

$\quad \mathbf{s} \leftarrow \text{applyAction}(\mathbf{s}, \mathbf{repL1}^*)$

$\quad \mathcal{L}_{\theta_L}^{ins1} \leftarrow -\sum_{w_i, w_{i+1} \in \mathbf{s}} \log \pi_{\theta_L}^{ins}(insL1_i^* | w_i, w_{i+1}, \mathbf{s}, \mathbf{d})$

$\quad \mathbf{s} \leftarrow \text{applyAction}(\mathbf{s}, \mathbf{insL1}^*)$

$\quad \mathcal{L}_{\theta_L}^{tok1} \leftarrow -\sum_{w_i \in \mathbf{s}, w_i = <mask>} \log \pi_{\theta_L}^{tok}(tokL1_i^* | w_i, \mathbf{s}, \mathbf{d})$

$\quad \mathbf{d} \leftarrow \text{applyAction}(\mathbf{d}, \mathbf{insH}^*)$

$\quad \mathcal{L}_{\theta_H}^{upd} \leftarrow -\sum_{\mathbf{s}_i \in \mathbf{d}} \log \pi_{\theta_H}^{upd}(updH_i^* | \mathbf{s}_i, \mathbf{d})$

$\quad \mathbf{s} \leftarrow \text{buildFrame}(\mathbf{updH}^*, \mathbf{d})$

$\quad \mathcal{L}_{\theta_L}^{rep2} \leftarrow -\sum_{w_i \in \mathbf{s}} \log \pi_{\theta_L}^{rep}(repL2_i^* | w_i, \mathbf{s}, \mathbf{d})$ ▷ Low Level

$\quad \mathbf{s} \leftarrow \text{applyAction}(\mathbf{s}, \mathbf{repL2}^*)$

$\quad \mathcal{L}_{\theta_L}^{ins2} \leftarrow -\sum_{w_i, w_{i+1} \in \mathbf{s}} \log \pi_{\theta_L}^{ins}(insL2_i^* | w_i, w_{i+1}, \mathbf{s}, \mathbf{d})$

$\quad \mathbf{s} \leftarrow \text{applyAction}(\mathbf{s}, \mathbf{insL2}^*)$

$\quad \mathcal{L}_{\theta_L}^{tok2} \leftarrow -\sum_{w_i \in \mathbf{s}, w_i = <mask>} \log \pi_{\theta_L}^{tok}(tokL2_i^* | w_i, \mathbf{s}, \mathbf{d})$

$\quad \theta \leftarrow \theta - \lambda \nabla [\mathcal{L}_{\theta_H}^{rep} + \mathcal{L}_{\theta_H}^{ins} + \mathcal{L}_{\theta_H}^{upd} + \mathcal{L}_{\theta_L}^{rep1} + \mathcal{L}_{\theta_L}^{ins1} + \mathcal{L}_{\theta_L}^{tok1} + \mathcal{L}_{\theta_L}^{rep2} + \mathcal{L}_{\theta_L}^{ins2} + \mathcal{L}_{\theta_L}^{tok2}]$

end while

Exploring the Vulnerability of Natural Language Processing Models via Universal Adversarial Texts

Xinzhe Li[1], **Ming Liu**[1,2], **Xingjun Ma**[1] and **Longxiang Gao**[1]

[1]School of IT, Deakin University, Australia
[2]Zhongtukexin Co. Ltd. , Beijing, China
{lixinzhe, m.liu,longxiang.gao}@deakin.edu.au
danxjma@gmail.com

Abstract

Universal adversarial texts (UATs) refer to short pieces of text units that can largely affect the predictions of Natural Language Processing (NLP) models. Recent studies on universal adversarial attacks require the availability of validation/test data which may not always be available in practice. In this paper, we propose two types of Data-Free Adjusted Gradient (DFAG) attacks to show that it is possible to generate effective UATs with manually crafted examples. Based on the proposed DFAG attacks, we explore the vulnerability of commonly used NLP models from two perspectives: network architecture and pre-trained embedding. The empirical results on three text classification datasets show that: 1) CNN-based and LSTM models are more vulnerable to UATs than self-attention models; 2) the vulnerability/robustness difference between of CNN/LSTM models and self-attention models could be attributed to whether or not they rely on training data artifacts for predictions; and 3) the pre-trained embeddings could expose vulnerability to both UAT and transferred UTA attacks.

1 Introduction

Deep neural networks (DNNs) have enabled significant advancement in a range of natural language processing (NLP) applications such as sentiment analysis (Yang et al., 2019; Xu et al., 2019) and topic classification (Sun et al., 2019). Despite the superior performance, DNNs are known to be vulnerable to adversarial perturbations (Szegedy et al., 2014; Goodfellow et al., 2015; Ma et al., 2018; Li et al., 2019; Ma et al., 2021), i.e., small changes on the input could lead to entirely incorrect predictions (Croce and Hein, 2020; Jiang et al., 2020). It has raised practical security concerns for the deployment of DNNs in safety-critical scenarios (Eykholt et al., 2018; Duan et al., 2020). Adversarially perturbed inputs are known as adversarial examples and the process of generating adversarial examples is known as adversarial attack. It has become a common practice to examine the vulnerability of DNNs to adversarial examples and mitigate the vulnerability by involving adversarial examples during the training process as a type of augmented data (Nie et al., 2020; Madry et al., 2018; Wang et al., 2019a; Zhang et al., 2019; Wang et al., 2019b; Croce et al., 2020).

Most adversarial attack methods for NLP models (Alzantot et al., 2018; Ebrahimi et al., 2018b; Jin et al., 2020) are sample-wise methods that craft adversarial examples by manipulating each clean example. Different from sample-wise attacks, universal adversarial attack (Behjati et al., 2019) aims to generate Universal Adversarial Texts (UATs) or universal triggers (Wallace et al., 2019) for each class or the entire dataset to fool NLP models. However, existing methods (Wallace et al., 2019; Song et al., 2021; Behjati et al., 2019) all require the validation/test dataset of the task or some proxy datasets in a similar domain to craft UATs.

To more easily and efficiently generate UATs, we propose Data-Free Adjusted Gradient (DFAG) attacks. According to the evaluation, our proposed DFAG attacks achieve a comparable performance as the original linear approximation method (Wallace et al., 2019) on most of the NLP models. We find that UATs generated by our method highly overlap with those from the original linear approximation method (Wallace et al., 2019). This indicates that the vulnerability of UATs may be inherent in the models. To better understand the vulnerability, we take text classification as an example and dive into different neural network architectures. Empirical results show that CNN and LSTM models are notebly more vulnerable to UATs than self-attention models. We also reveal that the effectiveness of UATs generated for LSTM and CNN models exposes certain training data artifacts, i.e., important words in the training data that are more closely correlated with the targeted class. In contrast, self-attention models are relatively more robust to UATs. This finding is consistent with previous study on model robustness to training data artifacts, so it is likely that self-attention models suffer less from training data artifacts.

Apart from the neural architectures, we also examine pre-trained embeddings, including static pre-trained word embeddings (Pennington et al., 2014; Mikolov et al., 2018) and contextualized ones from the pre-trained language model BERT (Devlin et al., 2018). These embeddings have been widely used in different NLP applications. Our experiments show that pre-trained word embeddings could deteriorate model robustness to UATs, and even self-attention models can become vulnerable with pre-trained embeddings. Upon further investigation, we find that UATs are often transferable among models that use the same pre-trained embeddings. This reveals one unique vulnerability of NLP models to UATs.

2 Generating Universal Adversarial Texts

Problem Formulation. Consider a text classifier f mapping from input $\mathbf{x}$ to label y. The goal of universal adversarial attack is to generate a small sequence of tokens $\mathbf{t} = (t_1, t_2, ..., t_k)$ (i.e., an UAT), which can be inserted into any clean example x to cause misclassification towards a targeted wrong label $\tilde{y}$. Previous work (Behjati et al., 2019; Wallace et al., 2019) showed the effectiveness of UAT when three words are inserted at the beginning of the input sequence. Here, we follow their settings and predetermine the adversarial target class $\tilde{y}$. The attack problem can be formally definedd as: for any clean example $\{(\mathbf{x}, y) | (\mathbf{x}, y) \in \mathcal{D} \text{ and } y \neq \tilde{y}\}$, we aim to make the classifier f predict the perturbed example $\mathbf{t} \oplus \mathbf{x}$ as the targeted label $\tilde{y}$, i.e., $f(\mathbf{t} \oplus \mathbf{x}) = \tilde{y}$. The problem can be solved by minimizing an adversarial loss $\mathcal{L}_{adv}(\mathbf{t} \oplus \mathbf{x}, \tilde{y})$, which is the cross-entropy loss defined with the targeted label.

$$\arg\min_{\mathbf{t}} \quad \mathbb{E}_{(\mathbf{x},y)\sim\mathcal{D}}[\mathcal{L}_{adv}(\mathbf{t} \oplus \mathbf{x}, \tilde{y})] \tag{1}$$

2.1 Gradient-based Attack

A UAT is composed of discrete tokens for which we search from the vocabulary $\mathcal{V} = w_1, w_2, \ldots, w_{|V|}$ ($|V|$ is the size of vocabulary). Each word w_i in the vocabulary is represented by a dense vector called embedding e_i. In order to find the optimal UAT, Behjati et al. (2019) applied gradient descent for $\mathbf{t}$ in the embedding space and identified the word in the vocabulary by projecting the nearest embeddings of the word. More efficiently, Wallace et al. (2019) proposed a linear approximation approach to generate gradients to approximate the loss of substituting $\mathbf{t}$ with $\mathbf{t}_{\text{update}}$, i.e., $\mathcal{L}_{adv}(\mathbf{t}_{\text{update}} \oplus \mathbf{x}, \tilde{y})$. According to the first-order Taylor approximation, we measure the effectiveness of the substitution by the inner product of the gradient $\nabla_{e_t}\mathcal{L}_{adv}$ with the embedding of t_{update}.

$$\arg\min_{e_t} \quad e_{t_{\text{update}}}^{\mathrm{T}} \nabla_{e_t}\mathcal{L}_{adv} \tag{2}$$

The approximation scores for all the possible substitution words in the vocabulary can be efficiently calculated via matrix multiplication, where $\mathbf{E} \in \mathbb{R}^{|V| \times m}$ denotes the embedding matrix with vocabulary size $|V|$ and embedding size m. It only needs one forward and backward pass to compute the gradients for all the positions of UAT tokens. The equation is shown below where $\nabla_{e_t}\mathcal{L}_{adv}$ has the dimensions for positions of UAT tokens and embedding size m.

$$\mathbf{A} = \mathbf{E} \times \nabla_{e_t}\mathcal{L}_{adv} \tag{3}$$

Both approaches require batches of data to update the UAT t. However, we can still use the linear approximation approach as a baseline for our experiment due to its efficiency. This approach requires a batch of examples to calculate the gradient for each update of the UAT, as shown in Equation (4) where n examples are consumed.

$$\nabla_{e_t}\mathcal{L}_{adv} = \frac{1}{n}\sum_{i=1}^{n} \nabla_{e_t}\mathcal{L}_{adv}(\mathbf{t} \oplus x_i) \tag{4}$$

2.2 Data-free Adjusted Gradient Attack

The universal property of UATs indicates that they reflect the inherent vulnerability of well-trained NLP models. Moreover, Wallace et al. (2019) reveals that UATs are a form of training data artifacts for natural language inference models. We suspect the validity of this conclusion across all text classification tasks, which is shown in Section 3.4.

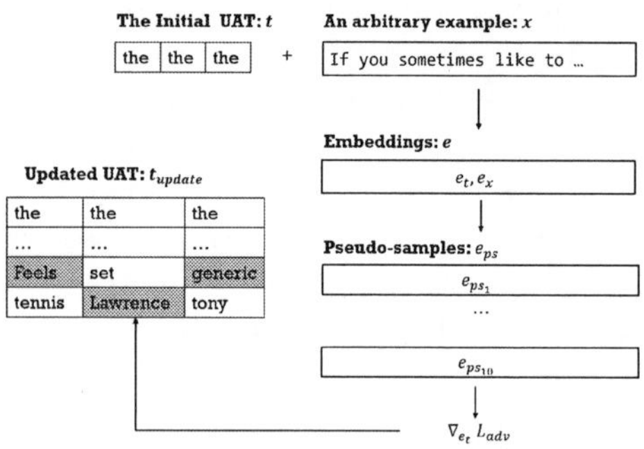

Figure 1: One iteration of the DFAG attack. The arbitrary example x is a positive movie review selected from the SST-2 test data, and the goal is to generate a UAT to make any non-negative (positive) reviews to be classified as negative ones. The UAT is generated by iterating the process: (1) concatenate the UAT t and the example x ; (2) generate dense text representation of $t \oplus x$, i.e., e_t, e_x; (3) generate pseudo-samples e_{ps} in the embedding space; (4) compute the gradient of adversarial loss w.r.t. e_t and finally find the updated UAT t_{updage} via the linear approximation method.

Therefore, using batches of data for universal attack might be redundant. Our proposed algorithm only requires an arbitrary example $\mathbf{x} = w_1, w_2, ..., w_l$ (l denotes the length of the text) which does not belong to the targeted class $\tilde{y}$ to generate effective UATs. In our experiment, we select the first valid sample from the test data. The attack could be *data-free* if the adversary chooses to manually craft the example. This is feasible because the only requirement for the example is that it does not belong to the targeted class. An interesting parallel work (Parekh et al., 2021) of data-free attack generates what they defined as "class impressions" for this purpose. We regard that the use of class impressions does lead to faster convergence but are not necessary, according to our experiments. Figure 1 demonstrates the process of updating the UAT in one iteration of our DFAG attack.

Unreliable gradients. The gradient for one single example might not be reliable since a DNN is usually not a smooth function. One most notable example is that an infinitesimal perturbation of the input could change its prediction. The issue also happens to the field of model interpretation, where they attribute input features for model prediction. Therefore, we generate pseudo-samples e_{ps} which are dense vectors $e_{ps1}, .., e_{psK}$ in the embedding space and compute more reliable gradient by aggregating the gradients of the pseudo-samples.

Generating pseudo-samples. We pass the $\mathbf{t} \oplus \mathbf{x}$ into the embedding layer, which outputs the dense representation $\mathbf{e}$ in the embedding space. We then manipulate $\mathbf{e}$ to generate K pseudo-samples $\mathbf{e}_{ps}$ in the embedding space during each iteration. The gradients of the pseudo-samples are then aggregated to apply the linear approximation attack. We refer to this approach as the DFAG (Data-Free Adjusted Gradient) attack.

We employ the following two techniques to generate pseudo-samples, which have been proved to be effective in approximating gradients for model interpretation (Smilkov et al., 2017; Sundararajan et al., 2017).

- Smooth noise: the Gaussian noise η is generated with mean 0 and standard deviation σ. We denote this method as DFAG (Smooth) to accredit the *SmoothGrad* method (Smilkov et al., 2017).

$$\mathbf{e}_{ps} = \{\mathbf{e} + \eta_i \mid i \in [1..K]\} \quad \text{where} \quad \eta_i \sim \mathcal{N}(0, \sigma^2) \tag{5}$$

- Path method: we sample K pseudo-samples evenly along the straight path from the origin to the given sample. We denote this method as *DFAG (Integrated)* to accredit the *Integrated Gradient* method (Sundararajan et al., 2017).

$$\mathbf{e}_{ps} = \{\mathbf{e}_{ps_i} \mid i \in [1..K]\} \quad \text{where} \quad \mathbf{e}_{ps_i} = \frac{i}{K} \times \mathbf{e} \tag{6}$$

3 Attacking Text Classification Models

This section introduces model configurations and attack settings, and analyzes the experimental results. We also publish the source code for all the settings and experiments on Github [1] to reproduce the result.

3.1 Modeling Setup

Tasks and Datasets. Our experiments include Stanford Sentiment Treebank (SST-2) (Socher et al., 2013), Yelp (Zhang et al., 2015) datasets for sentiment classification task, and AG-News constructed by (Zhang et al., 2015) for topic classification task.

[1] https://github.com/xinzhel/attack_alta

Task	Architecture	Pre-trained	Attack Success Rate			ASR Ratio
			Baseline	DFAG (Smooth)	DFAG (Integrated)	
SST-2	LSTM	/	0.53	0.53	0.52	1
		GloVe	0.43	0.44	0.3	**1.02**
		FastText	0.85	0.85	0.81	1
		BERT	0.43	0.25	0	0.58
	CNN	/	1	0	1	1
		GloVe	1	1	1	1
		FastText	1	0	1	1
		BERT	0.25	0.2	0.1	0.8
	Self-attention	/	0.43	0.43	0.43	1
		GloVe	1	1	1	1
		FastText	1	1	1	1
		BERT	0.16	0.15	0	0.94
Yelp	LSTM	/	0.55	0.26	1	**1.82**
		GloVe	0.81	0.89	0.13	**1.1**
		FastText	0.58	0.4	0.24	0.69
		BERT	0.16	0.14	0.05	0.88
	CNN	/	1	0	0	*0*
		GloVe	0.91	0	0.37	*0.41*
		FastText	1	0	0.98	0.98
		BERT	0.24	0.14	0.02	0.58
	Self-attention	/	0.15	0.15	0	1
		GloVe	0.97	0.97	0.68	1
		FastText	0.98	0.98	0	1
		BERT	0.1	0.07	0.03	0.7
AG-News	LSTM	/	0.3	0.3	0.3	1
		GloVe	0.3	0.18	0	0.6
		FastText	0.2	0.2	0.2	1
		BERT	0	0	0	/
	CNN	/	1	1	1	1
		GloVe	0.88	0.91	0.41	**1.03**
		FastText	1	0.98	1	0.98
		BERT	0.04	0.06	0	**1.5**
	Self-Attention	/	0.02	0.01	0	0.5
		GloVe	0	0	0	/
		FastText	0.1	0.38	0.13	**3.8**
		BERT	0	0	0	/

Table 1: Attack success rates on different NLP models. One targeted class is selected to attack for each task: "negative" class for SST-2, Yelp, "Business" class for AG-News. The baseline attack refers to Wallace et al. (2019), while the DFAG (smooth) and DFAG (integrated) attacks use the smooth noise and path method. We use the ASR ratio of the DFAG attack to the baseline attack to measure the effectiveness of our DFAG attacks. **The numbers in bold** indicate that our DFAG attacks are more effective than the baseline. The ratios of less than 0.5 are marked in *the italics and underlining*, which indicate that our DFAG attacks are much less effective than the baseline.

Model architectures. We use three classical neural networks as the text classifiers.

- LSTM: Two-layer LSTM with 512 hidden dimensions. We take the final hidden state of the last time step for fully connected and softmax layers to compute the probability distribution of all the classes.

- CNN (Zhang and Wallace, 2017): Four 1-dimensional convolution layers with filter sizes (2, 3, 4, 5) respectively. Each layer has six filters and is followed by the ReLU activation function and max-pooling layers. Therefore, the total output dimension is 24.

- Self-attention: One self-attention layer where we set 5 parallel attention heads (Vaswani et al., 2017) followed by a self-attentive pooling layer (McCann et al., 2017).

Pre-trained embeddings. We use static word embeddings GloVe (Pennington et al., 2014), FastText (Mikolov et al., 2018) and the contextualized embeddings from the last hidden layer of the pre-trained language model BERT (Devlin et al., 2018). The pre-trained embeddings can then be fed into the text classifiers. GloVe and FastText have different designs for obtaining word embeddings. GloVe embeddings are trained on a word co-occurrence matrix using a log-bilinear function where any pairs of word vectors are bilinearly mapped into the co-occurrence counts, while FastText embeddings are obtained by training a skip-gram model on word pairs from negative sampling.

All the pre-trained parameters are fixed without fine-tuning, as we aim to separate the vulnerability of the pre-trained embeddings from that of the model architectures and training. Specifically, we want to avoid propagating the information of the training data into pre-trained parameters, which would benefit the analyses of pre-trained embeddings and training data artifacts. In addition, when models use BERT embeddings with LSTM or CNN for classification, self-attention building blocks of BERT could interfere with our evaluation of architectures.

Training hyperparameters. We train all the models with the Adam optimizer, learning rate 5e-5, and batch size 64. The maximum number of training epochs is set to 5, and early stopping would occur when the validation accuracy has no improvement for one epoch.

3.2 Attack Setup

Attack hyperparameters. We select the first example from the attack data used by the baseline and then update the UATs in a maximum of 10 iterations with an early stop if there is no decrease of the loss $\mathcal{L}_{adv}$ for more than three iterations. We generate ten pseudo-samples during each iteration. The standard deviation of Gaussian noise is set as 0.01.

Constraints of substitution tokens. The vocabulary of BERT models has been built along with its pre-trained tasks, whereas we construct the word-level vocabulary from the training data for other models. Since sentiment words have strong indications for sentiment classification, sentiment words are filtered out following the practice in Wallace et al. (2019). In addition, our test examples are restricted to long sequences (>10 words) to preserve semantics to a large extent. BERT employs word-piece segmentation to process textual data into a sequence of sub-word units. However, when one or more sub-word are selected as the UAT tokens, the input may be re-segmented into a different sequence, such as the sub-word "##oot" which would be re-segmented into "#" "o" and "##ot". Our experiment shows that the word-level attack achieves similar performance, and tokens in the word unit cover 76.6% tokens in the BERT vocabulary. Therefore, we only consider substitution tokens in the word units to avoid the re-segmentation issue. The word-level substitutions also prevent that sub-words in UATs become unknown words during the UAT transfer attack.

Evaluation. We calculate Attack Success Rate (ASR) to measure the performance of the attack: the percentage of examples that are misclassified by the model as the targeted class among all the evaluation samples. We select evaluation examples that do not belong to the targeted class from the original test data.

3.3 Experimental Results

We first empirically verify the effectiveness of our attack on three neural network architectures, then evaluate the vulnerability of pre-trained embeddings via UAT transfer attacks.

Attack effectiveness. As shown in Table 1, our DFAG attacks with smooth gradients achieve competitive results on LSTM and self-attention models to the baseline. Moreover, the DFAG (Integrated) attack always performs better on CNN models, except the GloVe-CNN model on AG-News. Note that this finding does not involve BERT-based models since BERT composes of multi-head self-attention layers.

To quantify how much effectiveness our DFAG attacks achieve relative to the baseline attack, we also report the ASR ratio of our DFAG attack to the baseline, i.e.,

$$\frac{\text{ASR of the DFAG}}{\text{ASR of the baseline}}$$

Here, we choose the better one between the two DFAG attacks. It shows that our DFAG attacks achieve more than 50% effectiveness of the baseline in most cases. An ASR ratio of more than 1 indicates that our DFAG (Smooth) attack even outperforms the baseline on several models. Note that our DFAG attacks are proposed to more easily and efficiently examine the vulnerability of NLP models to universal adversaries, rather than competing the ASR with existing attacks.

Failure cases on CNN models. Both DFAG attacks exhibit low success rates against CNN models on the Yelp dataset. By contrast, the baseline attack achieves nearly 100% success rates on all CNN models, where only the GloVe embeddings drop around 10% success rates on Yelp and AG-News datasets. This marks some failure cases of our DFAG attacks.

Comparing UATs generated by the baseline and our DFAG attacks. By comparing the UATs, we find that they actually generate many overlapped UAT tokens, especially for SST-2 models, as shown in Table 3. We suspect that the low overlap rates for AG_News and Yelp models are due to their large vocabulary sizes.

The vulnerability of pre-trained embeddings. As shown in Table 1, the use of pre-trained word embeddings sometimes makes the models more vulnerable, especially for self-attention models. This counter-intuitive result indicates the existence of embedding vulnerabilities in pre-trained embeddings. Our UAT transfer attacks also confirm the vulnerability of pre-trained embeddings. The result in Table 2 shows that UATs tend to achieve the best transferability on models with the same pre-trained embeddings. This phenomenon is also observed for BERT, although the success rate drops.

Measuring UAT transfer attacks. The absolute transfer ASR is not suitable to measure transferability because vulnerable models tend to have low ASRs. Therefore, in Table 2, we normalize the absolute transfer ASR by dividing by the original ASR of the victim model. The higher the normalized ASR the more transferable the UATs are to the target models (columns of Table 2). Take the first row as an example: the absolute transfer ASR of the BERT-LSTM model is only 0.06, while the vulnerable models always have higher ASRs. The normalized ASRs remove the effect of the varying vulnerabilities of the target models since it would amplify the absolute transfer ASR for the robust models, causing the value for BERT-LSTM from 0.06 to 0.44 (0.06 dividing by 0.14).

3.4 Training Data Artifacts in UATs

Training data artifacts are hypothesis words that are highly correlated with the labels. The artifacts have been explored by neural NLP models as the shallow shortcut and spurious correlations for the predictions (Gururangan et al., 2018; Branco et al., 2021). Wallace et al. (2019) argues that effective UATs for Natural Language Inference (NLI) models expose training data artifacts. Through our analyses, we further prove that training data artifacts should be attributed to the existence of UATs. Interestingly, we also find that the self-attention architecture provides certain robustness to such training data artifacts.

Measuring training data artifacts of UATs. We follow Gururangan et al. (2018); Wallace et al. (2019) and compute the point-wise mutual information (PMI) between each word w and the targeted class $\tilde{y}$ as:

$$\text{PMI}(w, \tilde{y}) = \log \frac{p(w, \tilde{y})}{p(w)p(\tilde{y})}$$

The denominator is the expected probability of the word w appearing in class $\tilde{y}$. The numerator is the observed probability. PMI measures how much more the word w occurs in the targeted class than we expect. We measure the training data artifacts of UAT words by their PMI ranks. We rank all the words according to their PMI scores in descending order. Then, the high-rank words show a high correlation with the targeted class, i.e., indicating training data artifacts. We also measure the frequency of each trigger word (i.e., the frequency in a particular class vs. the total frequency) because PMI would amplify words with low frequency.

Self-attention is robust to training data artifacts. The training data artifacts are highly reflected on UATs generated for CNN and LSTM

	Dataset	FastText			GloVe			BERT		
		LSTM	CNN	Self-Attention	LSTM	CNN	Self-Attention	LSTM	CNN	Self-Attention
FastText-LSTM	Yelp	1	0.8	0.42	0.2	0	0.05	**0.44**	0.08	0
	SST	1	1	0.93	**0.7**	**0.91**	**1**	0.02	0.04	0.12
GloVe-LSTM	Yelp	**0.31**	0.07	0	1	0.31	0.73	**0.43**	0.08	0
	SST	**0.96**	**1**	**0.82**	1	0.96	1	0.02	0.04	0.12
BERT-LSTM	Yelp	0.08	0.1	0.02	**0.37**	0.18	0.15	1	0.67	0.7
	SST	0	0.1	0.05	0	0.01	0.01	1	1.16	1.56

Table 2: The vulnerability of pre-trained embeddings is reflected by the UAT transfer attack. Rows: Each row represents the source models on which the UATs are generated. Columns: each column specifies a target model of the transfer attack. For example, the first row of the second column demonstrates the normalized ASR when we apply UATs generated on the FastText-LSTM model to the FastText-CNN model.

	Overlap Rates	Total Tokens	Overlap Tokens	vocabulary Size
SST-2	76%	21	16	17,356
AG-News	33%	6	2	114,068
Yelp	12%	8	1	746,663

Table 3: Overlap rates of the UATs generated by the baseline and our DFAG attacks.

models, while self-attention models generate UATs with low training data artifacts. The result is shown in Table 4. In order to verify the robustness of self-attention models to training data artifacts, the top 5 tokens with high training data artifacts are manually selected to evaluate the LSTM, CNN, and self-attention models. Only the self-attention model shows 0 attack success rates, as can be inferred from Table 5. The robustness of self-attention models may be attributed to their contextualized token representations: each token is represented by attending all the input tokens based on the attention scores. This type of architectures prevents the model from leveraging shallow shortcuts (class-wise triggers) for predictions.

4 Related Work

Universal adversarial perturbations. Behjati et al. (2019); Wallace et al. (2019); Song et al. (2021) generated the input-agnostic perturbations of text for NLP models. These works follow the initial work (Moosavi-Dezfooli et al., 2017) of finding Universal Adversarial Perturbations (UAPs) for images. Compared to the instance-specific adversarial perturbations (Liang et al., 2018; Ebrahimi et al., 2018b,a; Li et al., 2020), UAPs is a more severe security issue (Ribeiro et al., 2020). Behjati et al. (2019) employed projected gradient descent for devising UATs. Wallace et al. (2019) followed the linear approximation to generate adversarial text (Ebrahimi et al., 2018b) to generate UATs, which converges faster than Projected Gradient Descent (PGD). Song et al. (2021) generated natural UATs with less grammatical errors and more fluency via Adversarially Regularized Auto Encoder (ARAE). In this paper, we refer to the gradient approximation method. The original idea was proposed by Ebrahimi et al. (2018b) called Hotflip and then utilized by Wallace et al. (2019) to generate universal triggers.

***Gradient x Embedding* scores for model interpretation.** The first-order Taylor approach and *Gradient x Embedding* scores are also used to generate the saliency map in the field of model interpretation (Sundararajan et al., 2017; Li et al., 2016; Smilkov et al., 2017). However, they aim to attribute the softmax output of a neural network to input features while we identify the important words for substitutions in terms of adversarial loss $\mathcal{L}_{adv}$. Hence, the gradient is calculated for the output logits of the correct class rather than the adversarial loss, and also they use the embeddings of the original input instead of substitution words.

Adversarial transferability. Empirical study also mentioned the transferability of universal adversarial perturbations (UAPs) across models with distinguished architectures and pre-trained modules, such as image adversaries from VGG-19 to GoogleLeNet (Moosavi-Dezfooli et al., 2017) or ResNets to other networks (Wu et al., 2020), and adversarial texts from GloVe-based Reading Comprehensive models to ELMo-based models. In terms of explanations for adversarial transferability, Liang

Tokens	Models	Frequencies	PMI Ranks
"appears"	LSTM	11.0 / 11.0	3664
"Feels"	CNN	12.0 / 12.0	3665
"Lawrence"	CNN	11.0 / 12.0	4747
"pleasurable"	**Self-Attention**	**0.0 / 4.0**	**17181**
"unique"	LSTM	13.0 / 14.0	4990
"refreshingly"	CNN	10.0 / 10.0	4305
"mess"	**Self-Attention**	**1.0 / 30.0**	**15939**

(a) SST-2

Tokens	Models	Frequencies	PMI Ranks
"quickinfo"	LSTM	1813.0 / 1813.0	13250
"Qtr"	LSTM	62.0 / 63.0	15775
"hellip"	LSTM,CNN	80.0 / 80.0	13187
"Spitzer"	CNN	220.0 / 238.0	16114

(b) AG-News

As shown in Table 1, self-attention models are robust to UATs. Therefore, there are no effective UATs listed for self-attention models.

Tokens	Models	Frequencies	PMI Ranks
"giving"	LSTM	8184.0 / 12057.0	338822
"Horrible"	LSTM	4136.0 / 4158.0	311571
"inedible"	LSTM	2035.0 / 2108.0	311733
"Slowest"	CNN	117.0 / 117.0	311557
"BUYER"	CNN	97.0 / 97.0	309895
"disrespected"	CNN	216.0 / 217.0	311570
"restrain"	**Attention**	**8.0 / 41.0**	**735421**

(c) Yelp

Table 4: Training data artifacts of UAT tokens. Frequencies: In-class frequencies are displayed relatively to the total frequencies.

et al. (2020) proved its correlation with knowledge transferability, which relates to pre-trained knowledge. Also, adversarial transferability between imitated models and victim models (Wallace et al., 2020; He et al., 2021) also enhanced the relationship between pre-trained, transferable knowledge and adversarial transferability. These works motivate us to study the effect of pre-trained embeddings via the UAT transfer attack. Yuan et al. (2021) also studies the transferability of different architectures and pre-trained modules. Different from our study, they generate the sample-wise adversarial texts. Interestingly, they achieve an opposite conclusion that architecture types are more sensitive than pre-trained embeddings to transfer attacks.

5 Conclusion

In this work, we investigated the vulnerability of Natural Language Processing (NLP) models to Universal Adversarial Texts (UATs). We proposed two types of Data-Free Adjusted Gradient(DFAG) attacks which can generate effective UATs without real data. Our DFAG attacks lower the requirement of using UATs to understand the vulnerability of NLP models. With DFAG-generated UATs, we found that the robustness of self-attention to words with training data artifacts and revealed the unique (transferable) vulnerability of pre-trained embeddings. Our findings could help build robust NLP models against adversarial attacks. Future work could expose whether the pre-trained vulnerability

PMI Ranks	Models	ASR
1	LSTM	0.2
	CNN	0.1
	Self-Attention	**0**
2	LSTM	0.1
	CNN	0.1
	Self-Attention	**0**
3	LSTM	0.1
	CNN	0.1
	Self-Attention	**0**
4	LSTM	0.2
	CNN	0.4
	Self-Attention	**0**
5	LSTM	0.2
	CNN	0.5
	Self-Attention	**0**

Table 5: Evaluating the performance of SST models with the top-5 words out of the whole vocabulary according to their PMI ranks.

could make UATs transferable across different NLP tasks. Moreover, our result should also be verified on large-scale models. More detailed analyses of different filter sizes and attention heads are also interesting future works.

References

Moustafa Alzantot, Yash Sharma, Ahmed Elgohary, Bo-Jhang Ho, Mani Srivastava, and Kai-Wei Chang. 2018. Generating natural language adversarial examples. In *Proceedings of the 2018 Conference on Empirical Methods in Natural Language Processing*, pages 2890–2896, Brussels, Belgium. Association for Computational Linguistics.

Melika Behjati, Seyed-Mohsen Moosavi-Dezfooli, Mahdieh Soleymani Baghshah, and Pascal Frossard. 2019. Universal adversarial attacks on text classifiers. In *ICASSP 2019-2019 IEEE International Conference on Acoustics, Speech and Signal Processing (ICASSP)*, pages 7345–7349. IEEE.

Ruben Branco, António Branco, João António Rodrigues, and João Ricardo Silva. 2021. Shortcutted commonsense: Data spuriousness in deep learning of commonsense reasoning. In *Proceedings of the 2021 Conference on Empirical Methods in Natural Language Processing*, pages 1504–1521, Online and Punta Cana, Dominican Republic. Association for Computational Linguistics.

Francesco Croce, Maksym Andriushchenko, Vikash Sehwag, Edoardo Debenedetti, Nicolas Flammarion, Mung Chiang, Prateek Mittal, and Matthias Hein. 2020. Robustbench: a standardized adversarial robustness benchmark. *arXiv preprint arXiv:2010.09670*.

Francesco Croce and Matthias Hein. 2020. Reliable evaluation of adversarial robustness with an ensemble of diverse parameter-free attacks. In *International conference on machine learning*, pages 2206–2216. PMLR.

Jacob Devlin, Ming-Wei Chang, Kenton Lee, and Kristina Toutanova. 2018. BERT: pre-training of deep bidirectional transformers for language understanding. *CoRR*, abs/1810.04805.

Ranjie Duan, Xingjun Ma, Yisen Wang, James Bailey, A Kai Qin, and Yun Yang. 2020. Adversarial camouflage: Hiding physical-world attacks with natural styles. In *IEEE/CVF conference on computer vision and pattern recognition*, pages 1000–1008.

Javid Ebrahimi, Daniel Lowd, and Dejing Dou. 2018a. On adversarial examples for character-level neural machine translation. In *Proceedings of the 27th International Conference on Computational Linguistics, COLING 2018, Santa Fe, New Mexico, USA, August 20-26, 2018*, pages 653–663. Association for Computational Linguistics.

Javid Ebrahimi, Anyi Rao, Daniel Lowd, and Dejing Dou. 2018b. Hotflip: White-box adversarial examples for text classification. In *Proceedings of the 56th Annual Meeting of the Association for Computational Linguistics, ACL 2018, Melbourne, Australia, July 15-20, 2018, Volume 2: Short Papers*, pages 31–36. Association for Computational Linguistics.

Kevin Eykholt, Ivan Evtimov, Earlence Fernandes, Bo Li, Amir Rahmati, Chaowei Xiao, Atul Prakash, Tadayoshi Kohno, and Dawn Song. 2018. Robust physical-world attacks on deep learning visual classification. In *IEEE conference on computer vision and pattern recognition*, pages 1625–1634.

Ian J. Goodfellow, Jonathon Shlens, and Christian Szegedy. 2015. Explaining and harnessing adversarial examples. In *3rd International Conference on Learning Representations, ICLR 2015, San Diego, CA, USA, May 7-9, 2015, Conference Track Proceedings*.

Suchin Gururangan, Swabha Swayamdipta, Omer Levy, Roy Schwartz, Samuel R. Bowman, and Noah A. Smith. 2018. Annotation artifacts in natural language inference data. In *Proceedings of the 2018 Conference of the North American Chapter of the Association for Computational Linguistics: Human Language Technologies, NAACL-HLT, New Orleans, Louisiana, USA, June 1-6, 2018, Volume 2 (Short Papers)*, pages 107–112. Association for Computational Linguistics.

Xuanli He, Lingjuan Lyu, Lichao Sun, and Qiongkai Xu. 2021. Model extraction and adversarial transferability, your BERT is vulnerable! In *Proceedings of the 2021 Conference of the North American Chapter of the Association for Computational Linguistics: Human Language Technologies, NAACL-HLT 2021, Online, June 6-11, 2021*, pages 2006–2012. Association for Computational Linguistics.

Linxi Jiang, Xingjun Ma, Zejia Weng, James Bailey, and Yu-Gang Jiang. 2020. Imbalanced gradients: A new cause of overestimated adversarial robustness. *arXiv preprint arXiv:2006.13726*.

Di Jin, Zhijing Jin, Joey Tianyi Zhou, and Peter Szolovits. 2020. Is bert really robust? a strong baseline for natural language attack on text classification and entailment. In *Proceedings of the AAAI conference on artificial intelligence*, volume 34, pages 8018–8025.

Jinfeng Li, Shouling Ji, Tianyu Du, Bo Li, and Ting Wang. 2019. Textbugger: Generating adversarial text against real-world applications. In *26th Annual Network and Distributed System Security Symposium, NDSS 2019, San Diego, California, USA, February 24-27, 2019*. The Internet Society.

Jiwei Li, Xinlei Chen, Eduard Hovy, and Dan Jurafsky. 2016. Visualizing and understanding neural models in NLP. In *Proceedings of the 2016 Conference of the North American Chapter of the Association for Computational Linguistics: Human Language Technologies*, pages 681–691, San Diego, California. Association for Computational Linguistics.

Linyang Li, Ruotian Ma, Qipeng Guo, Xiangyang Xue, and Xipeng Qiu. 2020. BERT-ATTACK: Adversarial attack against BERT using BERT. In *Proceedings of the 2020 Conference on Empirical Methods in Natural Language Processing (EMNLP)*, pages 6193–6202, Online. Association for Computational Linguistics.

Bin Liang, Hongcheng Li, Miaoqiang Su, Pan Bian, Xirong Li, and Wenchang Shi. 2018. Deep text classification can be fooled. In *Proceedings of the Twenty-Seventh International Joint Conference on Artificial Intelligence, IJCAI-18*, pages 4208–4215. International Joint Conferences on Artificial Intelligence Organization.

Kaizhao Liang, Jacky Y. Zhang, Oluwasanmi Koyejo, and Bo Li. 2020. Does adversarial transferability indicate knowledge transferability? *CoRR*, abs/2006.14512.

Xingjun Ma, Bo Li, Yisen Wang, Sarah M Erfani, Sudanthi Wijewickrema, Grant Schoenebeck, Dawn Song, Michael E Houle, and James Bailey. 2018. Characterizing adversarial subspaces using local intrinsic dimensionality. *arXiv preprint arXiv:1801.02613*.

Xingjun Ma, Yuhao Niu, Lin Gu, Yisen Wang, Yitian Zhao, James Bailey, and Feng Lu. 2021. Understanding adversarial attacks on deep learning based medical image analysis systems. *Pattern Recognition*, 110:107332.

Aleksander Madry, Aleksandar Makelov, Ludwig Schmidt, Dimitris Tsipras, and Adrian Vladu. 2018. Towards deep learning models resistant to adversarial attacks. In *6th International Conference on Learning Representations, ICLR 2018, Vancouver, BC, Canada, April 30 - May 3, 2018, Conference Track Proceedings*. OpenReview.net.

Bryan McCann, James Bradbury, Caiming Xiong, and Richard Socher. 2017. Learned in translation: Contextualized word vectors. In *Advances in Neural Information Processing Systems 30: Annual Conference on Neural Information Processing Systems 2017, December 4-9, 2017, Long Beach, CA, USA*, pages 6294–6305.

Tomas Mikolov, Edouard Grave, Piotr Bojanowski, Christian Puhrsch, and Armand Joulin. 2018. Advances in pre-training distributed word representations. In *Proceedings of the International Conference on Language Resources and Evaluation (LREC 2018)*.

Seyed-Mohsen Moosavi-Dezfooli, Alhussein Fawzi, Omar Fawzi, and Pascal Frossard. 2017. Universal adversarial perturbations. In *Proceedings of the IEEE conference on computer vision and pattern recognition*, pages 1765–1773.

Yixin Nie, Adina Williams, Emily Dinan, Mohit Bansal, Jason Weston, and Douwe Kiela. 2020. Adversarial NLI: A new benchmark for natural language understanding. In *Proceedings of the 58th Annual Meeting of the Association for Computational Linguistics, ACL 2020, Online, July 5-10, 2020*, pages 4885–4901. Association for Computational Linguistics.

Swapnil Parekh, Yaman Singla Kumar, Somesh Singh, Changyou Chen, Balaji Krishnamurthy, and Rajiv Ratn Shah. 2021. Minimal: Mining models for data free universal adversarial triggers. *arXiv preprint arXiv:2109.12406*.

Jeffrey Pennington, Richard Socher, and Christopher Manning. 2014. GloVe: Global vectors for word representation. In *Proceedings of the 2014 Conference on Empirical Methods in Natural Language Processing (EMNLP)*, pages 1532–1543, Doha, Qatar. Association for Computational Linguistics.

Marco Tulio Ribeiro, Tongshuang Wu, Carlos Guestrin, and Sameer Singh. 2020. Beyond accuracy: Behavioral testing of NLP models with CheckList. In *Proceedings of the 58th Annual Meeting of the Association for Computational Linguistics*, pages 4902–4912, Online. Association for Computational Linguistics.

Daniel Smilkov, Nikhil Thorat, Been Kim, Fernanda B. Viégas, and Martin Wattenberg. 2017. Smoothgrad: removing noise by adding noise. *CoRR*, abs/1706.03825.

Richard Socher, Alex Perelygin, Jean Wu, Jason Chuang, Christopher D. Manning, Andrew Ng, and Christopher Potts. 2013. Recursive deep models for semantic compositionality over a sentiment treebank. In *Proceedings of the 2013 Conference on Empirical Methods in Natural Language Processing*, pages 1631–1642, Seattle, Washington, USA. Association for Computational Linguistics.

Liwei Song, Xinwei Yu, Hsuan-Tung Peng, and Karthik Narasimhan. 2021. Universal adversarial attacks with natural triggers for text classification. In *Proceedings of the 2021 Conference of the North American Chapter of the Association for Computational Linguistics: Human Language Technologies*, pages 3724–3733, Online. Association for Computational Linguistics.

Chi Sun, Xipeng Qiu, Yige Xu, and Xuanjing Huang. 2019. How to fine-tune bert for text classification? In *China National Conference on Chinese Computational Linguistics*, pages 194–206. Springer.

Mukund Sundararajan, Ankur Taly, and Qiqi Yan. 2017. Axiomatic attribution for deep networks. In *International Conference on Machine Learning*, pages 3319–3328. PMLR.

Christian Szegedy, Wojciech Zaremba, Ilya Sutskever, Joan Bruna, Dumitru Erhan, Ian J. Goodfellow, and Rob Fergus. 2014. Intriguing properties of neural networks. In *2nd International Conference on Learning Representations, ICLR 2014, Banff, AB, Canada, April 14-16, 2014, Conference Track Proceedings*.

Ashish Vaswani, Noam Shazeer, Niki Parmar, Jakob Uszkoreit, Llion Jones, Aidan N Gomez, Ł ukasz Kaiser, and Illia Polosukhin. 2017. Attention is all you need. In *Advances in Neural Information Processing Systems*, volume 30. Curran Associates, Inc.

Eric Wallace, Shi Feng, Nikhil Kandpal, Matt Gardner, and Sameer Singh. 2019. Universal adversarial triggers for attacking and analyzing nlp. In *EMNLP-IJCNLP 2019 - 2019 Conference on Empirical Methods in Natural Language Processing and 9th International Joint Conference on Natural Language Processing, Proceedings of the Conference*, pages 2153–2162.

Eric Wallace, Mitchell Stern, and Dawn Song. 2020. Imitation attacks and defenses for black-box machine translation systems. In *Proceedings of the 2020 Conference on Empirical Methods in Natural Language Processing, EMNLP 2020, Online, November 16-20, 2020*, pages 5531–5546. Association for Computational Linguistics.

Yisen Wang, Xingjun Ma, James Bailey, Jinfeng Yi, Bowen Zhou, and Quanquan Gu. 2019a. On the convergence and robustness of adversarial training. In *International Conference on Machine Learning*, pages 6586–6595. PMLR.

Yisen Wang, Difan Zou, Jinfeng Yi, James Bailey, Xingjun Ma, and Quanquan Gu. 2019b. Improving adversarial robustness requires revisiting misclassified examples. In *International Conference on Learning Representations*.

Dongxian Wu, Yisen Wang, Shu-Tao Xia, James Bailey, and Xingjun Ma. 2020. Skip connections matter: On the transferability of adversarial examples generated with resnets. In *8th International Conference on Learning Representations, ICLR 2020, Addis Ababa, Ethiopia, April 26-30, 2020*. OpenReview.net.

Hu Xu, Bing Liu, Lei Shu, and Philip Yu. 2019. BERT post-training for review reading comprehension and aspect-based sentiment analysis. In *Proceedings of the 2019 Conference of the North American Chapter of the Association for Computational Linguistics: Human Language Technologies, Volume 1 (Long and Short Papers)*, pages 2324–2335, Minneapolis, Minnesota. Association for Computational Linguistics.

Zhilin Yang, Zihang Dai, Yiming Yang, Jaime Carbonell, Russ R Salakhutdinov, and Quoc V Le. 2019. Xlnet: Generalized autoregressive pretraining for language understanding. In *Advances in Neural Information Processing Systems*, volume 32. Curran Associates, Inc.

Liping Yuan, Xiaoqing Zheng, Yi Zhou, Cho-Jui Hsieh, and Kai-Wei Chang. 2021. On the transferability of adversarial attacks against neural text classifier. In *Proceedings of the 2021 Conference on Empirical Methods in Natural Language Processing*, pages 1612–1625, Online and Punta Cana, Dominican Republic. Association for Computational Linguistics.

Hongyang Zhang, Yaodong Yu, Jiantao Jiao, Eric Xing, Laurent El Ghaoui, and Michael Jordan. 2019. Theoretically principled trade-off between robustness and accuracy. In *International Conference on Machine Learning*, pages 7472–7482. PMLR.

Xiang Zhang, Junbo Jake Zhao, and Yann LeCun. 2015. Character-level convolutional networks for text classification. In *Advances in Neural Information Processing Systems 28: Annual Conference on Neural Information Processing Systems 2015, December 7-12, 2015, Montreal, Quebec, Canada*, pages 649–657.

Ye Zhang and Byron C. Wallace. 2017. A sensitivity analysis of (and practitioners' guide to) convolutional neural networks for sentence classification. In *Proceedings of the Eighth International Joint Conference on Natural Language Processing, IJCNLP 2017, Taipei, Taiwan, November 27 - December 1, 2017 - Volume 1: Long Papers*, pages 253–263. Asian Federation of Natural Language Processing.

Generating and Modifying Natural Language Explanations

Abdus Salam and **Rolf Schwitter** and **Mehmet A. Orgun**
Macquarie University, Sydney, Australia
{abdus.salam, rolf.schwitter, mehmet.orgun}@mq.edu.au

Abstract

HESIP is a hybrid explanation system for image predictions that combines sub-symbolic and symbolic machine learning techniques to explain the predictions of image classification tasks. The sub-symbolic component makes a prediction for an image and the symbolic component learns probabilistic symbolic rules in order to explain that prediction. In HESIP, the explanations are generated in controlled natural language from the learned probabilistic rules using a bi-directional logic grammar. In this paper, we present an explanation modification method where a human-in-the-loop can modify an incorrect explanation generated by the HESIP system and afterwards, the modified explanation is used by the symbolic component of HESIP to learn a better explanation.

1 Introduction

In recent years, the development of explanation systems has gained a lot of attention. Most of these explanation systems (Ribeiro et al., 2016, 2018; Lundberg and Lee, 2017) can explain predictions made by machine learning (ML) models. Researchers are focusing on building explanation systems for ML models, because these models have shown excellent performance for different prediction tasks (Zhang et al., 2020; LeCun et al., 2015) and most of these models are sub-symbolic black-box models that are not easily understandable, and therefore lead to difficulties explaining the predictions to the users. Explanation systems such as Lime (Ribeiro et al., 2016), Anchor (Ribeiro et al., 2018) and SHAP (Lundberg and Lee, 2017) use existing information of the datasets to explain predictions. However, sometime information that is not present directly in the dataset such as relation information can play an important role in the explanation; especially, in image prediction tasks as shown in LIME-Aleph (Rabold et al., 2019).

HESIP is a hybrid explanation system for image predictions. The HESIP system explains the predictions to the users using natural language explanations. The explanations are generated in a controlled natural language (CNL) (Kuhn, 2014) using a logic programming based bi-directional grammar that is similar to Schwitter (2018). The generated explanations of the HESIP system are human-understandable as well as machine-processable. Since the explanations are represented in a natural language, they are immediately understandable by all types of users. The bi-directional grammar of the HESIP system can also process a generated explanation that has been modified by the user. The HESIP system aims to generate an explanation for the predicted image that represents the object information together with the relation information. It is expected that such as system is not perfect, and HESIP is not an exception. HESIP sometimes generates wrong explanations. To the best of our knowledge, there is no explanation system that allows a user to modify an explanation in order to improve the explanation generation process of the system. It is important that a user can modify an incorrect explanation so that the system can learn how to generate a better explanation taking the feedback from the user into consideration. In this paper, we present a method that involves a human-in-the-loop who can fix incorrect explanations by modifying them.

2 HESIP: System Architecture

HESIP is a hybrid system that explains image predictions by integrating sub-symbolic and symbolic ML techniques in two separate components. For an input image, HESIP makes a prediction using a sub-symbolic ML model. Afterwards, HESIP uses a symbolic ML technique to learn symbolic probabilistic rules that are used to explain predictions. Based on a definition of hybrid systems introduced in Kautz's classification (Kautz, 2020), the HESIP system follows the architecture of a Type-3 hybrid system, since HESIP uses a sub-symbolic component to work on a task, and then a symbolic component to finalise that task. Figure 1 shows the architecture of the HESIP system. More details about the HESIP system can be found in (Salam et al., 2021).

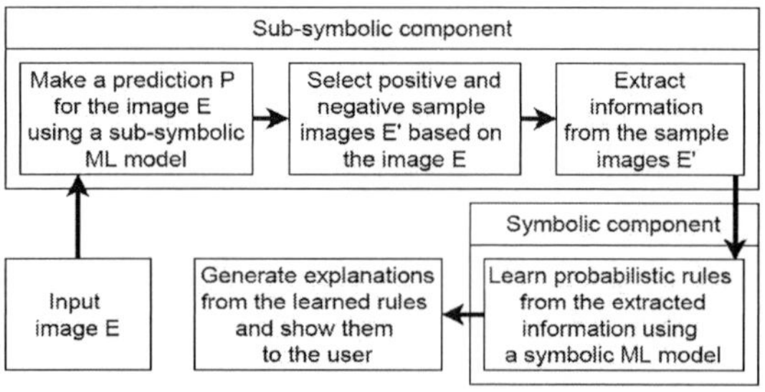

Figure 1: Architecture of the HESIP system

Rabold et al. (2019) have developed an explanation system called LIME-Aleph that explains image predictions using the learned rules. The HESIP system is motivated by the LIME-Aleph system and extends the architecture of LIME-Aleph in order to achieve a more generalised method. LIME-Aleph depends on two datasets that consist of synthetic images while the HESIP system can be applied to datasets that consist of real-world images. A detail comparison between the HESIP system and the LIME-Aleph system is provided in (Salam et al., 2021).

The steps of the HESIP system are demonstrated here using the PASCAL-Part dataset (Chen et al., 2014) that consists of real-world images. We want to learn the concept of a potted plant from the different parts of the concept that are present in an image. For this learning task, only those images that contain potted plants and bottles are used from the dataset. The potted plant concept has two parts: pot and plant. We say that there is a potted plant concept in an image, if it represents a pot that is located below a plant. Similarly, the bottle concept consists of two parts: body and cap. There are images of bottles in the dataset that contain only a body part. In our case, we work with the bottle images that contain both parts. Figure 2 shows images that contain a potted plant and a bottle.

2.1 The Sub-symbolic Component

As sub-symbolic ML model, HESIP uses an artificial neural network (ANN) (see Russell and Norvig, 2020, for an introduction) to make a prediction with a probability for an input image. Therefore, positive and negative images are selected from the dataset in order to learn explanatory probabilistic rules in the symbolic component. The sample images are selected based on the similarity to the input image. Predictions with their probabilities for all sample images are made with the ANN. A sample image is considered as a positive instance, if the prediction probability of the input image is less than or equal to the prediction probability of the sample image; otherwise, the sample image is considered as a negative instance.

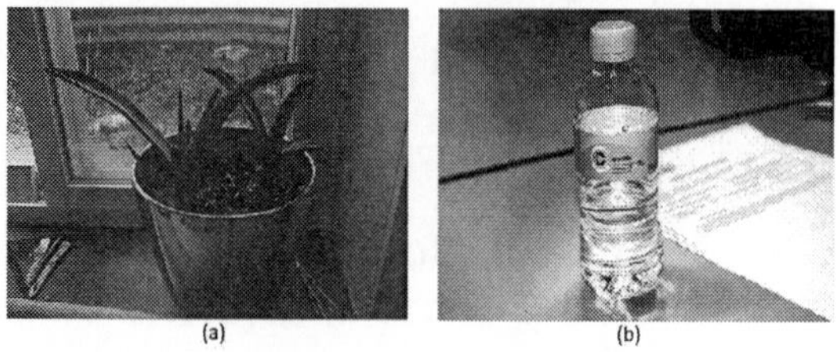

Figure 2: Example of a potted plant (a) and a bottle (b).

Once the sample images are selected, the HESIP system extracts all image information and represents it using an ontology. After that, the symbolic component uses this image information as data to learn the probabilistic rules. In the image information extraction step, the objects present in the image and their property information, the location information of the objects and the relations between the objects are extracted. The location of an object is determined from its position in the image grid considering the image as a grid. For an image, HESIP detects the objects and their location information using Detectron2 (Wu et al., 2019) that implements the Mask R-CNN (He et al., 2017) object detection algorithm. The relations between the objects in an image are determined using the location information of the objects. We assume that two objects are related in any of the following ways: *left of*, *right of*, *top of*, *bottom of*, *on*, *under* and *contain*. The relation between two objects is *on* or *under*, if one object is at the top or at the bottom of another object and they are adjacent.

2.2 The Symbolic Component

The symbolic component of the HESIP system learns the explanatory rules using the sample image information. As a symbolic component, HESIP uses *cplint* that is a probabilistic logic programming framework (Riguzzi and Azzolini, 2020). The information about the positive and negative sample images are used as data in the symbolic component that learns probabilistic rules and the predictions of the images are then explained using these rules. A probabilistic rule has the following form:

`h:p :- b1, ..., bn.`

where `h` is a head literal, $b_1, \ldots, b_n$ are body literals and `p` is a real number between `0` and `1` that indicates the probability of the rule. The *if*-symbol (`:-`) separates the head and the body of the rule. A colon (`:`) is used to associate the probability with the literal in the head of the rule.

To represent the sample image information, the HESIP system uses an ontology that has four predicates: `object/1`, `type/2`, `property/3` and `relation/3`. The predicates `object/1`, `type/2` and `property/3` are used to represent an object, the type of the object and the property of the object. The relation between two objects is presented using the predicate `relation/3`. The probabilistic rules learned in the HESIP system may contain either the predicate `type/2` or `relation/3` in the head of the rule and may contain any predicates of the ontology in the body of the rule. This ontology makes sure that the explanation generation method used in the HESIP system can be applied to different application domains.

Once the information of the sample images is represented with the help of the ontology, it can be used as data in the symbolic component where the information about each image represents an example instance. The decision of the sub-symbolic component is used to determine whether an example instance is a positive or negative instance. In our case, the images of the potted plant concept are determined as positive example instances while the images of the bottle concept are determined as negative example instances. Listing 1 shows a positive example instance for the potted plant concept in the symbolic component.

Listing 1: A positive example instance for the potted plant concept.

```
begin(model(pp1)).
  object(pp1_obj1).
  object(pp1_obj2).
  object(pp1_obj3).
  type(pp1_obj1, potted_plant).
  type(pp1_obj2, pot).
  type(pp1_obj3, plant).
  relation(pp1_obj1, pp1_obj2, contain).
  relation(pp1_obj1, pp1_obj3, contain).
  relation(pp1_obj2, pp1_obj3, under).
end(model(pp1)).
```

Using these example instances, the symbolic component of the HESIP system learns the probabilistic rule in Listing 2 for the potted plant concept. This rule specifies that an object A is of type potted plant with the probability `1`, if all the literals in the body of the rule are satisfied.

Listing 2: An example of a learned rule for the potted plant concept.

```
type(A, potted_plant):1.0 :-
  type(B, pot), object(B),
  type(C, plant), object(C),
  relation(B, C, under),
  relation(A, C, contain),
  relation(A, B, contain),
  object(A).
```

After the rule is learned in the symbolic component, the HESIP system uses this rule in the explanation generation module in order to generate a natural language description that will explain the image prediction. Before we go into details how this is done and how an explanation can be modified, we first present an overview of the user interface of the HESIP system in the following section.

3 HESIP: User Interface

A prototype of a graphical user interface for the HESIP system has been developed to illustrate the interaction between a user and the system for generating and modifying explanations. As illustrated in Figure 3, a user clicks on the "Choose File" button to select an image for predicting the image. After selecting the image, it is displayed and a new "Predict & Explain" button appears. When the user presses on the "Predict & Explain" button, the HESIP system predicts the image in the sub-symbolic component and learns a probabilistic rule in the symbolic component to explain the prediction. The prediction for the image and the explanation of the prediction along with the probability of the explanation are displayed in a panel (see Figure 3).

Because the interface of the HESIP system displays the predicted image, the prediction and the explanation together, the user can relate and inspect them immediately and can see whether the explanation is correct or not. After showing the prediction and the explanation to the user, two buttons "Modify Explanation" and "Confirm Explanation" are displayed (see Figure 3). After inspection, the user can either modify or confirm the explanation. If the user feels that there is something wrong with

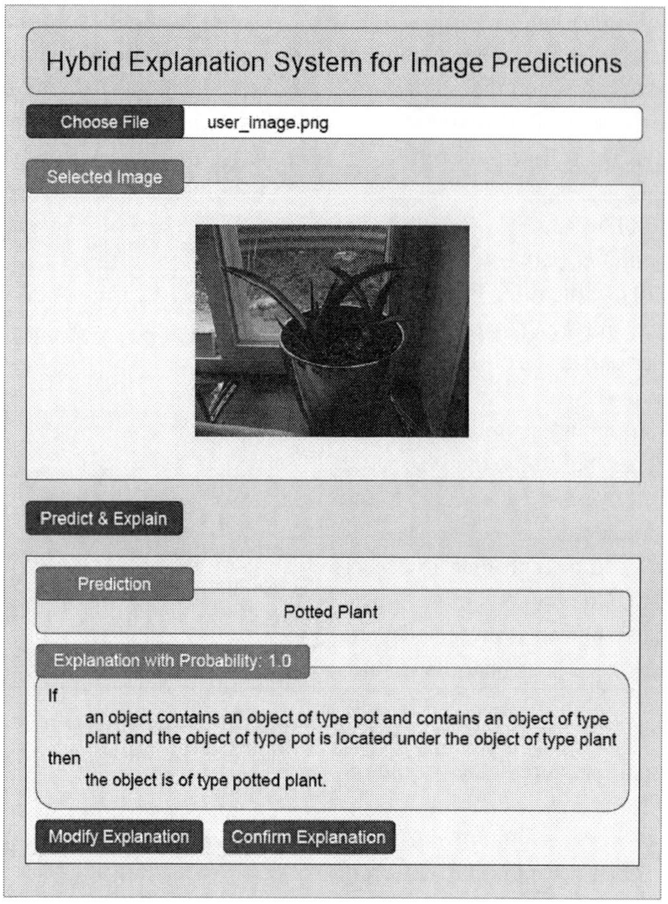

Figure 3: The HESIP system is displaying the prediction of the selected image and the corresponding explanation together with the probability.

the generated explanation, then they can fix the incorrect information so that the HESIP system can learn a better one.

After pressing the "Modify Explanation" button, the HESIP system shows the explanation inside a text editor that allows one to modify the explanation generated by HESIP. When the user uses the text editor to modify the explanation, the editor guides the user using appropriate word suggestions according to the grammar of the CNL used for generating the explanation (see Figure 4). There exist several projects where predictive editors have been developed to guide users for writing sentences in a CNL (Guy and Schwitter, 2017; Franconi et al., 2011; Bernstein and Kaufmann, 2006; Schwitter et al., 2003). When writing a CNL sentence, the next word is predicted and suggested to the user by the predictive editor. Since the explanations are expressed in a CNL, the text editor of the HESIP system can be developed as a predictive editor similar to the PENG^{ASP} system. The user can select a word from the suggested list of words or can write the word manually.

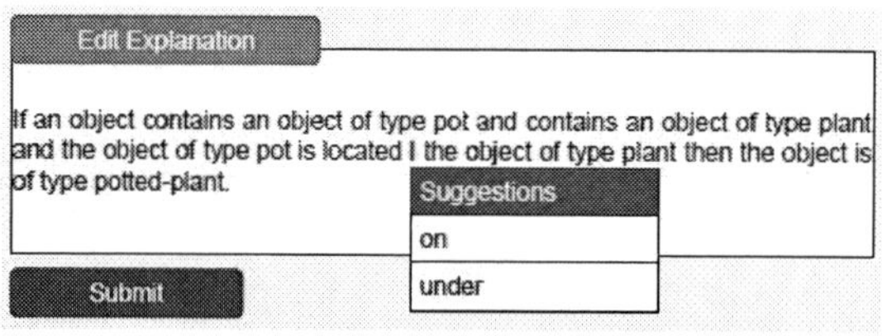

Figure 4: The HESIP system is showing suggestions to the user during the modification of an explanation.

The altered parts of the explanation are displayed as coloured text so that the user can easily identify which parts of the explanation are altered. The user clicks on the "Submit" button once they are done with the modification. Afterwards, HESIP learns a new explanatory rule for the predicted image by taking the modified explanation into account (see Section 5). The modified explanation is first processed using the bi-directional grammar that

Listing 4: Definite Clause Grammar Rule of the Bi-directional Grammar

```
np([mode:M, ctx:body, fcn:subj, def:_D, num:N, arg:X, clause:C1-C5, ante:A1-A4]) -->
  det([mode:M, morph:0, num:N, def:D, clause:C1-C2]),
  noun([mode:M, morph:_, num:N, arg:X, clause:C2-C3, ante:A1-A2]),
  prep([mode:M, ctx:head]),
  rnoun([mode:M, morph:_, num:N, arg:X, clause:C3-C4, ante:A2-A3]),
  { anaphora_resolution(det_noun_prep_rnoun, [M, D, X, C1, C4, C5, A1, A3, A4]) }.
```

produces a rule. Therefore, this rule is used to obtain the modified information and the example instances are updated accordingly in the symbolic component. Finally, the symbolic component uses these updated example instances to learn a new explanatory rule. HESIP generates a new explanation from the newly learned rule and displays it on the interface. The HESIP system compares the previous and the new explanation to identify the differences between them. If any difference was found, then the HESIP system shows that part as coloured text in order to highlight what is different with respect to the previous explanation. The message "*New explanation has been learned using the feedback.*" is displayed along with the new explanation to assure the user that the explanation has been learned taking the user's modified explanation into consideration. At this point, the user can press the "Confirm Explanation" button to approve the new explanation; otherwise, they can make further modifications to the explanation.

4 Generating Explanations

In Section 2, we showed how the HESIP system learns symbolic representation for generating explanations. Now let us have a closer look at how these explanations are generated. Once the explanatory rule is learned in the symbolic component, the HESIP system generates an explanation for the image prediction from the learned rule using a bi-directional logic grammar. The generated explanation can be processed with the same bi-directional grammar to produce a rule that is semantically equivalent to the learned rule from which the explanation was generated. This is important for the modification process, since we want to make sure that the grammar produces correct rules after processing the generated explanations as we will see in the following section.

The learned rule needs to be pre-processed before it can be used by the grammar for generating a natural language explanation. In the pre-processing steps, the literals of the rule are first reordered in a linguistically-motivated way; therefore, subject grouping is applied to remove redundant information in the reordered rule; and finally, variables that serve as names are added to the rule if required in order to resolve ambiguity of definite description. After pre-processing, HESIP sends the reconstructed rule to the grammar that generates the explanation. Listing 3 shows a reconstructed rule for the learned rule (see Listing 2) of the potted plant concept.

Listing 3: A reconstructed rule for the potted plant concept after pre-processing.

```
class(A, object), type(A, potted_plant) :-
  class(A, object),
  relation(A, B, contain),
  class(B, object), type(B, pot),
  relation(A, C, contain),
  class(C, object), type(C, plant),

  class(B, object), type(B, pot),
  relation(B, C, under),
  class(C, object), type(C, plant).
```

For the reconstructed rule in Listing 3, the grammar of the HESIP system generates the following explanation: *If an object contains an object of type pot and contains an object of type plant and the object of type pot is located under the object of type plant then the object is of type potted plant.*

Listing 4 shows an example of a grammar rule that generates a noun phrase in the subject position for a clause pattern that occurs in the body of a rule. In the generation mode (`mode:gen`), this grammar rule takes a class and a type (for example, `class(B, object)` and `type(B, pot)`) as input and generates an indefinite noun phrase (*an object of type pot*) or a definite noun phrase (*the object of type pot*) as output. The argument `clause` holds a difference list (`C1-C5`) with the incoming and outgoing literals. The argument `ante` holds a difference list (`A1-A4`) with the incoming and outgoing accessible antecedents. The call to `anaphora_resolution/2` updates these two difference lists. It is important to note that exactly the same grammar rule can also be used in the processing mode (`mode:proc`), since the grammar is bi-directional. In the processing mode, the grammar rule takes the generated verbalisation as input and produces a rule as output that is semantically equivalent to the rule from which the verbalisation was generated.

5 Modifying Explanations

The bi-directional property of the grammar enables the HESIP system to modify the generated explanations. In Section 3, we have shown how a human-in-the-loop can alter explanations that are displayed to the user for explaining image predictions. In this section, we show the steps (see Figure 5) that are performed by the HESIP system in order to generate a new explanation from a newly learned rule for the predicted image after modification by the user. Note that the explanation modification steps are completed in the symbolic component of the HESIP system.

Let us assume that a user wants to see the prediction and the explanation for an image shown in Figure 2a that represents a potted plant concept. As discussed in Section 2, HESIP selects sample images for a predicted image, extracts information of the sample images, represents the sample image information using an ontology. Finally, HESIP uses the information of the sample images as example instances in the symbolic component to learn the explanatory rule for explaining the image prediction. Let us assume that HESIP uses the example instances shown in Listing 5 and learns the explanatory rule in Listing 6 for explaining the prediction of the image in Figure 2a. In this case, HESIP generates the explanation "*If an object contains an object of type pot and contains an object of type plant and the object of type pot is located on the object of type plant then the object is of type potted plant.*" from the learned rule in Listing 6 using the bi-directional grammar after applying the pre-processing steps (as discussed in Section 4).

Listing 5: Three example instances that are used to learn the explanatory rule for the potted plant concept.

```
begin(model(pp1)).
  object(pp1_obj1).
  object(pp1_obj2).
  object(pp1_obj3).
  type(pp1_obj1, potted_plant).
  type(pp1_obj2, pot).
  type(pp1_obj3, plant).
  relation(pp1_obj1, pp1_obj2, contain).
  relation(pp1_obj1, pp1_obj3, contain).
  relation(pp1_obj2, pp1_obj3, on).
end(model(pp1)).

begin(model(pp2)).
  object(pp2_obj1).
  object(pp2_obj2).
  object(pp2_obj3).
  neg(type(pp2_obj1, potted_plant)).
  type(pp2_obj1, bottle).
  type(pp2_obj2, body).
  type(pp2_obj3, cap).
  relation(pp2_obj1, pp2_obj2, contain).
  relation(pp2_obj1, pp2_obj3, contain).
  relation(pp2_obj2, pp2_obj3, under).
end(model(pp2)).

begin(model(pp3)).
  object(pp3_obj1).
  object(pp3_obj2).
  object(pp3_obj3).
  neg(type(pp3_obj1, potted_plant)).
  type(pp3_obj2, pot).
  type(pp3_obj3, plant).
end(model(pp3)).
```

Listing 6: A learned explanatory rule for the potted plant concept.

```
type(A, potted_plant):1.0 :-
  type(B, pot), object(B),
  type(C, plant), object(C),
  relation(B, C, on),
  relation(A, C, contain),
  relation(A, B, contain),
  object(A).
```

When this explanation is displayed to a user, then the user may want to modify the explanation after noticing that the relation *on* between the pot and the plant objects is not correct. Let us assume, the user has changed the explanation to "*If an object contains an object of type pot and contains an object of type plant and the object of type pot is located* ***under*** *the object of type plant then the object is of type potted plant.*" where the preposition *on* is replaced by *under*. After submission of the modified explanation, HESIP processes the explanation using the bi-directional grammar to obtain a rule. The generated rule for the modified explanation is shown in Listing 7.

Listing 7: A rule obtained using the bi-directional grammar by processing the modified explanation for the potted plant concept.

```
type(C, potted_plant) :-
  class(C, object),
  relation(C, A, contain),
  class(A, object),
  type(A, pot),
  relation(C, B, contain),
  class(B, object),
  type(B, plant),
  relation(A, B, under).
```

The rule (see Listing 7) derived from the altered explanation is then compared with the rule previ-

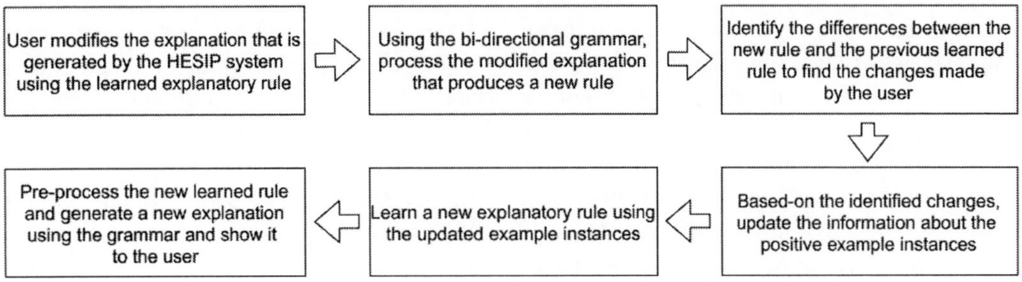

Figure 5: Steps for modifying explanations in the HESIP system.

ously learned by HESIP (see Listing 6) to identify the modifications. In this case, the user has updated the relation information and the rule in Listing 7 reflects that change. After identifying the changes, the amended information is updated in the example instances. In our case, we update the relation from *on* to *under* between the pot and the plant objects for all positive example instances. We do not update any information about the negative example instances, since the user modified an explanation in order to correct it and the positive example instances represent the correct information for the concept to be learned. Afterwards, an explanatory rule is learned using the updated example instances. The new rule is shown in Listing 8. We can see that the new rule is different from the previous one (see Listing 6) and that the preposition has been replaced.

Listing 8: A new explanatory rule learned for the potted plant concept after the explanation is modified by the user.

```
type(A, potted_plant):1.0 :-
  type(B, pot), object(B),
  type(C, plant), object(C),
  relation(B, C, under),
  relation(A, C, contain),
  relation(A, B, contain),
  object(A).
```

Once the new explanatory rule is learned, HESIP first pre-processes the new learned rule as discussed in Section 4 that results in a reconstructed rule. After that, HESIP verbalises the reconstructed rule to obtain a new explanation for the prediction. For this scenario, HESIP generates the new explanation "*If an object contains an object of type pot and contains an object of type plant and the object of type pot is located under the object of type plant then the object is of type potted plant.*" using the new learned rule in Listing 8. The new explanation is then displayed on the interface.

This example illustrates the explanation modification steps for changing the relation information. The HESIP system applies the same process to generate a new explanation for updating any information in the explanation. As mentioned earlier, a predictive editor is used in the HESIP system to modify an explanation that supports the user in making a modification. After generating an explanation for a prediction, it is possible that the explanation may have the following incorrect information and a user can update that information in the explanation:

- The user can update the relation information of an explanation as shown for the explanation of the potted plant concept.
- The user can modify the object property information (for example, the object colour information of a concept).
- The user can update the object type information in the conditional part of the explanation sentence.

Practically, in an explanation sentence, the user can update any content word introduced by the ontology used in the system. In the modification step, the predictive editor will ensure that the explanation is grammatically correct. In the case of updating the relation information, there should not be any issue, since the relevant relation words will be suggested by the predictive editor and the user can select the relation from a list of words. However, a problem may occur while updating any object property or type information in an explanation. An explanation may contain an anaphoric reference to an object. If the user updates the property or the type information of an object that is used as an anaphoric expression, then the user has to make sure that all the other parts of the explanation are also updated. Let us consider an example from a tower concept learning task (Rabold et al., 2019) to illustrate this scenario. In tower concept learning, an image consists of three squares with green, blue and pink colours, and if the image contains a square on top of another square without repeating the same colour, then the image represents a tower concept. For the tower concept, the HESIP system may generate the following explanation: "*If an object A contains a blue object and contains a green object and the blue object is located on the green object then the object A is of type tower.*" where the user may update the colour *green* to *pink* only for the first occurrence (*a green object* to *a pink object*). This will lead to incorrect information in the later part of the explanation (the noun phrase *the green object* should be changed to *the pink object*). The predictive editor usually will not identify this information as incorrect, since the sentence is grammatically correct. One possible solution to overcome this problem is to design the predictive editor in such a way that whenever a word related to an anaphoric expression will be updated, the editor will highlight all relevant anaphoric expressions in the explanation and the user can then fix the relevant words.

6 Evaluation

We evaluate the explanation generation and modification process of the HESIP system using four datasets: potted plant concept learning, house concept learning, tower concept learning and single relation learning. The LIME-Aleph system has used the tower concept learning and the single relation learning tasks in order to demonstrate their method. For the house concept learning task, an image consists of a triangle and a square, and if the image contains a triangle on top of a square, then the image represents a house concept. For single relation learning, if an image contains a green square on the left side of a blue square, then the image represents the *left of* relation. For evaluation, we use 382 test images for the potted plant concept and 1000 test images for all other concepts.

The explanation generation process is evaluated in two ways. First, if the generated explanation represents the literals that correspond to the literals of the image, then we consider the explanation as a correct one. Second, we check if the bi-directional grammar works in both directions using a technique known as semantic-round tripping (Hossain and Schwitter, 2020). Using this technique, we store the formal representation *R1* of an explanation. The explanation is then processed by the grammar that produces second formal representation *R2*. Therefore, we compare if *R1* and *R2* are semantically equivalent. For the 1000 test images, HESIP generates all correct explanations for single relation learning and tower concept learning, and 999 correct explanations for house concept learning leading to the accuracy of 100%, 100% and 99.9%. For the 382 test images of potted plant concept, HESIP generates 310 correct explanations with an accuracy of 81.15%.

To evaluate the explanation modification process, we take the test images for which the HESIP system could not generate the correct explanations. HESIP could not generated correct explanations for 1 test image of the house concept and for 72 test images of the potted plant concept learning. To check if the modification process works correctly, we first modify an incorrect explanation; therefore, HESIP learns a new explanatory rule taking the modified explanation into consideration and finally, we check if the explanation generated from the newly learned rule is correct or not.

Among the 72 test images of the potted plant concept for which HESIP could not generate the correct explanations, it generated 53 explanations with wrong relations. We discussed one such explanation in Section 5 where the explanation is learned for the relation *on* instead of the relation *under*. For all 53 explanations, we modified the explanations with correct relations and follow the steps discussed in Section 5 to generate the new explanations. We found that the HESIP system generated the new explanations with correct relations for all of them. For two test images, we could not modify the explanation using a correct relation, since the images contain only plants and there was no pot in these images. We also observe that there were 17 test images of potted plants for which the HESIP system learned incomplete explanatory rules and as a result, the system could not generate suitable explanations that can be modified to generate the correct explanations. We also notice a similar problem for one test image of the house concept for which the HESIP system could not generate a suitable explanation.

7 Conclusion

In this paper, we presented an explanation modification method for HESIP, a hybrid explanation system for image predictions. Using the prototype of the HESIP system, we showed how a human working in the loop can fix an incorrect explanation generated by the system. For an image prediction, the HESIP system learns an explanatory rule and generates an explanation in CNL using a bi-directional logic grammar. If the user decides that the generated explanation is wrong, then they can modify the explanation to fix it following the grammar rules of the CNL. After modifying the explanation, HESIP learns a new explanatory rule taking the user's modified explanation into account and generates an explanation from the new learned rule to better explain the image prediction. The result of the evaluation shows that the modification process of the HESIP system is very effective in learning better explanations in the symbolic component of the system.

References

Abraham Bernstein and Esther Kaufmann. 2006. GINO–a guided input natural language ontology editor. In *International Semantic Web Conference*, pages 144–157. Springer.

Xianjie Chen, Roozbeh Mottaghi, Xiaobai Liu, Sanja Fidler, Raquel Urtasun, and Alan Yuille. 2014. Detect what you can: Detecting and representing objects using holistic models and body parts. In *Proc. CVPR'14*, pages 1971–1978.

Enrico Franconi, Paolo Guagliardo, Sergio Tessaris, and Marco Trevisan. 2011. Quelo: an ontology-driven query interface. *Proceedings of the 24th International Workshop on Description Logics*, 745:488–498.

Stephen C. Guy and Rolf Schwitter. 2017. The PENG^{ASP} system: architecture, language and authoring tool. *Language Resources and Evaluation*, 51(1):67–92.

Kaiming He, Georgia Gkioxari, Piotr Dollár, and Ross Girshick. 2017. Mask R-CNN. In *2017 IEEE International Conference on Computer Vision (ICCV)*, pages 2980–2988.

Bayzid Ashik Hossain and Rolf Schwitter. 2020. Semantic round-tripping in conceptual modelling using restricted natural language. In *Australasian Database Conference*, pages 3–15. Springer.

Henry Kautz. 2020. The Third AI Summer, AAAI Robert S. Engelmore Memorial Lecture. *AAAI'20*. Retrieved November 13, 2021 from `https://www.cs.rochester.edu/u/kautz/talks/KautzEngelmoreLectureDirectorsCut.pdf`.

Tobias Kuhn. 2014. A survey and classification of controlled natural languages. *Computational Linguistics*, 40(1):121–170.

Yann LeCun, Yoshua Bengio, and Geoffrey Hinton. 2015. Deep learning. *Nature*, 521(7553):436.

Scott M. Lundberg and Su-In Lee. 2017. A unified approach to interpreting model predictions. In *Proceedings of the 31st International Conference on Neural Information Processing Systems*, NIPS'17, page 4768–4777. Curran Associates Inc.

Johannes Rabold, Hannah Deininger, Michael Siebers, and Ute Schmid. 2019. Enriching visual with verbal explanations for relational concepts–combining LIME with Aleph. In *Joint European Conference on Machine Learning and Knowledge Discovery in Databases*, pages 180–192. Springer.

Marco Tulio Ribeiro, Sameer Singh, and Carlos Guestrin. 2016. Why should I trust you?: Explaining the predictions of any classifier. In *Proceedings of the 22nd ACM SIGKDD International Conference on Knowledge Discovery and Data Mining*, pages 1135–1144. ACM.

Marco Tulio Ribeiro, Sameer Singh, and Carlos Guestrin. 2018. Anchors: High-precision model-agnostic explanations. In *Proceedings of the AAAI Conference on Artificial Intelligence*, volume 32.

Fabrizio Riguzzi and Damiano Azzolini. 2020. cplint Manual. *SWI-Prolog Version*. Retrieved November 13, 2021 from `http://friguzzi.github.io/cplint/_build/latex/cplint.pdf`.

Stuart Russell and Peter Norvig. 2020. *Artificial Intelligence: A Modern Approach*. Pearson.

Abdus Salam, Rolf Schwitter, and Mehmet A. Orgun. 2021. HESIP: a Hybrid System for Explaining Subsymbolic Predictions. In *34th Australasian Joint Conference on Artificial Intelligence, Sydney, Australia*. (accepted).

Rolf Schwitter. 2018. Specifying and verbalising answer set programs in controlled natural language. *Theory and Practice of Logic Programming*, 18(3-4):691–705.

Rolf Schwitter, Anna Ljungberg, and David Hood. 2003. Ecole: a look-ahead editor of controlled language. In *EAMT Workshop: Improving MT through other language technology tools: resources and tools for building MT*.

Yuxin Wu, Alexander Kirillov, Francisco Massa, Wan-Yen Lo, and Ross Girshick. 2019. Detectron2. Retrieved November 13, 2021 from `https://github.com/facebookresearch/detectron2`.

Ziwei Zhang, Peng Cui, and Wenwu Zhu. 2020. Deep Learning on Graphs: A Survey. *IEEE Transactions on Knowledge and Data Engineering*. DOI: 10.1109/TKDE.2020.2981333.

Does QA-based intermediate training help fine-tuning language models for text classification?

Shiwei Zhang
School of Computing Technologies
RMIT University, Australia
dr.shiwei.zhang@gmail.com

Xiuzhen Zhang*
School of Computing Technologies
RMIT University, Australia
xiuzhen.zhang@rmit.edu.au

Abstract

Fine-tuning pre-trained language models for downstream tasks has become a norm for NLP. Recently it is found that intermediate training based on high-level inference tasks such as Question Answering (QA) can improve the performance of some language models for target tasks. However it is not clear if intermediate training generally benefits various language models. In this paper, using the SQuAD-2.0 QA task for intermediate training for target text classification tasks, we experimented on eight tasks for single-sequence classification and eight tasks for sequence-pair classification using two base and two compact language models. Our experiments show that QA-based intermediate training generates varying transfer performance across different language models, except for similar QA tasks.

1 Introduction

The framework of fine-tuning pre-trained Language models (LMs), especially transformer-based LMs, for downstream tasks has shown state-of-the-art performance on many natural language processing (NLP) tasks (Devlin et al., 2019; Raffel et al., 2020). It is believed that the pre-training stage leads LMs to develop general-purpose abilities and knowledge that can then be transferred to downstream tasks (Raffel et al., 2020).

To further improve the performance of pre-trained LMs on target tasks, two novel training approaches have been recently researched, namely further pre-training and intermediate training. A further pre-training stage for LMs (Gururangan et al., 2020) is a stage between pre-training and fine-tuning, which further pre-trains LMs on an extra dataset using unsupervised objectives. It has been found that further pre-training LM on the target domain (domain-adaptive pre-training) leads to

*Corresponding author.

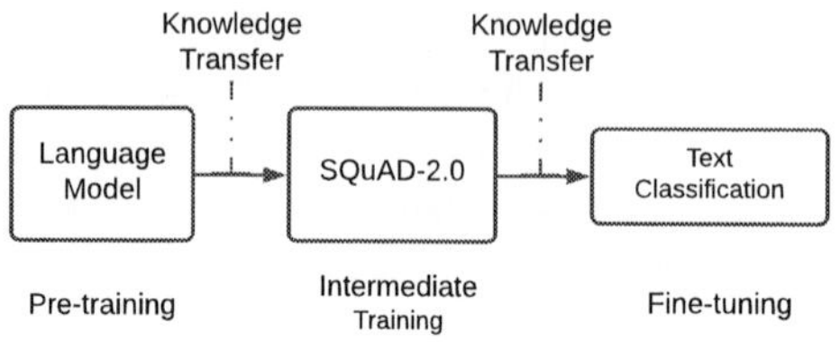

Figure 1: We experiment SQuAD-2.0 as the intermediate training task for text classification tasks.

improved performance on target tasks (Gururangan et al., 2020). Another effective transfer learning approach named intermediate training that chooses to train a LM model on an intermediate task via supervised manner and then fine-tune it on target tasks. This also leads to promising results across various NLP tasks including text classification, QA and sequence labeling (Phang et al., 2018; Vu et al., 2020; Pruksachatkun et al., 2020).

Text classification is the problem of classifying text into categories or classes which has been widely studied. In terms of input, there are mainly two forms of text classification problems: single-sequence classification tasks (e.g., sentiment classification and topic classification) and pairwise tasks (e.g., NLI and IR-related QA). In recent years, a common approach to tackle text classification problems is to fine-tune a pre-trained LM on target text classification tasks. Recently, advanced transfer learning-based approaches have been proposed to further improve the performance. For example, a recent work (Sun et al., 2019) has studied how to fine-tune BERT for text classification. They found that further pre-training LM using data within-task or in-domian can improve the performance of BERT for text classification tasks.

More recently, cross-task transfer learning technique for text classification has been investigated (Vu et al., 2020), and it is found that tasks that require high-level inference and reasoning abilities, such as natural language inference and question answering (QA) (Rajpurkar et al., 2018), are often the best intermediate tasks for text classification tasks. In a recent study (Pruksachatkun et al., 2020), it is found that natural language inference and QA tasks are generally helpful as intermediate tasks. Vu et al. (2020) showed that SQuAD-2.0 is the most favourable intermediate task for text classification. There are only a few text classifications tasks and only one language model (BERT) in their experiments, making it hard to conclude that SQuAD-2.0 as the intermediate task can generally improve the performance of all types of text classification tasks.

In this paper, we investigate the effectiveness of intermediate training for four different LMs – ELECTRA, RoBERTa, MobileBERT, and SqueezeBERT)– using the most popular QA resource SQuAD-2.0 as the intermediate task for eight target text classification tasks. We found that intermediate training shows varying transfer performance across different language models. Particularly contrary to previous thoughts, intermediate training with high-level inference QA tasks does not generally show positive transfer for low-level inference text classification tasks.

2 Related Work

As a large quantity of labeled data is not always available for training deep learning models, transfer learning becomes quite important for many of NLP problems. With transfer learning, widely available unlabeled text corpora containing rich semantic and syntactic information can be leveraged for learning language models, such as BERT (Devlin et al., 2019), GPT (Brown et al., 2020), and T5 (Raffel et al., 2020). Then, these language models are fine-tuned on downstream tasks, which is the dominant transfer learning method adopted in NLP at the moment. The second way of using transfer learning in NLP is to further pre-train pre-trained language models in domain data before fine-tuning on downstream tasks (Gururangan et al., 2020; Sun et al., 2019). The third approach, which is the method we investigate in our work, is to transfer models fine-tuned on an intermediate task for a target task (Pruksachatkun et al., 2020).

A recent work (Pruksachatkun et al., 2020) investigated when and why intermediate-task training is beneficial for a given target task. They experimented with 11 intermediate tasks and 10 target tasks, and find that intermediate tasks requiring high-level inference and reasoning abilities tend to work best, such as natural language inference tasks and QA tasks. Another recent work (Vu et al., 2020) has explored transferability across three types of tasks, namely text classification/regression, question answering and sequence labeling. They found that transfer learning is more beneficial for low-data source tasks and also found that data size, task and domain similarity, and task complexity all can affect transferability.

3 Methods

To find out whether using SQuAD-2.0 as the intermediate training task is generally helpful for text classification tasks for different language models, we experiment with 8 single-sequence text classification tasks and 8 sequence-pair text classification tasks, across four language models.

In SQuAD-2.0, each question is given a context from which to infer the answer. A QA system is expected to extract a span of text from that given context. More specifically, given a context C which consists of n tokens ($[t_1, t_2, ...t_n]$) and a question Q, a QA model is expected to predict the position of the start and end tokens of the answer in the context C. To correctly extract the answer span, on one hand an SQuAD-2.0 model needs to learn word-level dependencies between two sequences (semantic similarity); on the other hand it learns how to infer an answer from the context given a question. Training a transformer-based LM for SQuAD-2.0 intuitively enforces model's ability on inference and measuring semantic similarity, which is shown in previous studies (Pruksachatkun et al., 2020; Vu et al., 2020) to benefit text classification target tasks at the lower, sequence-level, either classification of single sequences or classification of the inference or similarity for sequence pairs.

When using transformer-based models for pairwise text classification, often a special token (e.g., [SEP]) is added between two sequences, similar to the QA input. We are interested in whether such a similarity between QA tasks and sequence-pair text classification tasks can make a difference. In terms of training procedure, we follow previous works (Phang et al., 2018; Vu et al., 2020). Specifically, we first fine-tune a pre-trained LM on SQuAD-2.0 (intermediate training stage) and then fine-tune it on each text classification tasks.

When adopting transformer-based language models (LM) for span extraction, we first load a

Table 1: Dataset Statistics

	Task	#DataSize (Training/Testing)	#Classes	Metric	Source
AGNEWS (Zhang et al., 2015)	Topic Classification	120000/7600	0: 31900, 1: 31900, 2: 31900, 3: 31900	Accuracy	News
SST2 (Wang et al., 2018)	Sentiment Classification	67349/872	0: 30208, 1: 38013	Accuracy	Movie Reviews
LIAR (Wang, 2017)	Fake News Detection	10269/1283	0: 2248, 1: 2390, 2: 2215, 3: 1894, 4: 1871, 5: 934	F1	POLITIFACT.COM
OFFENSIVE (Barbieri et al., 2020)	Offensive Speech Detection	11916/1324	0: 8595, 1: 4181	F1	Twitter
HATE (Barbieri et al., 2020)	Hate Speech Detection	9000/2970	0: 6935, 1: 5035	F1	Twitter
COLA (Wang et al., 2018)	Linguistic Acceptability	8551/1043	0: 2850, 1: 6744	Matthews Correlation	Books and Journal
EMOTION (Barbieri et al., 2020)	Emotion Detection	3257/1421	0: 1958, 1: 1066, 2: 417, 3: 1237	F1	Twitter
IRONY (Barbieri et al., 2020)	Irony Detection	2862/784	0: 1890, 1: 1756	F1	Twitter
MNLI (Wang et al., 2018)	Natural Language Inference	392702/9815	0: 134378, 1: 134023, 2: 134116	Accuracy	Multiple Text Corpus
QQP (Wang et al., 2018)	Quora Question Pairs	363846/40430	0: 255013, 1: 149263	F1	Quora
QNLI (Wang et al., 2018)	Question Answering	104743/5463	0: 55079, 1: 55127	Accuracy	Wikipedia
WIKIQA (Yang et al., 2015)	Question Answering	20360/2733	0: 25192, 1: 1333	F1	Wikipedia
BOOLQ (Wang et al., 2019)	Boolean Questions	9427/3270	0: 4790, 1: 7907	F1	Google search
MRPC (Wang et al., 2018)	Semantic Equivalence	3668/408	0: 1323, 1: 2753	F1	News
RTE (Wang et al., 2018)	Recognizing Textual Entailment	2490/277	0: 1395, 1: 1372	Accuracy	News and Wikipedia
WNLI (Wang et al., 2018)	Natural Language Inference	635/71	0: 363, 1: 343	Accuracy	Winograd Schema Challenge

pre-trained LM and then add a span classification head on top of it (a linear layer on top of the hidden-states output). A span classification head eventually generates two logits for each token, namely a logit for the start token and a logit for the end token. Learning a SQuAD-2.0 model performs classification at the token-level – classify a token either the start token or the end token. At inference stage, predictions are made based on logits (taking the token with the largest start logits as a start token and the token with largest end logits as an end token).

After we train a SQuAD-2.0 model, the next step is to transfer it for text classification tasks. When transferring a SQuAD-2.0 model, we only need to change a span classification head to a sequence classification head. The transferred transformer with a new sequence classification head will then be fine-tuned on text classification tasks. The weights of both the transferred SQuAD-2.0 model and the classification head will be updated during the fine-tuning stage. Therefore, the training process consists of three training stages, namely pre-training stage (pre-training a LM), intermediate training stage (fine-tuning on SQuAD-2.0), and fine-tuning stage (fine-tuning on each text classification tasks).

4 Experiments

4.1 Data and models

The dataset statistics and evaluation metrics for each task are shown in Table 1. We selected 8 single-sequence text classification tasks and 8 sequence-pair text classification tasks, covering binary and multi-class classification problems, balanced and imbalanced datasets, data-rich and data-scarce tasks, and different data sources. We select four pre-trained transformer-based LMs, namely ELECTRA (Clark et al., 2019), RoBERTa (Liu et al., 2019), MobileBERT (Sun et al., 2020), SqueezeBERT (Iandola et al., 2020).

4.2 Results

Experiment results (averaged over three runs) are reported in Table 2 and Table 3. Note that QQP, QNLI, MNLI, MRPC, WNLI, RTE, and COLA are sub-tasks of language understanding benchmark GLUE (Wang et al., 2018) widely used for LM evaluation. Our results are slightly different from (lower than) those reported in their paper, as we used the same setting of hyper-parameters (e.g., epoch, learning rate, input length, and batch size) for all LMs rather than tuning hyper-parameters, for fair comparison across all LMs.

According to Table 2, we can see that SQuAD2-tuned models for single-sequence text classification tasks have mixed results. On data-rich tasks, such as AGNEWS and SST2, the performance of SQuAD2-tuned models are slightly worse, except for RoBERTa(T) and MobileBERT(T) which have slightly better performance on SST2. On data-poor tasks, such as IRONY and EMOTION, transferred SQuAD2 models also tend to perform worse. In case of multi-class problems, such as AGNEWS and LIAR, the performance of models with SQuAD2 fine-tuning are not consistent. For example, ELECTRA(T), MobileBERT(T) and SqueezeBERT(T) improved the performance on LIAR, while RoBERTa(T) did not. Overall, we can see that SQuAD2-tuned models show varying transfer performance across four language models for single-sequence classification.

The results of sequence-pair text classification are reported in Table 3. Sequence-pair tasks can be roughly categorized into two groups, namely similarity tasks (e.g., QQP, MPRC) and inference tasks. Similarity tasks measure the semantic similarity between two sequences, while inference tasks measure the semantic relations between two sequences. Inference tasks have two sub-groups: natural language inference (e.g., WNLI, MNLI and RTE)

	AGNEWS	SST2	LIAR	OFFENSIVE	HATE	COLA	EMOTION	IRONY
ELECTRA	94.46	94.61	26.63	83.48	48.01	67.65	82.59	71.96
ELECTRA(T)	94.59^{+}	94.26^{-}	27.76^{+}	82.91^{-}	44.90^{-}	67.01^{-}	81.86^{-}	70.96^{-}
RoBERTa	94.84	93.00	27.65	83.18	44.19	58.84	82.75	71.41
RoBERTa(T)	$94.82^{=}$	94.15^{+}	27.35^{-}	83.45^{+}	46.62^{+}	57.17^{-}	81.79^{-}	69.35^{-}
MobileBERT	94.57	90.13	26.07	84.71	43.66	49.99	78.23	63.08
MobileBERT(T)	94.32^{-}	91.05^{+}	26.27^{+}	85.01^{+}	45.57^{+}	50.25^{+}	79.72^{+}	62.36^{-}
SqueezeBERT	94.68	89.90	27.26	84.09	41.97	44.50	78.72	66.07
SqueezeBERT(T)	94.09^{-}	89.10^{-}	27.72^{+}	83.61^{-}	40.54^{-}	35.37^{-}	77.73^{-}	66.44^{+}

Table 2: Performance(%) for single-sequence text classification tasks. Models with SQuAD2.0 intermediate tuning are denoted with T, $+$, $=$ and $-$ denote increase, equal and decrease in performance for SQuAD-tuned models.

	QQP	**QNLI**	WNLI	MNLI	**WIKIQA**	**BOOLQ**	MRPC	RTE
ELECTRA	91.69	92.09	47.88	88.52	46.04	84.16	88.60	77.61
ELECTRA(T)	91.45^{-}	$\mathbf{92.44}^{+}$	52.58^{+}	88.77^{+}	$\mathbf{50.43}^{+}$	$\mathbf{86.34}^{+}$	87.78^{-}	78.34^{+}
RoBERTa	91.24	92.04	56.34	87.69	43.41	84.22	89.56	75.33
RoBERTa(T)	91.14^{-}	$\mathbf{92.42}^{+}$	$56.34^{=}$	$87.65^{=}$	$\mathbf{52.45}^{+}$	$\mathbf{84.54}^{+}$	88.31^{-}	79.18^{+}
MobileBERT	89.09	89.18	46.48	82.63	40.18	77.65	83.69	56.68
MobileBERT(T)	88.94^{-}	$\mathbf{90.88}^{+}$	35.21^{-}	82.45^{-}	$\mathbf{52.60}^{+}$	$\mathbf{81.63}^{+}$	86.87^{+}	67.75^{+}
SqueezeBERT	89.32	89.16	52.11	80.49	41.70	79.45	83.62	68.11
SqueezeBERT(T)	89.07^{-}	$\mathbf{90.13}^{+}$	39.90^{-}	80.05^{-}	$\mathbf{50.89}^{+}$	$\mathbf{79.98}^{+}$	85.31^{+}	66.79^{-}

Table 3: Performance(%) for pairwise classification tasks. Models with SQuAD2.0 intermediate tuning are denoted with T, where $+$, $=$ and $-$ denote increase, equal and decrease in performance for SQuAD-tuned models. Note the positive transfer results on QA tasks QNLI, WIKIQA and BOOLQ.

and QA-related tasks (e.g., QNLI, WIKIQA and BOOLQ). We can see that SQuAD2-tuned models have consistently better performance for QA tasks QNLI, WIKIQA and BOOLQ. A possible explanation is when trained on SQuAD-2.0, if a question is unanswerable, the index of [CLS] token is usually set as the answer, which means that the representation of [CLS] token contains information about whether a question has the answer in the given context. On similarity tasks, SQuAD2-tuned models have worse performance on QQP (data-rich), but on MRPC (data-poor) SQuAD2-tuned models tend to have mixed performance. On natural language inference tasks, MNLI (data-rich) seems not benefit from SQuAD2 fine-tuning, but the performance on WNLI (data-poor) has shown some improvements. Our experiments show that SQuAD2-tuned models have seen consistent success on QA tasks, but generally sequence-pair tasks do not always benefit from this intermediate training, whether data rich or data-poor. Consequently, it is still hard to conclude that using SQuAD-2.0 as the intermediate training task is generally helpful for text classification.

5 Conclusion

We studied using the SQuAD-2.0 QA intermediate task for target text classification across different language models. Our experiments on eight classification target tasks and four language models show that SQuAD2-tuned models do not generally have better performance, whether single-sequence or sequence-pair, or data-rich or data-poor settings. This result highlights that high-level inference intermediate tasks may not generally produce positive transfer as previously thought. On the other hand, SQuAD-tuned models always have positive transfer results for QA tasks, which suggests further research is needed to investigate if task similarity rather than task complexity plays a significant role for intermediate training.

Acknowledgements

This initiative was funded by the Australian government Department of Defence and the Office of National Intelligence under the AI for Decision Making Program, delivered in partnership with the Defence Science Institute in Victoria.

References

Francesco Barbieri, Jose Camacho-Collados, Luis Espinosa Anke, and Leonardo Neves. 2020. Tweeteval: Unified benchmark and comparative evaluation for tweet classification. In *Proceedings of the 2020 Conference on Empirical Methods in Natural Language Processing: Findings*, pages 1644–1650.

Tom B Brown, Benjamin Mann, Nick Ryder, Melanie Subbiah, Jared Kaplan, Prafulla Dhariwal, Arvind Neelakantan, Pranav Shyam, Girish Sastry, Amanda Askell, et al. 2020. Language models are few-shot learners. *arXiv preprint arXiv:2005.14165*.

Kevin Clark, Minh-Thang Luong, Quoc V Le, and Christopher D Manning. 2019. Electra: Pre-training text encoders as discriminators rather than generators. In *International Conference on Learning Representations*.

Jacob Devlin, Ming-Wei Chang, Kenton Lee, and Kristina Toutanova. 2019. Bert: Pre-training of deep bidirectional transformers for language understanding. In *Proceedings of the 2019 Conference of the North American Chapter of the Association for Computational Linguistics: Human Language Technologies*, pages 4171–4186.

Suchin Gururangan, Ana Marasović, Swabha Swayamdipta, Kyle Lo, Iz Beltagy, Doug Downey, and Noah A Smith. 2020. Don't stop pretraining: Adapt language models to domains and tasks. In *Proceedings of the 58th Annual Meeting of the Association for Computational Linguistics*, pages 8342–8360.

Forrest Iandola, Albert Shaw, Ravi Krishna, and Kurt Keutzer. 2020. Squeezebert: What can computer vision teach nlp about efficient neural networks? In *Proceedings of SustaiNLP: Workshop on Simple and Efficient Natural Language Processing*, pages 124–135.

Yinhan Liu, Myle Ott, Naman Goyal, Jingfei Du, Mandar Joshi, Danqi Chen, Omer Levy, Mike Lewis, Luke Zettlemoyer, and Veselin Stoyanov. 2019. Roberta: A robustly optimized bert pretraining approach. *arXiv preprint arXiv:1907.11692*.

Jason Phang, Thibault Févry, and Samuel R Bowman. 2018. Sentence encoders on stilts: Supplementary training on intermediate labeled-data tasks. *arXiv preprint arXiv:1811.01088*.

Yada Pruksachatkun, Jason Phang, Haokun Liu, Phu Mon Htut, Xiaoyi Zhang, Richard Yuanzhe Pang, Clara Vania, Katharina Kann, and Samuel Bowman. 2020. Intermediate-task transfer learning with pretrained language models: When and why does it work? In *Proceedings of the 58th Annual Meeting of the Association for Computational Linguistics*, pages 5231–5247.

Colin Raffel, Noam Shazeer, Adam Roberts, Katherine Lee, Sharan Narang, Michael Matena, Yanqi Zhou, Wei Li, and Peter J Liu. 2020. Exploring the limits of transfer learning with a unified text-to-text transformer. *Journal of Machine Learning Research*, 21:1–67.

Pranav Rajpurkar, Robin Jia, and Percy Liang. 2018. Know what you don't know: Unanswerable questions for squad. In *Proceedings of the 56th Annual Meeting of the Association for Computational Linguistics (Volume 2: Short Papers)*, pages 784–789.

Chi Sun, Xipeng Qiu, Yige Xu, and Xuanjing Huang. 2019. How to fine-tune bert for text classification? In *China National Conference on Chinese Computational Linguistics*, pages 194–206. Springer.

Zhiqing Sun, Hongkun Yu, Xiaodan Song, Renjie Liu, Yiming Yang, and Denny Zhou. 2020. Mobilebert: a compact task-agnostic bert for resource-limited devices. In *Proceedings of the 58th Annual Meeting of the Association for Computational Linguistics*, pages 2158–2170.

Tu Vu, Tong Wang, Tsendsuren Munkhdalai, Alessandro Sordoni, Adam Trischler, Andrew Mattarella-Micke, Subhransu Maji, and Mohit Iyyer. 2020. Exploring and predicting transferability across nlp tasks. In *Proceedings of the 2020 Conference on Empirical Methods in Natural Language Processing (EMNLP)*, pages 7882–7926.

Alex Wang, Yada Pruksachatkun, Nikita Nangia, Amanpreet Singh, Julian Michael, Felix Hill, Omer Levy, and Samuel R Bowman. 2019. Superglue: A stickier benchmark for general-purpose language understanding systems. *Advances in Neural Information Processing Systems*, 32.

Alex Wang, Amanpreet Singh, Julian Michael, Felix Hill, Omer Levy, and Samuel Bowman. 2018. Glue: A multi-task benchmark and analysis platform for natural language understanding. In *Proceedings of the 2018 EMNLP Workshop BlackboxNLP: Analyzing and Interpreting Neural Networks for NLP*, pages 353–355.

William Yang Wang. 2017. "liar, liar pants on fire": A new benchmark dataset for fake news detection. In *Proceedings of the 55th Annual Meeting of the Association for Computational Linguistics (Volume 2: Short Papers)*, pages 422–426.

Yi Yang, Wen-tau Yih, and Christopher Meek. 2015. Wikiqa: A challenge dataset for open-domain question answering. In *Proceedings of the 2015 conference on empirical methods in natural language processing*, pages 2013–2018.

Xiang Zhang, Junbo Zhao, and Yann Lecun. 2015. Character-level convolutional networks for text classification. *Advances in Neural Information Processing Systems*, 2015:649–657.

Retrodiction as Delayed Recurrence: the Case of Adjectives in Italian and English

Raquel G. Alhama[1,2] **Francesca Zermiani** [2,3] **Atiqah Khaliq**[2]

[1]Tilburg University, Department of Cognitive Science & Artificial Intelligence, Tilburg, The Netherlands
[2]Max Planck Institute for Psycholinguistics, Language Development Department, Nijmegen, The Netherlands
[3]University of Stuttgart, Department of Teaching and Learning with Intelligent Systems, Stuttgart, Germany
rgalhama@tilburguniversity.edu, francesca.zermiani@ife.uni-stuttgart.de, atiqah.khaliq@mpi.nl

Abstract

We address the question of how to account for statistical dependencies in an online processing account of human language acquisition. We focus on descriptive adjectives in English and Italian, and show that the acquisition of adjectives in these languages likely relies on tracking both forward and backward regularities. Our simulations confirm that forward-predicting models like standard Recurrent Neural Networks cannot account for this phenomenon due to the lack of backward prediction, but the addition of a small delay (as proposed in Turek et al., 2019) endows the RNN with the ability to not only predict but also retrodict.

1 Introduction

Sensitivity to statistical regularities allows for efficient lexical processing. As a sentence unfolds, the experienced words convey information that humans use to anticipate upcoming words, and gain thereby processing speed. This has been evidenced in a long tradition of studies with human reading data, which reveal that words that are more predictable given their context are more likely to be read faster or even skipped (Ehrlich and Rayner, 1981).

The ability to track statistical regularities during language processing is present at a very young age, and can be recruited for language learning. Before their first birthday, infants are able to use this skill to identify words in unknown languages created with artificial (Saffran et al., 1996; Aslin et al., 1998) or natural words (Pelucchi et al., 2009b), demonstrating that this ability is useful for learning language-like stimuli (see Saffran, 2020 for a review). Studies have found that, before their second year of age, toddlers already engage in predictive processing to identify familiar words before they are complete (Swingley et al., 1999; Fernald et al., 2001), and are capable of anticipating upcoming words (Fernald and Hurtado, 2006; Lew-Williams and Fernald, 2007).

Given this relation between online processing and learning, it is perhaps unsurprising that children with more efficient lexical processing are also those with faster vocabulary growth (Fernald et al., 2006; Fernald and Marchman, 2012; Weisleder and Fernald, 2013; Donnelly and Kidd, 2020). From a cross-linguistic perspective, this suggests that typological variation on the statistical regularities of different languages should be either equally tracked during processing, or reflected in cross-linguistic differences in learning.

In our work, we focus on one such typological feature: in particular, word order of descriptive adjectives in English (which occur pre-nominally), and Italian (which appear mostly post-nominally, but also pre-nominally). We first show that this difference in word order bears a different pattern of statistical dependencies in these languages, related to the direction in which the words in these constructions are more predictable (forward in Italian, backward in English). We find that, despite this difference, children acquire nouns and adjectives in each language at the same pace, showing no advantage of either direction. Thus, in line with the relation between processing and learning sketched above, a computational approach needs to accommodate statistical tracking of dependencies that are both forward and backward. We then show limitations of standard recurrent models in dealing with backward dependencies, and propose the use of a Delayed Recurrent Neural Network (Turek et al., 2019) to capture this phenomenon.

2 Related work

Word order constraints in languages may favor regularities in either the *forward* direction (when words are predictable from their *earlier* context) or in the *backward* direction, (when words are more predictable from the context occurring *after* them). For instance, languages differ in whether they use prepositions (e.g. 'in Paris') or postpositions (e.g. 'Paris in'). The conditional probability of observing 'in' given 'Paris' is higher than that of observing 'Paris' given 'in' (since 'in' may be preceded or followed by any location name); thus, the construction with a postposition has higher forward predictability, while the construction with a preposition is more predictable in the backward direction.

Few studies focus on the role of backward dependencies in human processing and learning. Pelucchi et al. (2009a) found that 8-month-old infants can learn the words of an artificial language which can only be identified based on conditional probabilities in the backward direction. The experiments reported in Perruchet and Desaulty (2008) demonstrate that this ability is also present in adults. Another set of studies revealed that the word order patterns in the native language of speakers create learning biases that manifest when learning an artificial language. Using a carefully controlled artificial language that contained balanced cues in the forward and backward direction, Onnis and Thiessen (2013) found a significant difference between Korean and English speakers, manifested in a tendency to rely on dependencies that are consistent with the direction that best predicts constituency in those languages (forward for Korean and backward for English). 13 month-old children learning English also exhibit this bias (Thiessen et al., 2019).

French et al. (2011) reported successful simulations of the experiments in Perruchet and Desaulty (2008) with an autoencoder. This model used a form of recurrence that was conditioned on the reconstruction error, such that only internal representations of items with low error would be fed back to the model on the next step. Simulations involving standard recurrence were not successful in learning the backward dependencies (Perruchet and Peereman, 2004).

3 Corpus Analysis

First we confirmed that the adjective order in English and Italian was reflected in the conditional probabilities between adjectives and nouns. We extracted child-directed speech transcriptions from all the English and Italian corpora available in CHILDES (MacWhinney, 2000), using the `childesr` library (Sanchez et al., 2019) [1]. We focused on ages from 0 to 60 months old, and used the lemmatized, lowercased version of the words. Since part-of-speech information was not available for all the data, we used the part-of-speech tagger in spaCy [2] to annotate it. We applied additional manual revision to remove some words that were wrongly classified as descriptive adjectives [3]. We used the lemmatized version of the words since, unlike in English, nouns and adjectives have number and grammatical gender in Italian.

We selected all the adjective-noun pairs (for both languages), and noun-adjective pairs (for Italian only). We downsampled the adjective-noun pairs in English to be comparable in size to the Italian data. For each word pair w_1w_2 we computed its conditional probability as $P(w_i|w_j) = counts(w_1w_2)/counts(ctx)$, where $i = 2, j = 1, ctx = w_1$ for forward conditional probabilities and $i = 1, j = 2, ctx = w_2$ for backward conditional probabilities.

Figure 1 shows the distribution of the computed probabilities. Whereas forward conditional probabilities are significantly more reliable for adjectives occurring in the Italian canonical noun-adjective ordering ($p < 0.01$), the opposite is the case for English, in which predicting backwards is significantly more reliable ($p < 0.001$). In the case of the adjective-noun order in Italian, both forward and backward probabilities are equally informative. This is consistent with the highly formulaic nature of this syntactic pattern, since not all adjectives and nouns occur in this construction. To summarize, as expected, word order is reflected in the conditional probabilities between adjectives and nouns, at least in the canonical order: while noun-adjective in Italian is favoured by forward probabilities, adjective-noun in English is better predicted backwards.

[1] `http://childes-db.stanford.edu`

[2] `https://spacy.io`. Models: `it_core_news_sm` and `en_core_web_sm`.

[3] All the code used for data processing, analyses and models is available at `https://github.com/rgalhama/retro_adjs`.

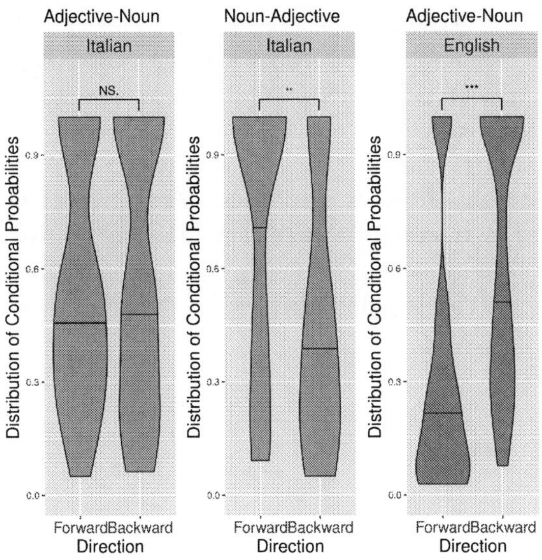

Figure 1: Distribution of conditional probabilities between words in adjective-noun and noun-adjective pairs, for English and Italian. Asterisks indicate if p-values are under significance levels (*: $p < 0.05$; **: $p < 0.01$; ***: $p < 0.001$; N.S.: $p > 0.05$).

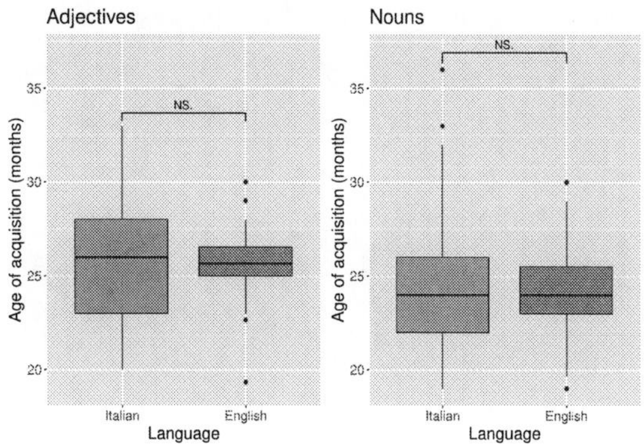

Figure 2: Age of Acquisition (AoA) of adjectives and nouns, as estimated from the CDIs in Wordbank.

As can be seen in Fig. 2, there is no significant difference between the AoA of adjectives and nouns in each language, even though we find more variability in Italian. This result suggests that children learning Italian must be employing their forward predictive skills, while children learning English need to draw upon their capacity to retrodict.

4 The Acquisition of Adjectives

Efficient processing correlates with faster vocabulary growth. Thus, if there is a difference in processing forward and backward dependencies, it should be reflected in a cross-linguistic difference in vocabulary acquisition (note that, once children start producing adjectives, they rarely produce them in incorrect word order, (Nicoladis, 2006)).

To analyze this, we used data collected with the MacArthur-Bates Communicative Development Inventory forms (CDIs). These forms contain checklists of common early acquired words. Parents complete the forms according to their estimation of whether their child produced each of those words at a given age. We used the 'Words & Sentences' CDIs from Wordbank (Frank et al., 2017)[4], for English and Italian. We excluded the forms involving twins (as significant differences have been observed in the language development of twins and singletons, Tomasello et al., 1986). We used the library in Wordbank to estimate the age of acquisition (AoA), considering that a word is acquired at the age at which at least 50% of the children in the sample produced a given word. Since differences in the acquisition of nouns could have an effect on the AoA of adjectives, we also report the estimated AoA of nouns.

[4]http://wordbank.stanford.edu/

5 Do RNNs Retrodict?

To account for the results in the previous section, models of online processing should predict but also retrodict. We first present simulations with a Recurrent Neural Network (RNN, Elman, 1990), which has a long tradition of use as a model of human sequential processing (with equivalent performance to variants with gated recurrence Aurnhammer and Frank, 2019). Although the RNN is trained exclusively in the forward direction, it is necessary to rule out the possibility that it can implicitly learn patterns that capture the backward regularities.

We trained the RNN on the child-directed data described in section 3, including sentences with and without adjectives. We downsampled the English data to have comparable training data size (41862 sentences). The RNN had an embedding layer (size:100), a hidden recurrent layer (size:250), and a softmax output layer over the whole vocabulary (size: 7875 (English); 7520 (Italian)). The model was trained to predict the next word in a sentence. We used cross-entropy loss, and updated the weights of the model with Stochastic Gradient Descent, until the loss became stable (around 60 epochs). We evaluated the trained model based on the entropy of the model prediction after the first word in adjective construction. Results are shown in Figure 3.

As can be seen, at the end of training, the RNN

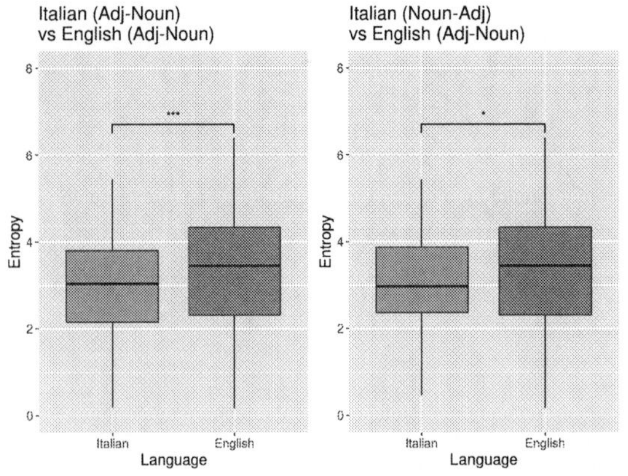

Figure 3: Entropy at the output layer of the RNN, after the first word in each adjective-noun or noun-adjective pair. Asterisks indicate if p-values are under significance levels (*: $p < 0.05$; **: $p < 0.01$; ***: $p < 0.001$; N.S: $p > 0.05$).

is significantly less successful in learning English than Italian (where success is quantified by low entropy). These results are consistent with our expectation: the model performs significantly worse for English, which —as shown in our analyses of conditional probabilities (section 3)— is less favoured by forward probabilities in the adjective-noun construction.

6 Retrodiction as Delayed Prediction

Our results indicate that a strictly forward model like the standard RNN cannot account for learning backward dependencies. An enhancement that could potentially capture the backward dependencies is the addition of a bidirectional recurrent layer (biRNN, Schuster and Paliwal, 1997). However, this would not constitute a realistic account of human processing, as this model peeks into the context which is not yet experienced.

Thus we explore an alternative account of retrodiction that functions as delayed prediction, based on the model presented in Turek et al. (2019), known as Delayed Recurrent Neural Network (dRNN). The dRNN extends the standard RNN in the following way. In the RNN, when an input word w_t is presented at time t, the model predicts the next word w_{t+1}, and the weights are updated immediately. In the dRNN, the weight update is performed at time $t + d$, where d is the pre-defined 'delay'. This entails that d extra words have been processed by the network before the error is backpropagated. This prevents the model from seeing future words during prediction, but it can effectively see them before the parameter update.

We implement a dRNN with the same hyperparameters as the RNN. We set a delay of one word and evaluate the model with the same entropy measure after similar number of epochs as the RNN (60 epochs). Results are shown in Fig. 4. As can be seen, there are no significant differences between these languages, suggesting that this model can account for learning adjective constructions in both languages.

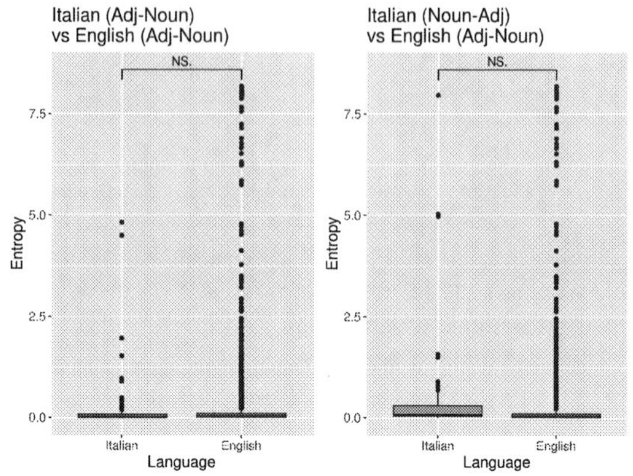

Figure 4: Entropy of the dRNN with $d = 1$, after the first word in each adjective-noun or noun-adjective pair. NS. (Not Significant) indicates p-value> 0.05.

Turek et al. (2019) noted that, for a large enough d, the dRNN can approximate the behavior of a biRNN. Since the biRNN explicitly processes the context after a word in the backward direction, similar performance provides further indication that the dRNN is learning backward dependencies. We thus replicate our simulations with a biRNN. Table 1 summarizes the mean entropy for all the models. As can be seen, the biRNN and the dRNN perform almost identically.

	RNN	biRNN	dRNN
ita: n-adj	3.01(1.08)	0.45(0.94)	0.42(1.20)
ita: adj-n	2.94(1.14)	0.15(0.27)	0.16(0.60)
ita: comb.	2.96(1.12)	0.26(0.61)	0.25(0.87)
eng: adj-n	3.33(1.29)	0.21(0.57)	0.24(0.92)

Table 1: Mean entropy (standard deviation) after the first word in adjectival constructions in Italian (noun-adjective, adjective-noun and both combined) and English (noun-adjective).

This is in line with the reported data, and offers an explanation to why the AoA of children does not show any differences despite the different word order patterns: while a classic RNN account shows an asymmetry depending on the directions of predictability, by delaying the prediction error update, the dRNN can take advantage of the backward dependencies in English, and strikes a good balance between the two directions in Italian.

7 Conclusions

Our work suggests that a full account of human processing and learning needs to address typological influences on distributional information, which require tracking of both forward and backward statistical dependencies. While we cannot account for these with standard RNN models, the dRNN can capture both forward and backward dependencies, offering a possible explanation for how humans are able to predict but also retrodict.

Acknowledgments

We are grateful to Evan Kidd for discussions and feedback on earlier versions of this paper. The authors also thank the International Max Planck Research School for Intelligent Systems (IMPRS-IS) for supporting Francesca Zermiani.

References

Richard N Aslin, Jenny R Saffran, and Elissa L Newport. 1998. Computation of conditional probability statistics by 8-month-old infants. *Psychological science*, 9(4):321–324.

Christoph Aurnhammer and Stefan L Frank. 2019. Comparing gated and simple recurrent neural network architectures as models of human sentence processing. *Proceedings of the 41st Annual Conference of the Cognitive Science Society.*

Seamus Donnelly and Evan Kidd. 2020. Individual differences in lexical processing efficiency and vocabulary in toddlers: A longitudinal investigation. *Journal of Experimental Child Psychology*, 192:104781.

Susan F Ehrlich and Keith Rayner. 1981. Contextual effects on word perception and eye movements during reading. *Journal of verbal learning and verbal behavior*, 20(6):641–655.

Jeffrey L Elman. 1990. Finding structure in time. *Cognitive science*, 14(2):179–211.

Anne Fernald and Nereyda Hurtado. 2006. Names in frames: Infants interpret words in sentence frames faster than words in isolation. *Developmental science*, 9(3):F33–F40.

Anne Fernald and Virginia A Marchman. 2012. Individual differences in lexical processing at 18 months predict vocabulary growth in typically developing and late-talking toddlers. *Child development*, 83(1):203–222.

Anne Fernald, Amy Perfors, and Virginia A Marchman. 2006. Picking up speed in understanding: Speech processing efficiency and vocabulary growth across the 2nd year. *Developmental psychology*, 42(1):98.

Anne Fernald, Daniel Swingley, and John P Pinto. 2001. When half a word is enough: Infants can recognize spoken words using partial phonetic information. *Child development*, 72(4):1003–1015.

Michael C Frank, Mika Braginsky, Daniel Yurovsky, and Virginia A Marchman. 2017. Wordbank: An open repository for developmental vocabulary data. *Journal of child language*, 44(3):677–694.

Robert M French, Caspar Addyman, and Denis Mareschal. 2011. Tracx: a recognition-based connectionist framework for sequence segmentation and chunk extraction. *Psychological review*, 118(4):614.

Casey Lew-Williams and Anne Fernald. 2007. Young children learning spanish make rapid use of grammatical gender in spoken word recognition. *Psychological Science*, 18(3):193–198.

Brian MacWhinney. 2000. *The CHILDES Project: Tools for Analyzing Talk*, 3 edition. Lawrence Erlbaum Associates, Mahwah, NJ.

Elena Nicoladis. 2006. Cross-linguistic transfer in adjective–noun strings by preschool bilingual children. *Bilingualism: Language and Cognition*, 9(1):15–32.

Luca Onnis and Erik Thiessen. 2013. Language experience changes subsequent learning. *Cognition*, 126(2):268–284.

Bruna Pelucchi, Jessica F Hay, and Jenny R Saffran. 2009a. Learning in reverse: Eight-month-old infants track backward transitional probabilities. *Cognition*, 113(2):244–247.

Bruna Pelucchi, Jessica F Hay, and Jenny R Saffran. 2009b. Statistical learning in a natural language by 8-month-old infants. *Child development*, 80(3):674–685.

Pierre Perruchet and Stéphane Desaulty. 2008. A role for backward transitional probabilities in word segmentation? *Memory & cognition*, 36(7):1299–1305.

Pierre Perruchet and Ronald Peereman. 2004. The exploitation of distributional information in syllable processing. *Journal of Neurolinguistics*, 17(2-3):97–119.

Jenny R. Saffran. 2020. Statistical language learning in infancy. *Child Development Perspectives*, 14(1):49–54.

Jenny R Saffran, Richard N Aslin, and Elissa L Newport. 1996. Statistical learning by 8-month-old infants. *Science*, 274(5294):1926–1928.

Alessandro Sanchez, Stephan C Meylan, Mika Braginsky, Kyle E MacDonald, Daniel Yurovsky, and Michael C Frank. 2019. childes-db: A flexible and reproducible interface to the child language data exchange system. *Behavior research methods*, 51(4):1928–1941.

Mike Schuster and Kuldip K Paliwal. 1997. Bidirectional recurrent neural networks. *IEEE transactions on Signal Processing*, 45(11):2673–2681.

Daniel Swingley, John P Pinto, and Anne Fernald. 1999. Continuous processing in word recognition at 24 months. *Cognition*, 71(2):73–108.

Erik D Thiessen, Luca Onnis, Soo-Jong Hong, and Kyung-Sook Lee. 2019. Early developing syntactic knowledge influences sequential statistical learning in infancy. *Journal of experimental child psychology*, 177:211–221.

Michael Tomasello, Sara Mannle, and Ann C Kruger. 1986. Linguistic environment of 1-to 2-year-old twins. *Developmental Psychology*, 22(2):169.

Javier S. Turek, Shailee Jain, Vy Vo, Mihai Capota, Alexander G. Huth, and Theodore L. Willke. 2019. Approximating stacked and bidirectional recurrent architectures with the delayed recurrent neural network.

Adriana Weisleder and Anne Fernald. 2013. Talking to children matters: Early language experience strengthens processing and builds vocabulary. *Psychological science*, 24(11):2143–2152.

Automatic Post-Editing for Vietnamese

Thanh Vu[1] and **Dai Quoc Nguyen**[2*]
[1]Oracle Digital Assistant, Oracle, Australia
[2]Oracle Labs, Oracle, Australia
[1]thanh.v.vu@oracle.com; [2]dai.nguyen@oracle.com

Abstract

Automatic post-editing (APE) is an important remedy for reducing errors of raw translated texts that are produced by machine translation (MT) systems or software-aided translation. In this paper, we present a systematic approach to tackle the APE task for Vietnamese. Specifically, we construct the first large-scale dataset of 5M Vietnamese translated and corrected sentence pairs. We then apply strong neural MT models to handle the APE task, using our constructed dataset. Experimental results from both automatic and human evaluations show the effectiveness of the neural MT models in handling the Vietnamese APE task.

1 Introduction

Recent research has placed significant advancements for automatic machine translation (Wu et al., 2016; Vaswani et al., 2017; Barrault et al., 2019). The high-quality MT output has been widely adopted by professional translators into their translation workflow to save time and reduce translation errors (Zaretskaya et al., 2016).

Translating Chinese novels to Vietnamese is an important task. In the last ten years, there are about 30K Chinese novels describing fiction stories, that are available in Vietnamese with $\sim$ 80K active readers and $\sim$ 600K novel chapter views daily from the three most popular Vietnamese websites for reading novels.[1][2][3] But, translating the Chinese novels to Vietnamese is still challenging. The reason is that in fact, readers prefer reading the novels translated using the traditional language style rather than the modern language style used in news articles (e.g. using "**tiểu nữ nhi**"$_{\textbf{little girl}}$ instead of "**cô bé**"$_{\textbf{little girl}}$). Note that current general-purpose MT systems (e.g., Google Translate), trained on modern language style-focused bilingual corpora, cannot satisfy the reader preference.

The well-known workflow/guideline used for translating the Chinese novels to Vietnamese consists of three steps:[4]

- In the first step, the Chinese text is converted into Sino-Vietnamese (i.e. Han-Viet)[5] text using a specialized software, such as TTV Translator.[6]
- In the second step, the Sino-Vietnamese text is further smoothed by replacing predefined Sino-Vietnamese phrases by dictionary-based Vietnamese phrases. The core content of the Vietnamese text generated as the output of the second step—namely software-aided **translated** text—can be generally understood by frequent readers who are familiar with reading the translated text. Note that the translated text does not fully follow the Vietnamese grammar and vocabulary, thus making it hard for new readers (and even fairly often for the frequent readers) to understand details of the text content.
- In the final step, the translated text is manually edited and polished following Vietnamese vocabulary and grammar. Here, we refer to the text generated as the output of the final step as the human-**corrected** text that can be accessed easily by readers with different reading levels.

Note that the final editing step is very time-consuming due to the large amount of human-manual work. Thus automatic post-editing (APE)

*Most of the work was done before two authors joined Oracle.

[1]https://truyencv.com

[2]https://truyenyy.com

[3]https://truyen.tangthuvien.vn

[4]http://www.tangthuvien.vn/forum/showthread.php?t=142168&page=2

[5]https://en.wikipedia.org/wiki/Sino-Vietnamese_vocabulary

[6]https://play.google.com/store/apps/details?id=vn.tangthuvien.ttvtranslate&hl=en_AU.

might be involved in this final step, helping to reduce the human effort in editing the translated text (Tatsumi, 2010). To the best of our knowledge, there is no previous study on APE for Vietnamese.

In this paper, we formulate the APE problem for Vietnamese as a monolingual translation task. We first construct a large-scale dataset consisting of translated and corrected sentence pairs. We then use our dataset to train a state-of-the-art neural MT model to automatically post-edit the translated sentences, and compare these models under various settings. Our contributions are summarized as:

- We are the first to tackle the APE task for Vietnamese to automatically improve the quality of the Vietnamese translated text of Chinese novels. We create a large-scale dataset of 5M translated and corrected sentence-level pairs extracted from 99.5K translated and corrected chapter-level pairs from 183 novels.
- We empirically evaluate neural MT models using our dataset, including a fully convolutional model (Gehring et al., 2017), "Transformer-base" and "Transformer-large" (Vaswani et al., 2017). We compare these models under automatic- and human-based evaluation settings as well as in-domain and out-of-domain schemes.

2 Our dataset

This section presents our large-scale dataset for the Vietnamese APE task.

Dataset construction

In almost all cases, the original Chinese novels are not publicly available to the readers of the Vietnamese websites for reading novels, thus *we cannot access those Chinese novels' texts*. Of 30K Chinese novels available in Vietnamese, there are currently only 283 novels available in both Vietnamese translated and corrected texts. We crawl all of those 283 novels. There is a ground-truth chapter-level alignment between translated and corrected chapter-level pairs from each of the 283 novels. We randomly sample from each novel 5 pairs of translated and corrected chapters and employ three annotators to manually evaluate the sampled chapters' editing quality on a 5-point scale. We select the top 183 novels having the highest average points over their sampled chapters to be included in our dataset.

We use all translated and corrected chapter-level pairs from the top 183 novels, i.e. a total of 99.5K chapter-level pairs. We then use RDRSegmenter (Nguyen et al., 2018) from VnCoreNLP (Vu et al., 2018) to segment each chapter text into individual sentences. In each chapter, to align the translated and corrected sentences, we compute an alignment score $\alpha = \frac{2 \times |I|}{|T| + |C|}$, where $|T|$ and $|C|$ denote the numbers of tokens in the translated and corrected sentences, respectively, while $|I|$ denotes the size of the intersection between them. Our sentence alignment process has two phases:

- In the first phase, we align every translated and corrected sentence pair with a score $\alpha >= 0.75$, i.e. alignment mode 1–1.
- In the second phase, for the remaining sentences, using a threshold $\alpha >= 0.5$, we only consider two alignment modes 1–2 and 2–1 for one translated sentence aligning two adjacent corrected sentences and two adjacent translated sentences aligning one corrected sentence, respectively.[7]

The alignment modes 1–1, 1–2 and 2–1 account for about 98% of the validation set.[8] In the end, our dataset consists of 5M (i.e. 5,028,749) translated and corrected sentence-level pairs in Vietnamese.

Dataset splitting

Our dataset of 5M Vietnamese translated and corrected sentence pairs is split into training, validation and test sets. We propose two splitting schemes which are *in-domain* and *out-of-domain*. For the in-domain scheme, the dataset is split based on the novel chapters, in which the first 92.5% chapters of each novel are used for training, the next 2.5% are for validation, and the last 5% are for testing. For the out-of-domain scheme, we split our dataset into training, development and test sets such that no novel overlaps between them. We select novels for training, validation and test sets so that the out-of-domain data distribution is similar to the in-domain data distribution. Basic in-domain and out-of-domain data statistics are detailed in tables 1 and 2, respectively.

3 Experimental setup

This section presents neural MT models as well as their training details that we employ for evaluation.

[7] We concatenate two adjacent sentences into a single one.

[8] We do not include the remaining 2% unaligned sentences into our dataset.

Item	Training set		Validation set		Test set	
	Translated	Corrected	Translated	Corrected	Translated	Corrected
#chapters(#novels)	92.2K (183)		2.5K (183)		4.8K (183)	
#sentences	4.65M		126.7K		248.0K	
#tokens	152.1M	143.7M	4.1M	3.9M	8.1M	7.6M
#tokens/sentence	32.7	30.9	32.7	31.0	32.6	30.8

Table 1: In-domain statistics of our dataset.

Item	Training set		Validation set		Test set	
	Translated	Corrected	Translated	Corrected	Translated	Corrected
#chapters(#novels)	91.5K (128)		2.8K (28)		5.1K (27)	
#sentences	4.66M		120.1K		245.6K	
#tokens	151.3M	143.0M	4.1M	3.8M	8.9M	8.4M
#tokens/sentence	32.5	30.7	33.7	31.6	36.3	34.2

Table 2: Out-of-domain statistics of our dataset.

Neural MT models

We formulate the final step of editing and polishing (i.e. post-editing) the translated sentence as a (monolingual) translation task. In particular, the translated and corrected sentences are viewed as the ones in the source and target languages, respectively. We employ strong neural MT models to handle the task. The first model is the well-known Transformer, in which we use its two variants of **"Transformer-base"** and **"Transformer-large"** (Vaswani et al., 2017). The second model is a fully convolutional model, named **"fconv"**, consisting of a convolutional encoder and a convolutional decoder (Gehring et al., 2017).

Training details

For each dataset splitting scheme, we train the models on the training set using implementations from the `fairseq` library (Ott et al., 2019). For each model, we employ the same model configuration as detailed in the corresponding paper (Vaswani et al., 2017; Gehring et al., 2017). We train each model with 100 epochs with the beam size of 5. We use the same shared embedding layer for both the encoder and decoder components of a neural MT model as both the translated and corrected sentences are in Vietnamese. We apply early stopping when no improvement is observed after 5 continuous epochs on the validation set. The model obtaining the highest BLEU score (Papineni et al., 2002) on the validation set is then used to produce the final scores on the test set.

We use standard MT evaluation metrics including TER—Translation Edit Rate (Snover et al., 2006), GLEU—Google-BLEU (Wu et al., 2016) and BLEU, in which lower TER, higher GLEU, higher BLEU indicate better performances.

4 Main results

Automatic evaluation

Table 3 shows in-domain and out-of-domain results for each model as well as for the translated text. In particular, with the in-domain scheme, the neural MT models produce substantially higher GLEU and BLEU scores and a lower TER score than the translated text. This indicates that APE helps improve the quality of the translated text. Among the MT models, "Transformer-large" achieves the best performance with the BLEU score of 49.686 which is 1.098 and 1.753 higher than "Transformer-base" and "fconv", respectively.

Regarding the out-of-domain scheme, Table 3 also shows a similar trend. In particular, all three neural MT models help improve the quality of the translated text with the absolute improvements of at least 7.5, 6.5, 9.0 points for TER, GLEU, BLEU, respectively. We also note that although "Transformer-large" consistently achieves the best TER, GLEU and BLEU scores, the out-of-domain score differences between the neural MT models are not as substantial as in the in-domain scheme.

Human evaluation

To better understand the performances of neural MT models, we conduct a human evaluation to manually evaluate the output quality of the three trained models. In particular, we collect a new set of 1K translated sentences which are randomly selected from 10 novels that are not in our dataset. To perform APE, we then apply each of the three

Model	In-domain			Out-of-domain		
	TER↓	GLEU↑	BLEU↑	TER↓	GLEU↑	BLEU↑
translated	46.027	39.816	35.834	50.678	36.174	31.591
fconv	36.539	49.188	47.933	43.106	42.654	40.502
Transformer-base	35.882	49.803	48.588	42.970	42.726	40.588
Transformer-large	**35.161**	**50.763**	**49.686**	**42.892**	**42.818**	**40.704**

Table 3: Experimental results on the test sets. "translated" denotes the result computed in using the raw translated sentence without post-editing correction.

models to produce a "corrected" candidate output for each "translated" sentence, resulting in three corrected candidates.[9]

We ask three annotators to independently vote the most suitable sentence among the translated sentence and its three corresponding corrected candidates (here, we do not show which sentence is the translated one or corrected by which model to the annotators), thus resulting in 3,000 votes in total. The best model is "Transformer-large" obtaining 1,405 votes (46.8%), compared to 815 votes (27.2%) for "Transformer-base", 780 votes (26.0%) for "fconv" and 0 vote for the translated sentences. We measure the inter-annotator agreements between the three annotators using Fleiss' kappa coefficient (Fleiss, 1971). The Fleiss' kappa coefficient is obtained at 0.350 which can be interpreted as *fair* according to Landis and Koch (1977). The results for the human evaluation are consistent with the results produced by the three models on the test sets, confirming the effectiveness of "Transformer-large" for APE in Vietnamese.

5 Related work

Our work is the first one to automatically handle the task of correcting the Vietnamese translated text of Chinese novels. However, APE is not new and has proved to be an effective approach to handle the inaccuracies of raw MT output (Simard et al., 2007; Lagarda et al., 2009; Pal et al., 2016; Nguyen et al., 2017; Correia and Martins, 2019).

APE approaches cover two main research directions including statistical MT-based models (Simard et al., 2007; Lagarda et al., 2009) and neural MT-based models (Pal et al., 2016; Correia and Martins, 2019). In particular, Simard et al. (2007) propose a statistical phrase-based MT system to post-edit the output of a rule-based MT system by handling the typical errors made by the rule-based one. Likewise, Lagarda et al. (2009) utilize statistical information from a pre-trained statistical MT model to post-edit the output of another statistical MT model. Pal et al. (2016) propose to use Bidirectional LSTM encoder-decoder for APE and found that it performs better than statistical phrase-based APE. Correia and Martins (2019) present an effective APE approach where they fine-tune pre-trained BERT models (Devlin et al., 2019) on both the BERT-based encoder and decoder.

[9]Note that we select the 1K translated sentences to ensure that the three corrected candidates are different.

6 Conclusion

We have presented the first work of APE for Vietnamese to automatically correct the Vietnamese translated text of Chinese novels. We construct the first large-scale dataset of 5M translated and corrected sentence-level pairs, extracted from 99.5K translated and corrected chapter-level pairs from 183 novels, for the Vietnamese APE task. We then compare three MT models using our dataset under in-domain and out-of-domain data splitting schemes. Experimental results from both the automatic and human evaluations show that the neural MT models help improve the quality of the translated text. Specifically, "Transformer-large" achieves the best performances w.r.t. the TER, GLEU, BLEU scores and human votes, helping to reduce the human effort in editing the translated novels, and serving as a strong model for future research and applications. We also publicly release our dataset and model checkpoints (*for research-only purpose*) at: `https://github.com/tienthanhdhcn/VnAPE`.

Acknowledgements

We thank the three anonymous reviewers for their valuable comments and suggestions which help improve the quality of the paper. We would also like to thank Dat Quoc Nguyen and his team for their help and support.

References

Loïc Barrault, Ondřej Bojar, Marta R Costa-Jussà, Christian Federmann, Mark Fishel, Yvette Graham, Barry Haddow, Matthias Huck, Philipp Koehn, Shervin Malmasi, et al. 2019. Findings of the 2019 conference on machine translation (wmt19). In *Proceedings of the Fourth Conference on Machine Translation (Volume 2: Shared Task Papers, Day 1)*, pages 1–61.

Gonçalo M Correia and André FT Martins. 2019. A simple and effective approach to automatic post-editing with transfer learning. *arXiv preprint arXiv:1906.06253*.

Jacob Devlin, Ming-Wei Chang, Kenton Lee, and Kristina Toutanova. 2019. BERT: Pre-training of deep bidirectional transformers for language understanding. In *Proceedings of NAACL*, pages 4171–4186.

Joseph L Fleiss. 1971. Measuring nominal scale agreement among many raters. *Psychological bulletin*, 76(5):378.

Jonas Gehring, Michael Auli, David Grangier, Denis Yarats, and Yann N Dauphin. 2017. Convolutional sequence to sequence learning. *arXiv preprint arXiv:1705.03122*.

Antonio-L Lagarda, Vicent Alabau, Francisco Casacuberta, Roberto Silva, and Enrique Díaz-de Liaño. 2009. Statistical post-editing of a rule-based machine translation system. In *Proceedings of Human Language Technologies: The 2009 Annual Conference of the North American Chapter of the Association for Computational Linguistics, Companion Volume: Short Papers*, pages 217–220.

J Richard Landis and Gary G Koch. 1977. The measurement of observer agreement for categorical data. *biometrics*, pages 159–174.

Dai Quoc Nguyen, Dat Quoc Nguyen, Cuong Xuan Chu, Stefan Thater, and Manfred Pinkal. 2017. Sequence to sequence learning for event prediction. In *Proceedings of the Eighth International Joint Conference on Natural Language Processing (Volume 2: Short Papers)*, pages 37–42.

Dat Quoc Nguyen, Dai Quoc Nguyen, Thanh Vu, Mark Dras, and Mark Johnson. 2018. A Fast and Accurate Vietnamese Word Segmenter. In *Proceedings of LREC*, pages 2582–2587.

Myle Ott, Sergey Edunov, Alexei Baevski, Angela Fan, Sam Gross, Nathan Ng, David Grangier, and Michael Auli. 2019. fairseq: A fast, extensible toolkit for sequence modeling. In *Proceedings of NAACL-HLT 2019: Demonstrations*.

Santanu Pal, Sudip Kumar Naskar, Mihaela Vela, and Josef van Genabith. 2016. A neural network based approach to automatic post-editing. In *Proceedings of the 54th Annual Meeting of the Association for Computational Linguistics (Volume 2: Short Papers)*, pages 281–286.

Kishore Papineni, Salim Roukos, Todd Ward, and Wei-Jing Zhu. 2002. Bleu: a method for automatic evaluation of machine translation. In *Proceedings of the 40th annual meeting of the Association for Computational Linguistics*, pages 311–318.

Michel Simard, Cyril Goutte, and Pierre Isabelle. 2007. Statistical phrase-based post-editing. In *Human Language Technologies 2007: The Conference of the North American Chapter of the Association for Computational Linguistics; Proceedings of the Main Conference*, pages 508–515.

Matthew Snover, Bonnie Dorr, Richard Schwartz, Linnea Micciulla, and John Makhoul. 2006. A study of translation edit rate with targeted human annotation. In *Proceedings of association for machine translation in the Americas*, volume 200. Cambridge, MA.

Midori Tatsumi. 2010. *Post-Editing Machine Translated Text in a Commercial Setting: Observation and Statistical Analysis*. Dublin City University. Faculty of Humanities and Social Science.

Ashish Vaswani, Noam Shazeer, Niki Parmar, Jakob Uszkoreit, Llion Jones, Aidan N Gomez, Łukasz Kaiser, and Illia Polosukhin. 2017. Attention is all you need. In *Advances in neural information processing systems*, pages 5998–6008.

Thanh Vu, Dat Quoc Nguyen, Dai Quoc Nguyen, Mark Dras, and Mark Johnson. 2018. VnCoreNLP: A Vietnamese Natural Language Processing Toolkit. In *Proceedings of NAACL: Demonstrations*, pages 56–60.

Yonghui Wu, Mike Schuster, et al. 2016. Google's Neural Machine Translation System: Bridging the Gap between Human and Machine Translation. *arXiv preprint*, arXiv:1609.08144.

Anna Zaretskaya, Mihaela Vela, Gloria Corpas Pastor, and Miriam Seghiri. 2016. Comparing post-editing difficulty of different machine translation errors in Spanish and German translations from English. *International Journal of Language and Linguistics*, 3(3):91–100.

Using Discourse Structure of Scientific Literature to Differentiate Focus from Background Entities in Pathogen Characterisation

Antonio Jimeno Yepes[1,2], Ameer Albahem[1], and Karin Verspoor[2,1]

[1]School of Computing and Information Systems, University of Melbourne
[2]School of Computing Technologies, RMIT University
Melbourne, Victoria, Australia

antonio.jimeno@gmail.com, ameer.albahem@gmail.com, karin.verspoor@rmit.edu.au

Abstract

In the task of *pathogen characterisation*, we aim to discriminate mentions of biological pathogens that are *actively studied* in the research presented in scientific publications. These are the pathogens that are the focus of direct experimentation in the research, rather than those that are referred to for context or as playing secondary roles. This task is an instance of the more general problem of identifying *focus entities* in scientific literature, in which key entities of interest must be discriminated from other potentially relevant entities of the same type mentioned in the articles.

In this paper, we explore the hypothesis that focus pathogens can be differentiated from other, non-actively studied, pathogens mentioned in articles through analysis of the patterns of mentions across different segments of a scientific paper, that is, using the discourse structure of the paper. We provide an indicative case study with the help of a small data set of PubMed abstracts that have been annotated with actively mentioned pathogens.

1 Introduction

Global monitoring of repositories of potentially harmful biological materials is an important component of ensuring the health and safety of our populations. In this context, we are building an information extraction system to identify information related to experimentation with potentially dangerous biological pathogens – e.g. viruses, bacteria, and biological toxins – as well as to detect facilities that may serve as repositories of harmful pathogens. This system will systematically scan open access data sets for evidence of research on those pathogens, thereby supporting gathering of information from public resources for biosecurity purposes (Jarrad et al., 2015).

A key requirement for automated characterisation of research on pathogens using text-based information sources, including the scientific literature, is to identify pathogens that are *actively studied*. An actively studied pathogen is defined as an organism that is subjected to direct physical experimentation in the research.

Recognition of potentially relevant entities is relatively advanced using biomedical named entity recognition tools that detect biological nomenclature such as the names of biological organisms (e.g. as studied in the context of BioCreative (Smith et al., 2008)). However, differentiating mentions of actively studied organisms from other, background or incidental mentions of organisms poses a deeper natural language processing challenge. In the context of chemical patents, it has been suggested that only ~10% of chemical mentions play a major role within the patent (Akhondi et al., 2019). It is insufficient to simply detect a mention of a potentially relevant pathogen name; it must also be decided whether that pathogen is a focus of the experiments. The main goal of our *pathogen characterisation* task is therefore to enable filtering out pathogens that are mentioned in articles but not considered to be actively studied in the described research.

Publications may refer to pathogens in various ways. In addition to mentions in the context of direct experimentation, pathogens may be mentioned as part of background knowledge or in the context of discussion or comparison. We propose that a key element of identifying actively studied pathogens is understanding where in a publication a pathogen is described (e.g. in a Methods segment vs. in the Background segment of the paper), and how the pathogen is relevant to the research (e.g. mentions of the pathogen being subjected to specific tests or examinations that reveal experimentation).

In this paper, we therefore explore the hypothesis that the context in a scientific paper where a potentially relevant entity is mentioned can provide clues about whether that entity is a *focus* (foregrounded)

entity, or an entity in the *background*; our notion of an actively studied entity assumes that it is a focus of the research described in a paper.

We investigate this hypothesis by comparing the distribution of focus and background entities across discourse segments, and apply association rule mining to identify combinations of segments that are relevant to identify focus entities. We present a small case study illustrating the proposed methodology, providing preliminary evidence of the value of discourse structure – consideration of *where* entities are mentioned – for identifying focus entities.

2 Related work

Identifying salient entities is a relevant component of information retrieval and text summarisation. The study of discourse structure has been suggested in previous work on entity salience (Boguraev and Kennedy, 1999; Walker and Walker, 1998). The work of (Dunietz and Gillick, 2014) evaluates a comprehensive set of features, showing that the discourse structure and centrality may support predicting entity salience. Our task differs in that we adopt a narrower focus specifically on identification of actively studied pathogens in scientific research papers.

Pathogen characterisation has been studied in recent shared tasks, such as the Bacteria Biotope task (Bossy et al., 2019). The tool GeoBoost (Tahsin et al., 2018) also addresses the identification of entities from GenBank, which includes largely information about viruses and bacteria. The main role of GeoBoost is to identify the location of these biological entities, which requires performing natural language processing tasks in addition to combining information from NCBI resources. This work does not address saliency of entity mentions.

In our work, we evaluate discourse features for direct identification of actively researched pathogens, covering a broad set of pathogen types.

3 Datasets

In our experiments, we constructed a dataset based on information obtained from the Biological Material Information Program (BMIP)[1] of the Defense Threat Reduction Agency (DTRA)[2].

[1]BMIP media article: https://globalbiodefense.com/2017/05/08/bmip-pathogen-repositories-worldwide

[2]https://www.dtra.mil/

3.1 Pathogen entity list

We were provided with a list of all pathogens tracked in the BMIP database, which we refer to as the BMIP list. To align these pathogens to publicly available resources, and normalise their representation, we mapped each pathogen in the list to the NCBI Taxonomy (Federhen, 2012) via direct lookup. These pathogens include viruses, bacteria, viroids, fungi and protozoa. In addition, there are mentions of toxins and PrPSc prions that were assigned a custom identifier.

3.2 Gold standard dataset

We have a small initial gold standard dataset that we use for our investigation. It consists of manual annotations of relevant pathogens over PubMed citations. *Relevance* is defined here as evidence of an actively studied pathogen, or focus entity.

This gold standard contains 87 PubMed citations (publication metadata) including titles and abstracts, each with an associated list of relevant pathogens. Out of these 87 citations, 35 have no actively studied pathogen, so we consider 52 citations in this study. There are a total of 69 relevant pathogen mentions, corresponding to 32 unique pathogens (individual NCBI Taxonomy IDs), identified across the remaining 52 articles. The maximum number of relevant pathogens annotated for a document is 5. Nineteen (19) pathogens are annotated only once; the pathogen with the largest number of annotations is *H1N1*, with total frequency of 11 (i.e. 11 citations are annotated with this pathogen). Most pathogens in the gold standard belong to the Influenza virus family.

4 Methods

We approach identifying focus entities of scientific articles as a two-stage process: pathogen identification and pathogen characterisation. Here, we describe our approach to each stage.

4.1 Pathogen identification

In the pathogen identification stage, the objective is to find all pathogens mentioned in a citation, irrespective of whether they are focus or background entities. Despite some pathogen mentions are available in author keywords and MeSH indexing, this information is sparse within the citations in MEDLINE or not mentioned at all. Both dictionary lookup and machine learning models learned from annotated data are possible for this step. Lacking annotated data specifically for the BMIP pathogen list, we utilise the dictionary-based ConceptMapper tool (Tanenblatt et al., 2010), found by Funk et al. (2014) to outperform other methods. We leverage the NCBI Taxonomy ConceptMapper annotation pipelines for the CRAFT corpus[3]. We construct the dictionary based on the BMIP list of relevant pathogens, mapped to the NCBI Taxonomy using the database downloaded from the OBO Foundry[4].

The BMIP list of pathogens also includes mentions of pathogens that are either toxins generated by pathogens or PrPSc prions, which are proteins with a pathological folding. Toxin mentions are identified using regular expressions that have higher recall than just using a dictionary matching while obtaining the same level of precision.

Using these strategies for identifying pathogens, we detect 49 mentions annotated as focus entities (out of the 69 from the 52 citations) and 9 mentions that we treat as background entities.

4.2 Pathogen characterisation

Given the list of pathogens in an abstract, the next step is to characterise which of these pathogens are focus entities, i.e. actively researched.

As described before, we hypothesise that focus pathogens are more likely to appear in some segments than others (e.g. in Methods segments vs. Fact segments), and that therefore the mention patterns of actively studied (focus) pathogens across segments are different from the mention patterns of not-actively studied (background) pathogens.

To model mention patterns, we adopt the method of association rule classification Liu et al. (1998)[5] to infer rules based on which discourse segments a pathogen is mentioned in that predict that the pathogen is a focus entity.

We treat the event of mentioning a pathogen once or more in a scientific article as a transaction event. Each transaction consists of items corresponding to the discourse structure labels of the different mentions of the pathogen. For instance, if the pathogen *Bacillus anthracis* is mentioned once in the title and once in the methods segment of a citation, we add a transaction to our dataset with the itemset (TITLE, METHOD). Given this transaction dataset, we employ association rule mining to mine top association rules for focus entities.

The class association rules (CAR) are obtained using a two-part algorithm. First, rules are generated using the APRIORI algorithm (Agrawal et al., 1994). The algorithm generates association rules that have enough support and confidence. The rules are generated without any target classification task under consideration, i.e. mention patterns for both focus and background entities are considered.

In the second part, the generated rules are used to build a classifier using the CAR M1 algorithm (Agrawal et al., 1994). The rules are sorted by confidence and then by support. Following this order, if a rule correctly classifies examples in the instance set, the rule is selected and those examples are removed. The total number of errors is recorded for the rule as the error of the rule on the instance set and the error of the default class (selected using the majority class of the remaining examples). Additional rules are selected using the remaining examples and this process continues until there are no more rules or examples. From the set of selected rules, the one with the lowest total numbers of errors is identified and the rules after that one are discarded, which reduces the error of the set. A rule is added at the end that returns the default class, which is the most frequent class not covered by the selected rules.

4.3 Discourse segment labeling

Ideally, we would hope to access articles with explicit discourse structure such as the introduction, methods, and results headings. However, such labelling is available for less than one quarter of PubMed abstracts (Jimeno Yepes et al., 2013). We therefore use automated discourse structure tagging to label segments in each abstract.

We build on existing work in scientific discourse tagging (Dasigi et al., 2017), which utilises a deep learning sequence-labeling model that identifies structure within experiment narratives in the scientific literature. A seven-label taxonomy is adopted from de Waard and pan der Maat (2012), containing GOAL, FACT, RESULT, HYPOTHESIS, METHOD, PROBLEM, and IMPLICATION. Li et al. (2019, 2021) extends the previous work, training on their SciDT dataset that contains 634 paragraphs and 6124 clauses. Their method combines a SciBERT (Beltagy et al., 2019) feature generator with a recurrent neural network to predict the scientific discourse labels.

[3]`https://github.com/UCDenver-ccp/ccp-nlp-pipelines`

[4]OBO NCBI taxonomy: `http://www.obofoundry.org/ontology/ncbitaxon.html`

[5]Using: `https://pypi.org/project/pyarc/`

Rule	Sup	Conf
method=1,title=1	0.21	1.00
title=1,result=1,goal=0	0.21	1.00
implication=1	0.17	1.00
title=1,result=1,fact=0	0.14	1.00
method=1,fact=1	0.10	1.00
title=1,fact=0,goal=1	0.10	1.00
title=1,fact=0	0.34	0.95
fact=1,goal=0	0.26	0.94
method=0,result=1,goal=0	0.24	0.93

Table 1: CAR M1 rules predicting that the pathogen is a focus entity. A value of 1 indicates that the pathogen appears in the corresponding discourse segment, while 0 indicates that the pathogen is absent from that type of segment. Rules have been selected and sorted based on the confidence (Conf) and support (Sup) values.

		Background		Focus	
Label	S.	Freq	%	Freq	%
METHOD	73	3	33.33	17	34.69
RESULT	186	4	44.44	29	59.18
FACT	51	2	22.22	21	42.86
IMPLICATION	44	0	0.00	10	20.41
GOAL	25	3	33.33	15	30.61
PROBLEM	8	0	0.00	3	6.12
HYPOTHESIS	15	0	0.00	1	2.04
TITLE	52	3	33.33	39	79.59
NONE	3	0	0.00	1	0.00
Pathogens	-	9	100.00	49	100.0

Table 2: Frequency (Freq) of the mentions of background and focus entities in various discourse segments of PubMed citations. The percentages indicate the proportion of pathogen mentions of each type occurring in each scientific discourse segment. "S." stands for the overall number of sentences per type in the 52 citations.

The scientific discourse tagger obtained an F1 of 0.841 on the SciDT dataset. They also added NONE label to allow for *none of the above*. We apply the scientific discourse tagger to assign one of the eight discourse labels to each sentence in an abstract. The TITLE label was assigned using the available citation metadata.

5 Results

We ran the CAR M1 algorithm on our data set annotated with pathogen mentions and present the inferred rules in Table 1. There are 9 rules that predict focus entities. The first rule means that if the pathogen is mentioned in the METHOD and TITLE segments of the citation, then it is a focus pathogen. The second rule means that if the pathogen is mentioned in the TITLE and RESULT segment but not in the GOAL segment, then it is a focus pathogen.

Doing an analysis of the rules, we find that most of the rules indicate that a pathogen being mentioned in the title is a sign that it is a focus pathogen, which is expected since the title denotes the most important concepts of the article. The rules also indicate that a mention of a pathogen in the results segment is relevant to the classification of the entity as a focus pathogen. Consideration of combinations of segments is more effective to identify focus entities than occurrence in any individual segment, apart from IMPLICATION.

Table 2 shows the frequency of pathogen mentions in the various discourse segments. We find that the focus pathogens are significantly more prevalent in the TITLE, RESULT and FACT segments, which correlates with the predicates of the inferred rules. Background pathogens seem to be equally prevalent in both the METHOD and GOAL segments when compared to the focus pathogens. Some of the labels, such as HYPOTHESIS, PROBLEM and NONE, have low frequency in our data set and did not participate in any of the generated rules.

6 Conclusion

We have proposed an approach to the problem of detecting focus versus ground entities using class association rules over entity mentions in discourse segments, specifically examining its use for pathogen characterisation. Focus pathogens tend to appear in the title and results segments of abstracts, where the key findings of research are highlighted. Our case study suggests that discourse information provides valuable cues to identify focus pathogens.

Given the small-scale data we have available, this work is only indicative of the promise of the approach. We are developing a larger data set, which will support comprehensive exploration of more refined rules. This data set would also support the exploration of additional existing methods, such as centrality and transformer based methods.

Acknowledgments

We acknowledge the funding support of the US Army International Pacific Centre, and the support of the US Defence Threat Reduction Agency Biological Materials Information Project team. We also thank Dr. Leyla Roohi for her work on an early version of this paper.

References

Rakesh Agrawal, Ramakrishnan Srikant, et al. 1994. Fast algorithms for mining association rules. In *Proc. 20th Int. Conf. Very Large Data Bases, VLDB*, volume 1215, pages 487–499. Citeseer.

Saber A Akhondi, Hinnerk Rey, Markus Schwörer, Michael Maier, John Toomey, Heike Nau, Gabriele Ilchmann, Mark Sheehan, Matthias Irmer, Claudia Bobach, Marius Doornenbal, Michelle Gregory, and Jan A Kors. 2019. Automatic identification of relevant chemical compounds from patents. *Database*, 2019. Baz001.

Iz Beltagy, Kyle Lo, and Arman Cohan. 2019. SciBERT: A pretrained language model for scientific text. In *Proceedings of the 2019 Conference on Empirical Methods in Natural Language Processing and the 9th International Joint Conference on Natural Language Processing (EMNLP-IJCNLP)*, pages 3615–3620, Hong Kong, China. Association for Computational Linguistics.

Branimir Boguraev and Christopher Kennedy. 1999. Salience-based content characterisation of text documents. *Advances in automatic text summarization*, pages 99–110.

Robert Bossy, Louise Deléger, Estelle Chaix, Mouhamadou Ba, and Claire Nédellec. 2019. Bacteria biotope at BioNLP open shared tasks 2019. In *Proceedings of The 5th Workshop on BioNLP Open Shared Tasks*, pages 121–131, Hong Kong, China. Association for Computational Linguistics.

Pradeep Dasigi, Gully APC Burns, Eduard Hovy, and Anita de Waard. 2017. Experiment segmentation in scientific discourse as clause-level structured prediction using recurrent neural networks. *arXiv preprint arXiv:1702.05398*.

Jesse Dunietz and Daniel Gillick. 2014. A new entity salience task with millions of training examples. In *Proceedings of the 14th Conference of the European Chapter of the Association for Computational Linguistics, volume 2: Short Papers*, pages 205–209, Gothenburg, Sweden. Association for Computational Linguistics.

Scott Federhen. 2012. The NCBI taxonomy database. *Nucleic Acids Research*, 40(D1):D136–D143.

Christopher Funk, William Baumgartner, Benjamin Garcia, Christophe Roeder, Michael Bada, K Bretonnel Cohen, Lawrence E Hunter, and Karin Verspoor. 2014. Large-scale biomedical concept recognition: an evaluation of current automatic annotators and their parameters. *BMC Bioinformatics*, 15(1):59.

Frith Jarrad, Samantha Low-Choy, and Kerrie Mengersen. 2015. *Biosecurity surveillance: quantitative approaches*. Cabi.

Antonio Jimeno Yepes, James Mork, and Alan Aronson. 2013. Using the argumentative structure of scientific literature to improve information access. In *Proceedings of the 2013 Workshop on Biomedical Natural Language Processing*, pages 102–110, Sofia, Bulgaria. Association for Computational Linguistics.

Xiangci Li, Gully Burns, and Nanyun Peng. 2019. Discourse tagging for scientific evidence extraction. *arXiv preprint arXiv:1909.04758*.

Xiangci Li, Gully Burns, and Nanyun Peng. 2021. Scientific discourse tagging for evidence extraction. In *Proceedings of the 16th Conference of the European Chapter of the Association for Computational Linguistics: Main Volume*, pages 2550–2562, Online. Association for Computational Linguistics.

Bing Liu, Wynne Hsu, and Yiming Ma. 1998. Integrating Classification and Association Rule Mining. In *Proceedings of the Fourth International Conference on Knowledge Discovery and Data Mining*, KDD'98, page 80–86. AAAI Press.

Larry Smith, Lorraine K Tanabe, Rie Johnson nee Ando, Cheng-Ju Kuo, I-Fang Chung, Chun-Nan Hsu, Yu-Shi Lin, Roman Klinger, Christoph M Friedrich, Kuzman Ganchev, et al. 2008. Overview of BioCreative II gene mention recognition. *Genome Biology*, 9(2):1–19.

Tasnia Tahsin, Davy Weissenbacher, Karen O'Connor, Arjun Magge, Matthew Scotch, and Graciela Gonzalez-Hernandez. 2018. GeoBoost: Accelerating research involving the geospatial metadata of virus GenBank records. *Bioinformatics*, 34(9):1606–1608.

Michael Tanenblatt, Anni Coden, and Igor Sominsky. 2010. The ConceptMapper approach to named entity recognition. In *Proceedings of the Seventh International Conference on Language Resources and Evaluation (LREC'10)*, Valletta, Malta. European Language Resources Association (ELRA).

Anita de Waard and Henk pan der Maat. 2012. Verb form indicates discourse segment type in biological research papers: Experimental evidence. *Journal of English for academic purposes*, 11(4):357–366.

Joshi Prince Walker and Marilyn I Walker. 1998. *Centering theory in discourse*. Oxford University Press.

Evaluating Hierarchical Document Categorisation

Qian Sun[♣] Aili Shen[♣] Hiyori Yoshikawa[◇] Chunpeng Ma[◇]
Daniel Beck[♣] Tomoya Iwakura[◇] Timothy Baldwin[♣]
[♣] The University of Melbourne
[◇] Fujitsu Limited
qiasun@student.unimelb.edu.au, {aili.shen, d.beck, tbaldwin}@unimelb.edu.au
{y.hiyori, ma.chunpeng, iwakura.tomoya}@fujitsu.com

Abstract

Hierarchical document categorisation is a special case of multi-label document categorisation, where there is a taxonomic hierarchy among the labels. While various approaches have been proposed for hierarchical document categorisation, there is no standard benchmark dataset, resulting in different methods being evaluated independently and there being no empirical consensus on what methods perform best. In this work, we examine different combinations of neural text encoders and hierarchical methods in an end-to-end framework, and evaluate over three datasets. We find that the performance of hierarchical document categorisation is determined not only by how the hierarchical information is modelled, but also the structure of the label hierarchy and class distribution.

1 Introduction

Document categorisation is a core task in information retrieval and natural language processing, whereby documents are categorised relative to a pre-defined set of labels. While the majority of research on document categorisation assumes a flat label structure, in practice in large-scale document categorisation tasks, there is often hierarchical label structure, in the form of either a tree or directed acyclic graph (Zhou et al., 2020; Azarbonyad et al., 2021), where "child" labels inherit the properties of their parents. The goal of hierarchical document categorisation is to classify documents into a set of labels, where there is a hierarchical relationship among the labels.

Hierarchical document categorisation methods explicitly capture the label structure during training. There has been a resurgence of interest in document categorisation in recent years, in part driven by breakthroughs in representation learning and pre-trained language models (Mikolov et al., 2013; Pennington et al., 2014; Peters et al., 2018; Kim, 2014; Wang et al., 2017; Devlin et al., 2019), which generate more expressive, general-purpose representations, thereby leading to performance gains across a range of NLP tasks. Despite this, there has been relatively little recent work specifically on hierarchical document categorisation. What recent work does has varied wildly in the choice of text encoder and dataset, with no systematic, controlled cross-dataset evaluation to be able to make solid conclusions as to whether the reported performance gains are attributable to the proposed hierarchical document categorisation method or just the text encoders used. Our work focuses on examining the capacity of existing methods dealing with labels with a hierarchical structure, which is different from the work of Yang et al. (2016), which focuses on modelling documents in a hierarchical way to perform classic document classification task.

In this work, we carry out systematic evaluation of a range of contemporary hierarchical document categorisation approaches, using a range of neural text encoders, based on three document collections with hierarchical label sets.

2 Related Work

Hierarchical document categorisation methods can be grouped into: flat approaches, local approaches, global approaches, and hybrid methods, based on how they utilise the label hierarchy.

2.1 Flat Approaches

Flat approaches (Eisner et al., 2005; Freitas and Carvalho, 2007) simply ignore the label hierarchy, and assume all classes are independent. As such, they are unable to capture the label structure and are poor at handling mutual exclusivity, especially among sibling nodes in multi-label categorisation tasks.

2.2 Local Approaches

Local approaches generally make predictions top-down recursively, along paths in the label hierarchy. They can be divided into three groups (Silla and Freitas, 2011): a local classifier per node (LCN), a local classifier per parent node (LCPN), or a local classifier per level (LCL). In LCN, there is a binary classifier for each node, which determines whether a document belongs to that node or not (Eisner et al., 2005; Freitas and Carvalho, 2007). In contrast, LCPN (Davies et al., 2007; Secker et al., 2010; Shimura et al., 2018; Banerjee et al., 2019) employs a multi-class classifier at each parent node, predicting which child node the document should be assigned to. Compared with LCN, LCPN significantly reduces the number of local classifiers, and can be applied in either single-label or multi-label settings. In contrast, LCL (Kowsari et al., 2017) employs a multi-class classifier at each layer in the hierarchy. This method usually fails to capture parent–child information between layers. For all three approaches, a top-down approach is often used to avoid label inconsistency, making them prone to error propagation.

2.3 Global Approaches

Global approaches (Mao et al., 2019; Zhou et al., 2020) optimise across all labels simultaneously, taking the label hierarchy into account. The simplest global approach converts the hierarchical categorisation task into a multi-label categorisation task, where each original label is replaced with its ancestors and itself. Similar to local approaches, this potentially results in label inconsistency during inference. A more popular global approach is to include a loss term which captures the hierarchy in some way (Gopal and Yang, 2013; Peng et al., 2018), such as an entropy term (Clare and King, 2003) or distance metric (Vens et al., 2008). For example, Zhou et al. (2020) proposed a hierarchy-aware structure encoder to model the label hierarchy as a directed graph. It can capture global hierarchical information as it models both top-down and bottom-up label dependencies. Moreover, all nodes are linked with each other, meaning that pairwise co-occurrence can be modelled in addition to parent–child relationships.

2.4 Hybrid Methods

There are also hybrid methods which combine the methods mentioned above (Wehrmann et al., 2018; Huang et al., 2019). For example, Gopal and Yang (2013) used simple recursive regularisation to encourage parameter smoothness between linked nodes, with positive results independently reported by Peng et al. (2018) and Zhou et al. (2020).

3 Experiments

3.1 Models

In our work, each model consists of a text encoder and a hierarchical method, where the text encoder is used to obtain text representations, and the hierarchical method makes predictions with the assistance of hierarchical label information.

3.1.1 Text Encoders

TextCNN (Kim, 2014): A CNN made up of convolutional and max-pooling layers. In this work, we apply convolution kernels with width 2, 3, and 4 (3 for each width size) to word embeddings, and use a max-pooling layer.

TextRNN: A single-layer Bi-LSTM (Wang et al., 2017) with a cell size of 64 where the concatenated hidden state at the last timestep makes up the document representation.

TextRCNN: A combination of TextCNN and TextRNN, where we first employ a single-layer Bi-LSTM with a cell size of 64 and obtain outputs across all timesteps by concatenating outputs from both directions, then apply convolution kernels with width 2, 3, and 4 (3 for each width size), followed by a max-pooling layer. This method has achieved state-of-the-art on RCV1 for both flat and hierarchical categorisation (Zhou et al., 2020).

BERT (Devlin et al., 2019): The hidden state of "CLS" from BERT is used as the document representation, using the base-uncased version.

3.1.2 Hierarchical Methods

Flat: Baseline method where all nodes are treated as candidate classes, ignoring hierarchical information.

Recursive Regularization (RR: Gopal and Yang (2013)): A hybrid method, utilising simple recursive regularisation to encourage parameter smoothness between linked nodes.

Hierarchical Multi-Label Classification Networks (HMCN: Wehrmann et al. (2018)): A hybrid local/global approach, where each level in

Dataset	|L|	Avg(|L|)	Depth	Training	Test
RCV1	103	3.24	4	23,149	592,688
SHINRA	237	3.16	4	390,433	43,382
WoS	141	2.00	2	42,286	4,699

Table 1: Statistics of datasets: "|L|" is the total number of labels; "Avg(|L|)" is the average number of labels per document; and "Depth" indicates the maximum hierarchy depth.

the model corresponds to a level in the label hierarchy. The global model consists of multiple linear layers with ReLU as the activation function. The input to each layer includes the original sequence and the output from its immediate last layer, where the hidden size for each layer is 384 as in Wehrmann et al. (2018). Passing information from the first layer to the last layer, we obtain the global output. In addition, the output from each layer is also fed into a local layer, where the hidden size is the number of nodes/classes in the corresponding hierarchical level. Then the sum of the global output and concatenated local outputs is fed into a sigmoid function to predict the classes.[1]

Hi-GCN (Zhou et al., 2020): An end-to-end hierarchy-aware global model that extracts the label hierarchy information to achieve label-wise text features. A graph convolutional network is used as the structure/hierarchy encoder, where each edge represents the correlation between a pair of nodes. There are three types of edges in the graph: top-down, bottom-up, and self-loop edges, where the weights for bottom-up and self-loop edges are 1, and the weights for top-down edges are determined by the predefined hierarchy and dataset distributions. To obtain label-wise text features, hierarchical text feature propagation is used. Specifically, the text representation from a text encoder is reshaped to act as the node input, which is updated through the hierarchy-aware structure encoder. The output of a node is based on its neighbourhood: itself, its child nodes, and its parent nodes. The output hidden state is then fed into the final classifier.

[1]In the original work of Wehrmann et al. (2018), the authors first apply the sigmoid function to the global output and local outputs, respectively, resulting into extremely bad performance in some settings, indicating that applying sigmoid separately to the global and local outputs is not as effective as applying it to the combined global and local information.

3.2 Datasets

We evaluate each text encoder+hierarchical method combination in an end-to-end framework over three datasets: RCV1 (Lewis et al., 2004), SHINRA (Sekine et al., 2020), and WoS (Kowsari et al., 2017). Here, RCV1 is a collection of news articles published by the Reuters News between 1996 and 1997. SHINRA contains English Wikipedia articles from the SHINRA2020-ML shared-task (Sekine et al., 2020), where each Wikipedia article is labelled according to a fine-grained named entity label set known as Extended Named Entity (ENE).[2] WoS is a collection of abstracts from academic papers across different research domains and areas. The statistics of each dataset is given in Table 1. Looking at the document distributions in terms of label hierarchy levels, we find that the relationship between the number of documents and label classes conforms to a power-law function for RCV1 and SHINRA, especially at lower (2+) levels. For WoS, the number of documents per class at level 1 and 2 is relatively balanced.

3.3 Evaluation Metrics

We evaluate model performance in terms of Micro-F_1 and Macro-F_1, two standard evaluation metrics for document categorisation. Micro-F_1 is instance-level F-score, and thereby gives more weight to frequent labels. Macro-F_1 is class-level F-score, and gives equal weight to all labels.

3.4 Experimental Settings

Each document is truncated/padded to a fixed length of 256 tokens, where stopwords are removed for all models except BERT. For all models except BERT, we use 100-dimensional pre-trained word embeddings from GloVe (Pennington et al., 2014) to initialise the word embeddings. The vocabulary contains at most 100,000 words ranked by frequency. For OOV words, the word embeddings are randomly initialised. We train all models with

[2]http://ene-project.info/ene8/?lang=en

Dataset	RCV1		SHINRA		WoS	
Method	Micro	Macro	Micro	Macro	Micro	Macro
TextCNN						
Flat	75.63	45.24	86.94	56.46	83.41	77.00
RR	75.56	50.81	85.31	56.62	83.51	77.32
HMCN	**78.22**	43.49	**87.03**	56.28	80.24	74.38
Hi-GCN	77.80	**51.34**	86.91	**58.61**	**84.09**	**77.37**
TextRNN						
Flat	78.46	49.18	88.43	60.11	83.72	77.55
RR	78.52	55.48	87.22	60.07	83.57	**78.08**
HMCN	80.52	48.97	88.71	59.76	82.09	75.90
Hi-GCN	**81.57**	**56.29**	**88.74**	**61.20**	**84.11**	77.95
TextRCNN						
Flat	79.92	51.54	88.12	60.34	84.05	77.95
RR	79.81	56.37	88.06	60.32	84.14	78.03
HMCN	81.13	50.44	88.56	59.71	82.86	76.11
Hi-GCN	**82.96**	**58.05**	**88.69**	**61.05**	**84.54**	**78.28**
BERT						
Flat	82.64	55.61	90.86	66.35	75.73	69.22
RR	82.13	59.41	90.70	66.59	75.77	69.43
HMCN	82.68	53.65	91.32	64.13	72.28	64.62
Hi-GCN	**83.20**	**60.32**	**91.90**	**67.79**	**75.94**	**70.81**

Table 2: Experimental results for different combinations of encoders and hierarchical document categorisation methods. The best result for each text encoder on each dataset is indicated in bold. Micro and Macro indicate micro and macro F_1 score, resp..

a batch size of 32 using Adam (Kingma and Ba, 2014), and an initial learning rate of 1e-3 (1e-5 for BERT) for at most 20 epochs.

For hierarchical categorisation methods, the penalty coefficient of recursive regularisation is set to 1e-6, while the output dimension of internal linear layers in HMCN is set to 384. For the hyper-parameters of Hi-GCN, we follow the recommendations of the authors in the original paper (Zhou et al., 2020). Note that in some cases, both HMCN and Hi-GCN suffer from the vanishing/exploding gradient problem, to counter which we apply batch normalisation to the outputs of the linear layers in HMCN and Hi-GCN where necessary.

3.5 Results

Table 2 presents the experimental results of different combinations of text encoders and hierarchical categorisation methods across the three datasets. Model performance is heavily influenced by the choice of text encoder, with BERT outperforming other encoders by a large margin on RCV1 and SHINRA in terms of both Micro-F_1 and Macro-F_1, but underperforming on WoS, irrespective of which hierarchical method it is combined with. We hypothesis that the performance drop for BERT on WoS is mainly due to domain shift, in that it has been pre-trained on Wikipedia articles and the Google Books corpus, which differ substantially from academic writing.[3] Among TextCNN, TextRNN, and TextRCNN, TextCNN underperforms TextRNN and TextRCNN on all three datasets, especially on RCV1 and SHINRA. The reason is that TextCNN can only capture local features, but the fine-grained hierarchical distinctions captured in the different label sets often require longer-distance semantic dependencies.

With regards to the hierarchical categorisation methods, compared with Flat on RCV1 and

[3]It would be interesting to experiment with SciBERT (Beltagy et al., 2019), which has been pre-trained on papers from the scientific domain, which we leave to future work.

SHINRA, RR improves Macro-F_1 in most cases at the cost of Micro-F_1, indicating that RR can improve the performance of classes with fewer training samples. In contrast, HMCN improves Micro-F_1 at the cost of Macro-F_1, indicating that HMCN is biased towards classes that are better represented in the dataset. However, on WoS, RR achieves better performance in terms of both Micro-F_1 and Macro-F_1— with the one exception of Micro-F_1 with TextRNN— while HMCN achieves worse performance in terms of both Micro-F_1 and Macro-F_1. All these results can be attributed to the fact that RR and HMCN leverage hierarchical information differently: RR utilises parent–child relationships, while HMCN adopts layer-wise hierarchical information. As a result of error propagation due to the greedy top-down approach, HMCN performs relatively worse the deeper the label hierarchy. For example, Flat with TextCNN achieves a Micro-F_1 of 88.53 at level-1 (7 classes) and a Micro-F_1 of 83.41 at level-2 (134 classes) on WoS, where both Micro-F_1 scores at these two levels are higher than 80.24 achieved by HMCN, indicating that the categorisation errors of HMCN at level-1 propagate to level-2 and lead to worse results on WoS.

Looking to Hi-GCN, we find that Hi-GCN with any text encoder consistently outperforms other methods on all three datasets in terms of both Micro-F_1 and Macro-F_1, by aggregating hierarchical information in a more flexible way. In addition to passing information from parent to child nodes, it also passes information from child to parent nodes, thereby improving categorisation performance at level-1 and categorisation at subsequent levels. Both RCV1 and SHINRA datasets have extremely imbalanced data distributions while WoS is relatively more balanced, which is also revealed by the greater differences between Micro-F_1 and Macro-F_1 on RCV1 and SHINRA, than on WoS.

These experiments indicate that the performance of hierarchical document categorisation not only depends on the text encoder and particular hierarchical methods, but also the intrinsic hierarchy label structure and the label distribution.

4 Conclusions

We examine various combinations of text encoders and hierarchical categorisation methods in an end-to-end fashion over three datasets. We find that the choice of text encoder is a strong determinant of performance than the choice of hierarchical method, and indeed that local hierarchical methods don't consistently outperform baseline flat classification methods. With regards to hierarchical methods, RR improves Macro-F_1 at the cost of Micro-F_1 on RCV1 and SHINRA, while HMCN improves Micro-F_1 at the cost of Macro-F_1 on RCV1 and SHINRA. An opposite trend is observed on WoS, namely an improvement for RR and deterioration for HMCN. These different behaviours are determined by how the hierarchical label information is modelled during training. The global model Hi-GCN achieves superior performance in terms of both Micro-F_1 and Macro-F_1 on all three datasets, indicating the necessity of capturing the hierarchy label structure holistically.

References

Hosein Azarbonyad, Mostafa Dehghani, Maarten Marx, and Jaap Kamps. 2021. Learning to rank for multi-label text classification: Combining different sources of information. *Natural Language Engineering*, 27(1):89–111.

Siddhartha Banerjee, Cem Akkaya, Francisco Perez-Sorrosal, and Kostas Tsioutsiouliklis. 2019. Hierarchical transfer learning for multi-label text classification. In *Proceedings of the 57th Annual Meeting of the Association for Computational Linguistics*, pages 6295–6300.

Iz Beltagy, Kyle Lo, and Arman Cohan. 2019. SciBERT: A pretrained language model for scientific text. In *Proceedings of the 2019 Conference on Empirical Methods in Natural Language Processing and the 9th International Joint Conference on Natural Language Processing*, pages 3615–3620.

Amanda Clare and Ross D King. 2003. Predicting gene function in saccharomyces cerevisiae. *Bioinformatics*, 19(suppl_2):ii42–ii49.

Matthew N Davies, Andrew Secker, Alex A Freitas, Miguel Mendao, Jon Timmis, and Darren R Flower. 2007. On the hierarchical classification of G protein-coupled receptors. *Bioinformatics*, 23(23):3113–3118.

Jacob Devlin, Ming-Wei Chang, Kenton Lee, and Kristina Toutanova. 2019. BERT: Pre-training of deep bidirectional transformers for language understanding. In *Proceedings of the 2019 Conference of the North American Chapter of the Association for Computational Linguistics: Human Language Technologies, Volume 1 (Long and Short Papers)*, pages 4171–4186.

Roman Eisner, Brett Poulin, Duane Szafron, Paul Lu, and Russell Greiner. 2005. Improving protein function prediction using the hierarchical structure of the gene ontology. In *Proceedings of the 2005 IEEE*

Symposium on Computational Intelligence in Bioinformatics and Computational Biology, pages 1–10.

Alex Freitas and André Carvalho. 2007. A tutorial on hierarchical classification with applications in bioinformatics. *Research and Trends in Data Mining Technologies and Applications*, pages 175–208.

Siddharth Gopal and Yiming Yang. 2013. Recursive regularization for large-scale classification with hierarchical and graphical dependencies. In *Proceedings of the 19th ACM SIGKDD International Conference on Knowledge Discovery and Data Mining*, pages 257–265.

Wei Huang, Enhong Chen, Qi Liu, Yuying Chen, Zai Huang, Yang Liu, Zhou Zhao, Dan Zhang, and Shijin Wang. 2019. Hierarchical multi-label text classification: An attention-based recurrent network approach. In *Proceedings of the 28th ACM International Conference on Information and Knowledge Management*, pages 1051–1060.

Yoon Kim. 2014. Convolutional neural networks for sentence classification. In *Proceedings of the 2014 Conference on Empirical Methods in Natural Language Processing*, pages 1746–1751.

Diederik P Kingma and Jimmy Ba. 2014. Adam: A method for stochastic optimization. *arXiv preprint arXiv:1412.6980*.

Kamran Kowsari, Donald E Brown, Mojtaba Heidarysafa, Kiana Jafari Meimandi, Matthew S Gerber, and Laura E Barnes. 2017. Hdltex: Hierarchical deep learning for text classification. In *16th IEEE International Conference on Machine Learning and Applications*, pages 364–371.

David D Lewis, Yiming Yang, Tony G Rose, and Fan Li. 2004. Rcv1: A new benchmark collection for text categorization research. *Journal of Machine Learning Research*, 5(Apr):361–397.

Yuning Mao, Jingjing Tian, Jiawei Han, and Xiang Ren. 2019. Hierarchical text classification with reinforced label assignment. In *Proceedings of the 2019 Conference on Empirical Methods in Natural Language Processing and the 9th International Joint Conference on Natural Language Processing*, pages 445–455.

Tomás Mikolov, Ilya Sutskever, Kai Chen, Gregory S. Corrado, and Jeffrey Dean. 2013. Distributed representations of words and phrases and their compositionality. In *Proceedings of Advances in Neural Information Processing Systems 26*, pages 3111–3119.

Hao Peng, Jianxin Li, Yu He, Yaopeng Liu, Mengjiao Bao, Lihong Wang, Yangqiu Song, and Qiang Yang. 2018. Large-scale hierarchical text classification with recursively regularized deep graph-cnn. In *Proceedings of the 2018 World Wide Web Conference*, pages 1063–1072.

Jeffrey Pennington, Richard Socher, and Christopher Manning. 2014. GloVe: Global vectors for word representation. In *Proceedings of the 2014 Conference on Empirical Methods in Natural Language Processing*, pages 1532–1543.

Matthew Peters, Mark Neumann, Mohit Iyyer, Matt Gardner, Christopher Clark, Kenton Lee, and Luke Zettlemoyer. 2018. Deep contextualized word representations. In *Proceedings of the 2018 Conference of the North American Chapter of the Association for Computational Linguistics: Human Language Technologies, Volume 1 (Long Papers)*, pages 2227–2237.

Andrew Secker, Matthew N Davies, Alex Alves Freitas, EB Clark, Jonathan Timmis, and Darren R Flower. 2010. Hierarchical classification of G-protein-coupled receptors with data-driven selection of attributes and classifiers. *International Journal of Data Mining and Bioinformatics*, 4(2):191–210.

Satoshi Sekine, Masako Nomoto, Kouta Nakayama, Asuka Sumida, Koji Matsuda, and Maya Ando. 2020. Overview of shinra2020-ml task. In *Proceedings of the NTCIR-15 Conference*.

Kazuya Shimura, Jiyi Li, and Fumiyo Fukumoto. 2018. Hft-cnn: Learning hierarchical category structure for multi-label short text categorization. In *Proceedings of the 2018 Conference on Empirical Methods in Natural Language Processing*, pages 811–816.

Carlos N Silla and Alex A Freitas. 2011. A survey of hierarchical classification across different application domains. *Data Mining and Knowledge Discovery*, 22(1):31–72.

Celine Vens, Jan Struyf, Leander Schietgat, Sašo Džeroski, and Hendrik Blockeel. 2008. Decision trees for hierarchical multi-label classification. *Machine Learning*, 73(2):185.

Zhiguo Wang, Wael Hamza, and Radu Florian. 2017. Bilateral multi-perspective matching for natural language sentences. In *Proceedings of the Twenty-Sixth International Joint Conference on Artificial Intelligence*, pages 4144–4150.

Jonatas Wehrmann, Ricardo Cerri, and Rodrigo Barros. 2018. Hierarchical multi-label classification networks. In *Proceedings of the 35th International Conference on Machine Learning*, pages 5075–5084.

Zichao Yang, Diyi Yang, Chris Dyer, Xiaodong He, Alex Smola, and Eduard Hovy. 2016. Hierarchical attention networks for document classification. In *Proceedings of the 2016 conference of the North American chapter of the association for computational linguistics: human language technologies*, pages 1480–1489.

Jie Zhou, Chunping Ma, Dingkun Long, Guangwei Xu, Ning Ding, Haoyu Zhang, Pengjun Xie, and Gongshen Liu. 2020. Hierarchy-aware global model for hierarchical text classification. In *Proceedings of the 58th Annual Meeting of the Association for Computational Linguistics*, pages 1106–1117.

BERT's The Word: Sarcasm Target Detection using BERT

Pradeesh Parameswaran, Andrew Trotman, Veronica Liesaputra, David Eyers
Department of Computer Science
University of Otago
New Zealand
[pradeesh,andrew,veronica,dme]@cs.otago.ac.nz

Abstract

In 2019, the Australasian Language Technology Association (ALTA) organised a shared task to detect the target of sarcastic comments posted on social media. However, there were no winners as it proved to be a difficult task. In this work, we revisit the task posted by ALTA using transformers—specifically BERT—given the current success of the transformer-based model in various NLP tasks. We conducted our experiments on two BERT models (TD-BERT and BERT-AEN). We evaluated our model on the data set provided by ALTA ('Reddit') and two additional data sets: 'book snippets' and 'Tweets'. Our results show that our proposed method achieves a 15.2% improvement from the current state-of-the-art system on the Reddit data set and a 4% improvement on Tweets.

1 Introduction

Sarcasm is a remark made by a certain person to ridicule or hurt another person's feelings (Cheang and Pell, 2008). A unique property of sarcasm lies in the way words are used. The result digresses from the conventional word order and alters the meaning of the whole sentence (Attardo et al., 2003). This very aspect also makes it very challenging to detect in a text. There has been a large number of studies that looked at automating sarcasm detection (Eke et al., 2020; Joshi et al., 2017) however there is less work done in identifying and extracting the target of sarcasm from the text.

The problem of sarcasm target detection was originally coined by Joshi et al. (2016a). The *target of sarcasm* is defined as an entity or a situation that is being ridiculed in a sarcastic text. The task of sarcasm target identification is to extract the subset of words that indicate the target of ridicule for a given sarcastic sentence. Identifying the target of ridicule can improve the detection of cyber-bullying and hate speech targeted towards minority communities such as people of colour, the LGBTQ+ community and others (Oliva et al., 2021; Hylton, 2018). However, this task is particularly challenging because of the following factors:

- **Multiple targets**—A sarcastic sentence may contain multiple targets. For instance in the following sentence, "*James is as good at cooking as Guy Feiri is at avoiding controversy*", the targets are both "*James*" and "*Guy Feiri*".

- **Lack of targets**—The target of sarcasm may not be present in the given sentence. For example in the sentence, "*I guess the kumara loves kayaking*", the speaker makes a sarcastic remark but the target of ridicule is unclear. When the sarcasm target does is not present or it is unclear, it is marked as OUTSIDE.

There have been various attempts to improve the performance of sarcasm target detection (Patro et al., 2019; Molla and Joshi, 2019; Bölücü and Can, 2020; Parameswaran et al., 2021) such as through the use of deep-learning models and rule-based methods. Given the successes of transformers, particularly BERT (Devlin et al., 2019), in NLP tasks such as Aspect-Based Sentiment Analysis (ABSA) (Sun et al., 2019a), and summarisation (Miller, 2019), we hypothesise that BERT-like models may also be good at this task.

Our experiments show that BERT models outperform the current state-of-the-art system on our Reddit data by 23.4% and give a 3% increase on our Tweets data.

2 Related Work

Sarcasm detection (i.e., distinguishing sarcastic texts from non-sarcastic texts) is widely studied in computational linguistics. Eke et al. (2020); Joshi et al. (2017) have presented a comprehensive overview in this field. To summarise, there are several approaches: semi-supervised learning (Bamman and Smith, 2015; Bharti et al., 2015; Ling and Klinger, 2016; Ghosh and Muresan, 2018), deep learning (Ghosh and Veale, 2016; Agrawal and An, 2018; Hazarika et al., 2018; Martini et al., 2018; Liu et al., 2019), and lately, with the advancement of transformers, researchers have used transformers to distinguish sarcastic texts from non-sarcastic texts (Baruah et al., 2020; Avvaru et al., 2020; Potamias et al., 2020).

Little work has been done to detect the target of sarcasm—in spite of the Australasian Language Technology Association (ALTA) organising a shared task challenge to encourage researchers to tackle this problem (Molla and Joshi, 2019). The approaches taken in prior work include a rule-based system that looks at Part-of-Speech (PoS) (Joshi et al., 2016b), deep learning (Patro et al., 2019), and an ensemble of machine learning and deep learning classifiers (Parameswaran et al., 2021). To the best of our knowledge, there is no research exploring the use of BERT models for sarcasm target detection, but we note that Parameswaran et al. (2021) used embeddings from BERT, but not the transformer.

BERT has shown success in Aspect-Extraction (AE) within ABSA tasks (Xu et al., 2019; Hoang et al., 2019). Our task is similar to Aspect-Extraction, but in our task, the targets may be absent from the given text, which makes it challenging. We consider two models from the ABSA literature for our experiments: TD-BERT (Gao et al., 2019) and BERT-AEN (Song et al., 2019). Initially our choice was guided by the fact that BERT-AEN works well with a smaller data set (Gao et al., 2019) and we chose TD-BERT as our second option as we have noticed similiar performance to BERT-AEN with a much simpler architecture by just extending it to include the aspect. Our choice to use these models is further motivated by the availability of a public repository[1] with standard implementations using *PyTorch*[2] (and therefore ease of reproducibility of our experiments).

[1] https://github.com/songyouwei/ABSA-PyTorch/

[2] https://pytorch.org/

	Tweets	*Books*	*Reddit*
Sentences	224	506	950
Avg. sentence length	13.06	28.47	25.30
Avg. target length	2.08	1.6	2.8
% OUTSIDE	10%	5%	35%

Table 1: Statistics of data sets

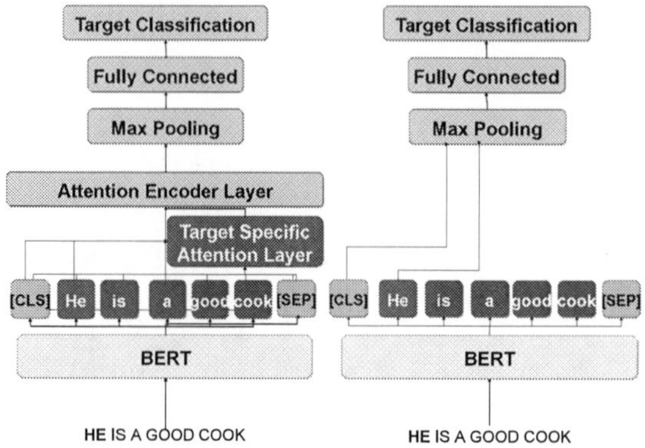

Figure 1: The architecture of BERT-AEN (Song et al., 2019) (left) and TD-BERT (Gao et al., 2019) (right)

We also note that Mukherjee et al. (2021) used the ABSA-PyTorch repository as the basis for reproducing the results of ABSA approaches.

3 Data Set

We consider the data sets released by Joshi et al. (2016b) and Molla and Joshi (2019). The sets consist of three different kinds of data: Tweets (*Tweets*), book snippets (*Books*) and also Reddit posts (*Reddit*). Table 1 shows the details of the collections.

4 Methodology

When predicting the target of sarcasm, like others (Patro et al. (2019) and Parameswaran et al. (2021)), we formulated the problem as a sequence labelling problem. We first represent a sarcastic sentence (S) as a sequence of words $\{w_1, w_2, \ldots, w_N\}$. We then append each word with a label indicating if it is a potential target. Consider the following example, *"He is a good cook"* with *'He'* as the potential target. The sentence is represented as {*'He'*, *'is'*, *'a'*, *'good'*, *'cook'*} and its label sequence is {*'He'*$_T$, *'is'*$_\emptyset$, *'a'*$_\emptyset$, *'good'*$_\emptyset$, *'cook'*$_\emptyset$}, where T is a potential target and $\emptyset$ is not. We feed both of these sequences as training input for our two BERT models (TD-BERT and BERT-AEN).

Model	*Tweets*	*Books*	*Reddit*
Baseline 1 (Patro et al., 2019)	0.831 ± 0.156	0.865 ± 0.188	0.623 ± 0.261
Baseline 2 (Parameswaran et al., 2021)	0.860 ± 0.165	0.879 ± 0.194	0.715 ± 0.260
TD-BERT	0.849 ± 0.123	**0.881** ± 0.195	0.663 ± 0.245
BERT-AEN	0.848 ± 0.102	0.864 ± 0.172	0.689 ± 0.274
TD-BERT (*PT*)	**0.891** ± 0.153	NA †	**0.824** ± 0.303
BERT-AEN (*PT*)	0.880 ± 0.183	NA †	0.785 ± 0.299

Table 2: Results of our experiments. The figures in each case indicate the mean DICE score and standard deviation. *PT* denotes that the model is further trained to understand the nuances of the data set. † denotes that the scores for non-*PT* and *PT* models are the same as we did not further train BERT on *Books*.

Since we are classifying whether each word in a sentence is a potential target of sarcasm, the first word of the sequence is appended with a unique `[CLS]` token which is used by BERT for classification tasks. As shown in Figure 1, in order to train the model, we transform the given sentence (S) into `[CLS]` $+ S +$ `[SEP]` and `[CLS]` $+ w_k +$ `[SEP]` along with the label, w_k, where k is $\{1 \ldots N\}$. As there can be multiple potential target terms, we introduce a max-pooling operation to the two BERT models. This takes into consideration which candidate targets are the best before it gets fed into the fully connected layer. Finally, we use a softmax layer in order to classify whether the current word is a potential target of sarcasm or not. We use $\text{BERT}_{\text{Base}}$ (Devlin et al., 2019) as our pre-trained model.

We briefly explain the architecture of the TD-BERT and BERT-AEN models below:-

- **BERT-AEN** (Song et al., 2019)—This model uses an attention encoder network to model the semantic interaction between the whole sentence and the potential target. The Target Specific Attention Layer is introduced so that it can compute the hidden states of the input embedding. The attentional encoder layer has two submodules: multi-head attention (MHA) and point-wise convolution transformation (PCT). The MHA performs multiple attention functionality that provides introspective context words modelling and perceptive target word modelling. According to Song et al. (2019), this is a lightweight solution as opposed to using LSTM. Then, PCT transforms the contextual information from MHA by incorporating context-perceptive target words. Additionally, BERT-AEN uses label smoothing regularisation (LSR) in the loss function. LSR reduces overfitting by replacing the 0 and 1 targets for the classifier with smoothed values (such as 0.1 and 0.9, respectively). This works well in our situation, where we have a limited amount of data.
- **TD-BERT** (Gao et al., 2019)—TD-BERT's architecture closely resembles that of BERT. The key difference is that TD-BERT incorporates the potential target information in its classification input, as described above.

Given the small number of sentences in our data sets, and the domain specific language used in *Reddit* and *Tweets*, we initially trained $\text{BERT}_{\text{Base}}$ to additionally understand the nuances of language use in those domains (Sun et al., 2019b). To do this we sampled 150,000 posts from Khodak's Reddit data set (Khodak et al., 2017) for *Reddit* and 100,000 tweets from The Edinburgh Twitter Corpus (Petrović et al., 2010) for *Tweets*. We further pre-trained $\text{BERT}_{\text{Base}}$ as a Mask Language Modelling task. We followed the recommendation of (Devlin et al., 2019), by masking 15% of all input tokens randomly. Additionally, we took the necessary steps to ensure that the sentences found in *Reddit* and *Tweets* were removed from Khodak's Reddit and the Edinburgh Twitter Corpus before training. We did no additional training for *Books* because $\text{BERT}_{\text{Base}}$ has already been trained on such content (Devlin et al., 2019).

We reserved 10% of our training set for the purpose of fine-tuning parameters. The best parameters we found were a batch size of 32, a maximum sequence length of 128, the maximum predictions per sequence being 20, and a learning rate of 10^{-5}.

Once we had trained the models for *Reddit* and *Tweets*, we then fine-tuned both of our BERT models to each of our three data sets using the training data provided in those data sets. We set the number of epochs to 3 and the *learning_rate* to be 10^{-5}

following the recommendation from Devlin et al. (2019).

5 Experimental Setup

We ran our experiments on an Intel Xeon E5-2690 v3 @ 2.00 GHz CPU with an NVIDIA Tesla T4 (CUDA Version 11.2, Driver Version 460.73) running on Debian 10 (Buster). We forked commit `9acab7e` of ABSA-PyTorch and modified it to suit our task. Our source code can be found on our GitHub page.[3]

We consider the current state-of-the-art models from Patro et al. (2019) and Parameswaran et al. (2021) as baselines for this task, that we called Baseline 1 and Baseline 2, respectively. We implemented the approaches of each author and compared our results to theirs. A one-way ANOVA showed no statistically significant difference at the 0.05 level, providing confidence in our implementations of their approaches.

We use DICE score to measure the accuracy as it has been used in past works (Joshi et al., 2016a; Molla and Joshi, 2019). All the results reported used five-fold cross-validation.

6 Results

We report our results in Table 2. It is not surprising that training BERT improves results for *Reddit* and *Tweets* as the model has learned the nuances of language used on those platforms (Sun et al., 2019b). From our experimental results, training TD-BERT gives a 15.2% improvement on state-of-the-art for *Reddit*, but only a modest improvement of 4% for *Tweets* and 0.22% for *Books*.

Surprising to us, TD-BERT performs best in all our tasks. We believe that the simple method of just incorporating a target's position helped the model to better understand the context of the sentences. Although the multiple attention mechanisms in BERT-AEN could be expected to outperform TD-BERT, it is unclear why this is not the case in our experimental results. One possible explanation is that the data set is small and the model has learned more noise. We leave for future work the exploration using larger data sets.

6.1 Evaluation on Kaggle

In addition to evaluating our models on the three data sets, we ran our best performing model (TD-BERT (*PT*)) on the data from the ALTA 2019 Shared Task, as seen on Kaggle. This allowed us to examine the generalisability of our solution *in the wild*. Table 3 presents our results and the results from previously published runs. A one-way ANOVA-test of our model with Baseline 1 and Baseline 2 did not find any statistically significant difference at the $p < 0.05$ level. However, our approach beats all the participants' runs (*Powers* and *Orangutan*) and the two baselines provided by the Shared Task (*Always* OUTSIDE, which always outputs 'no target', and *Pronouns*, which extracts and outputs the pronouns) at the $p < 0.05$ level.

System	Public	Private
Baseline 1 (Patro et al., 2019)	0.466	0.514
Baseline 2 (Parameswaran et al., 2021)	0.493	0.548
Always OUTSIDE	$0.367^{\dagger}$	$0.349^{\dagger}$
Powers	$0.386^{\dagger}$	$0.333^{\dagger}$
Orangutan	$0.371^{\dagger}$	$0.292^{\dagger}$
Pronouns	$0.209^{\dagger}$	$0.225^{\dagger}$
Ours (TD-BERT (*PT*))	**0.501**	**0.562**

Table 3: Evaluation on Kaggle Public and Private portions of the data set. † denotes a method that was included within the 2019 ALTA Shared Task Challenge

We further investigated the Kaggle score as our model's DICE score is much lower than the DICE score that we obtained in the other three datasets. First, we validated the scores in Table 2 by uploading our test portion to a private Kaggle contest and evaluating our run. The Kaggle score matched that in the table, giving confidence that our implementation of DICE is correct.

Next, we augmented our sentences with the subreddit information from Khodak et al. (2017) and compared that to the annotated public portion of *Reddit*. We observe that 23% of the private portion's subreddits are not in the public portion. We hypothesise that the model has learned the nuances of the subreddits it has seen, but cannot generalise this across all subreddits. However, we do not have the ground truth, so cannot form any solid conclusions.

6.2 Computational Costs

Figure 2 illustrates the comparisons of our chosen models' run-time and evaluation time on all three of the data sets. We can see that the much simpler TD-BERT performs faster than BERT-AEN in all the cases. The training and evaluation time for

[3]https://github.com/prasys/ABSA-PyTorch/

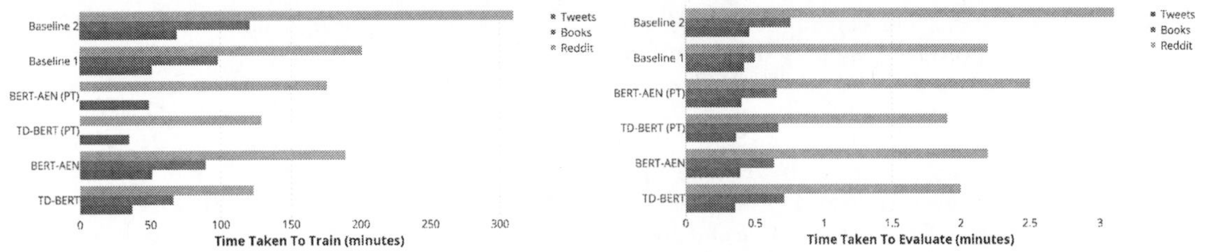

Figure 2: TD-BERT and BERT-AEN training time (left) and run time (right) comparison

non *PT* models are very similar to the *PT* ones. However, it is worth noting that training further on the *Reddit* data set took 336 minutes, and for *Tweets* took 240 minutes. We believe that the performance gain for both data sets easily justifies this modest training time. Hao et al. (2019) suggested that running more epochs can improve performance but we leave this for future work.

6.3 Failure Analysis

Compared to the untrained $\text{BERT}_{\text{Base}}$, we believe that our trained $\text{BERT}_{\text{Base}}$ can better understand the language used in various subreddits, where there are often novel words being coined. Consider the following example from the training set, "*Yeah, an ice cream is so much less creative than a* ***pokeball with eyes***" (target in bold). The further trained model predicted a partially correct answer of *"pokeball"* but the out of the box model missclassified this sentence, returning OUTSIDE.

However, there are instances where we did not obtain the correct target, regardless of the BERT model or any additional training and fine-tuning. For example, *"Yeah 0i have an i5 520m and Intel HD and you know, it really bugs the hell out of me when my fps goes below 20 like come on"*. The annotators mark it as OUTSIDE but both of our models predicted *"I"*, we believe the answer to be *"Intel HD"* as well as *"i5 520m"*.

In *Reddit*, the standard deviation of the DICE scores is higher than in the other data sets. This lends further evidence to our hypothesis that domain (subreddit) specific language is learned in training, and is not easily generalised. Patro et al. (2019) has demonstrated that a PoS tagger can help improve the quality of a sarcasm target detector, and we believe it might help here too. We leave the exploration of this for future work.

7 Conclusion

We presented our approach to sarcasm target detection. We used two different publicly available BERT models: TD-BERT and BERT-AEN, and fine-tuned them to the task using extra examples of data from the domains we explore. Finally, we evaluated our models on three publicly available data sets: *Tweets*, *Books*, and *Reddit*. Our empirical results show that this approach outperforms the current state-of-the-art on all three data sets.

Despite setting a strong baseline, we believe that there remains plenty of room for further work in this area. Firstly, we conducted our experiments on a small data set, therefore our proposed methodology needs to be tested when applied to a larger data set. Secondly, the use of user profiles, user history, context, and so on, might improve performance for *Reddit* and *Tweets* as detecting sarcasm is a difficult task and it requires more than content alone. Some users are more prone to sarcastic quips than others, and that could be mined from a person's past posts (Marwick and Boyd, 2011).

Acknowledgements

This material is based upon work supported by the Google Cloud Research Credits program with the award GCP19980904.

References

Ameeta Agrawal and Aijun An. 2018. Affective representations for sarcasm detection. In *41st International ACM SIGIR Conference on Research and Development in Information Retrieval, SIGIR 2018*, pages 1029–1032.

Salvatore Attardo, Jodi Eisterhold, Jennifer Hay, and Isabella Poggi. 2003. Multimodal markers of irony and sarcasm.

Adithya Avvaru, Sanath Vobilisetty, and Radhika Mamidi. 2020. Detecting sarcasm in conversation context using transformer-based models. In *Proceedings of the Second Workshop on Figurative Language Processing*, pages 98–103.

David Bamman and Noah A. Smith. 2015. Contextualized sarcasm detection on twitter. In *Proceedings of the 9th International Conference on Web and Social Media, ICWSM 2015*, pages 574–577.

Arup Baruah, Kaushik Das, Ferdous Barbhuiya, and Kuntal Dey. 2020. Context-aware sarcasm detection using bert. In *Proceedings of the Second Workshop on Figurative Language Processing*, pages 83–87.

Santosh Kumar Bharti, Korra Sathya Babu, and Sanjay Kumar Jena. 2015. Parsing-based sarcasm sentiment recognition in Twitter data. In *Proceedings of the 2015 IEEE/ACM International Conference on Advances in Social Networks Analysis and Mining, ASONAM 2015*, pages 1373–1380.

Necva Bölücü and Burcu Can. 2020. Sarcasm target identification with lstm networks. In *2020 28th Signal Processing and Communications Applications Conference (SIU)*, pages 1–4. IEEE.

Henry S Cheang and Marc D Pell. 2008. The sound of sarcasm. *Speech communication*, 50(5):366–381.

Jacob Devlin, Ming Wei Chang, Kenton Lee, and Kristina Toutanova. 2019. BERT: Pre-training of deep bidirectional transformers for language understanding. In *NAACL HLT 2019 - 2019 Conference of the North American Chapter of the Association for Computational Linguistics: Human Language Technologies - Proceedings of the Conference*, volume 1, pages 4171–4186.

Christopher Ifeanyi Eke, Azah Anir Norman, Liyana Shuib, and Henry Friday Nweke. 2020. Sarcasm identification in textual data: systematic review, research challenges and open directions. *Artificial Intelligence Review*, 53(6):4215–4258.

Zhengjie Gao, Ao Feng, Xinyu Song, and Xi Wu. 2019. Target-dependent sentiment classification with bert. *IEEE Access*, 7:154290–154299.

Aniruddha Ghosh and Dr. Tony Veale. 2016. Fracking Sarcasm using Neural Network. In *Proceedings of the 7th workshop on computational approaches to subjectivity, sentiment and social media analysis*, pages 161–169.

Debanjan Ghosh and Smaranda Muresan. 2018. "With 1 follower I must be AWESOME :P". Exploring the role of irony markers in irony recognition. *Icwsm*, (Icwsm):588–591.

Yaru Hao, Li Dong, Furu Wei, and Ke Xu. 2019. Visualizing and understanding the effectiveness of bert. *arXiv preprint arXiv:1908.05620*.

Devamanyu Hazarika, Soujanya Poria, Sruthi Gorantla, Erik Cambria, Roger Zimmermann, and Rada Mihalcea. 2018. CASCADE: Contextual Sarcasm Detection in Online Discussion Forums. In *Proceedings of the 27th International Conference on Computational Linguistics*, pages 1837–1848.

Mickel Hoang, Oskar Alija Bihorac, and Jacobo Rouces. 2019. Aspect-based sentiment analysis using bert. In *Proceedings of the 22nd Nordic Conference on Computational Linguistics*, pages 187–196.

Kevin Hylton. 2018. I'm not joking! the strategic use of humour in stories of racism. *Ethnicities*, 18(3):327–343.

Aditya Joshi, Pushpak Bhattacharyya, and Mark J. Carman. 2017. Automatic sarcasm detection: A survey. *ACM Computing Surveys*, 50(5):1–22.

Aditya Joshi, Pranav Goel, Pushpak Bhattacharyya, and Mark Carman. 2016a. Automatic Identification of Sarcasm Target: An Introductory Approach.

Aditya Joshi, Vaibhav Tripathi, Pushpak Bhattacharyya, Mark Carman, Meghna Singh, Jaya Saraswati, and Rajita Shukla. 2016b. How challenging is sarcasm versus irony classification?: A study with a dataset from English literature. In *Proceedings of the Australasian Language Technology Association Workshop 2016*, pages 123–127.

Mikhail Khodak, Nikunj Saunshi, and Kiran Vodrahalli. 2017. A large self-annotated corpus for sarcasm. *arXiv preprint arXiv:1704.05579*.

Jennifer Ling and Roman Klinger. 2016. An empirical, quantitative analysis of the differences between sarcasm and Irony. *Lecture Notes in Computer Science (including subseries Lecture Notes in Artificial Intelligence and Lecture Notes in Bioinformatics)*, 9989 LNCS:203–216.

Liyuan Liu, Jennifer Lewis Priestley, Yiyun Zhou, Herman E. Ray, and Meng Han. 2019. A2Text-Net: A Novel Deep Neural Network for Sarcasm Detection. In *2019 IEEE First International Conference on Cognitive Machine Intelligence (CogMI)*, pages 118–126.

Andrianarisoa Tojo Martini, Makhmudov Farrukh, and Hongwei Ge. 2018. Recognition of ironic sentences in Twitter using attention-based LSTM. *International Journal of Advanced Computer Science and Applications*, 9(8):7–11.

Alice E Marwick and Danah Boyd. 2011. I tweet honestly, i tweet passionately: Twitter users, context collapse, and the imagined audience. *New media & society*, 13(1):114–133.

Derek Miller. 2019. Leveraging bert for extractive text summarization on lectures. *arXiv preprint arXiv:1906.04165*.

Diego Molla and Aditya Joshi. 2019. Overview of the 2019 ALTA Shared Task : Sarcasm Target Identification. In *Proceedings of the The 17th Annual Workshop of the Australasian Language Technology Association*, pages 192–196.

Rajdeep Mukherjee, Shreyas Shetty, Subrata Chattopadhyay, Subhadeep Maji, Samik Datta, and Pawan Goyal. 2021. Reproducibility, replicability and beyond: Assessing production readiness of aspect based sentiment analysis in the wild. *arXiv preprint arXiv:2101.09449*.

Thiago Dias Oliva, Dennys Marcelo Antonialli, and Alessandra Gomes. 2021. Fighting hate speech, silencing drag queens? artificial intelligence in content moderation and risks to lgbtq voices online. *Sexuality & Culture*, 25(2):700–732.

Pradeesh Parameswaran, Andrew Trotman, Veronica Liesaputra, and David Eyers. 2021. Detecting the target of sarcasm is hard: Really?? *Information Processing & Management*, 58(4):102599.

Jasabanta Patro, Srijan Bansal, and Animesh Mukherjee. 2019. A deep-learning framework to detect sarcasm targets. In *Proceedings of the 2019 Conference on Empirical Methods in Natural Language Processing and the 9th International Joint Conference on Natural Language Processing (EMNLP-IJCNLP)*, pages 6335–6341.

Saša Petrović, Miles Osborne, and Victor Lavrenko. 2010. The edinburgh twitter corpus. In *Proceedings of the NAACL HLT 2010 workshop on computational linguistics in a world of social media*, pages 25–26.

Rolandos Alexandros Potamias, Georgios Siolas, and Andreas-Georgios Stafylopatis. 2020. A transformer-based approach to irony and sarcasm detection. *Neural Computing and Applications*, 32(23):17309–17320.

Youwei Song, Jiahai Wang, Tao Jiang, Zhiyue Liu, and Yanghui Rao. 2019. Attentional encoder network for targeted sentiment classification. *arXiv preprint arXiv:1902.09314*.

Chi Sun, Luyao Huang, and Xipeng Qiu. 2019a. Utilizing bert for aspect-based sentiment analysis via constructing auxiliary sentence. *arXiv preprint arXiv:1903.09588*.

Chi Sun, Xipeng Qiu, Yige Xu, and Xuanjing Huang. 2019b. How to fine-tune bert for text classification? In *China National Conference on Chinese Computational Linguistics*, pages 194–206. Springer.

Hu Xu, Bing Liu, Lei Shu, and Philip S Yu. 2019. Bert post-training for review reading comprehension and aspect-based sentiment analysis. *arXiv preprint arXiv:1904.02232*.

Cross-Domain Language Modeling: An Empirical Investigation

Vincent Nguyen[1,2] **Sarvnaz Karimi**[1] **Maciej Rybinski**[1] **Zhenchang Xing**[2]
[1]CSIRO Data61, Sydney, Australia
[2]The Australian National University, Canberra, Australia
{firstname.lastname}@csiro.au
{zhenchang.xing}@anu.edu.au

Abstract

Transformer encoder models exhibit strong performance in single-domain applications. However, in a cross-domain situation, using a sub-word vocabulary model results in sub-word overlap. This is an issue when there is an overlap between sub-words that share no semantic similarity between domains. We hypothesize that alleviating this overlap allows for a more effective modeling of multi-domain tasks; we consider the biomedical and general domains in this paper. We present a study on reducing sub-word overlap by scaling the vocabulary size in a Transformer encoder model while pretraining with multiple domains. We observe a significant increase in downstream performance in the general-biomedical cross-domain from a reduction in sub-word overlap.

1 Introduction

Contemporary language models are pretrained on massive, linguistically diverse corpora (Lan et al., 2020; Devlin et al., 2019a). It is not uncommon for these models to excel at benchmark downstream tasks (Wang et al., 2019a), given the use of contextual representations (Devlin et al., 2019b) that are trained on a variety of source *domains*—a term used to describe a distribution of language on a given topic or genre (for example BIOMEDICAL, SCIENTIFIC)—or GENERAL domain. However, the benefit of GENERAL domain pretraining for specialized application is questionable, as applying these language models (Gu et al., 2020) to specialized tasks is worse than using specialized counterparts (Beltagy et al., 2019). This degradation still occurs after sequential pretraining on specialized domains (Shin et al., 2020) when *fine-tuned* (updates to pretraining) to downstream tasks.

We hypothesize some of this degradation lies in the use of a *sub-word vocabulary* (Si et al., 2019). Sub-word vocabularies (Sennrich et al., 2016; Wu et al., 2016a,b) allow for efficient modeling of a source language distribution with a limited vocabulary size. However, problematically sub-words can be shared between different words—for example hypotension and hypocritical—with different meanings. This potentially conflates the vector representation of a sub-word (or *wordpiece*) causing *sub-word overlap*. When this overlap occurs with sub-words appearing in multiple domain contexts we call this *cross-domain sub-word overlap*.

As a pilot empirical study, we investigate reducing *cross-domain sub-word overlap*, by increasing vocabulary size, in language models pretrained in the GENERAL and BIOMEDICAL cross-domain. To evaluate the effect of sub-word overlap, general and biomedical domain benchmarks are used in this study as the *task distribution* includes different linguistic phenomena such as grammar, sentiment, textual similarity, natural language inference (Wang et al., 2019a). Interestingly, we find that disjoint sub-word vocabulary sets are not ideal. Some sub-word overlap is necessary and unavoidable, and a different level of overlap is ideal for each target domain. We also find a positive trend occurs when reducing cross-domain sub-word overlap, suggesting that there is a trade-off depending on the target downstream task and domain.

To better understand the results, we look at the impact of the pretraining data domain on downstream benchmark performance. Surprisingly, we found that inclusion of the general domain with a specialized domain improves downstream performance for that specialized domain's tasks, but *not* the other way around. This suggests that specialized domains should be trained in tandem with a general one.

Our contribution is a pilot study that investigates a pretraining strategy to reduce *cross-domain sub-word overlap* between GENERAL and BIOMEDICAL domains. We train cross-domain language models with varied vocabulary sizes and evaluate them on downstream classification tasks. We show that a significant improvement can be achieved on two benchmark datasets ((Wang et al., 2019a), (Peng et al., 2019)) when reducing overlap. Further experiments point to the importance of selecting appropriate pretraining data for specialized domains.

2 Related Work

We discuss strategies from the literature to adapt the GENERAL domain language model, in particular a Transformer (Vaswani et al., 2017) encoder (Devlin et al., 2019b), to a specialized domain.

Domain-specific pretraining Many studies have adapted BERT, a popular Transformer encoder, to a specialized domain. However, as BERT was pretrained with a general domain sub-word vocabulary and trained on general domain data (BookCorpus and Wikipedia), domain adaptation is needed. For example, in the BIOMEDICAL domain, BioBERT (Lee et al., 2019) benefited from additional pretraining of the pretrained BERT model on academic biomedical corpora (PubMed Open Access and MEDLINE), showing a marked improvement on downstream biomedical tasks. DAPT (Gururangan et al., 2020) showed similar improvements.

However, BioBERT's approach was less effective in clinical applications; thus, ClinicalBERT (Alsentzer et al., 2019) was trained on domain-specific clinical corpora to improve upon downstream clinical tasks. Similarly, BlueBERT (Peng et al., 2019) was pretrained on a combination of domain-specific data, including PubMed abstracts and clinical notes. However, these approaches were only specialized for narrow task distributions rather than the entire BIOMEDICAL domain (Nguyen et al., 2019) and were trained sequentially (general to biomedical) rather than combined initially, which may suffer from effects such as catastrophic forgetting (McCloskey and Cohen, 1989).

Vocabulary Insertion Other studies considered extending a Transformer-based model's vocabulary without repeating the expensive pretraining step. In particular, one study replaced unused vocabulary elements with medical suffixes and prefixes (Nguyen et al., 2019). Additional pretraining steps were used so that the model learned the new vocabulary. They found that vocabulary insertion did not help as much as an increase in pretraining data. A similar observation is found by Shin et al. (2020) and Beltagy et al. (2019). However, another study using a domain-specific tokenizer for vocabulary insertion (Tai, 2019) found improvements in the German legal domain. However, improvements from vocabulary insertion are minimal, as there is still an interaction between the original vocabulary embeddings and the embeddings added during the fine-tuning step, resulting in sub-word overlap.

Wang et al. (2019b) proposes an enrichment of the BERT vocabulary by using embeddings from other models and learns a projection to the BERT embedding space in a multilingual setting. exBERT (Tai et al., 2020) extends the embedding dimension with domain-specific vocabulary. The model's original weights and embeddings are frozen during extended vocabulary training. Within the same class of approaces, (Poerner et al., 2020) propose a method where general domain embeddings are aligned with target-domain-specific word2vec embeddings. However, vocabulary insertion approaches circumvent the pretraining stage with domain-specific data which may potentially be more important than a vocabulary change (Shin et al., 2020).

Domain-specific vocabulary pretraining An extension to these methods is to pretrain on a target domain corpus with a custom vocabulary. SciBERT (Beltagy et al., 2019) showed that pretraining from scratch with a domain-specific vocabulary is better than a general-purpose vocabulary despite having fewer combined pretraining examples. Similarly, BioMegatron (Shin et al., 2020) showed that a larger custom vocabulary is useful for biomedical named entity recognition tasks and that a domain-specific vocabulary is more valuable than a larger model. They also show that a larger vocabulary size caused a reduction in over-segmentation, a problem that occurs when using a general vocabulary on specialized tasks (Chalkidis et al., 2020) that increases sub-word overlap.

Our work is a pilot study that extends upon domain-specific vocabulary pretraining to investigate cross-domain sub-word modeling. We pretrain models with varying vocabulary sizes to reduce sub-word overlap. In particular, we focus on cross-domain pretraining, which was previously unexplored in vocabulary experiments.

3 Datasets and Tasks

We use the combined English snapshot of Wikipedia (a proxy for the general domain) and

PubMed Open Access Full-Text corpora (biomedical domain) taken on the 1st of April 2020 for pretraining the language models and tokenizers. The PubMed corpus, consisting of 8.3 billion tokens, is preprocessed to remove references, while the Wikipedia corpus, consisting of 2.0 billion tokens, is extracted and cleaned with *wikiextractor* (Attardi, 2015). We use this pretraining data combination as a cross-domain proxy of the GENERAL and BIOMEDICAL domain. We use the training and validation sets of the GLUE benchmark (Wang et al., 2019a) to fine-tune our models for general domain benchmarking. Likewise, we use the publicly available subset of the BLUE tasks collection for the biomedical domain (Peng et al., 2019).

4 Experiments

We perform pretraining with a cross-domain corpus with the ALBERT model, which results in a high degree of cross-domain sub-word overlap. In addition, we experiment with models that have different vocabulary sizes (5000 to 100,000), each with a varying degree of sub-word overlap during pretraining. In Transformer models, the embedding dimension is coupled with the model's hidden dimension, causing the vocabulary size to control the model size—a larger vocabulary size exponentially increases the model's size. To remedy this, we use the ALBERT model (Lan et al., 2020), which projects the embedding dimension to a latent vocabulary dimension before projecting it to the model's hidden dimension. This projection allows scaling of the vocabulary size without significantly impacting the model's size.

Task performance and vocabulary size After pretraining, for each vocabulary size, we then evaluate our language models on downstream BLUE and GLUE benchmark datasets to determine how downstream performance is affected by the amount of sub-word overlap.

Determining Sub-word Overlap To determine the amount of sub-word overlap in relation to vocabulary size, we tokenize each general domain and biomedical task in GLUE and BLUE for each vocabulary size and compute the Jaccard index (Jaccard, 1912). The GLUE and BLUE tasks, are used as a cross-domain proxy between the GENERAL and BIOMEDICAL domains.

Experimental Setup For each model (vocabulary size $|V|$), we train a separate tokenizer using Byte-Pair Encoding (Sennrich et al., 2016). We use masked language modeling to train the largest model, $\text{ALBERT}_{|V=100,000|}$, on the combined corpora of Wikipedia and PubMed for two weeks using four V100 GPUs with an effective batch size of 256. We use the LAMB (You et al., 2020) optimizer and a maximum model sequence length of 512. All other hyperparameters are left as default, as described by Lan et al. (2020). For each model, we select the checkpoint such that validation performance (perplexity) is equal for all models. We then evaluate each model on both general domain and biomedical benchmark tasks. Specifically, we fine-tune each model for a maximum of 15 epochs for all the biomedical tasks, taking the best model on the validation set for inference over the test set. For the general domain tasks, to reduce overfitting (false convergence), we train each task for five epochs and report the validation performance as the test set labels are not publicly available.

However, scaling vocabulary size itself can lead to performance increases (Shin et al., 2020). Hence, we use the checkpoint where validation performance for masked language modeling is equal across all models; meaning that all models have similar capacity for language modeling with the only difference being vocabulary size during downstream updates via fine-tuning. The increase in parameter count due to vocabulary embeddings is negligible as the embeddings are all projected into the same sized latent dimension before being used by the model.

The classification layer used is created for each individual task and is not shared by any model. We use the default classification layer, with the correct label output layer as provided by the huggingface library (Wolf et al., 2019).

$\|V\|$	CoLA	MNLI	MRPC	QNLI	QQP	RTE	SST-2	STS-B	WNLI
5000	13.7	64.9	79.6	64.3	75.7	**56.7**	78.0	17.7	53.5
10000	12.8	70.1	79.3	67.4	79.9	51.3	80.5	19.9	33.8
20000	9.30	70.8	78.6	78.8	**81.5**	51.6	83.4	61.0	46.5
30000	20.7	70.6	78.4	78.8	81.3	54.9	83.1	**63.7**	56.3
40000	14.8	71.2	**80.9**	78.7	80.0	54.5	82.3	21.3	43.7
50000	15.3	71.1	79.2	79.5	80.9	54.5	83.4	28.9	46.5
60000	16.9	**71.4**	77.3	79.6	80.3	53.1	82.1	25.6	42.3
70000	17.4	71.0	79.3	78.8	79.7	55.6	**85.7**	26.9	36.6
80000	17.3	71.0	80.3	79.0	81.3	53.8	84.8	31.0	**56.3**
90000	21.2	71.1	80.1	**79.6**	81.2	50.2	84.3	25.8	56.3
100000	**21.9**	71.3	79.0	79.0	80.4	52.4	83.7	34.5	46.5

Table 1: Evaluation of the general domain tasks against varied $|V|$ of the ALBERT model.

$\lvert V\rvert$	Jaccard Index	Num. Overlaps	Num. Overlaps/$\lvert V\rvert$	$\lvert V\rvert$ in use
5000	94.6	4710	94.2%	99.5%
10000	87.8	8730	87.3%	99.5%
20000	73.8	14600	73.0%	99.0%
30000	62.8	18480	61.6%	98.2%
40000	54.6	21200	53.0%	97.1%
50000	48.2	23100	46.2%	95.8%
60000	43.0	24360	40.6%	94.4%
70000	38.9	25200	36.0%	92.7%
80000	35.6	25840	32.3%	90.8%
90000	32.8	26280	29.2%	89.1%
100000	30.4	26600	26.6%	87.3%

Table 2: Jaccard Index and overlap proportion for varying vocabulary sizes.

5 Results and Discussion

We trained masked language models of varying vocabulary sizes, each with its own degree of sub-word overlap and evaluate on downstream general and biomedical language understanding benchmarks. We found that cross-domain sub-word overlap reduction benefited the cross-domain between the general (Table 1) and biomedical domain (Figure 1) as sub-word overlap decreased (Table 2).

In terms of sub-word overlap, we find that the Jaccard index decreases sharply with vocabulary size (Table 2), indicating that biomedical and general domain tasks share common elements. This overlap decreases rapidly, especially at larger vocabularies (26.6% overlap at $|V| = 100,000$). A similar overlap percentage is reported by Beltagy et al. (2019) when measuring overlap between scientific and general domain vocabulary.

We also report the sub-word overlap proportional to vocabulary size (Table 2) and observe that it also falls sharply in a similar pattern. Although sub-word overlap proportion decreases, at least 87.3% of the vocabulary is still used, meaning vocabulary elements are not underused. Generally, reducing the overlap from approximately 60% Jaccard Index ($|V| < 30000$) to 40% ($|V| \geq 70000$) increases effectiveness in the biomedical domain while producing small improvements in the general domain

Benchmark	Pretraining Corpora	Effectiveness
BLUE (F1)	Wiki	0.6973
	PubMed	0.6706
	PubMed+Wiki	**0.7186**†
GLUE (Acc)	Wiki	0.7090
	PubMed	0.7060
	PubMed+Wiki	0.6906

Table 3: Pretraining data selection and downstream benchmark performance. BLUE is measured in terms of F1-score, while GLUE is measured in Accuracy. The BLUE benchmarks have a confidence interval higher than 0.95 using a sign test.

Domain	Task	S	L	L-S
General Domain	CoLA	14.3	14.7	+0.40
	MNLI	69.5	71.1†	+1.60
	MRPC	79.4	79.6	+0.20
	QNLI	73.6	79.3	+5.70
	QQP	79.7	80.6	+0.90
	RTE	53.8	53.5	-0.50
	SST-2	81.5	84.0†	+2.50
	STS-B	36.7	28.8	-7.90
	WNLI	46.8	47.5	+0.70
Biomedical	biosses	13.6	19.0	+5.40
	chemprot	59.4	65.2	+5.80
	DDI	66.9	71.2†	+4.30
	HoC	81.4	82.1	+0.70
	MedNLI	67.6	70.2†	+2.60

Table 4: Performance of vocabulary sizes larger (L) than 50,000, and vocabulary sizes smaller (S) than 50,000 on language understanding general (GLUE) and biomedical (BLUE) tasks. An independent t-test is used to calculate statistical significance ($P < 0.05$) denoted by †. Metrics are given in Appendix 8.2.

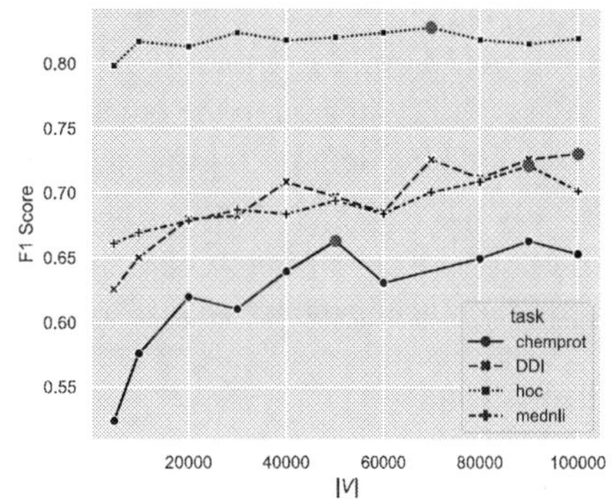

Figure 1: Evaluation of the biomedical tasks against varied $|V|$. A bold blue circle indicates the peak of the curve.

(Table 1). This indicates that reducing sub-word overlap does not reduce vocabulary usage and that downstream fine-tuning with a larger vocabulary size alleviates overlap and improves performance.

However, we find that few tasks perform best with a maximal separation of the biomedical and general domain vocabulary, with the only tasks performing well are CoLA (grammar detection), MedNLI (inference classification) and DDI (relation extraction). This suggests that a degree of overlap in a cross-domain is beneficial and that these domains share similarities. This shared similarity is also observed by Toews and Holland (2019).

BLUE tasks seem to benefit from a larger separation of vocabularies, as suggested by an improved F1-score with increased vocabulary size

($|V|$) in Figure 1. However, this benefit is less significant for GLUE tasks, as validation model selection (used in BLUE) could not be applied.

We find that GLUE results are worse when using combined (PubMed+Wiki) rather than individual pretraining corpora (see Table 3), while interestingly, the opposite appears to be true for BLUE. However, both benchmarks together show that the pretraining data and a larger vocabulary size helps in a cross-domain setting. Though it does not significantly *hurt* performance in the general domain, it significantly *improves* performance in the biomedical domain. Interestingly, pretraining with PubMed alone performed worse than pretraining with the Wikipedia corpus. A detailed table of results can be found in Appendix 5.

We observe that inference tasks fared better with a larger vocabulary (Table 4), indicating that inference tasks are more affected by sub-word overlap. For textual entailment (RTE) and paraphrase detection (QQP), larger $|V|$ had no positive effect. For SST-B (Textual Similarity) the model overfits as data size is small compared to the other tasks. Furthermore, while the default $|V|$ in transformers is 30,000, only a few tasks perform well at this size, suggesting that $|V|$ is an important consideration during pretraining depending on downstream task.

6 Limitations

This study only considers the biomedical and general domains; we hypothesize these principles can be applied to other domains, such as multilingual machine translation. One particular observation relevant to our setup is that the general domain corpus is smaller than that of the target domain, which should also be considered when extrapolating our findings. Another limitation is that training of the language models was not performed to completion. However, language modeling effectiveness was fixed for a fair comparison. These limitations will be explored in future work.

We are also aware that the fixed perplexity does not fully disentangle the impacts of vocabulary overlap and vocabulary size on the downstream effectiveness. We plan to extend our study with further experiments to ensure the robustness of results presented here.

7 Conclusions

When applying general domain Transformer language models to specialized ones, the use of sub-word modeling results causes sub-word overlap leading to decreased performance. We showed that increasing the vocabulary size of the model alleviates this performance penalty and improves downstream task performance on GENERAL and BIOMEDICAL benchmarks. Furthermore, we show that specialized domains improve significantly from a combination of specialized and general domain pretraining data. Our work is a pilot study into improving downstream performance on specialized domains with potential application in cross-domain tasks. In the future, we would extend this study to other applications such as machine translation and cross-lingual language modeling.

Acknowledgements

Vincent is supported by the Australian Research Training Program and the CSIRO Research Office Postgraduate Scholarship. This work is funded by the CSIRO Precision Health Future Science Platform.

References

Emily Alsentzer, John Murphy, William Boag, Wei-Hung Weng, Di Jindi, Tristan Naumann, and Matthew McDermott. 2019. Publicly available clinical BERT embeddings. In *Proceedings of the 2nd Clinical Natural Language Processing Workshop*, pages 72–78, Minneapolis, Minnesota, USA. Association for Computational Linguistics.

Giusepppe Attardi. 2015. Wikiextractor. `https://github.com/attardi/wikiextractor`.

Simon Baker, Ilona Silins, Yufan Guo, Imran Ali, Johan Högberg, Ulla Stenius, and Anna Korhonen. 2015. Automatic semantic classification of scientific literature according to the hallmarks of cancer. *Bioinformatics*, 32(3):432–440.

Iz Beltagy, Kyle Lo, and Arman Cohan. 2019. SciBERT: A pretrained language model for scientific text. In *Proceedings of the 2019 Conference on Empirical Methods in Natural Language Processing and the 9th International Joint Conference on Natural Language Processing (EMNLP-IJCNLP)*, pages 3606–3611, Hong Kong, China. Association for Computational Linguistics.

Ilias Chalkidis, Manos Fergadiotis, Sotiris Kotitsas, Prodromos Malakasiotis, Nikolaos Aletras, and Ion Androutsopoulos. 2020. An empirical study on large-scale multi-label text classification including few and zero-shot labels. In *Proceedings of the 2020 Conference on Empirical Methods in Natural Language Processing*, pages 7503–7515, Online.

Jacob Devlin, Ming-Wei Chang, Kenton Lee, and Kristina Toutanova. 2019a. BERT: Pre-training of deep bidirectional transformers for language understanding. In *Proceedings of the 2019 Conference of the North American Chapter of the Association for Computational Linguistics: Human Language Technologies, Volume 1 (Long and Short Papers)*, pages 4171–4186, Minneapolis, Minnesota. Association for Computational Linguistics.

Jacob Devlin, Ming-Wei Chang, Kenton Lee, and Kristina Toutanova. 2019b. BERT: Pre-training of Deep Bidirectional Transformers for Language Understanding. In *NAACL-HLT*, pages 4171–4186, Minneapolis, MN.

Alvar EllegaRd. 1960. Estimating vocabulary size. 16:219–244.

Yu Gu, Robert Tinn, Hao Cheng, Michael Lucas, Naoto Usuyama, Xiaodong Liu, Tristan Naumann, Jianfeng Gao, and Hoifung Poon. 2020. Domain-specific language model pretraining for biomedical natural language processing. *Computing Research Repository*.

Suchin Gururangan, Ana Marasović, Swabha Swayamdipta, Kyle Lo, Iz Beltagy, Doug Downey, and Noah A. Smith. 2020. Don't stop pretraining: Adapt language models to domains and tasks. In *Proceedings of the 58th Annual Meeting of the Association for Computational Linguistics*, pages 8342–8360, Online.

María Herrero-Zazo, Isabel Segura-Bedmar, Paloma Martínez, and Thierry Declerck. 2013. The ddi corpus: An annotated corpus with pharmacological substances and drug–drug interactions. *Journal of Biomedical Informatics*, 46(5):914 – 920.

Paul Jaccard. 1912. The distribution of the flora in the alpine zone.1. *New Phytologist*, 11:37–50.

Alistair Johnson, Tom Pollard, Lu Shen, Li-wei Lehman, Mengling Feng, Mohammad Ghassemi, Benjamin Moody, Peter Szolovits, Anthony Celi, and Roger Mark. 2016a. MIMIC-III, a freely accessible critical care database. *Scientific Data*, 3:160035.

Alistair EW Johnson, Tom J Pollard, Lu Shen, H Lehman Li-wei, Mengling Feng, Mohammad Ghassemi, Benjamin Moody, Peter Szolovits, Leo Anthony Celi, and Roger G Mark. 2016b. Mimic-iii, a freely accessible critical care database. *Scientific data*, 3:160035.

Martin Krallinger, O. Rabal, S. A. Akhondi, M. Pérez, J. Santamaría, Gael Pérez Rodríguez, G. Tsatsaronis, Ander Intxaurrondo, J. A. López, Umesh Nandal, E. V. Buel, A. Chandrasekhar, Marleen Rodenburg, A.G Lægreid, Marius A. Doornenbal, J. Oyarzábal, A. Lourenço, and A. Valencia. 2017. Overview of the biocreative vi chemical-protein interaction track. In *Proceedings of BioCreative*, pages 141–146.

Zhenzhong Lan, Mingda Chen, Sebastian Goodman, Kevin Gimpel, Piyush Sharma, and Radu Soricut. 2020. ALBERT: A Lite BERT for Self-supervised Learning of Language Representations. In *Proceedings of the 8th International Conference on Learning Representations*.

Jinhyuk Lee, Wonjin Yoon, Sungdong Kim, Donghyeon Kim, Sunkyu Kim, Chan Ho So, and Jaewoo Kang. 2019. BioBERT: A pre-trained biomedical language representation model for biomedical text mining. *Bioinformatics*, 36(4):1234–1240.

Michael McCloskey and Neal J. Cohen. 1989. Catastrophic interference in connectionist networks: The sequential learning problem. volume 24 of *Psychology of Learning and Motivation*, pages 109–165. Academic Press.

Vincent Nguyen, Sarvnaz Karimi, and Zhenchang Xing. 2019. Investigating the effect of lexical segmentation in transformer-based models on medical datasets. In *Proceedings of the 17th Annual Workshop of the Australasian Language Technology Association*, pages 165–171, Sydney, Australia. Australasian Language Technology Association.

Yifan Peng, Shankai Yan, and Zhiyong Lu. 2019. Transfer learning in biomedical natural language processing: An evaluation of BERT and ELMo on ten benchmarking datasets. In *Proceedings of the Workshop on Biomedical Natural Language Processing*, pages 58–65, Florence, Italy.

Nina Poerner, Ulli Waltinger, and Hinrich Schütze. 2020. Inexpensive domain adaptation of pretrained language models: Case studies on biomedical NER and covid-19 QA. In *Findings of the Association for Computational Linguistics: EMNLP 2020*, pages 1482–1490, Online. Association for Computational Linguistics.

Rico Sennrich, Barry Haddow, and Alexandra Birch. 2016. Neural machine translation of rare words with subword units. In *Proceedings of the 54th Annual Meeting of the Association for Computational Linguistics (Volume 1: Long Papers)*, pages 1715–1725, Berlin, Germany.

Hoo-Chang Shin, Yang Zhang, Evelina Bakhturina, Raul Puri, Mostofa Patwary, Mohammad Shoeybi, and Raghav Mani. 2020. BioMegatron: Larger biomedical domain language model. In *Proceedings of the 2020 Conference on Empirical Methods in Natural Language Processing (EMNLP)*, pages 4700–4706, Online.

Yuqi Si, J. Wang, H. Xu, and Kirk Roberts. 2019. Enhancing clinical concept extraction with contextual embedding. *Journal of the American Medical Informatics Association : JAMIA*.

Chin Man Yeung Tai. 2019. Effects of inserting domain vocabulary and fine-tuning bert for german legal language. Master's thesis, University of Twente, Netherlands.

Wen Tai, H. T. Kung, Xin Dong, Marcus Comiter, and Chang-Fu Kuo. 2020. exBERT: Extending pre-trained models with domain-specific vocabulary under constrained training resources. In *Findings of the Association for Computational Linguistics: EMNLP 2020*, pages 1433–1439, Online. Association for Computational Linguistics.

Daniel Toews and Leif Van Holland. 2019. Determining domain-specific differences of polysemous words using context information. In *Proceedings of the 25th International Working Conference on Requirement Engineering: Foundation for Software Quality*.

Ashish Vaswani, Noam Shazeer, Niki Parmar, Jakob Uszkoreit, Llion Jones, Aidan Gomez, Lukasz Kaiser, and Illia Polosukhin. 2017. Attention is all you need. *Computing Research Repository*, abs/1706.03762.

Alex Wang, Amanpreet Singh, Julian Michael, Felix Hill, Omer Levy, and Samuel R. Bowman. 2019a. GLUE: A multi-task benchmark and analysis platform for natural language understanding. In *In the Proceedings of International Conference on Learning Representations*, pages 353–355, Brussels, Belgium.

Hai Wang, Dian Yu, Kai Sun, Jianshu Chen, and Dong Yu. 2019b. Improving pre-trained multilingual model with vocabulary expansion. In *Proceedings of the 23rd Conference on Computational Natural Language Learning (CoNLL)*, pages 316–327, Hong Kong, China. Association for Computational Linguistics.

Thomas Wolf, Lysandre Debut, Victor Sanh, Julien Chaumond, Clement Delangue, Anthony Moi, Pierric Cistac, Tim Rault, Rémi Louf, Morgan Funtowicz, and Jamie Brew. 2019. Huggingface's transformers: State-of-the-art natural language processing. *Computing Research Repository*.

Yonghui Wu, Mike Schuster, Zhifeng Chen, Quoc V. Le, Mohammad Norouzi, Wolfgang Macherey, Maxim Krikun, Yuan Cao, Qin Gao, Klaus Macherey, Jeff Klingner, Apurva Shah, Melvin Johnson, Xiaobing Liu, Łukasz Kaiser, Stephan Gouws, Yoshikiyo Kato, Taku Kudo, Hideto Kazawa, Keith Stevens, George Kurian, Nishant Patil, Wei Wang, Cliff Young, Jason Smith, Jason Riesa, Alex Rudnick, Oriol Vinyals, Greg Corrado, Macduff Hughes, and Jeffrey Dean. 2016a. Google's Neural Machine Translation System: Bridging the Gap between Human and Machine Translation.

Yonghui Wu, Mike Schuster, Zhifeng Chen, Quoc V. Le, Mohammad Norouzi, Wolfgang Macherey, Maxim Krikun, Yuan Cao, Qin Gao, Klaus Macherey, Jeff Klingner, Apurva Shah, Melvin Johnson, Xiaobing Liu, Łukasz Kaiser, Stephan Gouws, Yoshikiyo Kato, Taku Kudo, Hideto Kazawa, Keith Stevens, George Kurian, Nishant Patil, Wei Wang, Cliff Young, Jason Smith, Jason Riesa, Alex Rudnick, Oriol Vinyals, Greg Corrado, Macduff Hughes, and Jeffrey Dean. 2016b. Google's Neural Machine Translation System: Bridging the Gap between Human and Machine Translation. *Computing Research Repository*, page arXiv:1609.08144.

Yang You, Jing Li, Sashank Reddi, Jonathan Hseu, Sanjiv Kumar, Srinadh Bhojanapalli, Xiaodan Song, James Demmel, Kurt Keutzer, and Cho-Jui Hsieh. 2020. Large batch optimization for deep learning: Training bert in 76 minutes. In *Proceedings of the 7th International Conference on Learning Representations*, Online.

George Zipf. 1936. *The Psychobiology of Language*. London, Routledge.

benchmark	collection	dataset	value
BLUE	Wikipedia+PubMED	Chemprot	60.0
		DDI	72.7
		HoC	83.1
		MedNLI	71.5
	PubMED	Chemprot	51.7
		DDI	66.3
		HoC	81.7
		MedNLI	68.4
	Wikipedia	Chemprot	56.6
		DDI	69.3
		HoC	82.0
		MedNLI	70.9
GLUE	Wikipedia+PubMED	MRPC	66.9
		QNLI	81.2
		QQP	85.8
		RTE	52.7
		SST-2	84.0
		WNLI	43.7
	PubMED	MRPC	65.0
		QNLI	79.7
		QQP	86.4
		RTE	51.3
		SST-2	85.0
		WNLI	56.3
	Wikipedia	MRPC	70.8
		QNLI	79.1
		QQP	86.3
		RTE	50.5
		SST-2	82.5
		WNLI	56.3

Table 5: Expanded results from Table 3.

8 Determining vocabulary size

Prior to pretraining, when building the wordpiece tokenizer. We estimated the upper limit of unique vocabulary tokens based on the assumptions that: (1) each corpora is english; (2) each corpora shares no tokens; and, (3) the corpora's token frequency follows a zipf distribution (Zipf, 1936). From, (EllegaRd, 1960) (Table 5), we calculated the upper limit for the vocabulary for each corpus given our second assumption and summed the result which gives a combined vocabulary size of approximately 90,000. We extend the vocabulary by an extra 10,000 to determine if our vocabulary size was sufficient.

8.1 Pretraining Data Experiments

We train separate models for each corpora, namely Wikipedia, PubMed and the combined corpora of Wikipedia and PubMed. We use the same training procedure as in our main experiments, but at a fixed vocabulary size of 40,000.

8.2 Downstream Tasks

We use the standard GLUE benchmark tasks and the BLUE language understanding tasks. We describe the BLUE tasks as follows:

Relation Extraction DDI (Herrero-Zazo et al., 2013), is a medical corpus consisting of texts from the Drugbank database and MeEDLINE abstracts annotated by experts for drug-drug interactions.

Chemprot (Krallinger et al., 2017), a classification task for five different chemical-protein interaction categories from PubMed abstracts.

Multilabel classification Hallmarks of Cancers (HoC) (Baker et al., 2015), a corpus of PubMed abstracts labeled with one or more of ten cancers.

Inference For inference-based tasks, we use Medical Natural Language Inference (MedNLI) (Johnson et al., 2016a) created from MIMIC-III (Johnson et al., 2016b) and annotated by radiologists with entailment, neutral and contradiction labels for each premise-hypothesis pair.

Metrics Generally, for the BLUE tasks, we use macro averaged F1-score, except for HoC where we report the micro averaged F1-score similar to that described in Peng et al. (2019). Evaluation of the GLUE benchmark is based on GLUE's official metrics (Wang et al., 2019a): F1-score for QQP and MRPC, Pearson and Spearman correlation for STS-B, Matthew's Correlation for CoLA, which measures binary agreement between prediction and observed from -1 (total disagreement) and +1 (perfect prediction), and accuracy for the remaining tasks.

9 Minimizing Sub-word overlap

We describe the intuition behind the reduction in sub-word overlap in more detail here and discuss some results.

9.1 Definitions

Sub-word overlap is a phenomena wherein tokens in a sub-word model will exhibit a polysemous, though it is closer to homonymy, effect where subwords will be shared by words that have different meanings. To combat this, we scale the vocabulary size, such that fewer sub-words are shared by different words. Chalkidis et al. (2020) also notes that in specialized contexts, general domain vocabularies tend to over-segment specialized terminology, such as diseases or medications.

$\|V\|$	Jaccard Similarity	Num. Overlaps	% Vocab Used	Num. Tokens used in GLUE tasks	Num. Tokens used in BLUE tasks
5000	94.6	4708	99.5	4970	4713
10000	87.8	8733	99.5	9893	8786
20000	73.8	14609	99.0	19418	14989
30000	62.8	18490	98.2	28457	19498
40000	54.6	21193	97.1	37057	22980
50000	48.2	23083	95.8	45239	25726
60000	43.0	24359	94.4	53109	27888
70000	38.9	25226	92.7	60545	29549
80000	35.6	25858	90.8	67563	30961
90000	32.8	26287	89.1	74369	32118
100000	30.4	26593	87.3	80842	33095

Table 6: Detailed results from Table 2, including statistics for the number of unique tokens used the BLUE and GLUE tasks.

9.2 Measuring Sub-word Overlap

We used Jaccard Index (Jaccard, 1912), to measure the set overlap between the GLUE and BLUE tasks. We found a decreasing trend in overlap when increasing vocabulary size, which was correlated with an increase in downstream task performance. We found that as vocabulary size increased, more vocabulary elements were used in terms of absolute quantities for both the GLUE and BLUE tasks. This could be attributed to fewer words being *broken up* into sub-word units as vocabulary size increases (Chalkidis et al., 2020).

9.3 Task Vocabulary Sizes

For each task, we used tokenized based on white-space to approximate the vocabulary size needed to represent all words in at task (Table 7).

Task	Unique Vocabulary Elements
CoLA	1948
MNLI	13693
MRPC	3858
QNLI	17837
QQP	38260
RTE	4510
sst-2	4293
sts-b	7073
WNLI	592
biosses	362
Chemprot	12385
DDI	3280
HoC	8288
MedNLI	2840

Table 7: Unique vocabulary elements (whole words delimited by spaces)

9.4 Discussions

By expanding the vocabulary dimension, fewer overlaps will occur which is shown in Table 2 as a proportion of the overall vocabulary size and Jaccard Index. Though, in absolute terms the number of overlaps increase, suggesting that some overlap between domains does exist and the overlap percentage being approached is similar to the one found in Beltagy et al. (2019). This is further reflected in Table 3 where the GLUE tasks perform similarly when pretrained on either PubMED or Wikipedia. Suggesting that the pretraining data on its own has enough data to pretrain a general domain model.

Although this not hold true for the specialized domain, which requires both the general domain and specialized domain. Our intuition for pretraining on both Wikipedia and PubMED simultaneously is to reduce the catastrophic forgetting effect (McCloskey and Cohen, 1989), which may be present in models such as BioBERT (Lee et al., 2019), and ClinicalBERT (Alsentzer et al., 2019) given that the models are trained sequentially with medical corpora.

Overview of the 2021 ALTA Shared Task: Automatic Grading of Evidence, 10 years later

Diego Mollá
Department of Computing
Macquarie University
diego.molla-aliod@mq.edu.au

Abstract

The 2021 ALTA shared task is the 12th instance of a series of shared tasks organised by ALTA since 2010. Motivated by the advances in machine learning in the last 10 years, this year's task is a re-visit of the 2011 ALTA shared task. Set within the framework of Evidence Based Medicine (EBM), the goal is to predict the quality of the clinical evidence present in a set of documents. This year's participant results did not improve over those of participants from 2011.

1 Introduction

Evidence Based Medicine (EBM) urges the medical practitioner to make use of the best available evidence for making decisions about the care of individual patients (Sackett et al., 1996). However, medical and biomedical research generates such a volume of publications that it is unrealistic for a medical doctor or researcher to be able to read all relevant publications in order to be up to date on the available medical evidence. For example, PubMed currently contains more than 33 million citations for biomedical literature[1]. A more recent collection, CORD-19, contains over 500,000 publications on topics related to COVID-19, SARS-CoV-2, and related coronaviruses[2].

An important step for determining the best clinical evidence is to grade the quality of the available evidence. To help address this problem, in 2011 the ALTA shared task launched the task of automatic evidence grading (Mollá and Sarker, 2011). The goal of the task was to build a system that predicts the grade of evidence available in a set of medical publications. Forward 10 years, in 2021, the task has been re-visited. The 2021 task uses the same training and test data sets as in 2011, and the evaluation framework has been re-created as closely as possible to match the 2011 evaluation framework.

We wanted to know whether the recent advances in machine learning over the last 10 years lead to an improvement in the accuracy of the automatic grading of evidence predictors. This paper describes the specific set up of the 2021 ALTA shared task, and shows the results of the participating systems. Back in 2011, no participating systems improved on a majority baseline. In 2021, the results of the participating systems appear to improve over the majority baseline, but the difference is not statistically significant. Section 2 gives more details about the automatic grading of evidence task. Section 3 presents related work since 2011. Section 4 details the evaluation framework. Section 5 presents the participating systems and their results, and Section 6 concludes this paper.

2 Evidence Grading

Several taxonomies have been defined to grade the quality of the medical evidence. The Strength of Recommendation Taxonomy (SORT) (Ebell et al., 2004), used in the 2011 ALTA shared task, is one such taxonomy. SORT uses a 3-point scale defined as follows:

A Recommendation based on consistent and good quality patient-oriented evidence.

B Recommendation based on inconsistent or limited quality patient-oriented evidence.

C Recommendation based on consensus, usual practice, opinion, disease-oriented evidence, and case series for studies of diagnosis, treatment, prevention, or screening.

In addition to the above definitions, Ebell et al. (2004) provides details on how to determine each grade, including a flowchart.

[1]https://pubmed.ncbi.nlm.nih.gov/

[2]https://www.kaggle.com/allen-institute-for-ai/CORD-19-research-challenge

Medical evidence is not necessarily bound to one publication only. There may be several publications related to a particular disease, treatment or diagnosis, and each of them may be of different quality. Further, it may indeed happen that each of the separate publications produces consistent results, but the evidence of the set of publications is inconsistent; when that happens the evidence grade cannot be of type A, as per the definitions above.

3 Related Work

The 2011 ALTA shared task overview paper (Mollá and Sarker, 2011) presents a short survey of related work prior to 2011. As we see in this section, there has been limited research since then.

None of the participants to the 2011 ALTA shared task (Mollá and Sarker, 2011) outperformed a majority baseline ("predict B", with an accuracy of 0.4863), and the participating systems did not publish the system descriptions.

A more sophisticated approach developed by the organisers of the 2011 shared task did manage to beat the baseline, reaching an accuracy of 0.6284. Their approach was based on cascaded Support Vector Machine (SVM) classifiers which were trained to separate class A and C from the default B with high precision. These SVM classifiers used combinations of the following features: n-grams of the abstract and title (with general medical semantic types replacing specific medical terms), and publication types (combining the publication types provided in the original abstracts with types generated by applying *ad-hoc* rules). The work was subsequently extended and published with more detail by Sarker et al. (2015).

Gyawali et al. (2012) reported an improved accuracy of 0.7377 on the same dataset by using a two-level stacking approach. In the first level, multiple SVM classifiers are trained using separate feature sets. Then, their output is fed to a second SVM classifier. Their feature sets included publication types, MeSH terms, title, abstract text, abstract method section, and abstract conclusion section. All of these features were as provided by the abstracts, except for the method and conclusion section, which were determined heuristically when not provided by the abstracts.

Byczyńska et al. (2020) reported an accuracy of 0.7541, again on the same dataset, after applying a wide range of different variants of stacked classifiers.

```
00001 B 10553790 15265350
00002 C 12804123 16026213 14627885
00003 B 15213586
00004 A 15329425 9058342 11279767
```

Figure 1: Sample training data. Each row indicates one evidence that needs to be graded. The first number is the evidence ID. This is followed by the evidence grade, and the list of PubMed IDs for the relevant documents.

Table 1 shows the results of the works mentioned in this section, with their confidence intervals as calculated by the Wilson score interval with continuity correction (Brown et al., 2001). According to the confidence intervals shown on the table, the difference between the systems by Gyawali et al. (2012) and Byczyńska et al. (2020) is not statistically significant.

4 Evaluation Framework

The data for the 2021 shared task includes a training set and a development set that were available to the participants. The final ranking was made on a separate test set and was available to the participants (without the target labels) for a limited time near the end of the shared task.

The training, development, and test sets were the same as for the 2011 shared task, after shuffling the rows and changing the row IDs. The corpus from which this data has been obtained has been described by Mollá et al. (2016). Figure 1 illustrates a fragment of the training data. Together with the data formatted as the samples of Figure 1, the participants were provided with the contents of the relevant abstracts as separate files.

The evaluation framework was implemented as a CodaLab competition[3]. The facilities available at CodaLab made it possible to specify our own evaluation script, and also gave us flexibility to design multiple phases and include a leaderboard and discussion forum. Additional information about the 2021 ALTA shared task was made available in the ALTA website[4].

The CodaLab competition was structured into two phases. In a first, development phase, all teams had access to the training and development sets and they could make an arbitrary number of submissions daily, for a maximum of 100 submissions in total. During the development phase, participant teams could submit the results of running their

[3]https://competitions.codalab.org/competitions/33739
[4]http://www.alta.asn.au/events/sharedtask2021/

System	Accuracy	95% CI
Majority Baseline	0.4863	0.4150–0.5583
Mollá and Sarker (2011)	0.6284	0.5564–0.6951
Gyawali et al. (2012)	0.7377	0.6696–0.7961
Byczyńska et al. (2020)	0.7541	0.6869–0.8108

Table 1: Accuracy and 95% confidence intervals of prior work. The confidence intervals were calculated using the Wilson score interval with continuity correction.

system on the development data, and the results could enter a public leaderboard. In the second, test phase, all teams had access to the test data set and each team could make a maximum of 3 submissions. The final ranking was made based on the best submission of each team made during the test phase. Table 2 shows the timeline and submission number limits of each phase.

The evaluation metric was accuracy.

5 Participating Systems

As in past ALTA shared tasks, submissions were made by teams in two categories: a student category, and an open category. In teams of the student category, all members must be university students and none of the team members could have a PhD. Teams that did not qualify for the student category could participate in the open category.

A total of 16 teams registered in the student category, and 5 teams registered in the open category. Of these, only 5 teams, all from the student category, submitted runs in the test phase for final ranking.

Table 3 shows the results of the systems by the participating teams. As can be observed, none of them improves the upper confidence interval of the majority baseline (0.5583). A McNemar's test for statistical significance confirmed that none of the submitted systems had a statistically significant difference with the majority baseline.

Of the 5 teams submitting in the final phase, 3 published a system description which is available in the 2021 ALTA proceedings. Team SarkerLab (Guo et al., 2021) experimented with the use of SVM and RoBERTa. Team Heatwave (Koto and Fang, 2021) applied an ensemble method with transformer variants including BioMed, RoBERTa, and ELECTRA. Finally, team OrangUtanV3 (Parameswaran et al., 2021) applied a cascaded approach that used BioBERT and SVM classifiers. Whereas team Heatwave's classifiers attempted to generate the final evidence grade of the collection of abstracts related to a question, the other two teams attempted to classify individual abstracts and the final result was obtained by combining the outputs of the individual classifications.

6 Conclusions

The participating systems appeared to obtain a score slightly better than the majority baseline but the difference was not statistically significant. These results underperformed those reported by the organisers of the 2011 shared task paper and subsequent work. The participating systems attempted to use some of the latest developments on machine learning algorithms and architectures. The reason of their relatively lower performance may be due to the choice of features. Possibly, better results could have been obtained by incorporating information such as the publication type, or by focusing on specific parts of the abstracts such as the methods or conclusions sections, as related work has shown to be most influential for this task.

References

Lawrence D. Brown, T. Tony Cai, and Anirban DasGupta. 2001. Interval Estimation for a Binomial Proportion. *Statistical Science*, 16(2):101 – 133.

Aleksandra Byczyńska, Maria Ganzha, Marcin Paprzycki, and Mikołaj Kutka. 2020. Evidence quality estimation using selected machine learning approaches. In *2020 Conference on Information Communications Technology and Society (ICTAS)*, pages 1–8.

Mark H Ebell, Jay Siwek, Barry D Weiss, Steven H Woolf, Jeffrey Susman, Bernard Ewigman, and Marjorie Bowman. 2004. Strength of recommendation taxonomy (SORT): a patient-centered approach to grading evidence in the medical literature. *The Journal of the American Board of Family Practice / American Board of Family Practice*, 17:59–67.

Yuting Guo, Yao Ge, Ruqi Liao, and Abeed Sarker. 2021. An ensemble model for automatic grading of evidence. In *Proceedings of the 2021 Australasian Language Technology Workshop*.

Phase	From	To	Submissions
Development	June 30, 2021	October 3, 2021	100
Test	October 4, 2021	October 11, 2021	3

Table 2: Dates and submission number limits of the CodaLab competition phases.

Rank	Team	Accuracy
1	SarkerLab	0.5355
2	Heatwave	0.5027
3	OrangUtanV3	0.4918
4	arana-initiatives	0.4863
	(Majority Baseline	0.4863)
5	nikss	0.4536

Table 3: Results of the participating systems plus the majority baseline.

Binod Gyawali, Thamar Solorio, and Yassine Benajiba. 2012. Grading the quality of medical evidence. In *BioNLP: Proceedings of the 2012 Workshop on Biomedical Natural Language Processing*, pages 176–184, Montréal, Canada. Association for Computational Linguistics.

Fajri Koto and Biaoyan Fang. 2021. Handling variance of pretrained language models in grading evidence in the medical literature. In *Proceedings of the 2021 Australasian Language Technology Workshop*.

Diego Mollá, María Elena Santiago-Martínez, Abeed Sarker, and Cécile Paris. 2016. A corpus for research in text processing for evidence based medicine. *Language Resources and Evaluation*, 50:705–727.

Diego Mollá and Abeed Sarker. 2011. Automatic grading of evidence: the 2011 ALTA shared task. pages 4–8. Australian Language Technology Association.

Pradeesh Parameswaran, Andrew Trotman, Veronica Liesaputra, and David Eyers. 2021. Quick, get me a Dr. BERT: Automatic grading of evidence using transfer learning. In *Proceedings of the 2021 Australasian Language Technology Workshop*.

David L. Sackett, William M. Rosenberg, Jamuir Gray, R. Brian Haynes, and W. Scott Richardson. 1996. Evidence based medicine: What it is and what it isn't. *BMJ*, 312:71–72.

Abeed Sarker, Diego Mollá, and Cécile Paris. 2015. Automatic evidence quality prediction to support evidence-based decision making. *Artificial Intelligence in Medicine*, 64:89–103.

Quick, get me a Dr. BERT: Automatic Grading of Evidence using Transfer Learning

Pradeesh Parameswaran, Andrew Trotman, Veronica Liesaputra, David Eyers
Department of Computer Science
University of Otago
New Zealand
[pradeesh,andrew,veronica,dme]@cs.otago.ac.nz

Abstract

We describe our methods for automatically grading the level of clinical evidence in medical papers, as part of the ALTA 2021 shared task. We use a combination of transfer learning and a hand-crafted, feature-based classifier. Our system ("*orangutanV3*") obtained an accuracy score of 0.4918, which placed third in the leaderboard. From our failure analysis, we find that our classification techniques do not appropriately handle cases when the conclusions of across the medical papers are themselves inconclusive.

We believe that this shortcoming can be overcome—thus improving the classification accuracy—by incorporating document similarity techniques.

1 Introduction

The recent COVID-19 pandemic has once again highlighted the importance of Evidence-Based Medicine (EBM) when deciding the course of treatment (Xu et al., 2020) as social media and television shows are being flooded by so-called experts, who have voiced unproven treatments for COVID-19 such as using hydroxychloroquine (Greenhalgh, 2020; Aquino and Cabrera, 2020). However, the main challenge with EBM is that it is a manual and tedious process and it is very hard for practitioners to keep up with the rise in medical research (Ghosh, 2004; Davies, 2007).

The challenges with EBM were no less true in 2011, when the Australasian Language Technology Association (ALTA) organised a shared task challenge to automatically grade evidence (Molla and Sarker, 2011). The task was to grade evidence based on an EBM framework which is the Strength Of Recommendation Taxonomy (SORT) (Ebell et al., 2004). ALTA decided to revisit the 2011 challenge again this year (2021), motivated by the leaps in Natural Language Processing (NLP) techniques that have occurred meanwhile (Torfi et al., 2020).

We investigate the following research questions with repsect to this challenge:

- *RQ1*: Can we solely use transformers to accurately perform SORT?
- *RQ2*: Can we improve the performance of Transformers by incorporating author and journal features?

Our experimental results suggest that these two approaches do not perform well. Our team placed third in the leaderboard with an accuracy score of 0.4918. None of the scores on the leaderboard beat the winning accuracy score in 2011, of 0.6284. This prompted us to perform an in-depth analysis of our approach, and how our work can be improved in the future to increase the overall accuracy of classification.

2 Related Work

In the medical literature, there are many different taxonomies that are used in order to rank the grade of a clinical study (Abrams et al., 2007; Guyatt et al., 2004). One of the commonly used taxonomies, due to its simplicity, is SORT (Ebell et al., 2004). SORT has been used in deciding whether to recommend root canal treatments (De-Deus and Canabarro, 2017), sports injury rehabilitation strategies (Bell et al., 2018; Rodriguez et al., 2019), and in evaluation of cognitive behavioural treatment (Chang et al., 2020; Baez et al., 2018). There are three grades: `A` (strong), `B` (moderate) and `C` (weak). Grade `A` reflects consistent and good-quality, patient-oriented evidence; Grade `B` reflects being based on inconsistent or limited quality patient oriented evidence; lastly, grade C reflects a recommendation based on consensus, usual practice, opinion or disease-oriented evidence.

The classification of SORT is manually done by medical practitioners, and automating it is still in its infancy. To the best of our knowledge, the only researchers who explored automating SORT are Molla and Sarker (2011). In their work, the authors used a set of classifiers that utilised different feature sets such as n-grams, publication type and titles and then applied multiple SVM classifiers. They obtained an accuracy score of 0.6284.

Transfer learning has shown vast improvement on a variety of downstream tasks such as summarization, translation, and question and answer interactions (Torfi et al., 2020). One popular transfer learning method that is widely adapted is BERT (Devlin et al., 2018). Driven by the success of BERT, Lee et al. (2020) introduced BioBERT (a biomedical focused version of BERT) for tasks such as biomedical Named Entity Recognition (NER), relation extraction, and summarization in the biomedical literature. Recently, Oniani and Wang (2020) demonstrated that BioBERT provides an effective method for chatbots answering questions related to COVID-19.

3 Data Set

The data set[1] provided by the organisers of the ALTA shared task consists of a collection of PubMed abstracts. There are 677 medical abstracts for training, 178 for development, and 183 for the testing set. The training and development data set come with the evidence ID, followed by SORT grade, and finally a list of PubMed IDs of the abstracts. The test data contains the same, except for the SORT grade.

We analysed both the development and training data sets to understand the characteristics of the data. Table 1 shows the distribution of the evidence that contains exactly one abstract and more than one abstract. We include the class distribution of both training and development sets. Across three data sets on average, the percentage of evidence IDs that contains more than one PubMed ID are 57%. From the visual inspection of our training set, we have observed that the majority of the queries (77%) tend to be graded as A and B. We have also noticed that the distribution of classes in development follows closely that of the training set.

Data Set	$=1$ abstract	>1 abstract	No of A	No of B	No of C
Train	293	384	212	311	154
Dev	113	65	48	80	50
Test	105	78	NA	NA	NA

Table 1: Distribution and abstracts in the data sets.

4 Methodology

We employed a two-phase approach to tackle the ALTA challenge. In the first phase, we used a pre-trained BioBERT model and in the second phase, we used an SVM classifier with handcrafted features such as h-index and the journal's impact factor. In this section, we describe our method in detail, along with the steps that we performed. We have made our system's source code publicly available on GitHub.[2]

4.1 Phase 1—BioBERT

We used a pre-trained BioBERT model *biobert-base-cased-v1.2*[3]. The two primary reasons for choosing this model is that the implementation is readily available via *huggingface*,[4] and that it has been trained on PubMed. Since our task relates to grading medical abstracts which are obtained from PubMed, this gives us further confidence that BioBERT would be the right choice for our task.

We first extract the abstracts using the PubMed IDs. If there are multiple PubMed IDs for a piece of given evidence, we treat each of them as independent from one another. This made the implementation easier. We then pre-processed the texts with *Scispacy*[5] by replacing entities of diseases with `[DISEASE]`, drug names as `[DRUGS]` and treatment plans with `[TREATMENT]`. Replacing these instances with a generic tag ensures that the classifier does not overfit or get influenced by these factors. We used the same pre-trained model for pre-processing. In addition to that, we replaced instances of sample size conducted in the studies by following the recommendation from Biau et al. (2008); Charan and Biswas (2013) into three generic tags: `[SMALL]` when the sample size is

[1] https://competitions.codalab.org/competitions/33739

[2] https://github.com/prasys/OrangUtanV3ALTASharedTask21

[3] https://huggingface.co/dmis-lab/biobert-base-cased-v1.2

[4] https://huggingface.co/

[5] https://allenai.github.io/scispacy/

less than 15, [MEDIUM] when it is between 15–100, and [LARGE] when it is greater than 100. These additional steps were done in order to prevent the model from over-fitting.

We then built two classifiers of BioBERT. The first classifier (C_1) distinguishes C-graded documents from non-C graded documents. As for the non-C graded documents, it is then fed to our second BioBERT classifier (C_2) which distinguishes A-graded documents from B-graded documents.

We evaluated the performance of our classifier using the validation data set. As for fine-tuning the classifier, we split 80% of our training data for training and the remaining 20% for fine-tuning. We froze all the layers of the model except for the final layer which is the classification layer. We used the Adam Optimizer with a learning rate of 10^{-5} for 10 epochs for C_1 and a learning rate of $10^{-3}$for 15 epochs for C_2. We set the batch size to be 64 for both C_1 and C_2. For both the classifiers, we used our validation set's accuracy score as an early stopping criterion. We stop the training if the score does not increase for 5 consecutive epochs or the maximum number of epochs has been reached. Our model was entirely implemented using huggingface 4.6.1.

4.2 Phase 2—SVM

In the second phase, we use an SVM classifier (C_3) with the following feature set; authors' h-index (averaged across all of the authors), journal's impact factor and also the journal rank. Past studies (Lee et al., 2002; Saha et al., 2003) have shown that these criteria can be used to judge the quality of medical literature and we hypothesise that these would further help to distinguish B graded articles from A graded articles given that the criteria for these grades are finer.

We made several assumptions when we derived our features. Firstly, given that the data set contains articles published from the late 1980s up to the late 2000s, the journal name at the time of publication may have changed. To tackle this problem, we obtained the current journal name using *google-scholar-crawler*[6] to crawl Google Scholar in order to retrieve the journal's current name, along with each author's h-index. This took us a considerable amount of time, as we were being rate-limited by the number of queries that Google allows, and to the best of our knowledge, there aren't any publicly available APIs for us to use.

We took the journal ranking and the impact factor from the 2020 SCImago[7] because we were unable to obtain the journals ranking and impact factor at the time of publication of the article.

We use sklearn 0.9.4[8] for implementation and kept the default kernel parameters of the SVM classifier as it yielded the best results based on our early experimentation. We used the same split as that in our phase one classifier.

System	Accuracy Score
$C_1 + C_2$	0.4494
$C_1 + C_3$	0.4228
$C_1 + C_2 + C_3$	**0.6573**

Table 2: System evaluation on development set.

System	Accuracy Score
$C_1 + C_2$	0.4808
$C_1 + C_3$	**0.5010**
$C_1 + C_2 + C_3$	0.4918

Table 3: System evaluation on test set.

4.3 Final Prediction

To make the final prediction, first we ran the abstracts through C_1 and then for those classified as non-C, we ran through C_2 and finally we ran the same set again through C_3. We set C_3 to have higher precedence than C_2. If a piece of evidence is categorised as A by C_2 and as B as C_1, we set the grade to B. If there are multiple abstracts for a given evidence ID, we assign a score of 3 for A, 2 for B and 1 for C. We then calculate the mean score and assign the grade closest to the score.

5 Results

ALTA chose CodaLabs as the submission platform. The organisers provided us with both the development and test set. In CodaLabs, participants are allowed to submit an unlimited number of times for the development set but are only limited to three submissions for the test set. The submissions are evaluated by using the accuracy score. We ran our experiments on Google Cloud Platform with 4 vCPUs, 16 GiB of RAM and an NVIDIA Tesla A100. We present our scores on

[6]https://github.com/geekan/google-scholar-crawler

[7]https://www.scimagojr.com/

[8]https://scikit-learn.org/stable/

the development set in Table 2 and summarise and present our final results on the test set in Table 3.

5.1 Discussion

From our experimental results on the development set, we found that our approach of using $C_1 + C_2 + C_3$ yielded the best results with a score of 0.6573 and a two-way ANOVA test confirmed that there are statistically significant differences between the systems ($p < 0.05$). Therefore, we picked $C_1 + C_2 + C_3$ to be used in the test portion.

When we evaluated our system on the test portion, we were surprised to see that we obtained a score of 0.4918. This suggested that our models are most likely over-trained or have not learnt to generalise very well. We went back to the drawing board to see if we could further improve the scores. Given the limited number of submissions, we decided to submit the other two models to see if they would fare better. To our surprise, $C_1 + C_3$ gave us the best results with a score of 0.5010. A one-way ANOVA showed no statistically significant difference between the scores at the 0.05 level and so we decided to look deeper at $C_1 + C_2 + C_3$ to have an understanding of what went wrong. We discuss this in subsection 5.2, 5.3 and 5.4.

5.2 Ambiguity in Classifying Different Grades

We first evaluated the performance of our three proposed systems ($C_1 + C_2$, $C_1 + C_3$, and $C_1 + C_2 + C_3$) on the development set containing only a single abstract and found that the best performing classifier is $C_1 + C_2$ with an accuracy score of 0.8314, followed by $C_1 + C_2 + C_3$ with an accuracy score of 0.8167, and finally $C_1 + C_3$ gave us a score of 0.7854. Our one-way ANOVA test also showed that there is a statistically significant difference ($p < 0.05$) between $C_1 + C_2 + C_3$ and the others.

Looking at the causes of failures with evidence containing a single abstract, we notice that distinguishing between A and B can be challenging. We observed that out of 13 A grades, we incorrectly classified 5 as B. As for B grades, out of 33, we misclassified 6 as A. Additionally, we have notice that 5% of the instances where C grade evidence are misclassified as A and B. We provide some examples of our findings from the development set in Table 5.

In the first example, the evidence is about diagnosing carpal tunnel syndrome. If we take a closer look at the abstract, we observe keywords that are commonly found in A and B graded evidence such as *"p-value"* , *"CI"* . However, unlike in many A and B graded papers, the authors of this paper mention that a *"future randomised control trial is required to validate the results"*. We observed that our model did not understand the context that the randomised control trial has not been performed and therefore classified it as B.

ID	Abstracts	Predicted	Actual
10111	Walker et al. (1993); Zajecka (2001); Ferguson et al. (2001)	A	B
10132	Frisancho (2000); Parsons et al. (1999); Hediger et al. (1999)	B	B

Table 4: Comparison of predictions made by our system and the actual label for evidence IDs with multiple abstracts.

This brings us to our second example, the evidence is on managing chronic fatigue syndrome in a primary care setting. Our classifier classifies it as C. From our visual inspection, we agree with the decision of the classifier. However, the annotators have graded it as B. Since none of the authors is an EBM practitioner, we cannot accurately determine the reason for this. We believe that an EBM practitioner would be able to provide us with how the decisions are derived, which can help to further improve our model. We'll leave this to be part of our future work.

As for the last example, this is an example of how authors' h-index and journal ranking influences the final grading of the evidence. Initially, the $C_1 + C_2$ classifiers labelled it as grade B but C_3 classifier classified it as A. Upon inspecting further, we find that C_3 classified it as A as the authors' h-index and the journal ranking fall in the A listing. We also observed that there are times where this information helped to correct the classification of phase one classifiers such as in evidence ID *10079* (Jackson et al., 1999) and *10042* (Orton and Omari, 2008). From our analysis, we hypothesise that these factors influence the grading of the paper in a similar way to the way funding source influences the quality of the study (Reed et al., 2007). Although SORT's assessment criteria do not mention this, our investigation suggests that this needs to be explored further.

5.3 Ablation study

To further understand the effect of the features that are used in C_3, we perform an ablation study on the development set that contains a single abstract. Keeping it with one single abstract allows us to separate our assumption with multiple documents per query. Additionally, we decided to only tune the C_3 classifier whilst keeping the other two classifiers as they are as we are interested in the impact of how different features influences the score. We summarise our results in Table 6.

For our ablation study, we looked at several aspects. First, we looked at using the impact on the accuracy score by solely using the primary author's h-index and averaging all the authors' h-index scores. We have noticed that if we were to use the primary author's h-index instead of calculating the mean h-index score of all the authors, the score decreased from 0.6603 to 0.6327. This is mainly because in the medical literature field, generally, the last author is the grand-holder or a prominent researcher in the field (Pina et al., 2019). From our test, we find no statistically significant difference ($p < 0.05$). However, given that the number of cases containing 1 abstract is small (n = 113), we think that the statistical power is limited, thus we decided to proceed on with our decision of averaging the h-index.

Additionally, we investigated independently the impact on journal ranking and h-index. We found that these two features have a high correlation coefficient (r) score of 0.92. However, if we removed one of the features, we notice that the scores decreases from 0.8167 to 0.7015 or to 0.6716. Our experimental results suggest that even highly correlated variables could carry non-redundant information, thus removing either degrades the overall information content.

5.4 Challenges with Averaging Method

Next, we repeated the experiment again—but this time solely focusing on evidence containing more than one abstract in order to test the effectiveness of our averaging method. From our experiments, we find that the best performing classifier (C_1 + C_2 + C_3) could only obtain an accuracy score of 0.4183—which is almost half the performance of the classifier on the queries containing a single abstract. This suggests that averaging the grading of each abstract is inadequate.

The score that we obtained only provides an indicator that our assumption needs to be redefined but it does not provide insights into why our performance is higher in the development set than in the test set. To answer this question, we looked at cases where prediction matches with annotators as well as the cases in which it does not match. We provide some examples of our findings from the development set in Table 4. Given that we have a limited amount of space—we provide a citation to the paper for the readers to examine instead of the complete abstract.

For the first example, the papers describe treatments of antidepressant-related sexual dysfunction. If we follow our method, all of the papers are graded as `A` since they fit the criteria to be graded as such. However, it was a surprise to us as to why the annotators classified it as `B`. Upon closely examining the three papers, we find that these papers suggest completely different mechanisms on how to address sexual dysfunction thus bumping down the grade to be `B` instead of an `A`. This finding prompted us to look closer into the way of how the final scores are calculated.

In the second example, the three papers describe the impact of obesity in children. If these are treated as a standalone, they are ranked `A`, `B` and `C` individually, based on SORT. In our method, we then average the grades to produce the final grade thus giving the evidence an overall score of `B`—matching the annotator's grade. However, we believe that this is purely by chance as when we visually inspect the abstracts—we find that the conclusions of the studies do not agree with one another, thus placing it in the `B` category. A better approach could be to use a Siamese Manhattan LSTM (Mueller and Thyagarajan, 2016) or even using Word Mover (Kusner et al., 2015) document similarity measures. Incorporating reinforcement learning might be able help our model to distinguish better as well. We will explore this as part of our future work.

6 Conclusion

We presented an approach to automatically grade evidence using a combination of transfer learning and a feature-based classifier. We competed in the ALTA 2021 Competition under the team name "*orangutanV3*". Despite achieving an accuracy score of 0.4918, we did not manage to beat the current state-of-the-art from ten years ago. The primary reason for our low score is attributed to our

Evidence ID	Abstract	Predicted	Actual
10141	Plaisance et al. (2000)	B	C
10169	Kroenke et al. (1988)	C	B
10091	D'Arcy and McGee (2000)	B	A

Table 5: Comparison of predictions made by our system and the actual label for an evidence ID with a single abstract.

h-index	Journal Rank	Impact Factor	Accuracy Score
Average	✗	✗	0.6603
1st Author	✗	✗	0.6327
✗	✓	✗	0.5042
✗	✗	✓	0.5565
Average	✓	✗	0.6716
1st Author	✓	✗	0.6654
Average	✗	✓	0.7015
1st Author	✗	✓	0.6968
Average	✓	✓	**0.8167**
1st Author	✓	✓	0.7669

Table 6: Ablation study of the features features used in C_3 which includes h-index (primary author's and average across all authors), the journal rank and the impact factor.

assumption of averaging the grades to obtain the final grade. As for our *RQ1*, we find that solely using a transformer on single abstracts is sufficient, as we obtained a score of 0.8314 in our development set. As for our *RQ2*, we obtained a score of 0.8167, although this gives us a lower score compared to using transformers alone. We still think that combining transformer along with the SVM classifier is a a better option. However, we do not have a high statistical power to support the claim that using two models improve the overall accuracy, as we only have a limited sample size. We plan to explore further with a larger data set as part of future work. Additionally, we plan to re-implement the technique used by (Molla and Sarker, 2011) in order to properly evaluate how our system compares, when focusing on queries with a single document.

Acknowledgements

Many thanks to Vaughan Kitchen and Lo Wei Hong for their time in proofreading this paper. We would like to thank Google Cloud, Dr Diego Molla-Aliod and the organisers for ALTA for their support.

References

P Abrams, S Khoury, and A Grant. 2007. Evidence-based medicine overview of the main steps for developing and grading guideline recommendations. *Prog Urol*, 17(3):681–4.

Yves SJ Aquino and Nicolo Cabrera. 2020. Hydroxychloroquine and covid-19: critiquing the impact of disease public profile on policy and clinical decision-making. *Journal of Medical Ethics*, 46(9):574–578.

Shelby Baez, Matthew C Hoch, and Johanna M Hoch. 2018. Evaluation of cognitive behavioral interventions and psychoeducation implemented by rehabilitation specialists to treat fear-avoidance beliefs in patients with low back pain: a systematic review. *Archives of physical medicine and rehabilitation*, 99(11):2287–2298.

David R Bell, Eric G Post, Kevin Biese, Curtis Bay, and Tamara Valovich McLeod. 2018. Sport specialization and risk of overuse injuries: a systematic review with meta-analysis. *Pediatrics*, 142(3).

David Jean Biau, Solen Kernéis, and Raphaël Porcher. 2008. Statistics in brief: the importance of sample size in the planning and interpretation of medical research. *Clinical orthopaedics and related research*, 466(9):2282–2288.

Cindy Chang, Margot Putukian, Giselle Aerni, Alex Diamond, Gene Hong, Yvette Ingram, Claudia L Reardon, and Andrew Wolanin. 2020. Mental health issues and psychological factors in athletes: detection, management, effect on performance and prevention: American medical society for sports medicine position statement—executive summary. *British journal of sports medicine*, 54(4):216–220.

Jaykaran Charan and Tamoghna Biswas. 2013. How to calculate sample size for different study designs in medical research? *Indian journal of psychological medicine*, 35(2):121.

Christopher A D'Arcy and Steven McGee. 2000. Does this patient have carpal tunnel syndrome? *Jama*, 283(23):3110–3117.

Karen Davies. 2007. The information-seeking behaviour of doctors: a review of the evidence. *Health Information & Libraries Journal*, 24(2):78–94.

G De-Deus and A Canabarro. 2017. Strength of recommendation for single-visit root canal treatment: grading the body of the evidence using a patient-centred approach. *International endodontic journal*, 50(3):251–259.

Jacob Devlin, Ming-Wei Chang, Kenton Lee, and Kristina Toutanova. 2018. Bert: Pre-training of deep bidirectional transformers for language understanding. *arXiv preprint arXiv:1810.04805*.

Mark H Ebell, Jay Siwek, Barry D Weiss, Steven H Woolf, Jeffrey Susman, Bernard Ewigman, and Marjorie Bowman. 2004. Strength of recommendation taxonomy (sort): a patient-centered approach to grading evidence in the medical literature. *The Journal of the American Board of Family Practice*, 17(1):59–67.

James M Ferguson, Ram K Shrivastava, Stephen M Stahl, James T Hartford, Frances Borian, John Ieni, and Darlene Jody. 2001. Reemergence of sexual dysfunction in patients with major depressive disorder: double-blind comparison of nefazodone and sertraline. *The Journal of clinical psychiatry*, 62(1):0–0.

A Roberto Frisancho. 2000. Prenatal compared with parental origins of adolescent fatness. *The American journal of clinical nutrition*, 72(5):1186–1190.

Amit K Ghosh. 2004. On the challenges of using evidence-based information: the role of clinical uncertainty. *Journal of Laboratory and Clinical Medicine*, 144(2):60–64.

Trisha Greenhalgh. 2020. Will covid-19 be evidence-based medicine's nemesis?

Gordon Guyatt, Deborah Cook, and Brian Haynes. 2004. Evidence based medicine has come a long way.

Mary L Hediger, Mary D Overpeck, Andrea McGlynn, Robert J Kuczmarski, Kurt R Maurer, and William W Davis. 1999. Growth and fatness at three to six years of age of children born small-or large-for-gestational age. *Pediatrics*, 104(3):e33–e33.

Lisa A Jackson, Patti Benson, Vishnu-Priya Sneller, Jay C Butler, Robert S Thompson, Robert T Chen, Linda S Lewis, George Carlone, Frank DeStefano, Patricia Holder, et al. 1999. Safety of revaccination with pneumococcal polysaccharide vaccine. *Jama*, 281(3):243–248.

Kurt Kroenke, David R Wood, A David Mangelsdorff, Nancy J Meier, and John B Powell. 1988. Chronic fatigue in primary care: prevalence, patient characteristics, and outcome. *Jama*, 260(7):929–934.

Matt Kusner, Yu Sun, Nicholas Kolkin, and Kilian Weinberger. 2015. From word embeddings to document distances. In *International conference on machine learning*, pages 957–966. PMLR.

Jinhyuk Lee, Wonjin Yoon, Sungdong Kim, Donghyeon Kim, Sunkyu Kim, Chan Ho So, and Jaewoo Kang. 2020. Biobert: a pre-trained biomedical language representation model for biomedical text mining. *Bioinformatics*, 36(4):1234–1240.

Kirby P Lee, Marieka Schotland, Peter Bacchetti, and Lisa A Bero. 2002. Association of journal quality indicators with methodological quality of clinical research articles. *Jama*, 287(21):2805–2808.

Diego Molla and Abeed Sarker. 2011. Automatic grading of evidence: the 2011 ALTA shared task. In *Proceedings of the Australasian Language Technology Association Workshop 2011*, pages 4–8, Canberra, Australia.

Jonas Mueller and Aditya Thyagarajan. 2016. Siamese recurrent architectures for learning sentence similarity. In *Proceedings of the AAAI conference on artificial intelligence*, volume 30.

David Oniani and Yanshan Wang. 2020. A qualitative evaluation of language models on automatic question-answering for covid-19. In *Proceedings of the 11th ACM International Conference on Bioinformatics, Computational Biology and Health Informatics*, pages 1–9.

Lois C Orton and Aika AA Omari. 2008. Drugs for treating uncomplicated malaria in pregnant women. *Cochrane Database of Systematic Reviews*, (4).

Tessa J Parsons, Chris Power, Stuart Logan, and CD Summerbelt. 1999. Childhood predictors of adult obesity: a systematic review. *International journal of obesity*, 23.

David G Pina, Lana Barać, Ivan Buljan, Francisco Grimaldo, and Ana Marušić. 2019. Effects of seniority, gender and geography on the bibliometric output and collaboration networks of european research council (erc) grant recipients. *PLoS One*, 14(2):e0212286.

Karen I Plaisance, Suneel Kudaravalli, Steven S Wasserman, Myron M Levine, and Philip A Mackowiak. 2000. Effect of antipyretic therapy on the duration of illness in experimental influenza a, shigella sonnei, and rickettsia rickettsii infections. *Pharmacotherapy: The Journal of Human Pharmacology and Drug Therapy*, 20(12):1417–1422.

Darcy A Reed, David A Cook, Thomas J Beckman, Rachel B Levine, David E Kern, and Scott M Wright. 2007. Association between funding and quality of published medical education research. *Jama*, 298(9):1002–1009.

Rosa M Rodriguez, Ashley Marroquin, and Nicole Cosby. 2019. Reducing fear of reinjury and pain perception in athletes with first-time anterior cruciate ligament reconstructions by implementing imagery training. *Journal of sport rehabilitation*, 28(4):385–389.

Somnath Saha, Sanjay Saint, and Dimitri A Christakis. 2003. Impact factor: a valid measure of journal quality? *Journal of the Medical Library Association*, 91(1):42.

Amirsina Torfi, Rouzbeh A Shirvani, Yaser Keneshloo, Nader Tavaf, and Edward A Fox. 2020. Natural language processing advancements by deep learning: A survey. *arXiv preprint arXiv:2003.01200*.

Parks W Walker, Jonathan O Cole, Elmer A Gardner, Arlene R Hughes, J Andrew Johnston, Sharyn R Batey, and Charles G Lineberry. 1993. Improvement in fluoxetine-associated sexual dysfunction in patients switched to bupropion. *The Journal of clinical psychiatry*.

Guogang Xu, Yongshi Yang, Yingzhen Du, Fujun Peng, Peng Hu, Runsheng Wang, Ming Yin, Tianzhi Li, Lei Tu, Jinlyu Sun, et al. 2020. Clinical pathway for early diagnosis of covid-19: updates from experience to evidence-based practice. *Clinical reviews in allergy & immunology*, 59(1):89–100.

John Zajecka. 2001. Strategies for the treatment of antidepressant-related sexual dysfunction. *Journal of Clinical Psychiatry*, 62:35–43.

An Ensemble Model for Automatic Grading of Evidence

Yuting Guo and **Yao Ge**
Computer Science
Emory University
Atlanta GA 30322, USA
yuting.guo@emory.edu
yao.ge@emory.edu

Ruqi Liao
Industrial and System Engineering
Georgia Institute of Technology
Atlanta GA 30332, USA
rliao34@gatech.edu

Abeed Sarker
Biomedical Informatics
Emory University
Atlanta GA 30322, USA
abeed@dbmi.emory.edu

Abstract

This paper describes our approach for the automatic grading of evidence task from the Australasian Language Technology Association (ALTA) Shared Task 2021. We developed two classification models with SVM and RoBERTa and applied an ensemble technique to combine the grades from different classifiers. Our results showed that the SVM model achieved comparable results to the RoBERTa model, and the ensemble system outperformed the individual models on this task. Our system achieved the first place among five teams and obtained 3.3% higher accuracy than the second place.

1 Introduction

Evidence-based medicine (EBM) requires the making of clinical decisions using the current best external evidence rather than solely relying on clinical experience and pathophysiologic rationale (Sackett et al., 1996). To adhere to EBM best practice, practitioners need to identify the best quality evidence associated with a clinical query. To grade the quality of evidence, Ebell et al. (2004) proposed the Strength of Recommendation Taxonomy (SORT). SORT has a three-levels for rating—A (strong), B (moderate), and C (weak), where A-level is based on high-quality studies with consistent results; B-level is based on high-quality studies with inconsistent results or some limitations; C-level is based on the studies with severe limitations. It is a straightforward grading system that allows clinical experts to rate individual studies or bodies of evidence based on quantity, quality, and consistency.

To address the challenging problem of automatically grading the quality of evidence, the Australasian Language Technology Association (ALTA) Shared Task 2021 organized a competition. The participants were required to develop a system to predict the grade of evidence given multiple related medical publications. Our team trained several supervised classifiers to address the problem. Our approach included traditional supervised classification models such as support vector machines (SVM) (Cortes and Vapnik, 1995), neural network models using pretrained models (RoBERTa) (Liu et al., 2019), and an innovative ensemble system which combines the predictions of multiple classifiers. Our results showed that the SVM model achieved comparable results to the RoBERTa model, and the ensemble system outperformed the individual models on this task. The ensemble model combines the prediction from multiple classifiers in a unique manner: grades (A, B or C) predicted by each classifier is first converted into a continuous number, and then all the numbers are added for each instance. Using the training data, the best separations for the numeric totals are computed. These numeric boundaries are then used to convert continuous scores in the test set to discrete evidence grades. Our system achieved the first place among five teams and obtained 3.3% higher accuracy than the second place.

2 Related Work

ALTA Shared Task 2021 is a re-visit of ALTA Shared Task 2011 (Molla and Sarker, 2011). Previous studies have developed several SVM-based systems for this task. Molla and Sarker (2011) used a sequential approach to combine multiple individual SVM models trained with the features from the titles, body of the abstracts, and publication types. Gyawali et al. (2012) expanded the feature set proposed by Molla and Sarker (2011) with the Medical Subject Headings (MeSH) terms and developed a stacking-based approach to integrate predictions from multiple SVM models. Byczyńska et al. (2020) experimented with a larger set of features and applied multiple machine learning techniques such as classical machine learning models, neural networks, game theory, and consensus methods. In our work, we trained SVM models on a feature set similar to Byczyńska et al. (2020). We also applied a pre-trained transformer-based model named RoBERTa (Liu et al., 2019), which has achieved state-of-the-art results in a wide range of natural language processing (NLP) tasks.

3 Data Description

The data for this shared task consisted of a set of evidence grades under the SORT criteria and a list of related publications associated with each evidence grade. The publications were obtained from PubMed [1] and were provided in the form of XML files which contained the title, the abstract, and some meta-data (*eg.*, publication types, MeSH terms). Some data statistics are shown in Table 1.

	Train (%)	Dev (%)	Test (%)
A	31.3	27.0	30.6
B	45.9	44.9	48.6
C	22.7	28.1	20.8
Total size	677	178	183

Table 1: The distribution of the three grades and data set sizes for the training, development, and test sets.

4 Method

4.1 SVM

We implemented the SVM models with Python 3.7 and the sklearn tool (Pedregosa et al., 2011). We trained multiple SVM models using different feature sets for each, which included the number of related publications (*npmid*), journal titles, and other features, as follows:

N-gram Features (*n-gram*) The n-gram features were generated from the texts of the titles and the bodies of the abstracts. Because one evidence grade can be based on multiple publications, we combined the titles and the abstracts of all publications to create sequences of titles and abstracts per evidence, respectively. Then, we computed the term frequency–inverse document frequency (TF-IDF) features from the n-grams ($n = 1, 2, 3, 4$) of the combined sequences.

Consistency Features (*cons*) As mentioned in Ebell et al. (2004), the consistency of experimental results can affect the evidence strength. Inspired by that, we detected the mentions of consistent results in the body of abstracts by keyword matching. For each evidence, if any of the publications matched the word "consistent" or "consistency" in the abstract, the consistency feature was set as 1; otherwise it was set to 0.

Publication Types (*pubtype*) As discussed in Molla and Sarker (2011) and Byczyńska et al. (2020), publication types can be a strong indicator of the evidence strength. We extracted the publication type terms tagged as *PublicationType* in the XML files and assigned a pseudo publication type "unknown" to the publications without any *PublicationType* tag. In addition, we used the PubMed tool [2] to retrieve the publication type IDs. We used one-hot encoding to encode the publication type terms and IDs, respectively. Also, we generated a publication type rank according to the level of evidence pyramid in Sarker and Mollá-Aliod (2010). The rank ranged from 0 to 5, where higher number indicates higher quality.

MeSH MeSH terms provide information regarding the topics covered in a publication. We used the PubMed tool to request MeSH term IDs and represented the MeSH feature by one-hot encoding.

4.2 RoBERTa

Encouraged by the success of the pre-trained transformer-based models in recent years, we developed a classifier using RoBERTa, one of the most popular pre-trained transformer-based models. The classification model architecture was the same as the model in (Liu et al., 2019). It consists of an encoder, which converted the input text sequence into an embedding vector, and a classification layer with softmax activation, which projected the embedding vector into a class probability vector. The inputs were the abstract texts of the publications associated with each evidence instance. However, if we attached the abstracts into one sequence, the input length often exceeded the maximum sequence length limitation of RoBERTa, which is 512 characters. Therefore, we re-organized the dataset by splitting the evidences involving multiple publications into different instances so that each instance only contained one evidence and one publication, as shown in Figure 1. During the inference phase,

[1] https://www.ncbi.nlm.nih.gov/pmc/tools/openftlist/

[2] https://www.ncbi.nlm.nih.gov/pmc/tools/get-metadata/

00004 A 15547167
00005 C 11392916
00006 A 8942774 8942775 8036464 7497161

⬇

00004 A 15547167
00005 C 11392916
00006 A 8942774
00006 A 8942775
00006 A 8036464
00006 A 7497161

Figure 1: An example of the data re-organization process. The first column contains the evidence IDs, the second column contains the SORT grades, and the third column contains the publication IDs.

for each evidence, the class probability vectors of multiple publications were averaged, and the class with the highest probability was chosen as the final prediction.

4.3 Ensemble

Because the classes A, B and C represent the strength of evidence from strong to weak, we considered the task of grading as a regression problem (rather than a classification problem) and converted the predictions from the classifiers into numbers on a numeric scale. Specifically, we represented the classes A, B, and C as the numbers 0, 1, and 2. For each instance, we computed a numeric score (rather than a discrete category) by adding up the converted predictions from all classifiers. Following this process, we performed grid search to find two thresholds in which the evidences with scores smaller the lower threshold were classified as A, those larger than the higher threshold were classified as C, and those with scores between the lower and upper thresholds were classified as B. Optimal values for the thresholds were based on the training set. In addition, considering the fact that the classifiers with low accuracies may hurt the performance of the ensemble model, we greedily removed the least accurate classifiers to find the classifier set that achieved the best performance on the training/development set.

5 Experiments

SVM We trained the SVM models for all possible combinations of the features and experimented with not using class weights and using the empirical class weights $W_A = 1.2$, $W_B = 1.2$, and $W_C = 1.0$. In total, we created 127 feature combinations and obtained 254 classification models. For each model, we performed grid search on the development set to find the best configuration for the regularization parameter $C \in \{1, 2, 4, 6, 8\}$ and the kernel type $K \in \{"linear", "rbf"\}$.

RoBERTa The specific version of RoBERTa we used was RoBERTa-large. According to the preliminary experiments, we set the batch size as 32, the learning rate as 8×10^{-6}, and the maximum sequence length as 256. The model was trained for 10 epochs with 3 random initialisations.

For both SVM and RoBERTa, we tuned the parameters based on the training set and the development set to find the optimal parameters, and we re-trained the model with the optimal parameters on the whole data set (i.e., the combination of the training set and the development set). The reported results of the test set were predicted by the models trained on the whole data set, and those of the development set were predicted by the models trained on the training set.

6 Results

Table 2 shows the results of the best individual SVM model, the RoBERTa model, and the ensemble model on the development set and the test set. For the SVM model, the best feature combination is *n-gram+pubtype+npmid*. The results show that the performance of the RoBERTa model is comparable to the SVM model, and the ensemble model outperformed the other two models. However, the differences between the three models were not statistically significant according to the 95% confidence intervals. Also, we observed that the performances were considerably lower for the test set compared to the development set. This suggests that the models may overfit on the training/development data because of the small data size.

For further error analysis, we plotted the confusion matrix for our best system (*ie.*, the ensemble model), shown in Figure 2. As we can see, the majority of errors can be attributed to the misclassification of the classes A and C. Most A-level and C-level evidences were predicted as B. This can be another indicator of overfitting because the majority evidences in the training set were graded as B.

Model	Dev	95% CI	Test	95% CI
SVM	0.63	0.48-0.76	0.48	0.34-0.60
RoBERTa	0.58	0.44-0.70	0.48	0.34-0.62
Ensemble	**0.7**	0.58-0.82	**0.54**	0.38-0.68

Table 2: The accuracies and 95% confidence intervals (CIs) on the development and test set.

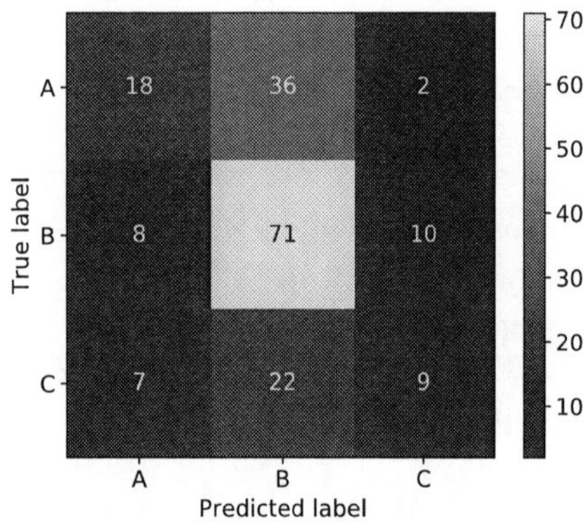

Figure 2: The confusion matrix for the result of the ensemble model on the test set.

7 Discussion

As illustrated in Table 6, the RoBERTa model did not outperform the SVM model on this task. This finding is somewhat surprising because many recent studies have shown that pre-trained transformer-based models can achieve the state-of-the-art performance on a wide range of natural language processing tasks (Liu et al., 2019; Devlin et al., 2019; Nguyen et al., 2020; Yang et al., 2019). A possible explanation for this can be that the most important factor for the evidence strength grading is the publication type and the consistency of the experiments (Ebell et al., 2004). In our experiments, the input for RoBERTa was only the abstracts, which rarely contained the publication type information. In contrast, in the abstracts, the consistency of the experiments are usually implicitly described by comparing the experimental results which involve numbers. It has been suggested that the pre-trained transformer-based models lack in the ability of effectively representing numbers (Wallace et al., 2019). Therefore, further studies will need to be undertaken to explore how to incorporate the meta-data information into transformer-based models and how to make such models understand/compare numbers.

Although we achieved the top place in this competition, some systems described in past publications achieved higher accuracies than our best result (Molla and Sarker, 2011; Gyawali et al., 2012; Byczyńska et al., 2020). We noted that all of these systems used the publication type features. Moreover, Byczyńska et al. (2020) showed that using the single publication type feature achieved 70% accuracy on the test set. However, in our experiments, our model with the single publication type feature only achieved 52% accuracy. We speculate that the cause of the performance gap might be due to the fact that we processed the publication type feature differently compared to the abovementioned publication. In our method, we simply used the publication type terms extracted from the XML files, while Byczyńska et al. (2020) used a rule-based system to identity the publication types from the titles and the abstracts. Further research is needed to explore effective methods for processing the publication type feature.

References

Aleksandra Byczyńska, Maria Ganzha, Marcin Paprzycki, and Mikołaj Kutka. 2020. Evidence quality estimation using selected machine learning approaches. In *2020 Conference on Information Communications Technology and Society (ICTAS)*, pages 1–8.

Corinna Cortes and Vladimir Vapnik. 1995. Support-vector networks. *Machine learning*, 20(3):273–297.

Jacob Devlin, Ming-Wei Chang, Kenton Lee, and Kristina Toutanova. 2019. BERT: Pre-training of Deep Bidirectional Transformers for Language Understanding. In *Proceedings of the 2019 North American Chapter of the Association for Computational Linguistics: Human Language Technologies.*

M. H. Ebell, J. Siwek, B. D. Weiss, S. H. Woolf, J. Susman, B. Ewigman, and M. Bowman. 2004. Strength of recommendation taxonomy (SORT): a patient-centered approach to grading evidence in the medical literature. *J Am Board Fam Pract*, 17(1):59–67.

Binod Gyawali, Thamar Solorio, and Yassine Benajiba. 2012. Grading the quality of medical evidence. In *BioNLP: Proceedings of the 2012 Workshop on Biomedical Natural Language Processing*, pages 176–184, Montréal, Canada. Association for Computational Linguistics.

Yinhan Liu, Myle Ott, Naman Goyal, Jingfei Du, Mandar Joshi, Danqi Chen, Omer Levy, Mike Lewis, Luke Zettlemoyer, and Veselin Stoyanov. 2019. RoBERTa: A Robustly Optimized BERT Pretraining Approach. *arXiv*, 1907(11692).

Diego Molla and Abeed Sarker. 2011. Automatic grading of evidence: the 2011 ALTA shared task. In *Proceedings of the Australasian Language Technology Association Workshop 2011*, pages 4–8, Canberra, Australia.

Dat Quoc Nguyen, Thanh Vu, and Anh Tuan Nguyen. 2020. BERTweet: A Pre-trained Language Model for English Tweets. In *Proceedings of the 2020 Conference on Empirical Methods in Natural Language Processing: System Demonstrations*, pages 9–14.

F. Pedregosa, G. Varoquaux, A. Gramfort, V. Michel, B. Thirion, O. Grisel, M. Blondel, P. Prettenhofer, R. Weiss, V. Dubourg, J. Vanderplas, A. Passos, D. Cournapeau, M. Brucher, M. Perrot, and E. Duchesnay. 2011. Scikit-learn: Machine learning in Python. *Journal of Machine Learning Research*, 12:2825–2830.

David L Sackett, William M C Rosenberg, J A Muir Gray, R Brian Haynes, and W Scott Richardson. 1996. Evidence based medicine: what it is and what it isn't. *BMJ*, 312(7023):71–72.

Abeed Sarker and Diego Mollá-Aliod. 2010. A rule based approach for automatic identification of publication types of medical papers. In *Proceedings of the ADCS Annual Symposium*, pages 84–88. Citeseer.

Eric Wallace, Yizhong Wang, Sujian Li, Sameer Singh, and Matt Gardner. 2019. Do NLP models know numbers? probing numeracy in embeddings. In *Proceedings of the 2019 Conference on Empirical Methods in Natural Language Processing and the 9th International Joint Conference on Natural Language Processing (EMNLP-IJCNLP)*, pages 5307–5315, Hong Kong, China. Association for Computational Linguistics.

Zhilin Yang, Zihang Dai, Yiming Yang, Jaime Carbonell, Russ R Salakhutdinov, and Quoc V Le. 2019. XLNet: Generalized Autoregressive Pretraining for Language Understanding. In H. Wallach, H. Larochelle, A. Beygelzimer, F. d'Alché-Buc, E. Fox, and R. Garnett, editors, *Advances in Neural Information Processing Systems 32*, pages 5753–5763. Curran Associates, Inc.

Handling Variance of Pretrained Language Models in Grading Evidence in the Medical Literature

Fajri Koto* **Biaoyan Fang***
School of Computing and Information Systems
The University of Melbourne
{ffajri,biaoyanf}@student.unimelb.edu.au

Abstract

In this paper, we investigate the utility of modern pretrained language models for the evidence grading system in the medical literature based on the ALTA 2021 shared task. We benchmark 1) domain-specific models that are optimized for medical literature and 2) domain-generic models with rich latent discourse representation (i.e. ELECTRA, RoBERTa). Our empirical experiments reveal that these modern pretrained language models suffer from high variance, and the ensemble method can improve the model performance. We found that ELECTRA performs best with an accuracy of 53.6% on the test set, outperforming domain-specific models.[1]

1 Background

Evidence-Based Medicine (EBM) is an approach by health practitioners to integrate individual clinical expertise and external evidence from medical literatures in making decisions about the care of patients (Sackett et al., 1996). In practice, understanding the current best evidence from the literature minimizes the unexpected risk of outdated treatments that can be detrimental to patients.

Strength of Recommendation Taxonomy (SORT) (Ebell et al., 2004) is one of the standard scale systems for grading evidence in medical literature and it has been used to assist the EBM approach. SORT groups a medical literature into one of three classes: **A** (*consistent* and *good-quality patient-oriented evidence*), **B** (*inconsistent* or *limited-quality patient-oriented evidence*) and **C** (*other evidence*, such as consensus guidelines, usual practice and opinion). While obtaining these grades on a wide-scale is expensive and requires in-depth medical expertise, previous works (Sarker et al., 2015) have attempted to automate the process by modelling the grading system with n-gram language model via SVM (Molla and Sarker, 2011) and ensemble method (Gyawali et al., 2012).

In this work, we focus on investigating the utility of various modern pretrained language models for modelling the evidence grading system in the medical literature. Although transformer (Vaswani et al., 2017) and pretrained language models such as BERT (Devlin et al., 2019), RoBERTa (Liu et al., 2019) have achieved impressive performance across various NLP tasks (Wang et al., 2018; Wang et al., 2019) and languages (Koto et al., 2020; Martin et al., 2020), we hypothesize that such evidence grading task is still challenging because of three reasons. First, in-depth medical expertise and knowledge are not always present in the language models. Second, it is very likely that machine learning models suffer from high variance as disagreement in assessing scientific literature is natural, even among the experts. Lastly, obtaining high-quality training data for this task is difficult, and the large transformer-based models potentially suffer from overfitting if the available data is limited.

To address the aforementioned challenges, we use three main strategies. First, we fine-tune domain-specific pretrained models (Gu et al., 2020) that are optimized for medical literature. Previous works (Gururangan et al., 2020; Gu et al., 2020; Alsentzer et al., 2019; Fang et al., 2021; Koto et al., 2021) have shown that such models contain domain-specific knowledge that can boost system performance. Second, we argue that discourse is prominent for this task because each of three SORT classes might have different document structure. For instance, patient-oriented literature and consensus guidelines potentially are written differently in

*equal contribution

[1] Our best result with ELECTRA (large) and ELECTRA (base) put us in the first and second rank on the leaderboard, respectively.

```
00667 A 10796398 11508437
00668 A 9036306
00669 C 7391096 11204962 7790481 6863528
00670 B 9569395 12069675
00671 B 11083602 10875559 15283004
```

Figure 1: Sample training data from ALTA 2021 shared task.

terms of flow and discourse. In this work, rather than employing a complicated discourse parser (Yu et al., 2018; Koto et al., 2019, 2021), we rely on modern pretrained language models such as ELECTRA (Clark et al., 2020) that contains a rich latent discourse representation (Koto et al., 2021). Lastly, similar to Gyawali et al. (2012), we also perform ensemble learning to tackle the high variance issue of models.

2 Dataset

We conduct our experiments based on the ALTA 2021 shared task[2] which aims to automatically grade evidence in the medical literature. The grading system follows the SORT framework (Ebell et al., 2004) with three classes: **A** (Strong), **B** (Moderate) and **C** (Weak).

As shown in Figure 1 each line in the training data is a single piece of evidence and consists of an ID, a SORT grade, and a list of resource/publication ID(s) from PubMed.[3] Each publication ID is mapped to an XML file containing bibliographic information (e.g. title, author, affiliation, etc.), abstract, and some meta-data such as type and status of the publication.

In Table 1, we present overall statistics of the train, development and test sets. First, nearly 45% of the train and development data are classified as class B. We also found there is no significant difference in terms of the number of resources and words between each subset.

	Train	Dev	Test
Evidences	677	178	183
in A	212	48	-
in B	311	80	-
in C	154	50	-
Ave. resources per evidence	2.4	2.5	2.3
Ave. words per abstract	269.9	262.6	274.1
Ave. words per evidence	655.9	653.7	643.9

Table 1: Overall statistics of the ALTA 2021 shared task dataset. Evidence classes in test dataset are withheld by the organizer. "Ave. resources per evidence" means the average number of XML files the evidence has. "Ave. words per abstract" means the average number of words per single abstract. "Ave. words per evidence" means the average number of words per evidence, including journal name, title and abstract.

3 Proposed Methods

Figure 2 describes the best model that we submit to ALTA 2021 shared task. We use filtered ensemble method over 3 domain-specific pretrained language models: 1) Biomed BERT (Gu et al., 2020), 2) Biomed RoBERTa (Gururangan et al., 2020) and 3) Biomed RoBERTa that is further pretrained with the training set for 400 epochs, denoted as Task Adaptive Pretraining (TAPT) model; and 3 domain-generic pretrained language models: 1) RoBERTa (Liu et al., 2019), 2) ELECTRA, and 3) ELECTRA (large) (Clark et al., 2020). The selection of RoBERTa and ELECTRA is based on their rich latent discourse representation as reported by Koto et al. (2021).

Given a list of resources or publications $R = \{r_1, r_2, .., r_n\}$ for evidence x, we construct an input sequence as follows. First, each resource r_i consists of journal name j_i, title t_i, and abstract a_i. We form an input sequence x as the concatenation of all texts $j_1 \oplus t_1 \oplus a_1 \oplus ... \oplus j_n \oplus t_n \oplus a_n$. We truncate a resource r_i if the tokens are more than 250, and set the maximum length of the input x to be 512.

To understand the variance of pretrained language models in this task, we fine-tune each model with 100 different random seeds. For ensemble learning, we first select models with accuracy more than hyper-parameter α (values range between 0 and 1) and apply two types of voting mechanism to aggregate the prediction: 1) simple voting based on majority classes, and 2) filtered voting. For the second approach, if the selected n models have an even class distribution, we set class B as the prediction, otherwise normal majority voting is applied. Mathematically, this even prediction is determined based on a threshold β as follows:

$$\frac{1}{3}(|y_A - y_B| + |y_A - y_C| + |y_B - y_C|) \leq \beta$$

where y_A, y_B, y_C are the occurrence of class A, B, and C in n models prediction, respectively (meaning $y_A + y_B + y_C = n$), and $|y_A - y_B|$ indicates the

[2] https://www.alta.asn.au/events/sharedtask2021/index.html

[3] https://pubmed.ncbi.nlm.nih.gov/

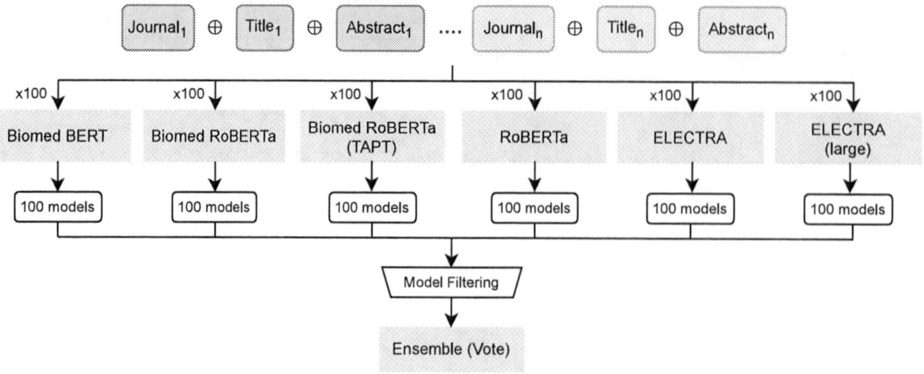

Figure 2: Filtered ensemble model used in this task.

absolute difference of class A and B occurrence. β is a hyper-parameter with values ranging between 0 and n, and $\beta < 0$ means normal majority voting is applied. All parameters (including α and β) are tuned based on the development set.

4 Experiments

4.1 Set-up

We use the huggingface Pytorch framework (Wolf et al., 2020) for the experiments.[4] In total, there are 6 models: 1) Biomed BERT,[5] 2) Biomed RoBERTa,[6], 3) Biomed RoBERTa (TAPT), 4) RoBERTa,[7] 5) ELECTRA,[8] 6) ELECTRA (large).[9] Each model is fine-tuned for 20 epochs with a batch size of 10, warm-up of 10% of the total steps, learning rate of 5e–5, Adam optimizer with epsilon of 1e–8, and early stopping with patience of 5.

In this work, accuracy is used as the primary evaluation metric, following ALTA 2021 shared task description.

4.2 Results over Development Set

In Table 2, we report the aggregate score (`mean`, `max`, `min`, `std`) of 100 runs of each models. First, we observe that Biomed RoBERTa has the highest average performance of 59.5, but only 0.3 higher than ELECTRA. In fact, Domain-generic models such as RoBERTa and ELECTRA outperform Biomed BERT and Biomed RoBERTa (TAPT), despite their domain/task-adaptive pretraning. We also found that even with 100 different random seeds, all models still have relatively high variance (`std`) with more than 2 points. ELECTRA (large) suffers worst from this issue, compared to the other models.

Model	Accuracy			
	Mean	**Max**	**Min**	**Std**
Biomed BERT	58.7	66.9	52.8	2.9
Biomed RoBERTa	**59.5**	67.4	55.1	2.5
Biomed RoBERTa (TAPT)	58.3	65.7	52.8	2.6
RoBERTa	59.1	64.6	53.9	2.2
ELECTRA	59.2	65.7	44.9	3.6
ELECTRA (large)	53.3	64.6	44.9	6.7

Table 2: Experiment results on development set over 100 different random seeds.

In Table 3, we describe the main experiment results. For baselines, we run unigram and bigram representation with Naive Bayes and Logistic Regression, and found the results are less optimal. For the ensemble method, we perform grid search over $\alpha \in \{0.60, 0.61, 0.62, 0.63, 0.64, 0.65\}$ and $\beta \in \{-1, 0, .., n\}$. n is number of models after filtered by parameter α. Ensemble results presented in Table 3 use the best combinations of α and β.

First, we perform ensemble method with all 500 "base" models from Table 2, and obtain accuracy of 69.7, 2 points higher than the best Biomed RoBERTa model (`max` in Table 2). 8 selected models after filtering with α are 2 Biomed RoBERTa, 2 Biomed RoBERTA (TAPT), 2 Biomed BERT, and 2 ELECTRA. In the next results, we also perform a grid search for each 6 pretrained language models (each initially has 100 models), and found that ELECTRA performs best with an accuracy of 70.2, outperforming all domain-specific models.

Another thing to note is that parameter β or fil-

[4] `https://huggingface.co/`
[5] `microsoft/BiomedNLP-PubMedBERT-base-uncased-abstract-fulltext`
[6] `allenai/biomed_roberta_base`
[7] `roberta-base`
[8] `google/electra-base-discriminator`
[9] `google/electra-large-discriminator`

Model	Hyper-parameters		Filtered models (n)	Acc.
	α	β		
Baseline				
Naive Bayes (unigram+bigram)	–	–	–	46.1
Logistic Regression (unigram+bigram)	–	–	–	51.1
Ensemble method				
All 500 "base" models	0.65	$\{-1, 0, 1\}$	8	69.7
Biomed BERT	0.62	$\{-1, 0, 1, 2, 3\}$	11	68.5
Biomed RoBERTa	0.63	2	7	67.4
Biomed RoBERTa (TAPT)	0.62	4	11	66.3
RoBERTa	0.64	$\{-1, 0, 1\}$	3	67.9
ELECTRA	0.63	$\{-1, 0, 1\}$	6	**70.2**
ELECTRA (large)	0.61	$\{-1, 0, 1, 2, 3, 4, 5\}$	18	67.4

Table 3: Results of baseline vs. ensemble methods on the development set. Parameter α and β are selected based on the grid search.

Model	Accuracy	
	Dev	Test
All 500 "base" models	69.7	49.7
ELECTRA	70.2	50.2
ELECTRA (large)	67.4	**53.6**

Table 4: Results of selected model (for shared task submission) on the development and test set.

tered voting mechanism is not significant except for Biomed RoBERTa. From Table 3 we can see that the optimal combinations of α and β for 5 ensemble models have $\beta = -1$, which indicates that the standard majority voting solely can yield the optimal result.

4.3 Results over Test Set

We pick the three best models for ALTA 2021 shared task submission as shown in Table 4. These models are the ensemble methods from Table 3: 1) All 500 "base" models, 2) ELECTRA, and 3) ELECTRA (large). We observe that the gap between development and test set is high, roughly 20 points, which can be due to overfitting problems and small training sets. The best models on the test set are ELECTRA and ELECTRA (large) with the accuracies of 50.2 and 53.6, respectively. Our best result with ELECTRA (large) put us in the first rank on the leaderboard.[10]

[10]The committee limits three submissions for each team. At the end of the competition, ELECTRA result with accuracy 50.2 is picked and put us in the second rank.

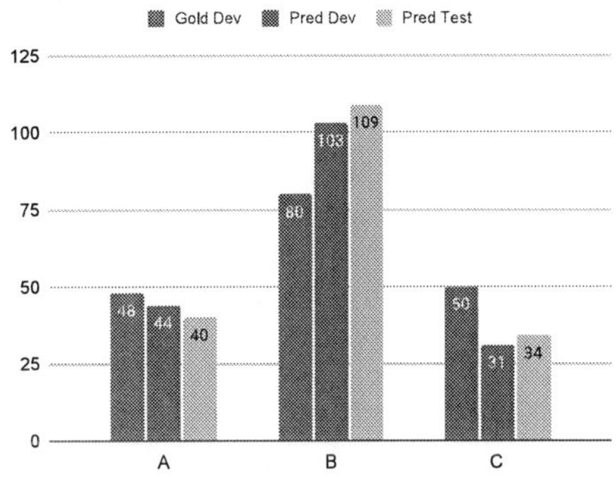

Figure 3: Label distributions on development and test set using ELECTRA (large).

5 Discussions and Conclusion

Figure 3 describes label distributions on development and test sets using our best model, ELECTRA (large). First, we found that the model tends to predict class B on the development, with a disparity of +23 instances with the gold label B. In contrast, the model only classifies 31 instances as class C, despite being there 50 gold labels C. Lastly, our final prediction in the test sets has a ratio of 40:109:34 of class A:B:C, respectively, and the graph in Figure 3 describes a similar shape with the development set prediction.

In conclusion, we have shown in this experiment that grading evidence in the medical literature is a challenging task, and modern pretrained language models suffer from high-variance issues. Interestingly, we found that ELECTRA, the domain-general models outperform domain-specific models through ensemble methods. We argue that this is because discourse is one of the relevant features for this task. This is in line with Koto et al. (2021) that has shown that the last layer of ELECTRA contains the richest latent discourse representation, compared to BERT, RoBERTa, ALBERT (Lan et al., 2019), GPT2 (Radford et al., 2019), BART (Lewis et al., 2020), and T5 (Raffel et al., 2019).

Acknowledgments

In this work, Fajri Koto is supported by the Australia Awards Scholarship (AAS), funded by the Department of Foreign Affairs and Trade (DFAT), Australia. Biaoyan Fang is supported by a graduate research scholarship from the Melbourne School of Engineering.

References

Emily Alsentzer, John Murphy, William Boag, Wei-Hung Weng, Di Jindi, Tristan Naumann, and Matthew McDermott. 2019. Publicly available clinical BERT embeddings. In *Proceedings of the 2nd Clinical Natural Language Processing Workshop*, pages 72–78, Minneapolis, Minnesota, USA. Association for Computational Linguistics.

Kevin Clark, Minh-Thang Luong, Quoc V Le, and Christopher D Manning. 2020. Electra: Pre-training text encoders as discriminators rather than generators. *arXiv preprint arXiv:2003.10555*.

Jacob Devlin, Ming-Wei Chang, Kenton Lee, and Kristina Toutanova. 2019. BERT: Pre-training of deep bidirectional transformers for language understanding. In *Proceedings of the 2019 Conference of the North American Chapter of the Association for Computational Linguistics: Human Language Technologies, Volume 1 (Long and Short Papers)*, pages 4171–4186, Minneapolis, Minnesota. Association for Computational Linguistics.

Mark H Ebell, Jay Siwek, Barry D Weiss, Steven H Woolf, Jeffrey Susman, Bernard Ewigman, and Marjorie Bowman. 2004. Strength of recommendation taxonomy (sort): a patient-centered approach to grading evidence in the medical literature. *The Journal of the American Board of Family Practice*, 17(1):59–67.

Biaoyan Fang, Christian Druckenbrodt, Saber A Akhondi, Jiayuan He, Timothy Baldwin, and Karin Verspoor. 2021. ChEMU-ref: A corpus for modeling anaphora resolution in the chemical domain. In *Proceedings of the 16th Conference of the European Chapter of the Association for Computational Linguistics: Main Volume*, pages 1362–1375, Online. Association for Computational Linguistics.

Yu Gu, Robert Tinn, Hao Cheng, Michael Lucas, Naoto Usuyama, Xiaodong Liu, Tristan Naumann, Jianfeng Gao, and Hoifung Poon. 2020. Domain-specific language model pretraining for biomedical natural language processing.

Suchin Gururangan, Ana Marasović, Swabha Swayamdipta, Kyle Lo, Iz Beltagy, Doug Downey, and Noah A. Smith. 2020. Don't stop pretraining: Adapt language models to domains and tasks. In *Proceedings of the 58th Annual Meeting of the Association for Computational Linguistics*, pages 8342–8360, Online. Association for Computational Linguistics.

Binod Gyawali, Thamar Solorio, and Yassine Benajiba. 2012. Grading the quality of medical evidence. In *BioNLP: Proceedings of the 2012 Workshop on Biomedical Natural Language Processing*, pages 176–184, Montréal, Canada. Association for Computational Linguistics.

Fajri Koto, Jey Han Lau, and Timothy Baldwin. 2019. Improved document modelling with a neural discourse parser. In *Proceedings of the The 17th Annual Workshop of the Australasian Language Technology Association*, pages 67–76, Sydney, Australia. Australasian Language Technology Association.

Fajri Koto, Jey Han Lau, and Timothy Baldwin. 2021. Discourse probing of pretrained language models. In *Proceedings of the 2021 Conference of the North American Chapter of the Association for Computational Linguistics: Human Language Technologies*, pages 3849–3864, Online. Association for Computational Linguistics.

Fajri Koto, Jey Han Lau, and Timothy Baldwin. 2021. IndoBERTweet: A pretrained language model for Indonesian twitter with effective domain-specific vocabulary initialization. *arXiv preprint arXiv:2109.04607*.

Fajri Koto, Jey Han Lau, and Timothy Baldwin. 2021. Top-down discourse parsing via sequence labelling. In *Proceedings of the 16th Conference of the European Chapter of the Association for Computational Linguistics: Main Volume*, pages 715–726, Online. Association for Computational Linguistics.

Fajri Koto, Afshin Rahimi, Jey Han Lau, and Timothy Baldwin. 2020. IndoLEM and IndoBERT: A benchmark dataset and pre-trained language model for Indonesian NLP. In *Proceedings of the 28th International Conference on Computational Linguistics*, pages 757–770, Barcelona, Spain (Online). International Committee on Computational Linguistics.

Zhenzhong Lan, Mingda Chen, Sebastian Goodman, Kevin Gimpel, Piyush Sharma, and Radu Soricut. 2019. Albert: A lite bert for self-supervised learning of language representations. *arXiv preprint arXiv:1909.11942*.

Mike Lewis, Yinhan Liu, Naman Goyal, Marjan Ghazvininejad, Abdelrahman Mohamed, Omer Levy, Veselin Stoyanov, and Luke Zettlemoyer.

2020. BART: Denoising sequence-to-sequence pre-training for natural language generation, translation, and comprehension. In *Proceedings of the 58th Annual Meeting of the Association for Computational Linguistics*, pages 7871–7880, Online. Association for Computational Linguistics.

Yinhan Liu, Myle Ott, Naman Goyal, Jingfei Du, Mandar Joshi, Danqi Chen, Omer Levy, Mike Lewis, Luke Zettlemoyer, and Veselin Stoyanov. 2019. Roberta: A robustly optimized bert pretraining approach. *arXiv preprint arXiv:1907.11692*.

Louis Martin, Benjamin Muller, Pedro Javier Ortiz Suárez, Yoann Dupont, Laurent Romary, Éric de la Clergerie, Djamé Seddah, and Benoît Sagot. 2020. CamemBERT: a tasty French language model. In *Proceedings of the 58th Annual Meeting of the Association for Computational Linguistics*, pages 7203–7219, Online. Association for Computational Linguistics.

Diego Molla and Abeed Sarker. 2011. Automatic grading of evidence: the 2011 ALTA shared task. In *Proceedings of the Australasian Language Technology Association Workshop 2011*, pages 4–8, Canberra, Australia.

Alec Radford, Jeffrey Wu, Rewon Child, David Luan, Dario Amodei, and Ilya Sutskever. 2019. Language models are unsupervised multitask learners. *OpenAI blog*, 1(8):9.

Colin Raffel, Noam Shazeer, Adam Roberts, Katherine Lee, Sharan Narang, Michael Matena, Yanqi Zhou, Wei Li, and Peter J. Liu. 2019. Exploring the limits of transfer learning with a unified text-to-text transformer. *Journal of Machine Learning Research*, 21(140):1–67.

David L Sackett, William MC Rosenberg, JA Muir Gray, R Brian Haynes, and W Scott Richardson. 1996. Evidence based medicine: what it is and what it isn't.

Abeed Sarker, Diego Mollá, and Cécile Paris. 2015. Automatic evidence quality prediction to support evidence-based decision making. *Artificial intelligence in medicine*, 64(2):89–103.

Ashish Vaswani, Noam Shazeer, Niki Parmar, Jakob Uszkoreit, Llion Jones, Aidan N Gomez, Łukasz Kaiser, and Illia Polosukhin. 2017. Attention is all you need. In *Advances in neural information processing systems*, pages 5998–6008.

Alex Wang, Yada Pruksachatkun, Nikita Nangia, Amanpreet Singh, Julian Michael, Felix Hill, Omer Levy, and Samuel R. Bowman. 2019. Superglue: A stickier benchmark for general-purpose language understanding systems. In *33rd Annual Conference on Neural Information Processing Systems, NeurIPS 2019*, volume 32, pages 3261–3275.

Alex Wang, Amanpreet Singh, Julian Michael, Felix Hill, Omer Levy, and Samuel Bowman. 2018. GLUE: A multi-task benchmark and analysis platform for natural language understanding. In *Proceedings of the 2018 EMNLP Workshop BlackboxNLP: Analyzing and Interpreting Neural Networks for NLP*, pages 353–355, Brussels, Belgium. Association for Computational Linguistics.

Thomas Wolf, Lysandre Debut, Victor Sanh, Julien Chaumond, Clement Delangue, Anthony Moi, Pierric Cistac, Tim Rault, Remi Louf, Morgan Funtowicz, Joe Davison, Sam Shleifer, Patrick von Platen, Clara Ma, Yacine Jernite, Julien Plu, Canwen Xu, Teven Le Scao, Sylvain Gugger, Mariama Drame, Quentin Lhoest, and Alexander Rush. 2020. Transformers: State-of-the-art natural language processing. In *Proceedings of the 2020 Conference on Empirical Methods in Natural Language Processing: System Demonstrations*, pages 38–45, Online. Association for Computational Linguistics.

Jianfei Yu, Luís Marujo, Jing Jiang, Pradeep Karuturi, and William Brendel. 2018. Improving multi-label emotion classification via sentiment classification with dual attention transfer network. In *Proceedings of the 2018 Conference on Empirical Methods in Natural Language Processing*, pages 1097–1102, Brussels, Belgium. Association for Computational Linguistics.

Association for Computational Linguistics
209 N. Eighth Street
Stroudsburg, Pennsylvania 18360

CURRAN ASSOCIATES INC. proceedings.com

ISBN 978-1-7138-9160-4

9 781713 891604